THE DEFENSE OF BERLIN

The
Defense of
BERLIN

BY JEAN EDWARD SMITH

THE JOHNS HOPKINS PRESS
Baltimore, Maryland
LONDON: OXFORD UNIVERSITY PRESS

"The experience of history teaches that when an aggressor sees that he is not being opposed he grows more brazen. Contrariwise when he meets opposition, he calms down. It is this historic experience that must guide us in our actions."

Nikita Khrushchev
August 7, 1961

ACKNOWLEDGMENTS

Many people have helped to make this book possible. Specifically, I am indebted:

To Professor John Seaman of Colorado State University, whose labors on behalf of style and clarity far exceed the call of friendship.

To Professor William M. Beaney of Princeton, who first encouraged me to undertake the writing of a political history of Berlin and who has seen the project through many difficult stages.

To Dr. Charles Burton Marshall of The Washington Center of Foreign Policy Research, who has read the entire manuscript and offered numerous friendly suggestions.

To Professor Quincy Wright of Columbia, for also reading the manuscript and saving me from many pitfalls of glibness and oversimplification.

To Professor Otto Kirchheimer, also of Columbia, for generously reading and carefully criticizing the several chapters dealing with the Allied occupation.

To General Lucius D. Clay and Lord Mayor Willy Brandt for a series of interviews concerning events in Berlin during the past two years.

To Colonel Harold B. Ayres, formerly Chief of Staff of the Allied Staff in Berlin (and my former Commanding Officer), for his never-failing kindness and advice.

To Dr. Arthur Siebens, Pastor of the American Church in Berlin, for allowing me to draw freely on his vast knowledge of Berlin and the Berliners.

To Dr. Wolfgang Stresemann, *Direktor of the Berliner Philhar-monisches Orchester*, Herrn Johannes Zinsel of the Goethe-Gymnasium, and Dr. Walter Winkler of the City Planning Division of the West Berlin City Government, for information concerning affairs in West Berlin during the years 1958–1961.

To my former Princeton classmates Norman Sepenuk, William Mackey, and Harry Moul who have read the manuscript in its earlier drafts and offered penetrating criticisms.

To Dr. Martin Sweig, Mr. James L. Harrison, and Mr. Robert Poston for kindnesses too numerous to mention.

To Gene Foreman of the *New York Times* for his careful reading of the manuscript for editorial flaws; to my agent, Llewellyn Howland, of The Sterling Lord Agency, for his constant support and advice.

To numerous public officials of all four Western powers who have generously assisted me but who, of necessity, must remain nameless.

To my father who has never failed to offer a word of kindly encouragement.

To my mother who has borne the entire typing burden and has spent many hours wrestling with a virtually illegible handwriting.

Finally, to my wife Christine. Were she not a Berliner, I'm sure she could not have endured the household trials of two years of authorship as cheerfully as she has.

Washington, D.C.   Jean Edward Smith

QUOTATION ACKNOWLEDGMENTS

The quotation from "Mending Wall" by Robert Frost (from *Complete Poems of Robert Frost*) 1939, is reproduced by permission of Holt, Rinehart and Winston; as are the quotations from *A Soldier's Story* by General Omar Bradley, 1951, Henry Holt and Co.

The sketch of occupation boundaries, drawn by President Roosevelt on the National Geographic Society Map of Europe and the Near East, is reproduced by courtesy of the National Geographic Society.

The quotations from Harry S Truman, *Year of Decisions*, 1955, and *Years of Trial and Hope*, 1956, are reprinted courtesy of Time, Inc.

The quotations from William D. Leahy, *I Was There*, 1950, William D. Leahy and Curtis Publishing Co., are reprinted courtesy of Brandt & Brandt.

The quotations from Walter Millis (ed.), *The Forrestal Diaries*, 1951, are reprinted courtesy of The Viking Press.

The quotations from Robert Sherwood, *Roosevelt and Hopkins*, 1948; and from Sumner Welles, *Seven Decisions that Shaped History*, 1950, are reprinted courtesy of Harper & Row.

The quotations from Frank Howley, *Berlin Command*, 1950, are reprinted courtesy of G. P. Putnam's Sons.

The quotations from Winston Churchill, *Triumph and Tragedy*, 1953, are reprinted courtesy of The Houghton Mifflin Co.

The quotations from Walter Bedell Smith, *Eisenhower's Six Great Decisions*, 1950, Longmans, Green, are reprinted courtesy of David McKay Company, Inc.

The quotations from Captain Butcher's *My Three Years With Eisenhower*, 1946, Simon & Schuster, are reprinted courtesy of Harry Butcher.

The quotations from W. Phillips Davison, *The Berlin Airlift*, 1958, The Rand Corporation; Herbert Feis, *Between War and Peace*, 1960, Princeton University Press; and Herbert Feis, *Churchill, Roosevelt, Stalin: The War They Waged and The Peace They Sought*, 1957, Princeton University Press, are made in accordance with the Resolution on Permissions of the Association of American University Presses.

The quotations from Field Marshal Montgomery, *Montgomery of Alamein*, 1958, World Publishing Co., are reprinted by permission of E. P. Dutton & Co.

The quotations from *My Road to Berlin* by Willy Brandt, as told to Leo Lania, 1960; from *Decision in Germany* by Lucius D. Clay, 1950; from *Crusade in Europe* by Dwight D. Eisenhower, 1948, Doubleday & Company, Inc.; and from *Roosevelt and the Russians* by Edward R. Stettinius, copyright 1949 by The Stettinius Fund, Inc., are made by permission of Doubleday & Co.

The quotations from the *Memoirs* of Cordell Hull, 1948, are reprinted by permission of The Macmillan Company.

CONTENTS

THE DEFENSE OF BERLIN

Something there is that doesn't love a wall,
That wants it down! I could say "elves" to him,
But it's not elves exactly, and I'd rather
He said it for himself. I see him there,
Bringing a stone grasped firmly by the top
In each hand, like an old stone savage armed.
He moves in darkness, as it seems to me,
Not of woods only and the shade of trees.

Robert Frost, *Mending Wall.*

1

The Defense of Berlin

(Setting the Scene)

DURING THE SECOND WEEK OF AUGUST, 1961, an atmosphere of expectancy hung over Berlin. The flight of refugees from the Soviet zone, increasing steadily since the Vienna Conference between President Kennedy and Premier Khrushchev, was now at record proportions.

During June and July, more than fifty thousand persons had come over to the West. Another sixteen thousand arrived during the first eleven days of August. On Saturday, August 12, 1961, a new twenty-four hour record was set when over three thousand disenchanted East Germans made their way to the reception center in West Berlin to ask for asylum.[1] Only in the summer of 1953, the summer of the violent uprising in East Germany, had more people fled the Socialist Utopia of Walter Ulbricht.

As in 1953, reports of unrest throughout the Soviet zone were rife. Even the heavily censored East German press made little effort to conceal the rising tide of popular discontent. From Halle, the Communist newspaper *Freiheit* reported that people in East Germany were clamoring for reunification before a separate peace treaty with the Soviet Union. In Leipzig, workers publicly demanded an end to the Iron Curtain between East and West. In East Berlin, the same construction workers who had touched off the revolt on Stalin Allee on June 17, 1953, warned Khrushchev against trying to settle the German question unilaterally.[2]

Each of the refugees now coming to West Berlin also brought stories of unrest in the Communist zone. Many even reported an imminent East German move to seal the frontier. These reports, as it happened, were not without foundation. In the past twelve years over two and a half million people had left the Communist zone of East Germany; since 1945, more than four million. The population of the so-called "German Democratic Republic," almost eighteen million in 1949, numbered little more than sixteen million by mid-1961.[3]

The drain of labor and skilled workers represented by this extraordinary emigration was more than the East German regime could endure. Most of those who were leaving had been usefully employed. Over half were under twenty-five years old and represented a particularly serious loss in terms of future productivity. Of the others, many were senior craftsmen, highly trained artisans, physicians, teachers, and engineers. All were desperately needed in the sagging economy of Walter Ulbricht and could not easily be replaced.*

Perhaps as important as its effect on the East zone's economy was the effect of the great exodus on world opinion. The shortcomings of communism, as practiced in the "German Democratic Republic," were being exposed daily by the thousands who were rejecting it for the freedom of the West. As a result, the Communist crusade among the neutral and uncommitted nations was being seriously undermined.

The role of Berlin in promoting the refugees' escape was well known. At no other point was the Iron Curtain so easily breached. A would-be refugee from the Soviet zone had only to catch a train to East Berlin, transfer to an intracity subway (U-Bahn) or elevated (S-Bahn), and

---

* Among the 30,415 persons who fled from East Germany during July, 1961, there were: 65 physicians, 29 dentists, 6 veterinarians, 12 pharmacists, 332 teachers, two university professors, six lawyers, two judges, 455 engineers and 186 university students.

By source of employment, the total was broken down as follows: industry and handicrafts, 21.8%; trade and transport, 11.4%; domestic and health service workers, 4.2%; farmers, 4.1%; administrative employees, 3.1%; engineers and technicians, 2.8%; artists, intellectuals and university students, 2.5%; other occupations, 9.7%; housewives, 10%; children, 24.5%; pensioners, 5.9%; (*New York Times,* August 13, 1961.)

then ride freely into the Western sectors. If he wanted, he could even walk across or take a taxi. Border controls between the sectors were rigid but free movement was one of the attributes of Berlin's four-power status. Once in the Western sectors, it was an easy bus ride to the refugee center, a short period of processing, and then out by air from Tempelhof to West Germany and a new existence.

As long as the border to West Berlin remained open, residents from the East came there *en masse*. Aside from the refugees, one hundred and fifty thousand came daily. Many worked there; others came simply for a look, a shopping trip or a visit with friends. For most people in East Germany, a trip to West Berlin was at least an annual ritual. They returned afterward with their spirits recharged. They had seen the miracle of West Berlin, had sampled its flavor, and experienced its exhilaration. They had seen the showcase of liberty at first hand.

The contrast between life in West Berlin and life in the Soviet zone was striking. For the people of East Germany, West Berlin represented Western civilization—the civilization to which they belonged. Its prosperity was a fact that Communist propaganda could not conceal. Indeed, West Berlin was the best argument against communism in the arsenal of the West. So long as it remained open and flourishing, communism in East Germany could not prosper. In the twelve years since the puppet regime of Walter Ulbricht officially came into existence, communism still had not taken root.

At his Vienna meeting with President Kennedy in June, 1961, Nikita Khrushchev acknowledged as much. The "abnormal" situation in West Berlin, he insisted, must be ended this year.[4] Following Vienna, Khrushchev began the third Soviet offensive since the end of the war to bring this about. A propaganda campaign unusual in its intensity even for the Soviet Union was launched against the continued Allied occupation of West Berlin.

As Khrushchev's verbal attacks mounted in fury during June and July, so did the exodus of refugees from the Communist zone. By August, the stream had turned into a flood. It was a self-fulfilling prophecy; by increasing the tension around Berlin, Khrushchev was increasing the flow of refugees. By increasing the flow of refugees, he was making the position of the Ulbricht regime untenable. By making the position of the Ulbricht regime untenable, he was giving himself a justification to seal the border between East and West Berlin. By the second weekend of August, Communist action to do just that seemed imminent.*

Shortly after midnight, Sunday, August 13, 1961, the blow fell. The East German News Agency published a special announcement: The Council of Ministers of the German Democratic Republic, at the request of the Warsaw Pact, was putting into effect "those control measures . . . usually introduced along the borders of every sovereign state." The border of the "capital of the German Democratic Republic" (East Berlin) with the Western sectors would be included. Citizens of the GDR (German Democratic Republic) would be permitted to cross this border only with special permission. A simultaneous decree of the East Berlin city government banned all persons living in East Berlin from working in West Berlin.[5]

No sooner had the announcements been published than measures were under way to put the decrees into effect. At thirty-five minutes past midnight units of the East German Peoples Army rolled into the Potsdamer Platz in the center of Berlin. By two-thirty in the morning the border between the East and Western sectors had been sealed. From Tegel in the north to Rudow in the south East German military units were deployed along the border in tactical formation, deployed as if to withstand an assault by an approaching enemy.

Several hundred yards behind them hard core factory militia (*Betriebskampfgruppen*) in brown uniforms mounted a rear guard against possible attack by disgruntled East Berliners, and tanks and machine guns were emplaced at strategic intersections. East Berlin was an armed camp. Barbed wire was strung and light obstacles emplaced. Of the eighty crossing points that had previously existed, only thirteen remained. These were all one way—for West Berliners and foreigners only.

The border closure was at once effective. The flow of refugees was reduced overnight to an insignificant trickle. Fewer than one hundred managed to cross into West Berlin in the first twenty-four hours after the new measures went into effect. Most of these crossed in the early

---

* This did not prevent life from going on much as usual among the Allied forces in Berlin. On August 12, the American command was busily engaged in the climactic phases of a youth carnival organized and conducted for the benefit of the children of American personnel. Brigadier General Frederick O. Hartel, Commander of the Berlin Command, was personally involved. While the carnival was going on he granted an interview to Harry Gilroy of the *New York Times*. "Emphasize one thing," Hartel told Gilroy, "we are not excited." (*New York Times*, August 13, 1961.)

hours before the controls were complete. In the following days their numbers would be counted in tens and twenties instead of hundreds and thousands.

The Communists moved rapidly to consolidate their gains. At 4 A.M. Monday morning, August 14, all telephone and postal service between East and West Germany was suspended. Later in the afternoon, the Brandenburg Gate was closed to traffic by an armed cordon of East German Peoples Police (*Volkspolizei*) supported by tanks and armored cars. The number of crossing points was reduced to twelve. At several of these the street already was being torn up, reducing traffic to a single lane.

At one o'clock Tuesday morning, August 15, all West Berlin vehicles were banned by the East German Ministry of Interior from entering East Berlin. This announcement marked the first direct attack on the rights of Western movement within the city since the border closure began. The puppet regime of Walter Ulbricht was getting bolder. Several hours later, East German police fired for the first time on escaping refugees attempting to make their way into the American sector.

By Tuesday evening the border between East and West had become a fortified frontier. The hasty barbed wire entanglements of Sunday morning were replaced with concrete slabs and formidable antitank barriers, and the entire work took on an appearance of permanence.

For the next several days Communist preparations continued. On Wednesday, movable barriers were installed at each of the twelve remaining crossing points. On Thursday, East German workers began tearing out the rail sections of three elevated (S-Bahn) lines crossing into West Berlin. On Friday, August 18, the Wall itself began to appear. Thousands of laborers worked round the clock pouring cement into prefabricated forms, and by Tuesday evening, August 22, it was virtually complete. A concrete barrier six feet high, one foot wide, and twenty-eight miles long now separated the two sectors of the city. It had arisen in less than five days, and the entire Communist action had taken place in less than ten. Within that time East Berlin physically had been incorporated into the "German Democratic Republic."

The remaining vestiges of four-power occupation in Berlin were quickly reduced by the East German regime to manageable proportions. Until now, little effort had been made to interfere with Allied movement throughout the city. On Wednesday, August 23, however,

the number of crossing points between East and West Berlin was reduced from twelve to seven, all further restricted as to purpose: four
for West Berliners, two for West Germans, and one for foreigners, the
category into which the Western Allies were neatly fitted. Thus, where
formerly they had been free to travel between the two sectors of the
city with relative ease, the Western powers now found themselves unable to enter the self-styled "capital of the German Democratic Republic" except through one gate; a gate manned not by their co-occupiers,
the Soviet Union, but by the minions of the puppet East German
satellite.

The following day, Thursday, August 24, the first refugee was shot
and killed attempting to escape. The "abnormal" situation had been
brought under control.

For Nikita Khrushchev, the sealing of the East Berlin sector boundary represented a major triumph; the construction of the Wall between
East and West Berlin an even greater one. With free movement within
the city now a thing of the past, the four-power status of the former
German capital was over, and East Berlin passed almost unnoticed behind the Iron Curtain. The boundary of the Soviet zone, a boundary
separate and distinct from the territory of Greater Berlin, had been extended to include the eastern sector of the city within its realm. An
area of 154 square miles containing 1.1 million people had been annexed unilaterally by the satellite regime of Walter Ulbricht.

But the physical annexation of East Berlin by the German Democratic Republic was only one of the victories of August 13, 1961. By
successfully sealing the border between East and West Berlin, the
ruinous flow of East German refugees had been halted. The tottering
East German government was bolstered, and dissident elements within
the Soviet zone now could be brought under control. With the border
closed, the satellite bloc could be consolidated. Indeed, with access to
West Berlin denied, East Germany itself has been condemned to the
prison of international communism.

One effect of the border closure was immediate. Sixty thousand new
workers for labor-short East German industry appeared overnight.
These were the persons living in East Berlin who formerly had worked
in West Berlin. While many were menials, many also were highly

skilled technicians who had continued to live in the East only because it was their home—an important consideration in housing-scarce Berlin. The sudden windfall represented by these workers more than offset the increased exodus caused by Khrushchev's post-Vienna bluster.

Of perhaps more far-reaching importance, the erection of the East German state frontier between East and West Berlin forced the Western Allies into a position of dealing directly with the hitherto unrecognized Ulbricht regime. After August 13, 1961, the Soviet Union was conspicuously absent from the affairs of East Berlin. The unchallenged border closure effected by the so-called German Democratic Republic thus amounted to a virtual *de facto* acceptance of East Germany by the Western powers.

In addition, the Communist action of August 13 presented a direct threat to the freedom and viability of West Berlin itself. The immediate effect of the border closure on the sinking morale of West Berlin is well known. In part, this resulted from the Berliners' frustration at their own inability to counteract the East German measures. In part, the Berliners' reaction also reflected a feeling of having been betrayed by their Allies. Primarily, however, their despondency derived from a realization that much of the basis for West Berlin's existence suddenly had disappeared.

On July 25, 1961, three weeks before the East German action took place, President Kennedy said that West Berlin "has many roles."

> It is more than a showcase of liberty, a symbol, an island of freedom in a Communist sea. It is even more than a link with the free world, a beacon of hope behind the Iron Curtain, an escape hatch for refugees.
> West Berlin is all of that. But above all it has now become, as never before, the great testing place of Western courage and will, a focal point where our solemn commitments . . . and Soviet ambitions now meet in basic confrontation.[6]

After August 13, however, many of the roles which President Kennedy had so eloquently proclaimed no longer fitted. The escape hatch for refugees was closed. The beacon of hope had been dimmed. West Berlin as a link with the free world for the people behind the Iron Curtain no longer existed.

With the border closed, the people of East Germany were prevented from visiting West Berlin. Prevented from visiting West Berlin, they were deprived of experiencing the wonders of freedom so vigorously in evidence there. The message of the city, the striking contrast between East and West, between communism and democracy, was stilled. The showcase of liberty had lost its lustre.

There was therefore reason for despair in West Berlin immediately following the border closure, for the city might well wither on the vine. With access from the East shut off, access from the West seemed to diminish in importance. Worse, there was danger that the West Berliners, now leery of Allied determination, might panic from the city. Such a flight would only further undermine what was left of West Berlin's resiliency. The West, regardless of its determination, would then be left with an empty and decaying shell.

By sealing the border between East and West Berlin on August 13, 1961, the Communist regime materially altered the balance of power in Central Europe. West Berlin was no longer a bone in Khrushchev's throat. Its disrupting influence among the Communist satellites had been contained. What was formerly an offensive sally port for the Western powers was now, at best, a defensive bastion.

With Berlin's role partially changed, the considerations involved in its defense have also changed. The right of Western access, previously the keystone of the Allied position, is important today only if the economic and spiritual vitality of West Berlin can be preserved, and this can be guaranteed only if West Berlin continues to be a place where people choose to live. West Berlin will be a place where people choose to live only if those who do live there have confidence in its future, are certain of its freedom, and are convinced it will not be forsaken. Accordingly, for the Western Allies, a new dimension has been added to the problem of maintaining the freedom of West Berlin. It is a problem which, to a large degree, the Western powers brought on themselves. Had their response to the events of August 13, been different, it would not be necessary at this late date to prove again their determination to remain.

In many respects, the Allied position in West Berlin is so enmeshed in subtleties, past precedents, and out-dated agreements that a true understanding of exactly what is at stake at any given time or in any given situation is frequently obscured. Certainly, this was true on August 13. It was not for several weeks after the border closure, in fact, that a full realization of what had happened actually dawned in the West.

In an article appearing in the *Saturday Evening Post* in December of 1961, former President Dwight Eisenhower remarked: "Others may find it possible to discuss intelligently the current world debates centering about Berlin without reference to its early postwar history. I find this impossible." [7] To this statement one might add that an understanding of the present Western position in Berlin cannot be obtained except through a historical perspective.

It is well known, of course, that the location of Berlin 110 miles behind the Iron Curtain is one of the legacies of World War II. The occupation boundaries, the location of Berlin within the Soviet zone, and the sector divisions within the former German capital all were determined while the war was still in progress (with the exception of the French sector of Berlin [see Chapter VI]). The legal basis for the present Western position in Berlin rests on these agreements. By the same token, the basis for the present crisis may also be found there.

2

Wartime Agreements Regarding the Occupation of Berlin

ALLIED DISCUSSIONS ON POSTWAR GERMANY began in Moscow in mid-December, 1941. The occasion was hardly propitious. Hitler's invasion of Russia was then less than six months old, and the great German offensive which began on June 22 already had ground its way to within sight of the Kremlin. Only the week before it had been halted, and elements of the Fourth Army of Field Marshal von Kluge were still lodged in the city's western suburbs; foreign embassies and legations had been evacuated, and victory seemed within the Nazi grasp.[1]

Elsewhere, the tide also was running against the Allies. In the North Atlantic, Hitler's submarines were taking a dreadful toll of Allied shipping. In Africa, El Alamein was almost a year ahead. In the Pacific, the wreckage of Pearl Harbor was less than two weeks old. American forces were in retreat in the Philippines, the garrisons at Guam and Wake Island were under sustained attack, the fall of Singapore and the invasion of the Dutch East Indies were imminent.

It was in this context—on December 16, 1941—that British Foreign

Secretary Anthony Eden arrived in Moscow to discuss future Allied co-operation. Much to his surprise, Eden quickly learned that the Soviet government had other considerations in mind. At his first meeting with Marshal Stalin on the afternoon of December 16, the Soviet Premier launched into a discussion of Russian territorial expectations once Germany was defeated. The question of whether Germany would be defeated, ironically seems not to have entered the Communist dictator's mind.

In particular, Stalin was interested in Russia's western boundary. The war, he advised Eden, already had cost Russia untold suffering for which she would have to be compensated. The future boundary between Poland and the Soviet Union, Stalin said, must be based on the old Curzon line of 1919, meaning that Russia would retain almost all of that part of eastern Poland overrun in 1939. The portion of Finland taken by Russia in 1940, the Baltic states, and the Rumanian province of Bessarabia also were to remain within the Soviet Union after the war. In addition, Stalin told his British guest that extraterritorial arrangements for Soviet military forces would have to be concluded with Finland and Rumania, and that East Prussia, at least as far as Koenigsberg, would be annexed directly.[2] As subsequent events have made clear, Stalin's demands that bleak December day offer a surprisingly accurate forecast of the shape of things to come.

Eden reported Russian territorial desires to Prime Minister Churchill, who was then en route to Washington for a meeting with President Roosevelt. The American government, or at least the State Department, was also informed.[*]

On December 20, Churchill replied to Eden from the *Duke of York* in mid-Atlantic. The Prime Minister's message indicates his feeling for the sensibilities of his American ally.[**] Said Churchill:

[*] Mr. Llewellyn Thompson, then Second Secretary of the American Embassy in Moscow, had remained behind when the rest of the Embassy was evacuated. During the course of the Eden-Stalin discussions (December 16–28, 1941) he was kept informed of their general drift by the British Embassy. Eden's reports to London were also shown to American Ambassador John G. Winant. See U.S. Department of State, *Foreign Relations of the United States—Diplomatic Papers, 1941,* Vol. I (Washington: Government Printing Office, 1958), pp. 198–205.

[**] Washington had learned of the plans for Eden's visit to Moscow on December 4. When informed, Secretary of State Cordell Hull became concerned that Eden might be led into a commitment on Soviet territorial demands. Accordingly, on December 5, and with the approval of the President, he cabled Ambassador Winant in London to advise Eden that the United States felt it would be a mistake to con-

1. Naturally you will not be rough on Stalin. We are bound to the United States not to enter into secret and special pacts. To approach President Roosevelt with these proposals would be to court a blank refusal, and might cause lasting trouble on both sides.

2. The strategic security of Russia on her Western border will be one of the objects of the Peace Conference. . . . The separation of Prussia from South Germany, and the actual definition of Prussia itself, will be one of the greatest issues to be decided. But all of this lies in a future which is uncertain and probably remote. We have now to win the war by a hard and prolonged struggle. To raise such issues publicly now would only be to rally all Germans round Hitler.

3. Even to raise them informally with President Roosevelt at this time would, in my opinion, be inexpedient. This is the line I should take [with Stalin], thus avoiding any abrupt or final closing of interviews. . . .[3]

There is no indication of whether President Roosevelt was informed of Stalin's demands. As Churchill's cable suggests, Mr. Roosevelt preferred to postpone postwar settlements until victory had been won. In this he was supported both by Secretary of State Hull and the military chiefs of staff.[*]

For over a year following Eden's visit to Moscow the question of postwar Germany lay dormant. It was revived briefly by President Roosevelt at Casablanca in January, 1943, when he announced the doctrine of "Unconditional Surrender." But the phrase "unconditional surrender" was extremely vague as to future Allied aims and quite likely was announced by President Roosevelt deliberately to remove

---

clude any agreement on specific postwar settlements. American war aims, said Hull, were outlined in the Atlantic Charter to which Britain was a party. Above all, he insisted, there must be no secret agreement. Hull's message was delivered by Winant to Eden on December 6. *Foreign Relations of the United States—Diplomatic Papers, 1941,* Vol. I, *op. cit.,* pp. 192–95. Vol. IV, p. 1027. Also see Herbert Feis, *Churchill, Roosevelt, Stalin: The War They Waged and the Peace They Sought* (Princeton: Princeton University Press, 1957), p. 25.

[*] According to the late Sumner Welles, who was American Under Secretary of State during the early years of the war, as well as a close personal friend of President Roosevelt, the Joint Chiefs of Staff were among the foremost of the Presidential advisers who endorsed this position. "It was altogether natural," Welles states, "that the Joint Chiefs of Staff should constantly warn the President that, whatever the theoretical future advantages of trying to settle political and territorial problems during the war, these were offset by the immediate dangers of the controversies with Russia which might be aroused." Sumner Welles, *Seven Decisions That Shaped History* (New York: Harper and Bros., 1950), p. 134. Also see Cordell Hull, *Memoirs* (New York: Macmillan, 1948), pp. 1570–79; Albert C. Wedemeyer, *Wedemeyer Reports* (New York: Henry Holt, 1958), pp. 89–96.

the question of specific postwar demands from Allied discussions. The effect of this action was to conceal Allied differences regarding Germany for almost another year.[4]

Two months after Casablanca, Anthony Eden arrived in Washington for further consultations. In the series of conferences which followed, President Roosevelt advised Eden that American troops would remain in Germany after the war as part of an Allied occupation force. This marked the first time that the President actually had committed the United States to take part in Germany's occupation and Eden replied he was glad to hear it.[5]

Harry Hopkins' notes of Eden's visit include an entry dated March 17, 1943, reporting a tea attended by Eden, Secretary of State Hull, himself and the President, in the President's study. According to Hopkins:

> We discussed, for some time, the question of precisely what our procedure in Germany during the first six months after the collapse of Germany should be.
> I said I thought there was no understanding between Great Britain, Russia and ourselves as to which armies would be where and what kind of administration should be developed. I said that unless we acted promptly and surely I believed one of two things would happen—either Germany would go Communist or an out and out anarchic state would set in. . . . I said I thought it required some kind of formal agreement and that the State Department should work out the plan with the British and the one agreed upon between us should then be discussed with the Russians. The President agreed that this procedure should be followed.[6]

Seven months after Eden's visit to Washington, the Foreign Ministers of the United States, Great Britain, and Russia convened in Moscow for their first meeting. In spite of Hopkins' suggestion, however, the American and British positions on postwar Germany still had not been co-ordinated. To a large extent, official Washington at this time shared President Roosevelt's opinion that postwar settlements should be postponed until later. Joint Anglo-American planning toward Germany therefore had been neglected in favor of the more pressing military matters then at hand. What few efforts had been made were largely directed toward the creation of *ad hoc* advisory committees and reflected little overall co-ordination.*

* At the time of America's entry into the war, an "interdivisional" policy committee on postwar problems was established within the Department of State. In

The Moscow Conference was designed as a preliminary to the first meeting of the Big Three, scheduled to be held in Tehran the following month, and may legitimately be said to mark the beginning of three-power planning toward Germany. On October 17, 1943, the day the Conference began, Secretary Hull gave a tentative draft of so-called *Basic Principles Regarding Germany's Surrender* to Russian Foreign Minister Molotov, saying: "This is not a formal United States proposal but something to show a slant of mind. It is just a personal suggestion you and I can talk about. Then, if you like, we can talk to Eden about it and see what he thinks. I can make the proposal mine, or you can make it yours." [7]

For the most part, Hull's suggestions were exceedingly general. Germany was to be occupied by all three nations but no mention was made of how this was to take place. No zonal boundaries were proposed and no mention was made of Berlin. The question of Germany's postwar frontiers was touched on in one sentence: "This is a matter which should come within the purview of a general settlement." [8]

The Moscow Conference made little effort to reach concrete agreement on Hull's recommendations. Eden told Hull he thought the proposals were well drawn but needed further analysis. For this purpose, he suggested the formation of a tripartite commission, known as the European Advisory Commission (EAC), to consider the problems of conquered enemy countries in greater detail. The Commission, as Eden proposed it, was to be primarily a negotiating body and its recommendations were to be presented to the Big Three for final decision. [9]

Eden's suggestion was quickly agreed to and the European Advisory Commission began functioning shortly after it was approved at Tehran the following month. Although it later became the scene of a bitter jurisdictional dispute, it was in the EAC that the final zonal arrangement in Germany was actually drafted.

Following the Moscow Conference, planning for Germany took on a greater importance. On November 13, 1943, two weeks after the close

---

1942, President Roosevelt appointed a special public advisory committee on post-war problems under the sponsorship of the Council on Foreign Relations. Neither of these groups were favored with Administration interest, however, and their findings, at least until late 1943, seldom reached the upper levels of government. See especially Harley A. Notter, *Postwar Foreign Policy Preparation: 1939–1945*, U.S. Department of State Publication 3580 (Washington: Government Printing Office, 1949).

of the Foreign Ministers' meeting, President Roosevelt embarked for Tehran from Hampton Roads, Virginia, on the battleship *USS Iowa*. In addition to Harry Hopkins and the President's personal staff, the *Iowa's* passengers included Army Chief of Staff General George C. Marshall, Chief of Naval Operations Admiral Ernest King, the President's personal Chief of Staff, Admiral William D. Leahy, General H. H. Arnold, then Chief of the Army Air Force, and sixty other military staff planners. Neither Secretary of State Hull nor any of the other State Department participants in the Moscow Conference were present.[10]

The long sea cruise across the Atlantic was intended to allow the President sufficient time to discuss the major issues of global strategy with his military staff prior to meeting the British and Russian delegations at Tehran.[11] Staff discussions were held daily throughout the trip, culminating in two meetings between President Roosevelt and the Joint Chiefs of Staff on November 15 and November 19, 1943. In the course of these two meetings, the subject of postwar Europe was discussed in detail. According to the official history of this period prepared by the Department of the Army, President Roosevelt gave the military leaders "the fullest guidance on politico-military issues he had given them since America's entry into the war." [12]

During the November 19th meeting, the President was asked by his military advisers for information on the problem of Allied zones of occupation in Germany.[13] Before them was a military paper prepared in London by the staff (COSSAC) which had been set up to prepare for the invasion of France.* The occupation boundaries of the COSSAC plan were similar to the division of Germany today. This particular arrangement had been developed earlier in 1943 by a British Cabinet Committee working under the direction of Deputy Prime Minister Clement Attlee.[14] It had no relation to the plan recommended by Secretary Hull in Moscow the previous month.[15] Under the Attlee plan, the Soviet zone of occupation would include the provinces of Mecklenburg, Pomerania, Brandenburg, Saxony-Anhalt, Thuringia, Saxony, Silesia

---

* COSSAC, i.e., Chief of Staff to the Supreme Allied Commander (Designate). At this time, General Eisenhower had not yet been appointed Supreme Commander in Europe. Until such time as a commander was selected, however, a small staff group had been established in London to begin planning. This staff was given the code name COSSAC and became the nucleus around which General Eisenhower later built his headquarters.

and East Prussia. At its western terminus near the city of Eisenach, the proposed Soviet zone extended to a point less than one hundred kilometers from the Rhine. In all, it included a territory consisting of forty percent of Germany's 1937 land area, thirty-six percent of her population and thirty-three percent of her productive resources.[16]

The American zone, which was to be located in southern Germany, included the provinces of Bavaria, Baden-Wuerttemberg, Hesse, the Rhinish Palatinate and possibly Austria. Great Britain itself would occupy the northwestern part of Germany, Schleswig-Holstein, Lower Saxony, the Ruhr, North Rhine-Westphalia and the great centers of commerce and industry located there. The Attlee proposal also recommended that Berlin be jointly occupied by all three powers as a symbol of Allied unity although it did not delineate actual city boundaries. It made no mention of Western access to the German capital which, of course, was located well within the Russian zone.

President Roosevelt told the Joint Chiefs of Staff that he did not agree with the British arrangement. In particular, he did not agree with the provision that Great Britain, and not the United States, should occupy the northwestern part of Germany. The President was anxious to provide for American access to the sea. He was concerned both with the problem of supplying the occupation force and with the need to ship U.S. troops to the Far East when the war in Europe was over. For these reasons he wanted to control the ports of Hamburg and Bremen. Also, President Roosevelt is reported to have been concerned about the stability of the French government and did not want American supply lines in Germany dependent upon France, as they would be if the United States occupied the southern zone.

Interestingly, the President also discussed Berlin. To the military chiefs he predicted that there would "be a race for Berlin" and that regardless of the outcome "the United States should have Berlin." These statements are recorded in a memorandum of the meeting prepared by Major General Thomas T. Handy, Acting Army Assistant Chief of Staff for Operations, from notes given him immediately afterward by General Marshall.[17]

To set forth more clearly his ideas as to how the future zonal boundaries should be drawn, President Roosevelt penciled-in his proposed lines of demarcation on a National Geographic Society map. In the President's sketch, the United States would occupy a considerably larger zone than the Attlee draft had suggested and it would be in northwestern Germany instead of the south; Great Britain would occupy the south, and Russia, a smaller zone in eastern Germany. Berlin, in Mr. Roosevelt's sketch, was not located within the Russian zone as the British plan had proposed but on the frontier *between* the American and Russian zones. The President anticipated that perhaps a million U.S. troops would remain in Germany "for at least one year and possibly two." * [18]

Significantly, no representatives of the State Department attended the meeting on the *Iowa* when President Roosevelt discussed occupation policy. To a large extent, this represented a deliberate effort on the part of the President to restrict the role of the State Department in Allied planning. It also reflected his feeling that occupation policy was primarily a concern of the military. Mr. Robert Sherwood, a close friend and confidant of the President, reports that the State Department had fallen from grace with Roosevelt. The ancient bureaucratic machinery of the Department was little suited for time of war and FDR felt that many of the senior career officers of the diplomatic service were hostile to the Administration. The prewar handling of Hitler and Mussolini by the State Department, and especially its overriding concern for diplomatic nicety, had upset him on numerous occasions.[19]

Secretary Hull at this time also had faded from a leading position in the Administration. Frequently he was by-passed by Mr. Roosevelt in his dealings with foreign governments. When the President embarked for Tehran, he therefore purposely left Hull in Washington.** Little effort was made to keep the State Department informed of what was happening, and planning for the occupation of Germany soon took off

---

* Of the discussions on board the *Iowa,* the Army documentary history states:

> It is interesting to note that the President's idea of an American zone in postwar northwest Germany portended a U.S. occupation in force, to be conducted, like the American approach to the European war itself, with a minimum of time, expense, and political complications in European affairs.

Maurice Matloff, *Strategic Planning for Coalition Warfare, 1943–1944,* Office of the Chief of Military History, Department of the Army (Washington: Government Printing Office, 1959), p. 342.

** On August 17, 1944, Secretary Hull told Secretary of the Treasury Henry Morgenthau, Jr., that he had "never been permitted to see the minutes of the Teheran Conference," that he was "not told what is going on," and that he had been informed that the planning of occupation policy toward Germany was a military affair. See John L. Snell, *Dilemma in Germany* (New Orleans: Hauser, 1959), p. 72.

in two separate directions; one pursued by the Department of State
and one by the President and his military advisers.[20]

The Tehran Conference convened on November 28, 1943. For the
most part, Churchill, Roosevelt and Stalin limited themselves to military arrangements for continuing the war in Europe. In particular,
planning centered on the establishment of a "Second Front" in Western
Europe by the forces of the United States and Great Britain. Postwar
Germany was discussed but briefly. As Prime Minister Churchill has
stated:

> At this time the subject seemed to be purely theoretical. No one
> could foresee when or how the end of the war would come. The
> German armies held immense areas of European Russia. A year
> was to pass before British or American troops set foot in Western
> Europe, and nearly two years before they entered Germany. . . .[21]

Whether the Attlee proposals were discussed at Tehran is not clear.
Certainly, they were not approved.[22] There was merely a general understanding by the Big Three that Germany should be occupied by the
three Allies, each in a separate zone, and that Berlin should be jointly
controlled by all three.[23] According to Harry Hopkins, who was present,
the discussion on postwar Germany "ended up nowhere; it was decided
that the subject should be considered further by the European Advisory Commission in London." [24]

The European Advisory Commission, it will be recalled, had been
created at the Moscow Conference of Foreign Ministers. In referring
the question of postwar Germany to it, the Big Three were getting rid
of a hot potato. As American representative to the EAC, President
Roosevelt designated John G. Winant, the former Governor of New
Hampshire who had succeeded Joseph P. Kennedy as American Ambassador to the Court of St. James. Mr. Winant was to serve on the
Commission simultaneously with his other duties in London as Ambassador. Although he had been present at Tehran as an official ob-
server, it is doubtful whether Winant was familiar with President
Roosevelt's ideas on occupation boundaries.[25] The map which FDR
had drawn on the *Iowa* was given to General Handy who subsequently
returned it to Washington where it was kept in the records of the
Army's Operations Division (OPD) in the Pentagon.[26]

From the beginning, American policy toward the European Advisory
Commission was ambivalent. President Roosevelt and the military

ROOSEVELT'S CONCEPT OF POSTWAR OCCUPATION ZONES *for Germany drawn in pencil by
the President himself on a National Geographic Society map while en route to the Cairo conference.*

chiefs considered occupation boundaries primarily a military affair.*
The EAC was a diplomatic rather than a military creation and therefore soon found itself in the middle of the hiatus which had developed
in Washington. The American delegation to the EAC received its instructions from the Department of State. Because of the split between
Secretary Hull and the President, however, it seldom was informed of
Administration policies.

In addition to Ambassador Winant, the American delegation to the
European Advisory Commission included a full complement of political
and economic advisers. Mr. George F. Kennan, recent United States
Ambassador to Yugoslavia, author of the containment policy of the
Truman Administration, and a postwar Ambassador to the Soviet Un-
ion, was appointed as Winant's deputy. Kennan was later succeeded by
Mr. Philip Mosely, now with the Council on Foreign Relations.

The Russian delegation to the EAC was headed by Fedor Tarasovich
Gousev, then Soviet Ambassador to London. His Majesty's representative was Sir William Strang, later Lord Strang, who at that time was
the Permanent Under Secretary in the British Foreign Office.**

The first formal meeting of the European Advisory Commission was
held on January 14, 1944. At this meeting Sir William Strang introduced
the Attlee committee proposals on zonal boundaries † which President Roosevelt had rejected on the *Iowa*—the plan calling for the division of Germany into three separate zones with the United States

---

* At the Cairo Conference following Tehran, the American and British Chiefs of
Staff (i.e., the Combined Chiefs of Staff) discussed zonal boundaries within
Germany and officially referred the subject back to COSSAC headquarters in
London for further consideration. Minutes, 134th Meeting of the Combined
Chiefs of Staff, 4 December 1943, quoted in Matloff, *op. cit.*, p. 491. Also see
U.S. Department of State, *The Conferences at Cairo and Tehran* (Washington:
Government Printing Office, 1961), pp. 688, 786–87, 810–15.

** The first informal organizational meeting of the European Advisory Commission
was held in London on December 15, 1943; the first formal session one month
later. In all, the Commission held 20 formal and 97 informal meetings and was
finally dissolved by the Potsdam Conference in August, 1945. It concluded twelve
tripartite agreements dealing with the relative surrender and peace settlements in
Austria, Bulgaria and Germany. See Philip E. Mosely, "The Occupation of
Germany," *Foreign Affairs*, Vol. 28, No. 4 (July, 1950), p. 582n.

† The policy-making machinery of the British government, it should be noted,
was a great deal more integrated than that of the United States. For this reason,
the question of jurisdiction over occupation policy, or indeed, over any phase
of wartime planning, did not arise there. See Robert E. Sherwood, *Roosevelt and
Hopkins* (New York: Harper & Bros., 1948), pp. 755–57. Also see Lord Strang,
Home and Abroad (London: Andre Deutsch, 1956), p. 208.

zone located in the south and the boundary of the Soviet zone as it is today.

In January of 1944, the war in Europe was very much a Russian affair. The landings of American, British, and Canadian troops in France were still five months away. The great battles of Stalingrad, Leningrad and Moscow had been won and the Red Army already was at the prewar Russo-Polish frontier. Accordingly, the British government did not consider the Attlee proposals to be overly favorable to Russia. Indeed, there were many in London who considered them the very minimum that the Soviet Union would accept.[27]

When the Attlee proposals were transmitted to the EAC, the dispute in Washington as to jurisdiction over occupation policy had come to the surface. In December, the Department of State set up a special committee known as the Working Security Committee (WSC) to transmit instructions to the American delegation. (The name "Working Security Committee" had been selected as a cover-name to veil the true purpose of the committee.) The War and Navy Departments agreed to furnish representatives to the Committee on an "informal basis." [28] From the beginning, however, the Committee had been the scene of discord, unable to agree on what matters it should consider, and what matters should be forwarded to Mr. Winant. There were several reasons for this.

First, the Army representatives to the Committee insisted that occupation policy was a military consideration. They said it would be handled by the Joint Chiefs of Staff and not the European Advisory Commission. They said it was no concern of Ambassador Winant, or for that matter, of the WSC. Accordingly, they refused to discuss any question pertaining to occupation policy and declined to concur in any messages sent to Mr. Winant in which it was mentioned.[29]

Second, the Committee was established at an extremely low level in the Washington bureaucracy. The Army permanent representative was a lieutenant colonel; the Navy representative a lieutenant. The representatives of the State Department, who were slightly higher in rank, changed frequently and were themselves usually in the dark as to Administration policy. Like the military, they were also extremely jealous of their prerogatives and were very hesitant in sharing what they believed to be their policy-making responsibilities.[30] Differences between the State Department and the military therefore were magnified, perhaps out of proportion, and compromise became impossible.[31]

A third factor contributing to the difficulty was the extremely complicated procedure of the WSC. According to the War Department:

> On questions pertaining to military affairs, the Working Security Committee had to get comments from the State, War, and Navy Departments, the JPWC [Joint Post-War Committee of the Joint Chiefs of Staff], the Civil Affairs Division, and any other interested Washington agency. It then prepared papers incorporating these and its own comments and circulated them either to the JPWC, in cases involving primarily military problems, or to the Civil Affairs Division, in cases involving civil affairs. These agencies could then prepare papers for the JCS [Joint Chiefs of Staff] and the JCS could refer those acceptable from a military view back to the State Department. The State Department then, if it wished, could give its final approval to such papers and send them to Ambassador Winant as a basis for negotiations in the European Advisory Commission.[32]

As a result of the discord in the WSC, Ambassador Winant was left in London without instructions. Not even President Roosevelt's feelings on occupation boundaries announced on the *Iowa* were transmitted to him.

Throughout the months of December, January, and February, the deadlock in Washington continued. The War Department representatives to the WSC resolutely maintained that the question of occupation policy was a purely military affair.[33] The anomaly of this position, of course, was that simultaneously in London, the subject of occupation boundaries was being considered in detail by Winant's British and Russian colleagues.

On February 18, 1944, while the impasse in Washington continued, Soviet Ambassador Gousev announced to the European Advisory Commission that Russia was prepared to accept the zonal boundaries proposed in the Attlee report.[34] Gousev also spelled out the detailed arrangements that the Soviet Union proposed for Berlin.* In effect, the

---

* The Soviet reply of February 18, 1944, was the first time the problem of Berlin had been discussed in detail. "There shall be established around Berlin," it stated, "a 10 to 15 kilometer zone which shall be occupied jointly by the armed forces of the Union of Soviet Socialist Republics, the United Kingdom and the United States of America." The draft then went on to delineate actual city boundaries. It contained no mention of Western access.

Soviet Union had accepted without bargaining the entire package on
zonal boundaries which the British government had prepared! American participation in the proceedings thus far had been minimal, and
there is little to indicate how Winant himself felt at this time. If he
objected to the boundaries of the Attlee plan, he did not communicate
his objections to Washington.

Further talks between the British and Soviet delegations soon resulted in a draft protocol on zonal boundaries which was drawn up
and presented to the Commission. As a result, the United States was
confronted with an agreement on zones of occupation in which two of
the three member governments already concurred. By having refused
earlier to forward any instructions on occupation boundaries to London, the War Department had become an unwilling accomplice to an
agreement to which it objected.

In Washington, the deadlock in the WSC between the representatives of the State Department and the War Department continued until
late February—almost two weeks after Soviet acceptance of the British
proposals had been announced. At this point the War Department reversed its position and presented to the WSC a military plan for the
drawing of occupation boundaries. Under this plan the three Allied
zones of occupation would meet in Berlin and radiate outward like
spokes of a wheel.[35] The representatives of the State Department on
the WSC were hostile to the plan and dispatched it to London ten days
later without recommendation.*

When Ambassador Winant received the plan in London he declined
to present it. Instead, he cabled the State Department requesting further instructions, but none were forthcoming. When he asked for a
supporting memorandum, none was provided, and the WSC was again
deadlocked. The War Department insisted, and perhaps properly, that
it was a State Department function to prepare such documents. The
State Department, not in sympathy with the draft in the first place,

---

* Mr. Philip Mosely, later Winant's deputy, reports that the sketch was represented
by the military as being in accordance with President Roosevelt's ideas on occupation policy. Colonel Edgar P. Allen, the War Department representative who
carried the document to the WSC is on record as saying that he did not recall
mentioning the President's name but "thinks that all papers of this nature from
the Joint Chiefs went through the White House." Cf. Mosely, *op. cit.*, p. 591;
and Albert L. Warner, "Our Secret Deal Over Germany," *Saturday Evening Post*,
August 2, 1952, p. 66.

claimed that the War Department should provide them since it was a military proposal.[36]

Throughout March, while the British and Russian drafts on occupation boundaries were being reconciled, Winant declined to present the American proposal. Among other things, Winant and his advisers contended that the Soviets would never agree to it. The size of the Russian zone was greatly reduced from that of the Attlee proposal. The Army's plan also disregarded the normal political and administrative boundaries within Germany. The fact that the Russians had already announced their approval of the earlier British plan was cited as an additional reason for not confusing the issue with a new Western proposal.[37]

Having delayed action throughout the entire month of March, at the beginning of April Winant sent his deputy, George Kennan, back to Washington to place the issue before the President. With the State Department's approval, Kennan met with Mr. Roosevelt on April 3, 1944. He advised the President of events in London, of the earlier British proposal which the Soviet Union had accepted, and of the American delegation's opinion that the Soviets would most certainly reject the sketch prepared by the War Department. Following Mr. Kennan's presentation, the President gave in and stated that he had no objection to accepting the boundaries of the Soviet zone, since the others had already agreed.[38]

For all practical purposes, this settled the boundary of the Soviet zone and the location of Berlin one hundred and ten miles within it. Had the War Department's sketch been presented earlier, had Winant been informed of the President's policy views immediately after Tehran, had the friction in Washington over occupation boundaries not existed, the division of Germany today might be different.

Presumably, the mission of George Kennan to Washington in April was not so much to seek instructions as to convince the President to accept the British proposals. As it was, Mr. Roosevelt only partly gave in, and even after indicating to Kennan his willingness to go along with the boundaries of the Soviet zone, continued to insist that the United States occupy the northwestern zone rather than the southwestern one which the British had proposed.

Following Kennan's meeting with President Roosevelt on April 3,

the Attlee proposals once more were referred to the Joint Chiefs of
Staff. This time, the American military added their approval providing
that the United States occupy the area of northwestern Germany. On
May 1, the State Department advised Ambassador Winant in London
that the United States was prepared to accept the boundaries of the
Soviet zone as provided in the Attlee draft. Unwillingly, the United
States had become a party to an agreement to which the responsible
Administration at that time was opposed. If the governmental machinery had been able to translate this opposition into effective action
in London, that agreement would not have been reached. If the State
Department had proven itself capable of following Administration
direction in the years before the war, the situation probably would
not have arisen in the first place.[39]

In all of this, nothing had been said about Western access to Berlin.
The original Attlee draft made no mention of it. The Soviet reply of
February 18, ignored it. The American approval transmitted on May
1, was similarly silent. The problem was not raised, in fact, until later
in May when Ambassador Winant returned to Washington. During
the course of his visit, Winant went to the Pentagon to discuss occupation policy with the military authorities. According to Major General
John H. Hilldring, Chief of the Army's Civil Affairs Division and later
Assistant Secretary of State for Occupied Areas, the discussions with
Winant resulted in agreement that access to Berlin should be provided
for.*

When Winant returned to London, however, he made no effort to
raise the matter of access to Berlin in the EAC. Mr. Robert Murphy,
who subsequently became Under Secretary of State, is reported by
General Clay to have mentioned the question to Winant later in 1944.
At the time, Murphy was stationed in London as political adviser
to General Eisenhower. Afterwards, he went to Berlin with General
Clay. According to Clay's account,

---

* Philip Mosely, who was not present at the discussions in the Pentagon, gives
a different account. According to Mosely, Ambassador Winant raised the question
of access only to be told that it was a "military matter" which would be decided
"at the military level." In view of the fact that the War Department had already
acquiesced to the jurisdiction of the EAC over occupation boundaries, however,
it would appear that General Hilldring's version is substantially correct. Cf.
Mosely, *op. cit.*, pp. 593–94.

Ambassador Winant believed that the right to be in Berlin carried with it right of access and that it would only confuse the issue to raise it in connection with the agreement. He felt strongly that it would arouse Soviet suspicion and make mutual understanding more difficult to attain. He believed it possible to develop a mutual friendly understanding in which differences would disappear.[40]

In any event, Mr. Winant did not raise the question of Western access to Berlin during the proceedings in London.* During June and July, 1944, the European Advisory Commission went forward with the detailed negotiations regarding the Allied sectors in Berlin.** Since this was an extended and laborious process, it is probable that the question of access to the German capital presented itself to the members of the American delegation.[41] Sir William Strang, the British delegate to the EAC, has stated, however, that at that time "it was not our expectation that the zones would be sealed off from one another. This was a Soviet conception which only became apparent in the late summer of 1945 when the occupation was an accomplished fact." [42]

Because of the Western hesitancy to mention the matter of access, the draft protocol on zones of occupation finally concluded by the EAC made no reference to it. Under the protocol, Germany was divided according to the original Attlee proposals with the boundary of the Soviet zone as it is today. Berlin also was divided into three sectors, although again, as in the question of the Western zones, the assignment of the particular Western sectors awaited final determination.

On September 12, 1944, the first "Protocol on Zones of Occupation" was signed in London by Winant, Gousev, and Strang. It simply left blank the name of the particular Western power occupying each of the Western zones. In spite of the fact that it contained no provision for access, this Protocol is basic to the present four-power status of

---

* In later correspondence, Mr. Robert Murphy has stated that Winant did not raise the issue of access to Berlin in the EAC because he thought that "once established in Berlin, our ingress and egrees would be a natural corollary." See Warner, *op. cit.*, p. 68.

** In referring to "zones" and "sectors," normal postwar usage has restricted "zone" to mean the divisions of the prewar state of Germany. The term "sector" is reserved for the division within the city of Berlin itself. Hence, the Soviet zone and the Soviet sector are two separate entities.

Berlin.* As has been indicated, it was based largely on an initial British proposal but secured early and complete Soviet acceptance. According to the Protocol:

> The Governments of the United States of America, the United Kingdom of Great Britain and Northern Ireland, and the Union of Soviet Socialist Republics have reached the following agreement . . .

> 1. Germany, within her frontiers as they were on the 31st December, 1937, will, for the purposes of occupation, be divided into three zones, one of which will be allotted to each of the three Powers, and a special Berlin area, which will be under joint occupation by the three Powers.
> 2. The Boundaries of the three zones and of the Berlin area, and the allocation of three zones as between the U.S.A., the U.K. and the U.S.S.R. will be as follows:

✿   ✿   ✿

> *The Berlin area (by which expression is understood the territory of "Greater Berlin" as defined by the Law of the 27th April, 1920) will be jointly occupied by armed forces of the U.S.A., U.K., and U.S.S.R., assigned by the respective Commanders-in-Chief.* For this purpose the territory of 'Greater Berlin' will be divided into the following three parts:–[Italics added.]

> *North-Eastern part of "Greater Berlin"* (districts of Pankow, Prenzlauerberg, Mitte, Weissensee, Friedrichshain, Lichtenberg, Treptow, Köpenick) will be occupied by the forces of the U.S.S.R.:

> *North-Western part of "Greater Berlin"* (districts of Reinickendorf, Wedding, Tiergarten, Charlottenburg, Spandau, Wilmersdorf) will be occupied by the forces of _____ _____:

> *Southern part of "Greater Berlin"* (districts of Zehlendorf, Steglitz, Schöneberg, Kreuzberg, Tempelhof, Neukölln) will be occupied by the forces of _____:

✿   ✿   ✿

> 5. An Inter-Allied Governing Authority (Komandatura) consisting of three Commandants, appointed by their respective Commanders-in-Chief, will be established to direct jointly the administration of the 'Greater Berlin' Area.[43]

✿   ✿   ✿

* France was added later as an occupying power. See *infra.*

When the draft Protocol was signed, Ambassador Winant took it immediately to Quebec where President Roosevelt and Prime Minister Churchill were conferring. The purpose for doing so was to settle British-American differences over the two Western zones.

The Quebec Conference had been arranged largely at the insistence of Prime Minister Churchill. With the war in Europe drawing to a close, with France liberated and Allied forces knocking at the German frontiers, the British government strongly desired to review the final phases of European strategy. Among other things to be discussed were the role of Great Britain in the Pacific, the continuation of American Lend-Lease assistance to Britain after the war, and the course of Allied occupation policy toward Germany.

Much of the conference, as it turned out, was devoted to the question of the coming occupation of Germany. To Mr. Churchill's surprise, the President had brought with him to Quebec Secretary of the Treasury Henry Morgenthau, Jr. "I had been surprised when I arrived at Quebec," Mr. Churchill has written, "that the President was accompanied by Mr. Morgenthau, the Secretary of the United States Treasury, though neither the Secretary of State nor Harry Hopkins was present. But I was glad to see Morgenthau, as we were anxious to discuss financial arrangements between our two countries for the period between the conquest of Germany and the defeat of the Japanese. The President and his Secretary of the Treasury were however much more concerned about the treatment of Germany after the war." [44]

In the ensuing discussions the President and Morgenthau pressed on Mr. Churchill what has since become known as the "Morgenthau Plan"—a plan calling for the destruction of German industry after the war and for the turning of Germany into an agricultural "pastoral" nation. The Morgenthau Plan had been drafted by Harry Dexter White, Morgenthau's Special Assistant in the Treasury Department.* Although he at first opposed it, Churchill finally accepted the plan after he had been promised substantial American financial assistance during the postwar period. According to the Prime Minister, "At first I violently opposed this idea. But the President, with Mr. Morgen-

---

* Harry Dexter White figures prominently in American planning for the occupation of Germany. According to Eugene Davidson, the Morgenthau Plan bore a "strong resemblance" to an earlier Soviet plan for Germany prepared in Moscow by Eugene Varga, a Soviet economist. Eugene Davidson, *The Death and Life of Germany* (New York: Alfred A. Knopf, 1959), pp. 37–38.

thau—from whom we had so much to ask—were so insistent that in
the end we agreed to consider it." [45]

Following Mr. Churchill's ostensible acceptance of the "Morgenthau
Plan" (he later rejected it), President Roosevelt agreed to accept the
southern zone in Germany for the United States. While there may
have been other considerations, it seems fair to say that the President's
sudden reversal of position was in large part determined by Churchill's
decision.[46]

Before finally accepting the southern zone, however, President
Roosevelt insisted that the port cities of Bremen and Bremerhaven
(which were located in north Germany) be included under American
jurisdiction as separate enclaves. The American Joint Chiefs of Staff
also demanded iron-clad agreements from the British guaranteeing
American access through the British zone. These requirements were
incorporated into the final report of the Quebec Conference prepared
by the Combined Chiefs of Staff.

Paradoxically, the military chiefs did not demand the same rights
from the Russians. When the overall zonal structure in Germany was
reviewed at Quebec by the Combined Chiefs, the right of Allied access
to the German capital was not questioned.[47] As for the Soviet boundaries, Quebec merely ratified the earlier accord reached by the
European Advisory Commission in London.

The Quebec Conference thus settled the relative location of the
American and British zones. This agreement was embodied in a
November 14th amendment to the original Protocol on Zones of Oc-
cupation. Likewise, it was signed in London by Winant, Gousev, and
Strang. In it, Great Britain also accepted the northwestern sector of
Berlin, and the United States the southern sector. The Russian sector
in Berlin and the Russian zone in Germany remained unchanged.

In light of the earlier Allied failure to raise the question of access
to Berlin, the insistence of the American military on transit rights
through the British zone is the most significant portion of the November 14th amendment. Specifically, it stated:

> For the purpose of facilitating communications between the
> South-Western Zone and the sea, the Commander-in-Chief of the
> United States forces in the South-Western Zone will
>
> (a) exercise such control of the ports of Bremen and Bremer-
> haven and the necessary staging areas in the vicinity thereof as

may be agreed hereafter by the United Kingdom and United States military authorities to be necessary to meet his requirements:

(b) enjoy such transit facilities through the North-Western Zone as may be agreed hereafter by the United Kingdom and United States military authorities to be necessary to meet his requirements.[48]

Shortly after Quebec, President Roosevelt acted to curtail the role of the European Advisory Commission in occupation planning. In a memorandum to Secretary Hull on September 29, 1944, he specifically prohibited the EAC from considering the problem of postwar economic policy toward Germany.[49] This was followed on October 20, by a second Presidential memorandum in which Mr. Roosevelt took the Commission to task for its earlier activities. Five days later a third note from the President put a complete stop to the postwar planning for Germany then being pursued by the American delegation in London. According to Philip Mosely, the decision by the President "cut the ground completely from under the EAC and from under the policy . . . of Mr. Winant."[50] One may well speculate what might have happened had this decision been taken six months earlier. Probably, the occupation boundaries in Germany would have been negotiated by the military authorities and a zonal arrangement much closer to that which President Roosevelt initially proposed would have resulted.*

As a result of the President's action, the responsibility for planning occupation policy was returned to the military. By this time, however, the damage had been done and the boundary of the Soviet zone as it exists today had been agreed to. On February 1, 1945, the Joint Chiefs of Staff met with their British counterparts at Malta. The meeting was preparatory to the final Big Three Conference of Roosevelt, Churchill and Stalin which was to take place shortly afterwards at

---

* Later, at Yalta, President Roosevelt once more indicated his distaste for the European Advisory Commission. According to the then Secretary of State, Edward R. Stettinius, the President "made it clear that he felt the European Advisory Commission, established by the Moscow Pacts of 1943, had not been a success. . . ." When Ambassador Winant cabled Mr. Roosevelt expressing regret that he had not been invited to Yalta, "The President, on receipt of Winant's message, remarked that it was not necessary for the Ambassador to Great Britain to be present." Edward R. Stettinius, *Roosevelt and the Russians—The Yalta Conference* (Garden City, N.Y.: Doubleday & Co., 1949), pp. 88, 289.

Yalta. Although the question of the occupation of Germany was discussed, no mention was made of Berlin, or of the necessity to provide for access to it.[51] And when the plans were reviewed during a similar pre-Yalta policy meeting—this time at Marrakech, French Morocco—Secretary of State Stettinius and his key advisers from the State Department agreed that the question of Western access to Berlin was one which should be left to the military authorities.[52]

Thus, when the Yalta Conference convened, most of the plans about the future zones of occupation in Germany had been completed. The Soviet Union had accepted its zone of occupation almost one year before. At Quebec, four and a half months before Yalta, President Roosevelt and Prime Minister Churchill had agreed on the respective location of the American and British zones. Formal acceptance by the Big Three of the protocols prepared by the European Advisory Commission was therefore a foregone conclusion. What little debate there was at Yalta regarding zones of occupation did not concern Berlin or the Soviet zone but developed over Western proposals to include France as an equal partner in Germany's occupation.[53]

The military situation when the Yalta Conference convened was again favorable to the Soviet Union. The Red Army had just reached the banks of the Oder River on a thirty-five mile front less than fifty miles from Berlin. The great Soviet winter offensive of 1944–45 was still in progress. In the West, the Allies had not finished restoring the positions in the Ardennes which Field Marshal von Rundstedt had overrun during the Battle of the Bulge. The Rhine had not been breached. Every factor indicated that the armies of General Eisenhower faced another several months of heavy fighting. In this situation the Western leaders were little disposed to question anew the proposed boundaries of the Soviet zone or the location of Berlin within it. Accordingly, the previously drafted protocols of the European Advisory Commission on zones of occupation were quickly approved.

The zonal boundaries in Germany were also reviewed at Yalta by the American Joint Chiefs of Staff and approved on February 7, with the following statement: ". . . there are no reasons from a military viewpoint why the Draft Protocol of the European Advisory Commission relative to zones of occupation in Germany and Administration of Greater Berlin should not be approved." [54]

In considering the question of access to Berlin, the American Joint

Staff (a staff group working under the Joint Chiefs of Staff) prepared the following memorandum:

> The U.S. Forces in Berlin and certain other areas will be isolated from the main areas of U.S. occupation by territory occupied by other than U.S. forces. There will be need for regular transit by road, air, and rail across this intervening territory. The U.S. Chiefs of Staff propose that the general principle be accepted of freedom of transit by each nation concerned between the main occupied area and the forces occupying Berlin and similar isolated areas. They further propose that the details be worked out by the local commanders.[55]

When the question was raised by the Joint Chiefs with their British and Russian counterparts, however, the Russians proved reluctant to discuss it and the matter was dropped. No further action was taken and apparently no significance was attached to the Russian reluctance.[56]

The decision of the Yalta Conference to admit France to the military occupation of Germany came only after the Western Allies had agreed that whatever zone France might occupy would be taken from the area already allotted to the Western powers. As a result, the United States and Great Britain began the task of creating a third Western zone. The province of Baden-Wuerttemberg in the American zone was split giving the French the southwestern portion which was adjacent to France. The Saar and the Rhinish-Palatinate from the British zone also were ceded to France, forming a barely contiguous zone of about half the size of the other three.

In the division of Baden-Wuerttemberg, the Joint Chiefs of Staff demonstrated once more their concern for securing the right of American access. In this case they insisted that the Munich-Karlsruhe-Frankfurt autobahn, and the main trunk railway from Frankfurt to Munich, be kept solely in American hands. This led to the splitting of Baden-Wuerttemberg along purely logistical lines and was opposed by the State Department on the grounds that such a split would only further complicate the administration of the territories affected.[57]

With the location of the French zone agreed to, the occupation boundaries in Germany were complete. From their inception, these boundaries had been opposed by the responsible Administration in Washington. Their subsequent acceptance by the United States had been reluctant and hesitant. The differences between the State Department, and the President and his military advisers, had been present throughout the entire process. When the boundaries of the Soviet zone were first proposed, the conflict in Washington prevented President Roosevelt's ideas from being transmitted to London. When the Administration position later was forwarded, the opinion of the London delegation prevented it from being introduced into the proceedings.

The fact that President Roosevelt later ordered the American delegation to the European Advisory Commission to cease planning for the occupation of Germany and transferred the matter to the Joint Chiefs of Staff is indicative that the activity of Ambassador Winant and his associates was not approved in Washington. Once the planning of occupation policy was returned to the military, the Joint Chiefs did not neglect to provide for American access through both the British and French zones in the agreements which were subsequently concluded.* Their failure to secure similar guarantees from the Russians can only be attributed to a desire to avoid raising any subject which might weaken Soviet desires to contribute to the overall Allied effort. The war with Japan loomed ominously on the horizon and the American Chiefs were more than anxious to obtain prompt Soviet intervention.

The wartime agreements regarding the occupation of Germany set the stage for the drama in Berlin which has since developed. In retrospect, it is clear that many of these agreements were ill-considered. It is hardly worth while, however, to resurrect these decisions, or the processes through which they were made, with the intent of finding scapegoats for the present crisis. At the time the decisions were made, there were few in the West who would have suggested that America's emphasis on winning the war might have been better placed on securing the peace.

If any one factor may be singled out above all others as contributing to the unhappy outcome of the wartime negotiations, it would have to be the lack of overall coordination which then existed in Washington. The total inability to translate the policy announcements of Presi-

* The November 14th Amendment in which the right of access through the British zone was guaranteed was approved at Malta on February 1, 1945.

dent Roosevelt on the *Iowa* into effective action at the scene of the negotiations in London exposes a weakness in our governmental process which recent events have shown to be a luxury we can hardly afford.

3

The Military Decision
to Halt at the Elbe

THE ATTLEE PROPOSALS on zonal boundaries within Germany were devised in mid-1943, presented to the European Advisory Commission at the beginning of 1944, accepted by the Soviets February 18, 1944, and approved by the United States three months later. The first protocol reflecting these agreements was signed in London on September 12, 1944. At Quebec shortly afterward, Churchill and Roosevelt agreed upon the location of the British and American zones and then at Yalta, with Stalin, reviewed and approved the entire zonal set-up in Germany.

Immediately following Yalta, however, the military situation in Europe changed considerably. The armies of General Eisenhower, so hard pressed in December and January, suddenly resumed the offensive and, as German resistance rapidly disintegrated, the offensive turned into a *blitzkrieg*. What had looked at Yalta like a prolonged campaign, soon showed promise of early victory. In this situation, the British government, and especially Winston Churchill, began to question the wisdom of the Attlee proposals. Even at Yalta the Prime Minister had begun to grumble about the advance of Russia into Central Europe. With victory in the offing, the growling of the British Lion turned into a roar.

Originally, Allied military plans envisaged a final drive toward Berlin by the Western powers. Preinvasion plans prepared by the Supreme Headquarters of the Allied Expeditionary Force (SHAEF) listed Berlin as the ultimate military goal of the American and British forces.[1] Following the invasion, Berlin remained the number one objective. According to the late General Walter Bedell Smith, Eisenhower's able Chief of Staff at SHAEF:

> From the day our invasion broke over the beaches of Normandy, the goal of every Allied soldier had been Berlin. The Supreme Commander, the Staff, and all the troops shared a driving ambition to seal the defeat of Nazi Germany by seizing the capital of the Reich itself. During our planning days in England, there seemed every reason to believe that after the Ruhr was encircled and its troops destroyed, we could end the war by taking the political heart—Berlin.[2]

In September, 1944, after the fall of Paris, Field Marshal Montgomery suggested a lightning thrust toward Berlin, but General Eisenhower replied that he preferred to reduce the industrial areas of the Ruhr and Rhine before pushing on to the German capital. From a military standpoint, the Supreme Commander was on firm ground. Unquestionably, however, Eisenhower recognized the importance of Berlin. "Clearly Berlin is the main prize," he wrote Montgomery, "and the prize in defense of which the enemy is likely to concentrate the bulk of his forces. There is no doubt whatsoever, in my mind," that after the Ruhr has been conquered, "we should concentrate all our energies and resources on a rapid thrust to Berlin."[3]

The idea of a final drive on Berlin was based on sound strategic reasoning. The terrain separating Berlin from the Ruhr was ideal for offensive operations. Unlike the other regions of Germany where mountain barriers and forests tended to restrict armored activity, the area west of Berlin was generally open and rolling. Except for the Weser and Elbe rivers, it was devoid of natural obstacles.[4]

At the end of January, 1945, General Eisenhower sent his Chief of Staff, General Walter Bedell Smith, to the Anglo-American conference

then underway at Malta. Smith's purpose was to brief the Western
leaders on the course of future military operations. In so doing, he
advised them that the Allied forces would very likely advance beyond
the zonal boundary which the European Advisory Commission had
established. As reported by General Eisenhower: "We felt that if our
political superiors agreed with us they might decide to insist upon
their right to occupy a greater portion of the German territory than
then recommended. General Smith's presentation obviously changed
no ideas; the advisory commission's plan, outlining boundaries as they
now exist . . . was to stand." [5]

Shortly after Smith's presentation, the Allied Expeditionary Force
regained the initiative, and by the beginning of March, the German
Army was reeling in retreat from the North Sea to the Swiss frontier.
On March 3, General William H. Simpson's Ninth U.S. Army reached
the Rhine near Düsseldorf, shortly thereafter American troops captured Cologne, and on March 5, General Patton's Third Army, driving
down the Moselle, reached the Rhine at Coblenz.

Two days later, March 7, 1945, the 9th Armored Division pushed
into the battered Rhineland town of Remagen. To their surprise, the
Ludendorff railway bridge across the Rhine was still standing. This
was a break for the West; in two days, five divisions of the First Army
were pushed across and a bridgehead three miles deep on the other
side was secured.

Two weeks after the capture of the bridge at Remagen, all organized
resistance west of the Rhine was over.[6] Simpson's Ninth Army and
the First Army of General Courtney Hodges were now driving for
a link-up in the Ruhr which would isolate an estimated force of
twenty-one German divisions—an army greater than that which Field
Marshal von Paulus had surrendered at Stalingrad.

The advance continued without respite. The bridges over the Main
River and the powerful concrete fortifications at Aschaffenburg in
Bavaria were captured intact by the 4th Armored Division on March
25. Other elements of the Third Army captured the vital rail terminus
of Darmstadt. Frankfurt was cleared of enemy resistance on March
29, as were Giessen to the north, and Mannheim to the south.[7]

The sudden collapse of German resistance in the West caused
General Eisenhower and those near him at SHAEF to review the
earlier tactical plans for a final push to Berlin. American intelligence
estimates placed forward elements of the Red Army across the Oder

River and only twenty-eight miles from the outskirts of the German capital.[8] With the occupation boundaries already agreed to, there was little inclination at SHAEF to engage the Soviets in a race for Berlin.[9] It was not known, of course, that the Russians would be held on the Oder for the next six weeks as Hitler scraped together every remaining formation for a final desperate stand.

With the fall of Berlin believed imminent, however, other objectives loomed into view. The possibility of continuing Nazi resistance in a so-called "National Redoubt," reports of which had disturbed SHAEF for over a month, caused American strategists at General Eisenhower's headquarters to turn their attention toward the Bavarian Alps. An American intelligence summary received on March 11 specifically warned that the Nazis would make a last stand in Bavaria. The report itself read like science fiction:

> Here [in the Bavarian mountains], defended by nature and by the most efficient secret weapons yet invented, the powers that have hitherto guided Germany will survive to reorganize her resurrection; here armaments will be manufactured in bomb-proof factories, food and equipment will be stored in vast underground caverns and a specially selected corps of young men will be trained in guerilla warfare, so that a whole underground army can be fitted and directed to liberate Germany from the occupying forces.[10]

The subsequent capture of several general officers of the German Army who denied any knowledge of a defensive position in the Alps was simply interpreted by military intelligence as a further verification. According to the intelligence appraisal, it would be the SS elite troops and not the German Army who would hold these positions, and their construction therefore was being kept secret from the Army.[11]

Belief in the National Redoubt dominated American military thinking until well into April. At a background briefing to a press conference in Paris on the twenty-first of April, 1945, General Bedell Smith emphasized the importance of the National Redoubt in Allied strategy. Admitting that precise information about the region was sketchy, Smith stated:

> Just what we will find down there we do not know. We are beginning to think a lot more than we expect. You have seen the underground installations around Mosbach and Schweinfurt, where we have been just bombing the hell out of the ball bearing plants

up there and doing a marvelous job of hitting buildings, and finding eighty-five percent were underground, beautifully underground. We may find when we get down there a great deal more underground than anticipated; I am thinking we will.

Our target now, [Smith continued,] if we are going to bring this war to an end and bring it to an end in a hell of a hurry, is this National Redoubt, and we are organizing our strength in that direction. . . . From a purely military standpoint . . . Berlin . . . doesn't have much significance any more—not anything comparable to that of the so-called National Redoubt.* [12]

General Eisenhower himself was also disturbed over the reports regarding the National Redoubt. In recalling his reasons for deciding not to push on to Berlin the Supreme Commander has written,

> For many weeks we had been receiving reports that the Nazi intention . . . was to withdraw the cream of the SS, Gestapo, and other organizations fanatically devoted to Hitler, into the mountains of southern Bavaria, Western Austria, and northern Italy. There they expected to hold out indefinitely against the Allies. . . . The evidence was clear that the Nazi intended to make the attempt and I decided to give no opportunity to carry it out.[13]

In reality, the National Redoubt existed only in the propaganda blasts of Dr. Goebbels. Postwar studies by the Allied Military Government clearly indicate that the Berchtesgaden area was being turned into a refuge, not a stronghold.[14] But it was not until the war was over that the phantom of the National Redoubt was exposed. According to General Omar Bradley, "the Redoubt existed largely in the imagination of a few fanatic Nazis. It grew into so exaggerated a scheme that I am astonished we could have believed it as innocently as we did." [15]

In addition to the National Redoubt, other factors intervened in

---

* In his subsequent book on the war in Europe, General Smith, who undoubtedly was closer than anyone else to the decision-making process at Eisenhower's headquarters, cites the concern with the "National Redoubt" as the reason, "above all," in determining to push south toward Dresden rather than on to Berlin. Although he admits that the extent of the so-called National Redoubt "remained something of an unknown quantity" at SHAEF during March and April (the British never accepted it as genuine), Smith recalls having received reconnaissance photographs which showed that the Germans were constructing extensive bunkers in the Berchtesgaden area. The fact that many government bureaus were quitting Berlin and setting up in Berchtesgaden and the reports of feverish activity by the Germans along the Danube and in Munich added further to this belief. See Walter Bedell Smith, *Eisenhower's Six Great Decisions* (New York: Longmans, Green & Co., 1956), pp. 186–89.

March to cause SHAEF to reconsider the possibility of a drive on Berlin. Since much of Germany's arms production had been moved from the Ruhr to Saxony and Thuringia, these areas became attractive targets. Also, an attack on Berlin, if it were made, would fall under the direct command of Field Marshal Montgomery whose Twenty-first Army Group held that section of the Allied front. South of Montgomery, command was vested in General Omar Bradley. Intoxicated by the rapid advance to the Rhine, United States public opinion at this time was crying out for further American victories. A thrust by Montgomery to Berlin would mean that the Ninth American Army, located in the center of the front, could not be given to Bradley but would remain under British control. Such an event would fly directly in the face of popular sentiment. The individualistic personality of Field Marshal Montgomery, compared with the somewhat closer relationship which existed between Eisenhower's and Bradley's headquarters, may also have influenced a decision at SHAEF in favor of Bradley.

In any event, in early March, 1945, Bradley returned to Supreme Headquarters at Rheims for a final review of Western strategy. Asked by Eisenhower for his opinion of a drive on Berlin, Bradley replied that it might cost 100,000 lives. "A pretty stiff price to pay for a prestige objective, especially when we've got to fall back and let the other fellow take over." [16]

In his account of the meeting at Rheims, the scholarly Bradley describes how he and Eisenhower, bending over a map together, selected the Elbe near Dresden as the final objective for the Allied forces.* "I could see no political advantage accruing from the capture of Berlin," Bradley writes, "that would offset the need for quick destruction of the German army on our front. As soldiers we looked naively on the British inclination to complicate the war with political foresight and nonmilitary objectives." [17]

Following Bradley's visit to Rheims, the Allied staff at Supreme

---

* Considering that Bradley's Twelfth Army Group was to lead the thrust toward Dresden, the official historian of the Department of the Army has pointedly remarked that "it is not surprising that General Bradley's advice stressed the difficulties of the advance on Berlin and the value of striking toward Dresden." See Forrest C. Pogue, *Command Decisions* (Kent R. Greenfield, ed.) Office of the Chief of Military History, Department of the Army (Washington: Government Printing Office, 1960), p. 483.

Headquarters prepared plans to shift the major Anglo-American effort south of Berlin, driving instead toward a link-up with the Russians near Dresden.* In the words of General Smith, "Berlin was officially abandoned as an objective." [18]

At about the same time as the meeting in Rheims, Prime Minister Churchill began to inquire about the final phases of Allied strategy. Churchill alone among the Western leaders recognized the danger latent in the continued advance of the Red Army. The impending destruction of German military power was bringing with it fundamental changes in the face of Europe. As the common enemy disappeared, so too did the bond of union which had cemented the Grand Alliance together. The final political settlement in Germany loomed greater than ever on the horizon. Churchill expressed his concern in the following homily: "When wolves are about the shepherd must guard his flock, even if he himself does not care for mutton." [19]

On March 17, the Prime Minister asked the British Chiefs of Staff what the nature of the final German resistance was likely to be. "All kinds of rumors, only slightly sustained by our reports," Mr. Churchill states, "were rife about Hitler's future plans. I had thought it prudent to have them searchingly examined, because I heard that they were counting for much at Eisenhower's headquarters." [20]

Several days later the British Chiefs reported back to the Prime Minister that a prolonged German campaign, "or even guerilla" warfare, in the Bavarian mountains was highly unlikely.[21] Having received this information and thus verified for himself that in all probability there would be no final stand in the so-called "Bavarian Redoubt," Churchill asked Eisenhower what direction the final Allied advance would take.

On March 30, the Supreme Commander replied that he was planning to launch his major attack to the south of Berlin toward Dresden.

---

* In explaining his decision of that March to strike toward Dresden rather than Berlin, Eisenhower wrote in 1948 that while the German capital may have been important as a political and psychological objective, ". . . it was not the logical or the most desirable objective for the forces of the Western Allies." "Military plans," as he phrased it, "should be devised with the single aim of speeding victory." The proximity of the Russians to Berlin, combined with what he considered the resulting Allied logistical problems, made an attack on Berlin in his words, "more than unwise, it was stupid." Dwight D. Eisenhower, *Crusade in Europe* (Garden City, N.Y.: Doubleday & Co., 1948), p. 396.

Following the encirclement of the Ruhr, Eisenhower said, the First, Third, and Ninth American Armies would drive eastward along the line Kassel-Leipzig-Dresden toward the Elbe and attempt a link-up with Soviet forces in that area. The entire operation would be controlled by Bradley's Twelfth Army Group, while Montgomery would support the left flank, and the Seventh Army of General Jacob Devers, the right flank. The purpose of Bradley's drive, as Eisenhower explained it, would be to cut the German military strength in half as soon as possible and, "will not involve us in crossing the Elbe." Berlin, as a result, would be left to the Russians.[22]

Two days previously, on March 28, 1945, Eisenhower announced his new tactical plan in a direct telegram to Marshal Stalin. This was the first time that SHAEF had dealt directly with the head of the Soviet government and it would soon have its consequences. In his reply, Stalin advised Eisenhower that he wholly agreed with SHAEF's latest proposal. According to Stalin, Eisenhower's plan to avoid Berlin "entirely coincides with the plan of the Soviet High Command. Berlin has lost its former strategic importance. The Soviet High Command therefore plans to allot secondary forces in the direction of Berlin." [23]

When SHAEF's plan was received in London, British reaction was immediate. Churchill and the British Chiefs of Staff were concerned not only that its major concept was to by-pass Berlin, but also that it had been communicated directly to Marshal Stalin. Eisenhower's cable to Stalin, it should be noted, was dispatched two days prior to his message informing Churchill that he had decided to drive south toward Dresden.*

London considered Eisenhower's telegram to Stalin as a transgression of an earlier authorization that had been given to him by the Combined Chiefs of Staff to deal directly with Russian military authorities on military matters. Churchill felt that the information communicated by Eisenhower to Stalin went far beyond the military sphere. Although ostensibly concerned with the juncture of the two

---

* Dr. Herbert Feis, noted authority on the diplomatic history of World War II, has suggested that Eisenhower may have dispatched his message to Stalin on March 28, "in order to end all chance of further argument" with the Prime Minister about taking Berlin. The cable to Stalin was sent on the Supreme Commander's own initiative on March 28 without informing either his deputy, British Air Marshal Tedder, or the Combined Chiefs of Staff. Herbert Feis, *op. cit.*, p. 603. The complete text of Eisenhower's cable to Stalin is printed in John Ehrman, *Grand Strategy*, Vol. VI (London: H. M. Stationery Office, 1956), p. 132.

armies, the Supreme Commander, as Churchill saw it, was settling major strategic problems which had decided political implications.[24]

However disturbed the Prime Minister may have been over what he considered Eisenhower's intrusion into the political sphere, his greatest fire was directed at the substance of the plan itself. Writing to General Lord Ismay, his personal Chief of Staff, on March 31, the Prime Minister stated: "It seems to me that the chief criterion of the new Eisenhower plan is that it shifts the axis of the main advance upon Berlin to the direction through Leipzig to Dresden. . . . It also seems that General Eisenhower may be wrong in supposing Berlin to be largely devoid of military and political importance. Even though German Government departments have to a great extent moved to the south, the dominating fact on German minds of the fall of Berlin should not be overlooked. The idea of neglecting Berlin and leaving it to the Russians to take at a later stage does not appear to me correct." [25]

The British Chiefs of Staff had previously notified Washington of their disagreements with SHAEF's new strategy. On March 29, General Marshall cabled the British concerns to Eisenhower. The following day, Eisenhower replied that since he was the responsible commander on the spot, he felt authorized in pursuing his present course. After disclaiming any change in plans, General Eisenhower pointed out that he felt Berlin was ". . . no longer a particularly important objective. Its usefulness to the German has been largely destroyed and even his government is preparing to move to another area. What is now important is to gather up our forces for a single drive. . . ." Concluding his cable in the time honored method of successful field commanders who feel they are being interfered with at home, Eisenhower said that "naturally" his plans were flexible and that as the tactical commander, it was essential for him to retain the freedom of action necessary to meet changing situations. By implication, the shift south from Berlin to Dresden was one of these situations.[26]

In Washington, General Eisenhower's position received immediate support. Replying to the British Chiefs of Staff on behalf of the United States, General Marshall not only upheld the right of Eisenhower to communicate directly with Stalin but also approved, in substance, Eisenhower's latest plan. In what could, according to the Army's official history, "easily be interpreted as a dig at the strategic views of the British Chiefs of Staff," Marshall pointed to the successful conclusion of the battle on the Rhine as a vindication of Eisenhower's military judgment. According to Marshall: "The battle of Germany is now at a point where it is up to the Field Commander to judge the measures which should be taken. To deliberately turn away from the exploitation of the enemy's weakness does not appear sound. The single objective should be quick and complete victory. While recognizing there are factors not of direct concern to SHAEF, the U.S. Chiefs consider his strategic concept is sound and should receive full support. He should continue to communicate freely with the Commander-in-Chief of the Soviet Army [Marshal Stalin]." [27]

The American Joint Chiefs of Staff were products of the same military tradition as General Eisenhower and shared his sentiments on strategic planning. To them, SHAEF's plan of driving toward a juncture with the Red Army was infinitely more realistic than the somewhat politically tainted British desire to capture Berlin. Perhaps they also did not look adversely on concentrating the last big push under Bradley's American command rather than under the Twenty-first Army Group of Field Marshal Montgomery.

In spite of Marshall's reply, however, opposition to SHAEF's plan continued in London. Berlin, the British felt, should remain the principal Allied objective, and on March 31, 1945, Churchill wrote to Eisenhower at Rheims and announced once more his preference for:

> . . . the plan on which we crossed the Rhine, namely, that the Ninth U. S. Army should march with the Twenty-first Army Group [Montgomery] to the Elbe and beyond Berlin.
>
> I do not know why it would be an advantage not to cross the Elbe. If the enemy resistance should weaken, as you evidently expect and which may well be fulfilled, why should we not cross the Elbe and advance as far eastward as possible? This has an important political bearing. . . . Further, I do not consider myself that Berlin has yet lost its military and certainly not its political significance. The fall of Berlin would have a profound psychological effect on German resistance in every part of the Reich. While Berlin holds out great masses of Germans will feel it their duty to go down fighting. The idea that the capture of Dresden and the junction with the Russians there would be a superior gain does not commend itself to me. The parts of the German government departments which have moved south can very quickly move southward again. But while Berlin remains under the German flag

it cannot, in my opinion, fail to be the most decisive point in Germany.[28]

The following day, April 1, 1945, the Prime Minister carried his appeal to President Roosevelt. After disclaiming any desire to detract or discredit the military ability of SHAEF and reaffirming "the complete confidence felt by His Majesty's Government in General Eisenhower," Churchill launched into a direct attack on the strategy which Eisenhower proposed.

> Hitherto the axis [of advance] has been upon Berlin. General Eisenhower . . . now wishes to shift the axis somewhat to the southward and strike through Leipzig, even perhaps as far south as Dresden. He withdraws the Ninth United States Army from the northern group of Armies [Montgomery] and in consequence stretches its front southward. . . . I say quite frankly that Berlin remains of high strategic importance. Nothing will exert a psychological effect of despair upon all German forces of resistance equal to the fall of Berlin. It will be the supreme signal for the German people. On the other hand, if left to itself to maintain a siege by the Russians among its ruins, and as long as the German flag flies there, it will animate the resistance of all Germans under arms.[29]

Turning to the political considerations involved, the British head of government stated: "There is moreover another aspect which it is proper for you and me to consider. The Russian armies will no doubt overrun all Austria and enter Vienna. If they also take Berlin will not their impression that they have been the overwhelming contributor to our common victory be unduly imprinted in their minds, and may this not lead them into a mood which will raise grave and formidable difficulties in the future? *I therefore consider that from a political standpoint we should march as far east into Germany as possible, and that should Berlin be in our grasp we should certainly take it.*" [30]

Churchill concluded his message to the President with a statement that although this was a personal message and not "a staff communication," he had no objection to Roosevelt's showing it to General Marshall. The Prime Minister was later to learn, although he was not aware of it at the time, that the President's health had failed to such an extent that it was General Marshall and not Mr. Roosevelt who answered his message.[31]

Marshall's reply stressed only the immediate military considerations involved in striking toward Dresden. According to the notes of the War Department, it was dispatched by the White House exactly as Marshall had written it.[32]

On the same date that Churchill was writing to President Roosevelt, General Eisenhower attempted to refute the Prime Minister's charges. The Supreme Commander insisted he had not changed plans but was simply taking advantage of the recent changes in the military situation. Although Eisenhower said he recognized the political considerations which had been mentioned by Mr. Churchill, he still preferred to exploit the idea of a central thrust under Bradley's control along the axis Kassel-Leipzig-Dresden.[33]

The following day Churchill conceded. British military forces in Europe at this time were outnumbered three to one by the Americans and, as Churchill said, "I felt it my duty to end this correspondence between friends." * [34] On April 5, as the Allied attack toward Dresden began, the Prime Minister cabled President Roosevelt that he considered the matter closed. "To prove my sincerity," Churchill stated, "I will use one of my very few Latin quotations: *Amantium irae amoris integratio est.*" [35] This was translated by the War Department as "Lovers' quarrels are a part of love." [36]

Mr. Churchill's avowals did not end the matter, however. Likewise suspicious at the alacrity with which Marshal Stalin had agreed to Eisenhower's proposal, the British Chiefs of Staff began to urge a reconsideration of SHAEF's new strategy on military grounds. Their pleas, as it turned out, were in vain. The American Chiefs of Staff refused to intervene.[37] In their reply to the British,** the U.S. military chiefs stated that "only Eisenhower is in a position to know how to

* In his message to Eisenhower, however, the Prime Minister left little doubt as to his own opinion. Referring to Stalin's earlier cable to SHAEF, Churchill stated, "I am however all the more impressed with the importance of entering Berlin, which may well be open to us, by the reply from Moscow to you, which in paragraph 3 says, 'Berlin has lost its former strategic importance.' *This should be read in the light of what I mentioned of the political aspects. I deem it highly important that we should shake hands with the Russians as far to the east as possible.*" Winston Churchill, *Triumph and Tragedy*, p. 467. [Italics added.]
** The official history of the U.S. Army in World War II presents the position of the American Joint Chiefs clearly: "On the broader political question of getting to Berlin before the Russians," it states, "the U.S. Chiefs of Staff reacted as they had done formerly in regard to proposals of Balkan operations. Their view was that the business of the armed forces was to get the war ended as soon as possible and not to worry about the matter of prestige which would come from entering a particular capital." Forrest Pogue, *Command Decisions*, p. 444.

fight his battle," and Eisenhower, on April 7, with the Allied advance moving at high speed, once more stuck to his position: "I regard it as militarily unsound at this stage of the proceedings to make Berlin a major objective, particularly in view of the fact that it is only 35 miles from the Russian lines." [38]

In Washington there was no disagreement with General Eisenhower's analysis, and certainly, no inclination on the part of the Joint Chiefs of Staff to overrule him.[39] But the British continued to persist, and the following day, in a message to General Eisenhower, Field Marshal Montgomery took up the attack where Churchill left off. He rephrased the question in purely military terms. Could he have ten divisions for a lightning dash to Berlin? Eisenhower was unsympathetic and replied as follows: "You must not lose sight of the fact that during the advance on Leipzig you have the role of protecting Bradley's northern flank. It is not his role to protect your southern flank." As for Berlin, "I am quite ready to admit," Eisenhower said, "that it has political and psychological significance but of far greater importance will be the location of the remaining German forces in relation to Berlin. It is on them that I am going to concentrate my attention." [40]

When Eisenhower replied to Montgomery, German resistance had virtually collapsed. The closing of the Ruhr pocket on April 2, tore a gap of over 200 miles in the German front. Field Marshal Model and 325,000 men had been surrounded, and for all practical purposes, six German corps of seventeen divisions ceased to exist as a military force. Into this gap in the German lines had poured the First and Ninth American armies under Bradley's unified control.

As the British predicted, only scattered resistance remained. The enemy fell apart and waited to be overrun. The German High Command no longer retained operational control and even regimental headquarters had difficulty knowing the exact locations of their troops. As General Jodl later explained, with the surrender of Army Group B, the OKW (*Oberkommando der Wehrmacht*) in Berlin was no longer able to contain the Allied forces.[41]

On April 6, the Ninth American Army crossed the Weser River below Hanover in force, and by April 11, Magdeburg had been reached.[42] The following day as the American First Army, which was supposedly spearheading the Allied attack, drove into Leipzig, Simpson's Ninth Army crossed the Elbe River in three places. One week after the offensive had begun, American forces were fifty-three miles from Berlin.[43]

It was at this point that SHAEF issued a second order not to push onward to the German capital. Russian forces were still no closer to Berlin than they had been two months before. The city now lay equidistant between both armies and since Hitler had withdrawn everything to the East, there was little opposition in the West. But when General Simpson asked permission to continue the advance, the Supreme Commander was again resolute. Simpson was ordered to hold on the Elbe, and instead of advancing on Berlin to turn his forces toward Lübeck in the north and the National Redoubt in the south.[44]

On April 15, 1945, General Eisenhower told the War Department that he thought both of these targets to be "vastly more important than Berlin." In his words, to plan an immediate push toward Berlin "would be foolish in view of the relative situation of the Russians and ourselves. . . . While it is true that we have seized a small bridgehead over the Elbe, it must be remembered that only our spearheads are up to the river; our center of gravity is well back." * [45] "At that time," General Bradley wrote later, "we could probably have pushed on to Berlin had we been willing to take the casualties Berlin would have cost us." [46]

Indicative of the attitude of SHAEF at this time is Bradley's account of the following conversation which took place during a visit of his to Simpson's command post near Magdeburg. According to Bradley, the telephone rang.

> Big Simp listened for a moment and clamped his hand across the mouthpiece. "It looks as though we might get the bridge in Magdeburg. What'll we do if we get it Brad?"

* When asked during a briefing shortly afterwards—and before Berlin had fallen to the Russians—whether the Allies intended a full scale march on Berlin, General Bedell Smith responded:

. . . At the moment, except politically and psychologically, Berlin has lost a great deal of its significance. . . . The center, that is, the so-called "thrust on Berlin," from a purely military standpoint has ceased to be of any great importance to us. . . . There isn't any place along this front that we are going to rush to at the cost of lives and material in order to get there before the Russians do, unless our masters tell us differently. . . . We are handling it as a strictly military campaign. I think that's all we can do, don't you? After all, General Eisenhower has these lives entrusted to him and he will fight this campaign as economically as he can.

"Hell's Bells," I answered, "we don't want anymore bridgeheads on the Elbe. If you get it you'll *have* to throw a battalion across it, I guess. But let's hope the other fellow blows it up before you find you're stuck with it."

Thirty minutes later as I was putting on my helmet to leave, the phone rang again. Simpson's bony face split into a broad smile. "No need to worry, Brad," he laughed as he hung up the receiver, "the Krauts just blew it up." [47]

As a result of General Eisenhower's decision not to push on to Berlin, the American Ninth Army waited for the Russians on the banks of the Elbe for almost two weeks. The juncture was finally accomplished at 4:40 P.M. on April 25, at Torgau, an Elbian city some seventy-five miles south of Berlin, when patrols of the American 67th Division met advance units of the Russian 58th Guards Division.

Significantly, the Red Army did not begin its long awaited offensive until April 17, six days after the Ninth Army had crossed the Elbe. In the early morning hours of April 17, over one million men swarmed to the attack on a front 200 miles long in the last great Soviet offensive of the war. The very size of this attack belied Stalin's earlier disclaimer that the Russians considered Berlin no longer important.

The decision of General Eisenhower to halt the advance of the Ninth Army on the Elbe was made on purely tactical grounds. While it is true that the faulty interpretation of intelligence estimates at SHAEF may have encouraged this decision, the desire of the Supreme Commander to close with what remained of the German forces south of Berlin and complete a juncture with the Russians was sound military strategy. The mission which had been assigned to him by the Combined Chiefs of Staff was to "undertake operations aimed at the heart of Germany and the destruction of her armed forces." It was not, nor had it ever been, to maintain or restore the balance of power in central Europe.

The messages which General Eisenhower received from Washington at this time emphasized that purely tactical decisions were to be preferred. He received no political directives regarding Berlin either from Washington or the Combined Chiefs of Staff.* The agreements

* In a letter to Forrest C. Pogue, dated February 20, 1952, General Eisenhower stated that no political directive was given him to stop at the Elbe or to go on to Berlin (or Prague). See Forrest C. Pogue, *Command Decisions*, p. 490n.

on occupation boundaries also carried no provision about the capture
of Berlin. It was there for whomever got there first. In his book,
Eisenhower's Six Great Decisions, General Walter Bedell Smith has
remarked:

> It has been suggested on a great many occasions and from a
> great many sources that we deliberately avoided Berlin because of
> a political agreement that the Russians rather than the Western
> Allies, were to capture the Nazi capital. Nothing could be further
> from the truth. There was no political consideration involved and
> there was no agreement on this score with the Russians. General
> Eisenhower's decision to destroy the remaining enemy forces
> throughout Germany and, above all, to seal off the National Re-
> doubt, was based on a realistic estimate of the military situa-
> tion.* [48]

Later in April, when the British Chiefs of Staff once more sought
to push beyond the line determined by the Supreme Commander for
what they considered political advantages vis-a-vis the Russians, General Marshall in Washington strongly objected. In transmitting the
British proposal to Eisenhower, the Army Chief of Staff stated:
"Personally and aside from all logistics, tactical or strategical implications I would be loath to hazard American lives for purely political
purposes." Marshall's statement was in full accord with the policy

---

* The implications of General Eisenhower's decision of April, 1945, not to
push onwards to Berlin has recently been raised in connection with the publication by the State Department on August 18, 1961, of a background pamphlet
entitled *Berlin–1961.* The pamphlet describes the event in this way:

> The Western Armies could have captured Berlin or at least joined in capturing
> it. But the Supreme Allied Commander, General Eisenhower, believed that
> they could be more usefully employed against the major German forces else-
> where. As a result the Soviets captured Berlin. . . .

When asked about this analysis on September 11, 1961, General Eisenhower,
according to the *New York Times,* "betrayed no irritation" over the implication
that this decision "had proved to be a primary cause" of the present difficulties
over Berlin. Acknowledging his responsibility for the tactical military decision,
the former Supreme Commander stated that the final determination of the zones
of occupation had been made by the political leaders of the Allied powers. "We
were soldiers, not politicians. And to say that this was a military decision is a
rewriting of history."

As for the arrangements for the subsequent occupation of Berlin, General
Eisenhower was on firm ground. While the tactical military decision to halt was
Eisenhower's, the final occupation agreement certainly was not. The State Department announced the passage would be rewritten. (*New York Times,* September
12, 1961.)

which had been followed by the American Joint Chiefs of Staff throughout the war.[49]

In retrospect, the decision of General Eisenhower to halt at the Elbe was one of the great decisions—possibly even the greatest single decision of the war in Europe. It is certainly not true, however, that had it been made otherwise, today's situation in Berlin would not exist. What the effects of his decision may have been cannot be accurately determined. The fact that the decision was made, and made on tactical military grounds, should not be surprising. To an extent, it was an outgrowth of the American policy which had been followed throughout the war. The entire United States war effort had been based on the premise that the fighting must be ended—and ended in victory—as soon as possible.

In a sense, the decision not to drive on to Berlin was even more an outgrowth of America's peacetime military tradition. The Supreme Commander, his military superiors in Washington, his American associates at SHAEF, all, in fact, of the professional Army officers of that generation had been meticulously trained in a tradition which confined the problems of the military exclusively to the field of battle. To the senior American generals of that period (MacArthur was the exception to prove the rule), war was fought by professional military officers seeking specific military goals in a clearly defined sphere free from political intrusions. When political issues arose, they were to be settled by the proper political authorities. Conversely, within the tactical theater of the battle, "military" reasoning was to prevail. "Battles," as Bedell Smith phrased it, were "fought to defeat armies, to destroy the enemy's ability to go on fighting. With the German Government evacuated, Berlin became a terrain objective empty of meaning. To send armies crashing into its Western suburbs could have no tactical significance."

Unlike their European counterparts who had been trained in the tradition of the great soldier-statesmen of the nineteenth century, the professional American officer of the Second World War tended to look on everything beyond the tactical military sphere as alien domain. Prewar training had been limited to the most esoteric of military studies.[50] Garrison life during the twenties and thirties had been isolated from civilian contact; many Army officers declined even to vote in national elections. A narrow military society had, in fact, grown up in America during the prewar years; a society which was insulated completely from all contact with public and international affairs.*

Field Marshal Montgomery was later to comment: "The Americans could not understand that it was of little avail to win the war strategically if we lost it politically. . . . War is a political instrument; *once it is clear that you are going to win, political considerations must influence its further course.*" [51]

To General Eisenhower, as to Marshall, Bradley, and Smith, however, there was no worse opprobrium which could be applied than that of being a "political general." In 1945, the ghost of McClellan still stalked the American officer corps. Ten years later, in an epilogue to his earlier work on Eisenhower, General Smith summarized Eisenhower's views in this regard. The Supreme Commander, according to Smith:

> . . . was, and always considered himself, strictly a military commander. . . . I make this point because I have occasionally heard the question raised as to why the Americans did not rush for Berlin and seize it before the Russians could take the German capital. The reason, as has been pointed out in an earlier chapter [of the 1946 edition] was purely "military." And, a purely military operation meant "finding, engaging and destroying the enemy armies wherever they could be encountered." [52]

Politically, when Washington had been informed of General Eisenhower's decision in 1945, there was no question but that the Supreme Commander should be supported. Admiral Leahy, the personal Chief of Staff to the President, wrote that, "he [Eisenhower] made a military decision in the field to rest on the Elbe. . . . My notes do not show that the matter ever came before the Combined Chiefs of Staff." [53]

Later in April when the question of continuing beyond the Elbe once more arose, Washington again indicated that it preferred a

---

* Walter Bedell Smith was later to write of the effect which had been made on him by a lecture delivered at the War College by one of the military greats of the First World War. According to Smith, this "senior American general" concluded his address by saying, "I devoutly hope that our country may never again be involved in a great war, but if this should be our fate, I pray that we may meet it without the incumbrance of Allies." Smith, *op. cit.*, p. 227.

"military solution," rather than a "political" one, in the deployment of American troops. Much to Churchill's discomfiture, President Truman (who had succeeded Mr. Roosevelt on April 12) denied the request of the Prime Minister that the Allied forces continue to advance as far as possible into what was to be the Soviet zone in order to make the Russians more willing to share the anticipated food surplus of their zone with the rest of Germany. In reviewing this incident in his *Memoirs,* President Truman stated that after examining the Prime Minister's proposal, he could not "see any useful purpose in interfering with successful operations." [54] Since Mr. Truman had been in office only one week when Churchill's message arrived, it is probable, just as the Prime Minister later contended, that "the purely military view received an emphasis beyond its proper proportion." [55]

On the last day of April when Mr. Churchill suggested penetrating as far as possible into Czechoslovakia to keep that country from going "the way of Yugoslavia," President Truman referred the suggestion to the military for their opinion.[56] Prague especially was sought by Churchill for its future political value, but again the military declined to expand the scope of operations for political purposes. General Eisenhower, who had been asked for his opinion, stated that it was the Russian General Staff who anticipated operations in the Prague area and that he planned to continue to destroy any remaining enemy forces in Germany. "If a move into Czechoslovakia is then desirable, and if conditions here permit, our logical initial move would be on Pilsen and Karlsbad [not Prague]. I shall not attempt any move which I deem militarily unwise merely to gain a political advantage unless I receive specific orders from the Combined Chiefs of Staff." [57] Needless to say, no such orders were forthcoming.

The failure of the American military to recognize the political implications of the actions they took, or failed to take, in the spring of 1945, no doubt has played a part in the subsequent history of central Europe and Berlin. Whether a different course by the military at that time would have materially altered the situation in Berlin today is, at best, problematical. The conference of the heads of government at Yalta already had given the final stamp of approval to the zones of occupation which had been hammered out by the European Advisory Commission in London. In that case, as in this, the blame, if blame there was, lies not only in the misconceived notions of Soviet intent then prevalent at all levels of the American government, but also in the failure to understand the close connection between political and military decisions which was prevalent as well.

Even had the Allied forces moved beyond the Elbe, even had they liberated Berlin or assisted in its liberation, the present Allied position there would hardly be altered. In the light of the earlier diplomatic agreements on Germany, these moves would have proved valuable only as bargaining instruments. The previously concluded occupation agreements made it abundantly clear which power would occupy which area. Berlin patently was to be under joint four-power occupation and was to be located 110 miles within the Soviet zone. Public feeling in the United States at the time would not have permitted these agreements to have been breached.

Commenting on this subject, General Bedell Smith has stated, "In the atmosphere of friendship which was supposed to exist at that period [April, 1945] between the Eastern and Western cobelligerents, the violation on our part of an agreement already reached would have been interpreted by our own people, as well as by the Russians, as gross ill faith. In the ensuing outcry, I personally feel sure we could not have stood our ground." [58]

4

"An Iron Curtain Is Drawn Down Upon Their Front . . ."

FOLLOWING THE DECISION OF SHAEF to concentrate the major Allied thrust in the direction of Leipzig and Dresden rather than Berlin, Anglo-American military leaders turned to the problem of how to effect a peaceful meeting with the Soviet Armies.

On April 5, 1945, General Eisenhower informed the Combined Chiefs of Staff that it would be impractical to keep the American advance within the zonal boundaries previously decided upon. He suggested that both the Allied Expeditionary Force and the Russian Army continue to advance until contact was made. To minimize the danger of an inadvertent attack by one side upon the other, he recommended the line of the Elbe River beyond Leipzig as the best place to meet.* A natural barrier, such as a river line, would be easily recognizable on the ground by both sides and would make contact

* This line previously had been selected by General Eisenhower and General Bradley at their meeting in Rheims.

easier. Once the armies had met, Eisenhower said, then either the Red Army or SHAEF, on its own initiative, could request the other to withdraw. Based purely on operational necessity, the withdrawal would then take place.[1]

Eisenhower's proposal eliminated entirely any advantage which the Western Allies might have gained as a result of their further military advance. As might be expected, British opposition to SHAEF's plan was immediate. To Prime Minister Churchill, Eisenhower's proposal not only was "premature" but "exceeded the immediate military needs" as well. In a note to General Lord Ismay, written on April 7, the Prime Minister summarized his disapproval:

> When the forces arrive in contact and after the preliminary salutations have been exchanged, they should rest opposite each other in those positions.
>
> Thus if we crossed the Elbe and advanced to Berlin, or on a line between Berlin and the Baltic, which is well within the Russian zone, we should not give this up *as a military matter*. It is a matter of State to be considered between the three governments. . . .
>
> There cannot be such a hurry about our withdrawing from a place we have gained that the few days necessary for consulting the Governments in Washington and London cannot be found. I attach great importance to this, and could not agree to proposals of this kind [being decided] on a Staff level. They must be referred to the President and me.[2]

Four days later, on April 11, the formal reply of the British Chiefs of Staff to Eisenhower's proposal was forwarded to Washington. It repeated Churchill's objections and suggested that the Allied and Russian armies stand in place until ordered to withdraw by their respective governments. In short, the British stressed that the evacuation from the Soviet zone should be a political consideration to be decided by the heads of state and not by the military commanders.[3]

When the British reply was received in Washington, both the Department of State and the War Department vigorously objected. To them, the proposal of the British Chiefs of Staff was "Churchiavellian." It marked the injection of political considerations vis-a-vis the Russians that Washington preferred to avoid. "For governments to direct [this] movement of troops," according to officials of the European and Russian Affairs divisions of the Department of State, "definitely indicated *political* actions." "*Such movements,*" these officials advised the Joint Chiefs of Staff, "*should remain a military considera-tion.*" [4] [Italics in original.]

As Washington saw it, the position of the Allied armies in Germany when hostilities ended was not something to be used for political leverage. "Our State Department," a later cable from the White House to London stated, "does not believe that the matter of retirement of our respective troops to our zonal frontiers should be used for bargain-ing purposes." [5]

Unlike the discussions over the direction of the Allied advance toward Berlin, this time the British government remained adamant. Mr. Churchill renewed his argument against what he considered a premature withdrawal of Allied forces directly to President Truman. In office little more than a week, Mr. Truman replied to the Prime Minister on April 23 that he preferred to withdraw the American forces from the Soviet zone on a purely tactical basis, and as soon as the military situation permitted. In his message to Churchill the President also enclosed a draft note to that effect which he proposed sending Marshal Stalin. Interestingly, both Mr. Truman's reply and the draft text of the message to Stalin were prepared by the Joint Chiefs of Staff. [6]

The Prime Minister however stood his ground. The withdrawal of Allied troops from the Soviet zone was a political issue and should await a decision by the heads of government. The following day he replied to the White House emphasizing once more the political ad-vantages to be gained by the West from waiting until the end of hostilities before agreeing to such a move.

On April 23, while Washington and London negotiated, General Eisenhower cabled President Truman recommending that the with-drawal be handled along military lines. "I do not understand," Eisen-hower stated, "why the Prime Minister has been so determined to intermingle political and military considerations in attempting to es-tablish a procedure for the conduct of our own and Russian troops when a meeting takes place. My original recommendation submitted to the CC/S [Combined Chiefs of Staff] was a simple one and I thought provided a very sensible arrangement." [7]

The tenaciousness of the Prime Minister temporarily won out, and Washington reluctantly agreed to await the end of hostilities before beginning the withdrawal. On April 27, 1945, with President Truman's hesitant approval, Churchill cabled Marshal Stalin that the troops of the Western Allies would withdraw to their respective zones, not as might be decided by SHAEF and the respective commanders of the Red Army opposite (which Eisenhower had proposed), but only upon the termination of hostilities. American and British troops were to remain in place following contact with the Russian Army, and major adjustments would be made only upon the approval of the Combined Chiefs of Staff.[8]

Instructions were to come from the Combined Chiefs of Staff rather than the heads of government because of Washington's insistence that the matter remain in military hands.[9] Since a decision of the Combined Chiefs would require British concurrence, however, many in London took hope that the evacuation could await future political adjustments. They were soon disappointed. It is no secret that in April of 1945 Washington was not prepared to accept Mr. Churchill's judgment about future Soviet intentions. To the American military, referral of the evacuation decision to the Combined Chiefs, rather than SHAEF, simply meant transferring it from one military level to another. As Washington saw it, the evacuation decision still was to be a military one and did not involve matters of state.

When Churchill's message arrived in Moscow, Stalin did not answer. For almost a week the Soviet Premier waited, and when his reply did come, it was noncommittal. In contrast to his earlier message to Eisenhower, Stalin neither agreed nor disagreed with Churchill's proposals. "I should inform you," Stalin said, "that the Soviet High Command has issued instructions that when the Soviet and Allied forces meet the Soviet Command should immediately establish contact with the Command of the American or English forces." That was all. There was no mention whatever of Allied troop locations in the Soviet zone nor indeed, anything that would indicate an acknowledgment of Churchill's message.[10]

On May 4, 1945, two days after the Russian reply was received, Prime Minister Churchill expressed his fears about the attitude of the Soviet Union in a letter to Anthony Eden:

> I fear terrible things have happened during the Russian advance through Germany to the Elbe, [Churchill said]. The proposed withdrawal of the United States Army to the occupational lines

which were arranged . . . would mean the tide of Russian domination sweeping forward 120 miles on a front of 300 or 400 miles. This would be an event which, if it occurred, would be one of the most melancholy in history.

We have several powerful bargaining counters on our side, the use of which might make for a peaceful arrangement. First, the Allies ought not to retreat from their present positions to the occupational line until we are satisfied about Poland, and also about the temporary character of the Russian occupation of Germany. . . .[11]

The death of President Roosevelt on April 12, 1945, already had seriously complicated the state of Anglo-American relations in dealing with Russia. The late President had been confident he understood the Russians and could handle them. He had recognized the signs of Soviet expansion and was troubled by them, but he hoped to temper these tendencies by the force of his own dynamic leadership and the personal relations which he had so laboriously cultivated with Marshal Stalin.

During the latter days of February and March, 1945, the President's failing health had greatly affected his ability to give direction to American policy and it was at this time that the U.S. most needed firm guidance in response to the increasingly aggressive designs of the Soviet Union. Prime Minister Churchill has eloquently captured the tragic spirit of those fateful days:

As a war waged by a coalition draws to its end political aspects have a mounting importance. In Washington especially longer and wider views should have prevailed. . . . At this time the points at issue did not seem to the United States Chiefs of Staff to be of capital importance. They were of course unnoticed by and unknown to the public, and were all soon swamped, and for the time being effaced by the flowing tide of victory. Nevertheless, as will not now be disputed, they played a dominating part in the destiny of Europe, and may well have denied us all the lasting peace for which we had fought so long and hard. We can see now the deadly hiatus which existed between the fading of President Roosevelt's strength and the growth of President Truman's grip of the vast world problem. In this melancholy void one President could not act and the other could not know. Neither the military chiefs nor the State Department received the guidance they required. The former confined themselves to their professional sphere; the latter did not comprehend the issues involved. The indispensable political direction was lacking at the moment when it was most needed. The United States stood on the scene of victory, master of world fortunes but without a true and coherent design. Britain, though still very powerful, could not act decisively alone." [12]

One of the great enigmas of the latter days of the war is what might have been the subsequent shape of Western policy had President Roosevelt lived and witnessed the blatant course of Communist aggression which Russia soon demonstrated she was pursuing. In a final cable, written in his own hand shortly before his death on April 12, Mr. Roosevelt had informed Churchill: "I would minimize the general Soviet problem as much as possible because these problems, in one form or another, seem to arise every day and most of them straighten out. . . ." [13] At this time, however, the President's health had deteriorated to such an extent that most of his wartime responsibilities already had been delegated to the military authorities.

Following the death of President Roosevelt, Mr. Truman at first also was unwilling to accept at face value Churchill's warnings about the Soviet Union. To some extent, President Truman felt himself pledged to carry on with the policies that the Roosevelt Administration had begun. To a much larger extent he was completely unprepared to assume the burdens of the Presidency, which suddenly fell upon him. Unlike later incumbents of the Vice Presidency, Mr. Truman had not been made a part of the Executive branch of the government. He was unfamiliar with the belligerent turn which Soviet policy had taken and, like the general public, shared a hope that everything would be peacefully settled. He had not been informed in detail of the earlier agreements which had been negotiated regarding Germany and therefore, during his first weeks in office, was unwilling to act in these matters on his own responsibility.

Instead, he chose to rely upon his professional advisers and particularly, upon his professional military advisers. These unfortunately, as Mr. Churchill has suggested, were insufficiently aware of the larger political considerations then at stake. Those advisers of the political departments of State and Treasury whose business it was to know what was at stake, often feared that Britain and not Russia was the greater danger to world peace. Few of the top level officials of those departments were ready to renounce their past idealistic aspirations for working together in cooperation with the Soviet Union. None were prepared to confront the Russian behemoth in a test of wills, or to maintain large American armies in Germany until the Soviet government, in Churchill's words, "satisfied our wishes and eased our anxieties."

As Dr. Herbert Feis has noted, these advisers judged the course which Churchill would have followed to be "inadvisable, ineffective, and impractical": inadvisable because it might provoke a harsh dispute with Soviet authorities; ineffective because the Soviet armies could close us out of Berlin; impractical because American opinion expected a rapid return of the soldiers from Europe.[14]

Alger Hiss and Harry Dexter White at this time were still high in the councils of the American government. Gerhart Eisler, later to become deputy propaganda chief of the puppet East German regime, was chief of the broadcasting station of the Office of War Information. Irving Kaplan, later identified as a Communist agent, served as Economic Adviser on Liberated Areas to the Department of the Treasury.[15] With the possible exception of Harry Dexter White, it is reasonable to assume that these men had little effect on the formulation of American policy.* Their contribution, if any, lay in seconding the voices of anti-British and pro-Russian sentiment then prevalent in Washington; prevalent, it should be added, among those whose basic loyalty to the United States is clearly beyond doubt.

Harry Hopkins, special confidant of President Roosevelt; Secretary of the Treasury Henry Morgenthau, Jr.; Secretary of Commerce Henry Wallace; former Ambassador to Moscow Joseph E. Davies, and Fleet Admiral Ernest King all were highly distrustful of British imperialistic ambitions and highly receptive to ideas of Russian good faith. Nor were they alone. General Marshall, Secretary of War Henry L. Stimson, and Mobilization Director James F. Byrnes also shared the optimism of the late President regarding future Soviet intentions. All of these advisers had experienced the fruits of co-operation with Russia at first hand. For the past three years there had been almost no international issue that the Big Three had not settled. World government,

---

* Harry Dexter White, as Special Assistant to Secretary Morgenthau, was directly responsible for all foreign affairs as they affected the Treasury Department. Original drafter of the Morgenthau Plan, it was through White that a set of American plates for Allied occupation currency in Germany was made available to the Russians.

in effect, was already a reality and few wished to sacrifice it to the cold realism of postwar politics.*

The prevailing temper of the times was reflected by United States Justice Hugo Black of Alabama. Addressing an audience in the Hollywood Bowl, Justice Black compared Prime Minister Churchill's fear of Russia to the anti-Bolshevik tirades of Hitler which had "kept nations divided within and suspicious of one another." [16]

The American military in the spring of 1945 were also far too concerned with closing off hostilities in Europe to be interested in questions of Soviet intent. General Marshall, the Army Chief of Staff and, upon President Roosevelt's death, the virtual director of the American war effort, sought immediate Soviet assistance in the war which was still in progress against Japan and tried to avoid questions that might endanger that assistance. Admiral Leahy and the other members of the Joint Chiefs shared this desire.[17] In Europe, General Eisenhower and his associates at SHAEF simply were politically out-distanced by Mr. Churchill in the appraisal of Communist aims.

General Eisenhower's personal opinion of the Soviet Union at this time was recorded by his Naval Aide, Captain Harry Butcher, USNR, in a diary entry dated "Paris, Friday, May 25, 1945." According to Butcher:

> Last night, the General and I had an old fashioned bull session that lasted until too late this morning. We talked about Russia. Ike said he felt that the American and British relationship with Russia was about at the same stage of arms-length dealing that

---

* Ambassador to Moscow Averell Harriman and Secretary of the Navy James V. Forrestal were notable exceptions. Forrestal reports a White House meeting on April 23, 1945, during which President Truman asked those present for their views on Soviet policy toward Poland. According to Mr. Forrestal, "The Secretary of War [Stimson] said that it was such a newly posed question . . . he found great difficulty in making positive recommendations but he did feel that we had to remember that the Russian conception of freedom . . . was quite different from ours or the British and that he hoped we would go slowly and avoid any open break. He said that the Russians had carried out their military engagements quite faithfully and was sorry to see this one incident project a breach between the two countries.

"I gave it as my view," Forrestal said, "that this was not an isolated incident but was one of a pattern of unilateral action on the part of Russia . . . and I thought we might as well meet the issue now as later on.

"Ambassador Harriman expressed somewhat the same views. Admiral Leahy took the view, on the other hand, more or less the same as that of the Secretary of War . . ." *The Forrestal Diaries*, Walter Millis, ed. (New York: Viking Press, 1951), pp. 48–50.

marked the early contacts between Americans and the British
when we first got into the war. As we dealt with each other, we
learned the British ways and they learned ours. A common understanding developed and eventually we became Allies in spirit as
well as on paper. Now the Russians, who have had relatively little
contact, even during the war, with the Americans and British, do
not understand us, nor do we them. The more contact we have
with the Russians, the more they will understand us and the
greater will be the cooperation. The Russians are blunt and forthright in their dealings, and any evasiveness arouses their suspicions. It should be possible to work with Russia if we follow the
same pattern of friendly cooperation that has resulted in the great
record of Allied unity demonstrated first by AFHQ [Air Force
Headquarters] and subsequently by SHAEF.[18]

When seen in this context of official and unofficial sentiment it is not
surprising that President Truman at first avoided the firm policy toward Russia that Churchill proposed.*

With the beginning of May, hostilities in Germany rapidly drew to
a close. The Nazi hierarchy did not attempt a last stand in the Bavarian
Redoubt and with Hitler's death the will to resist quickly ebbed. The
successor government of Admiral Doenitz at Flensburg made plans to
capitulate. Following a brief period of negotiations, the formal Instrument of Surrender was signed in General Eisenhower's headquarters
at Rheims at 0241 hours on May 7, 1945. Colonel General Alfred Jodl,
Chief of Operations of the German High Command, and Grand Admiral Hans von Friedeburg, Commander-in-Chief of the German Navy,
represented the tottering Doenitz government. General Walter Bedell
Smith signed for the Allies. Witnessing his signature were General Ivan
Susloparov of the Soviet Union and General Francois Sevez of France.
The following day a second surrender ceremony demanded by the

---

* By the following month Harry Truman was firmly in the driver's seat. When
Secretary Morgenthau, the sponsor of the ill-fated plan for the pastoralization
of Germany, wanted to go to Potsdam to take part in the discussions on Germany,
the President informed him that the place for the Secretary of the Treasury was
in Washington, not Potsdam. According to the President:

"He [Morgenthau] replied that it was necessary for him to go and that if he
could not he would have to quit.
"'Allright,' I replied, 'I'll accept your resignation right now.' And I did.

"That was the end of the conversation and the end of the Morgenthau Plan."
Harry S Truman, *Year of Decisions* (Garden City, N.Y.: Doubleday & Co., 1955),
p. 327.

Soviet Union was held in Berlin. This time Field Marshal Keitel represented Germany; Marshal Zhukov and Air Marshal Tedder signed for
the two Allied Commands; General de Lattre de Tassigny and General
Spaatz signed as witnesses for France and the United States. At the
time, little significance was attached to the Soviet Union's insistence
on a separate ceremony.

On May 12, with the hostilities ended, Prime Minister Churchill renewed once more his request that the American and British forces not
be withdrawn from the Soviet zone until suitable political agreements
regarding the future of Germany had been concluded. In a telegram
to President Truman, Mr. Churchill referred for the first time to the
"Iron Curtain" which he said had descended along the Russian front.
Churchill requested that he and Truman meet at once with Stalin to
discuss a general European settlement. Until such time as the meeting
was held, the Prime Minister urged that Western troops remain in
place.*

"I am profoundly concerned about the European situation," Mr.
Churchill wrote:

> I learn that half the American Air Force in Europe has already
> begun to move to the Pacific theatre. The newspapers are full of
> the great movements of the American armies out of Europe. Our
> armies also are, under previous arrangements, likely to undergo a
> marked reduction. The Canadian Army will certainly leave. Any-
> one can see that in a very short space of time our armed power on
> the Continent will have vanished, except for moderate forces to
> hold down Germany.
>
> Meanwhile what is to happen about Russia? I have always
> worked for friendship with Russia, but, like you, I feel deep
> anxiety because of their misinterpretation of the Yalta decisions.
> their attitude towards Poland, their overwhelming influence in the
> Balkans, excepting Greece, the difficulties they make about Vienna.
> the combination of Russian power and the territories under their
> control or occupied, coupled with the Communist technique in so
> many other countries, and above all their power to maintain very
> large armies in the field for a long time. What will be the position
> in a year or two, when the British and American armies have
> melted and the French has not yet been formed on any major
> scale, when we have a handful of divisions mostly French, and

---

* "Of all the public documents I have written on this issue," Churchill later stated,
"I would rather be judged by this." Winston Churchill, *Triumph and Tragedy,*
p. 572.

when the Russians may choose to keep two or three hundred on active service?

An iron curtain is drawn down upon their front, and we do not know what is going on behind. There seems to be little doubt that the whole of the regions east of the line Lübeck, Trieste, Corfu will soon be completely in their hands. To this must be added the further enormous area conquered by the American armies between Eisenach and the Elbe, which will, I suppose, in a few weeks be occupied, when the Americans retreat, by the Russian power. . . . And then the curtain will descend again to a very large extent, if not entirely.

Meanwhile the attention of our people will be occupied in inflicting severities upon Germany, which is ruined and prostrate. . . . Surely it is vital now to come to an understanding with Russia, or see where we are with her, before we weaken our armies mortally or retire to the zones of occupation.

The Prime Minister then went on to request an immediate meeting with Stalin to discuss these problems.[19]

President Truman, however, felt a meeting with Marshal Stalin was premature. By Washington's direction, American forces would withdraw from the Soviet zone when the military situation made it advisable. With hostilities now ended, it was time for the withdrawal to take place. Two day later, on May 14, Mr. Truman formally declined Churchill's request. It was better to discover the true aim of Soviet policy, Truman said, before risking a final rupture. For this purpose, he told Churchill, Harry Hopkins was going to Moscow to discuss recent differences with Marshal Stalin. The policy of the Roosevelt Administration temporarily would be continued.[20]

In declining Churchill's proposal to meet with Stalin prior to the withdrawal of Allied troops, President Truman was yielding both to the counsel of his advisers and to the attitude of the American people. The United States still was not willing to use its military position for political purposes.

The net result of the exchange of cables between the Prime Minister and President Truman was that SHAEF would arrange the Allied withdrawal before any Big Three conference could be held. The advance position of Western forces, the hold by the United States Army on that great area of central Germany between Eisenach and the Elbe, would be yielded to the Red Army as a military consideration. Included in this region were the provinces of Saxony, Saxony-Anhalt and Thuringia, containing the great industrial cities of Leipzig (1939 population 701,606), Dresden (625,174), and Magdeburg (334,358); an area with the second greatest concentration of German industry outside the Ruhr. It was an area of over 20,000 square miles, a region as large as the combined land areas of Massachusetts, Connecticut and New Jersey with a prewar population exceeding 12.5 million people. Today it comprises almost half of the total land area of the East German satellite state and nearly two-thirds of its present population.

Clearly, the decision of the United States to proceed with the evacuation of American troops from the Soviet zone was one of the major decisions of the early postwar period. The subsequent communization of Central Europe could not have taken place had the Allied forces remained where they were. The fall of the democratic government in Czechoslovakia three years later can be directly attributed to the power vacuum created by the withdrawal of Western military power.

Similarly, the decision to withdraw American forces from the Soviet zone prior to a meeting with Stalin is indicative of what might have happened had the Western Allies continued on to Berlin while the war was still in progress. Berlin, had it been captured, likewise would have been yielded to Soviet authority.

In retrospect, considering the temper of the times, the attitude of the American people and the policy of the American government, it is indeed possible that General Eisenhower was correct in halting the Allied advance on the Elbe. The advantages which might have accrued to the Western powers from the capture of Berlin certainly would not have been realized. General Bradley estimated that to take Berlin might have cost one hundred thousand casualties. Bradley may have exaggerated the figure but the fact remains that the cost could have been high. Given the drift which official American policy assumed in 1945, it is extremely doubtful if this prize would have been used to later advantage. The roots of the present Berlin crisis in the wartime and the immediate postwar periods, are found not in decisions made by military men on the field of battle, but in decisions *not made* in Washington.

In the heady atmosphere of May, 1945, with peace in Europe so recently secured, few in the West were prepared to recognize the situation in Germany for what it was. The menace of Communist aggression as yet was little understood, and the political advantage of military strength—the role of the military as a guarantor of peace—as yet was little appreciated. America did not understand the nature of the world that it had suddenly been called upon to lead. In 1945 we still assumed that Western concessions would be taken by the Russians as signs of friendship. Few were willing to believe that to the Soviet Union Western concessions appeared as signs of weakness, encouraging communism to drive an even harder bargain. Prime Minister Churchill's cable requesting an immediate meeting with Stalin arrived in Washington less than one week after the final Instrument of Surrender in Germany had been concluded. In the prevailing atmosphere of joy and celebration it is not surprising that so few took it seriously.

For the most part, the American people were still thinking of our wartime good fellowship, and like Mr. Truman, they were little prepared for the difficulties that were then developing. War as a means of policy was morally wrong, and the United States had been at war only because she had been attacked. Now, with victory assured, America was not going to become involved in what many considered the petty, imperialistic quarrels of Europe. As one distinguished critic of this era has written, the American people "were quite unready to face the necessity of engaging in a prolongation of the struggle to protect the freedom of European peoples, and to preserve a safe strategic position and balance of power against the Allied nation to whose survival they had contributed so much." [21]

In Berlin, the fighting had stopped on May 2, 1945. On that date, *General der Artillerie* Erich Weidling, German Military Commander of Berlin, representing the remnant of the German Army which had resisted the Russian onslaught for over two weeks, signed the formal capitulation of the city at Tempelhof. Two days before, on April 30, Adolph Hitler had committed suicide. Simultaneous with Hitler's death, Walter Ulbricht, puppet czar of the present East German regime arrived in the baggage of the Red Army. One tyranny was over but another was about to begin.

The Berlin which surrendered to the Russian Army on May 2, 1945, seemed unlikely ever to recover from the war's destruction. The Inner City, a broad expanse of ancient buildings, parks, and governmental structures stretching from the Alexander Platz to the Tiergarten was a smoking ruin. Only twisted shambles remained of the international quarter, the *Hansa Viertel,* and the downtown shopping area. Scarcely a home had been left untouched. Of the 1,500,000 dwellings which formerly existed in Berlin, seventy-six percent were no longer inhabitable; twelve percent had been totally destroyed. Entire blocks had been leveled to the ground. Whole streets, passageways and courtyards had vanished.[22]

Of the 150 bridges which had once connected the various parts of Berlin, 128 were destroyed. Gas, water and electricity had ceased to function, and telephone service was virtually unknown. Untreated sewage created a further problem. Buses and street cars were no longer in operation, and transportation from one part of the city to another was impossible.

In May of 1945, the population of Berlin, formerly 4.3 million, numbered little more than two million. Less than ten percent of these were under thirty years of age. Death from causes other than war had increased from a level of 13.3 per thousand persons in 1939 to 76.2 per thousand in 1945. Cases of typhus and tuberculosis increased threefold. Hospital and medical facilities were seriously over-taxed. Stores and businesses, closed when the fighting began, remained shuttered with their proprietors usually in hiding.

For the better part of a week the Red Army ran loose in a reign of terror. Only gradually was order restored; then the looting became systematic. Reparations succeeded rape as the Communist Order of the Day. Ninety percent of Berlin's steel industry, 75 percent of its printing industry, 85 percent of the machinery of the electrical and optical industries were loaded onto flatcars for shipment to the Soviet Union.

Ten weeks later when President Truman arrived in Berlin for the Potsdam Conference he was staggered by the destruction he found. "I never saw such desolation," he wrote. "Our drive . . . took us past the Tiergarten, the ruins of the Reichstag, the German Foreign Office, the Sports Palace, and dozens of other sites which had been world famous before the war. Now they were nothing more than piles of rubble. A more depressing sight than that of ruined buildings," he continued, "was the long, never-ending procession of old men, women, and children wandering aimlessly along the autobahn . . . carrying, pushing, or pulling what was left of their belongings. In that two-hour drive I saw evidence of a great world tragedy, and I was thankful that the

United States had been spared the unbelievable devastation of this war." [23]

To Fleet Admiral William D. Leahy, war-hardened Chief of Staff to the President, the scene was equally appalling. "As we toured the ruins of Berlin," Leahy reported, "every building we saw was badly damaged or completely destroyed. This one-time great and beautiful metropolis, capital of a proud nation which many times I had desired to visit, was wrecked beyond repair. . . . I had never seen anything like it in my long naval career."

And just as President Truman had noted, Leahy also found that:

> . . . much more distressing than the view of devastated Berlin was a long procession of old men, women and children, presumably evacuated from their homes by their Russian conquerors. They were marching in great numbers along the country roads, carrying their pitifully small belongings and their infants, probably to an unknown destination and probably without hope. There were no young men among them. Any men we saw were all beyond military age or crippled and lame. These helpless people seemed to be prodded by some urge to get some place where they could find food or shelter—anything, apparently, to get out of the Soviet occupied territory.
>
> It was noticeable to me, as the President's own personal party at dinner that evening discussed scenes we had witnessed, [Leahy continued,] that there was no mood of vindictiveness or revenge, but rather a realization . . . of the horrible destructiveness of modern conflict.[24]

Gradually Berlin awakened. Beneath the rubble and destruction, under the ruin and chaos, much had remained intact. The war had taken its toll and the first few days of the Russian occupation even more, but the foundations of the city had survived. What was underground was usually only flooded; what was severed could be joined; what was broken could be mended. Most important, however, was that through it all the citizen of Berlin somehow had managed to survive. In him the heart of the city remained intact.

Slowly, life in Berlin was restored. Restaurants and cabarets, soon to become places of entertainment for the troops, had been ordered reopened by Russian authorities on May 2, and the distribution of rations was organized shortly afterward. On May 4, Radio Berlin resumed broadcasting under Soviet control. Public transportation was resumed on May 13, and the first U-Bahns (subways) began to operate the following day. On May 22, the first Russian film was shown in postwar Berlin. The Berlin Philharmonic gave its first concert on the twenty-sixth, and the following day the Renaissance Theatre reopened. For the most part, however, the theatres and the cabarets were only for the soldiers of the Red Army. Life for the Berliners was bleak beyond description.[25]

The governmental apparatus of Berlin also was quickly reorganized by the Soviets and set to work. No mention was made to the Berliners that the Americans, British and French would be coming later to join in the occupation of the city. For the present, all of Berlin belonged to the Communists.

District mayors were appointed by the Russians in each of the city's twenty boroughs. New department heads in each borough were appointed—usually from a previously selected cross-section of middle class doctors, lawyers and trade unionists known by the Soviets to be sympathetic with the "proletariat." Of those who were so selected, most were advanced in age and without previous political experience. The key positions in each borough were retained by the Communist Party. Personnel directors in eighteen out of the twenty boroughs were Communists. Education and police always remained in Communist hands.

The central city government likewise was reorganized. As Lord Mayor, an inconspicuous Arthur Werner, sixty-seven-year-old retired architect with no previous governmental experience was chosen. The deputy mayor however and six out of thirteen executive department heads of the central city government were Communists. Paul Markgraf, a former German Army officer who had been captured at Stalingrad and indoctrinated in the Soviet Union, became Police President. Trade unions and political parties were revived at this time and likewise came under the closest Communist supervision.

Soviet controlled newspapers quickly began publication. The *Tägliche Rundschau*, a German-language daily of the Red Army, was the first to appear. The *Berliner Zeitung*, the official organ of the city government, followed shortly afterwards. In all, there were five local newspapers, each under strict Soviet supervision, when the Western Allies arrived.

The Soviets also used the distribution of food as a device to further

Communist aims. For ration purposes, the Berliners were divided into five categories. Those in the highest category, politicians, Party officials, most teachers, and those who were performing hard labor, received 2,485 calories a day. Those in the lowest category—those who were unemployed, overage, or who had incurred Communist displeasure—were allowed only 1,248 calories. Those in the lower two ration categories, a total of almost one million people, lived on the borderline of starvation.[26]

Significantly, the Berliners resisted Communist pressure even then. Perhaps they had endured too much in one lifetime to trade-in one form of totalitarianism for another. As a result of the actions of the Red Army, the people of Berlin were permanently estranged from the Soviet Union. Even before the Western powers arrived, Russia already had lost her chance of capturing Berlin. Although she had captured it militarily, the first few weeks of looting and raping prevented forever her capturing it ideologically. The aims of international communism had been subverted by the soldiers of the Russian Army. Longingly, Berlin waited for the Western Allies.

5

The Occupation Begins

WHILE THE RUSSIANS HAD Berlin to themselves, the Western Allies fell
to debating how best to begin Germany's four-power occupation. As
has been noted, President Truman's cable to Prime Minister Churchill
announcing Washington's decision to withdraw the Allied forces from
the Soviet zone was dispatched on May 14. Two days later, on May 16,
General Eisenhower returned to London to review the situation with
Mr. Churchill and the British Chiefs of Staff.

As Eisenhower explained it, the problem of dealing with Germany
needed settling quickly. First, the present occupation setup was impossible. Everyone knew the area of Germany they were to occupy but
as yet no order to do so had been given. Not even the four-power Control Council had been established. SHAEF, he said, was still in command of the entire Western front and was having to administer not
only the three Western zones but a great deal of the Soviet zone as
well. This was creating numerous problems and was only delaying the
establishment of a workable four-power occupation. Equally important,
Eisenhower said, the terms of the surrender had not yet been announced. Until they were, the occupation could not go forward on a

legal basis. The problem of governing Germany was thus still hanging fire.[1]

Eisenhower recommended to Churchill that SHAEF (the joint head-quarters for the Allied troops) be dissolved and that the United States, Britain and France immediately assume the responsibilities for their particular zones.* As long as the SHAEF command structure remained, Eisenhower said, he was still the military superior both of Field Marshal Montgomery and General de Lattre de Tassigny, the designated British and French Commanders-in-Chief. Clearly, this arrangement would not work if all four zones were to be considered politically equal.

General Eisenhower also pointed out to the Prime Minister the difficulty which the present situation created in dealing with the Soviets who at that time had to refer everything to Moscow for decision. Eisenhower felt that once four-power government was established the Russian High Command would be able to act on its own initiative—greatly facilitating the handling of occupation problems. Accordingly, he proposed to Churchill that the four-power Control Council designed for governing Germany be activated as soon as possible.**

* Much earlier in the war, General Eisenhower had favored the continuance of SHAEF to govern the occupation of Germany as a combined command but had been turned down in Washington. See Forrest C. Pogue, *The Supreme Command,* pp. 348–51; Lucius D. Clay, *Decision in Germany,* p. 10; Dwight D. Eisenhower, *Crusade in Europe,* p. 218.
** The Allied Control Council for Germany had been authorized in the "Agreement on Control Machinery in Germany" drafted by the European Advisory Commission and signed in London on November 14, 1944. Under the provisions of this agreement, supreme authority in Germany was to be exercised by the four military Commanders-in-Chief, "each in his own zone of occupation, and also jointly, in matters affecting Germany as a whole. . . ." When acting jointly, the four Commanders-in-Chief would constitute the Allied Control Council. The precise nature of the Control Council was spelled out in Article 3 of the EAC agreement. It stated:

Article 3.

(a) The four Commanders-in-Chief, acting together as a body, will constitute a supreme organ of control called the Control Council.
(b) The functions of the Control Council will be:—
(i) to insure appropriate uniformity of action by the Commanders-in-Chief in their respective zones of occupation;
(ii) to initiate plans and reach agreed decisions on the chief military, political, economic and other questions affecting Germany as a whole, on the basis of instructions received by each Commander-in-Chief from his Government;
(iii) to control the German central administration, which will operate under the direction of the Control Council and will be responsible to it for ensuring compliance with its demands;

Prime Minister Churchill agreed that the situation in Germany was urgent, but he did not feel that SHAEF should be abolished just yet. The Prime Minister said he did not wish to make any move which might give the Soviets grounds for demanding the withdrawal of Allied troops from their advance positions in the Russian zone. He therefore told Eisenhower that he thought they should just wait and see how the situation developed. In the meantime, SHAEF should continue as a tactical headquarters with all Allied troops remaining under its control.[2]

It is clear that Churchill was still worried about Russian expansion. Eisenhower, who did not share the Prime Minister's alarm, reported Churchill's reaction to Washington and, with noticeable irritation, remarked that the Prime Minister "did not appear to be in any real hurry" to have four-power occupation begin.[3]

The Supreme Commander waited a week, however, before raising the issue again. Then, on May 23, he advised Washington that he "could not carry out his mission much longer" in the absence of four-power government. He suggested that SHAEF be abolished and that the withdrawal from the Russian zone begin immediately.

The British, of course, were opposed. The following day the Foreign Office recommended a compromise. The four Commanders-in-Chief, they suggested, should convene in Berlin the next week in order to establish the Control Council and then continue to meet as they deemed necessary. According to the British plan, however, the Control Council would only consider organizational matters and in the meantime, the Allied forces should remain in place under SHAEF's control until certain "outstanding questions" were discussed with the Soviet Government.[4]

London had agreed to a meeting of the Commanders-in-Chief, hoping thereby to persuade the United States to postpone the early with-

---

(iv) to direct the administration of "Greater Berlin" through appropriate organs.

(c) The Control Council will meet at least once in ten days; and it will meet at any time upon request of any one of its members. *Decisions of the Control Council shall be unanimous.* The chairmanship of the Control Council will be held in rotation by each of its four members.

(d) Each member of the Control Council will be assisted by a political adviser, who will, when necessary, attend meetings of the Council. Each member of the Control Council may also, when necessary, be assisted at meetings of the Council by naval or air advisers. [Italics added.]

drawal of Allied troops from the Soviet zone. But in Washington their proposal fell on deaf ears, and the War Department, with the approval of the President and the Joint Chiefs, went ahead with their plans for the dissolution of SHAEF and the return of American troops to the designated U.S. zone.

Washington did agree with the British, however, that the four military Commanders-in-Chief should meet as soon as possible. After another exchange of cables, the meeting was arranged for Berlin on June 5, 1945.[5]

On June 2, preparatory to the Berlin meeting, General Eisenhower asked Washington for a definite date on which Allied forces would withdraw from the Soviet zone. To General Marshall he cabled:

> It is anticipated that one of the questions which will be raised at Berlin meeting, will be date on which forces will begin their withdrawal from the Russian zone. It is possible that the Russians may establish such withdrawal as a corollary to the establishment of the Control Council on a functioning basis in Berlin and to turning over the several zones [sectors] in Berlin to the forces to occupy these zones [sectors]. Any cause for delay in the establishment of Control Council due to the delay in withdrawal would be attributed to us and might well develop strong public reaction. We have as yet no instructions covering such withdrawal. It is believed desirable that separate instructions be given to me as American Commander and to the British Commander prior to Berlin meeting as to how we should reply to this question if it is raised.[6]

The following day, the Joint Chiefs of Staff, with President Truman's approval, told Eisenhower that the Allied troops should not withdraw from the Soviet zone before the establishment of the Control Council, or the take-over of the sectors in Berlin. Instead, the Council itself, once established, should handle this as a matter of military convenience. "If the Russians raise the point," General Marshall stated, "you should state in substance that the matter of withdrawal of forces to their own zones is one of the items to be worked out in the Control Council. As to the actual movement of U.S. Forces, you should state that this, in your view, is primarily a military matter; its timing will be in accordance with U.S. ability to withdraw their forces from other than their own zone and British and Russian ability to take over." [7]

On June 4, one day before the meeting of the four military Commanders-in-Chief was to take place, Prime Minister Churchill repeated his misgivings to President Truman over "the retreat of the American Army to our line of occupation in the central sector, thus bringing Soviet power into the heart of Western Europe and the descent of an iron curtain between us and everything to the eastward. I hoped that this retreat, if it has to be made, would be accompanied by the settlement of many great things which would be the true foundation of world peace. Nothing really important has been settled yet, and you and I will have to bear great responsibility for the future." [8]

Washington was not impressed, however, and on June 5, the four Commanders-in-Chief met in Berlin as scheduled. Each of the three Western commanders looked forward to their first encounter with Marshal Zhukov, the great military leader of the Red Army. But in a somewhat different and perhaps more prophetic vein, General Lucius Clay, who accompanied Eisenhower that day, recalls: "When we climbed into the planes [at Frankfurt] we remembered Soviet reluctance to participate in the first surrender ceremony in Rheims and Soviet insistence on a second ceremony in Berlin, and we could not but wonder what might lie ahead." [9]

The three Western Commanders-in-Chief landed separately at Tempelhof airfield in Berlin on the morning of June 5. Upon arrival, each was escorted to Marshal Zhukov's headquarters in Karlshorst, one of the suburban districts in the eastern part of the city. The meeting itself was scheduled to convene at twelve noon.

In preparation for the meeting the European Advisory Commission had drawn up three separate documents for the military commanders to sign. The first of these was a "Declaration Regarding the Defeat of Germany"; it amounted to the assumption of supreme authority by the Allies as a result of Germany's unconditional surrender. The second document divided Germany into four zones of occupation and provided for the joint occupation of Berlin. The third established various organs of control machinery to be used by the Allies during the course of the occupation. Under its provisions, supreme authority in Germany was to be exercised by an Allied Control Council made up of the four Commanders-in-Chief. Decisions of the Council were to be unanimous and its chairmanship was to rotate on a regular basis.

Instead of commencing the conference at the scheduled hour, however, the Russians began to delay. Each of the three Western Commanders-in-Chief, General Eisenhower, Field Marshal Montgomery and General de Lattre de Tassigny was kept waiting in his respective quarters until late in the afternoon. Gradually becoming angry at the delay, Eisenhower and Montgomery finally sent a joint ultimatum to Zhukov demanding that the conference begin or else they would leave. According to Field Marshal Montgomery:

> That produced quick results and we were summoned to the conference, which was held in a clubhouse nearby. But, on arrival, there was a further delay owing to Russian objection to one word in the English text which disagreed with the Russian version. I had no idea what the word was, or what effect it had on the general problem. But I was so fed up with the whole affair that I suggested the offending word be deleted from the text; this suggestion was at once agreed to by the Russians and by everyone else, and to this day I do not know what difference it made.[10]

With the texts reconciled to the Russians' satisfaction the ceremony began, and in the glare of arc lamps, each of the four Commanders-in-Chief signed the documents. Afterward, they withdrew for a private meeting. Marshal Zhukov, who was presiding at this meeting, asked if there were any other matters to be discussed, and Eisenhower replied, "The installment of the Control Council in Berlin."

"No," answered Zhukov, "not until your troops will have been evacuated from the areas in the Soviet Zone they now illegally occupy."

"Why not then talk about both questions?" asked Eisenhower.

"No," Zhukov replied, "I cannot discuss the first until the second is settled." He said he could not do so "until all forces in Germany had been homed within their zones, or at least a date fixed for that event." [11]

For all practical purposes this meant that the Allied Control Council for Germany could not get underway for some time. As Eisenhower had suspected, the Soviets were making the establishment of the Control Council contingent upon the withdrawal of Allied forces from the Soviet zone.

As the meeting concluded, General Eisenhower said that American and British troops would withdraw from the Soviet zone at the same time they entered Berlin, but Zhukov would not discuss this until the date of the withdrawal had been settled. According to General Clay, Eisenhower did not press the issue further "since it was obvious that Marshal Zhukov was not prepared to discuss it." The meeting in Berlin ended with the agreement that the problem of the redistribution of forces was one which would be settled at the governmental level. Each of the military Commanders-in-Chief was to refer it to his respective government for further action.[12]

Following his return to Frankfurt that evening, General Eisenhower advised Washington that he thought the Russians would not agree to the activation of the Control Council in Germany until they had been satisfied about the withdrawal of Allied troops from the Soviet zone. He also pointed out that Allied Military Government had become a fact in Germany with the signature of the declaration establishing supreme authority, and requested that SHAEF be dissolved as soon as possible.

At this time, both General Eisenhower and his political adviser, Mr. Robert Murphy, thought it would be unwise to continue to keep the American forces in the Soviet zone. Murphy's own report to the State Department after the meeting in Berlin stated:

> For the Department's secret information I believe that General Eisenhower does not consider that the retention of our forces in the Russian zone is wise or that it will be productive of advantages. I believe that it is pretty obvious to all concerned that we really are desirous of removing our forces and that it is only a question of time when we will inevitably do so. The Russians on the other hand may well be content temporarily to consolidate their present position in the territory they hold. In the interim, no progress would under such circumstances be made in the organization of the quadripartite control of Germany, to which we are committed.

On June 8, 1945, three days after the Berlin meeting, Harry Hopkins, who had stopped off in Frankfurt on his return from Moscow, informed President Truman of General Eisenhower's preference for an early withdrawal. The Supreme Commander was convinced, Hopkins reported, that the present "indeterminate status for the date for withdrawal of Allied troops from area assigned to the Russians is certain to be misunderstood by Russia as well as at home." Until such a withdrawal was carried out, Hopkins advised the President, the Allied control machinery could not be started and any delay in the establishment of the control machinery "would interfere seriously with the development of government administrative machinery for Germany."

Hopkins suggested that in the withdrawal firm arrangements should be made with the Soviets for the simultaneous arrival of Western troops in Berlin. "As a concurrent condition to our withdrawal," Hopkins said, "we should specify a simultaneous movement of our troops to Berlin under an agreement between the respective commanders which would provide us unrestricted access to our Berlin area from Bremen and Frankfurt by air, rail and highway on agreed routes." [13]

In spite of a further warning from Prime Minister Churchill on June 9 that they should not withdraw, President Truman adopted the Eisenhower–Hopkins proposal. Unconsciously anticipating the American decision by one day, Churchill advised the British Foreign Office on June 11 that he was "still hoping that the retreat of the American centre to the occupation line can be staved off till 'the Three' meet. . . . Of course at any moment the Americans may give way to the Russian demand, and we shall have to conform. . . . We ought not to let ourselves be hurried into a decision which touches issues so vast and fateful." [14]

The following day, the Americans gave way. President Truman pointedly told the Prime Minister that he did not feel it possible to delay the withdrawal of United States forces for political purposes. "In consideration of the tripartite agreement as to zones of occupation in Germany, approved by President Roosevelt after long consideration and detailed discussion with you," Mr. Truman stated, "I am unable to delay the withdrawal of American troops from the Soviet zone in order to use pressure in the settlement of other problems."

Referring to the report he had just been given by Hopkins, the President said that "advice of the highest reliability is received that the Allied Control Council cannot begin to function until Allied troops withdraw from the Russian zone."

"I am also convinced," Mr. Truman continued, "that the military government now exercised by the Allied Supreme Commander should, without delay, be terminated and divided between Eisenhower and Montgomery, each to function in the zone occupied by his own troops."

"I am advised that it would be highly disadvantageous to our relations with the Soviets to postpone action in the matter until our meeting in July."

Truman then proposed a message to Stalin (written by General Marshall) stating that he was prepared to order all American troops in Germany to start their withdrawal to the American zone on June 21, in accordance with arrangements to be made "between the respective commanders." These arrangements were to include provisions for the simultaneous movement of the Allied garrisons into Greater Berlin and for the free access to Berlin by air, road, and rail from Frankfurt and Bremen. Mr. Churchill was asked by the President for his concurrence in the draft message before it was dispatched.[15]

"This struck a knell in my breast," Churchill later recalled, "but I had no choice but to submit." [16] On June 14, he sent his reply to Washington. "Obviously," Churchill said, "we are obliged to conform to your decision, and the necessary instructions will be issued." The Prime Minister quickly took issue with part of Truman's message, however. "It is not correct to state," he said, "that the tripartite agreement about zones of occupation in Germany was the subject of 'long considerations and detailed discussion' between me and President Roosevelt. References made to them at Quebec were brief, and concerned only Anglo-American arrangements which the President did not wish to raise by correspondence beforehand. These were remitted to the Combined Chiefs of Staff and were certainly acceptable to them."

"I sincerely hope," Churchill concluded, "that your action will in the long run make for a lasting peace in Europe." * [17]

In Washington, Churchill's surrender to the American decision caught the White House by surprise. According to Admiral Leahy, "Churchill's action in agreeing to our withdrawal was entirely unexpected. His acceptance of the President's decision, after repeated British insistence that we remain in the Soviet zone, indicated to me a possibility that the great Englishman was not in vigorous health. It was

---

* In writing subsequently of this immediate postwar decision, Prime Minister Churchill magnanimously has indicated many of the considerations which prompted President Truman's action. According to Churchill:

> It must not be overlooked that President Truman had not been concerned or consulted in the original fixing of the zones. The case as presented to him so soon after his accession to power was whether or not to depart from and in a sense repudiate the policy of the American and British governments agreed under his illustrious predecessor. He was, I have no doubt, supported in his action by his advisers, military and civil. His responsibility at this point was limited to deciding whether circumstances had changed so fundamentally that an entirely different procedure should be adopted, with the likelihood of having to face accusations of breach of faith. Those who are only wise after the event should hold their peace.

Triumph and Tragedy, pp. 606–8.

not in his nature or in accord with his past performance to give up so easily, even when he was plainly wrong,—as he was in this matter." [18]

As soon as Churchill's reply was received in Washington, the draft message to Stalin setting the date for the American withdrawal from the Soviet zone on June 21, was dispatched. The Prime Minister reluctantly sent a similar message to Moscow in which he stated that he was prepared to act in conjunction with the United States and that, if arrangements could be made between the tactical commanders, he would order General Montgomery to begin the withdrawal of British troops simultaneously. Both messages were received by the Kremlin on June 15.

On the following day, Marshal Stalin replied. His answer shocked both Washington and London. The Russians were not ready for the Allies to come to Berlin. July 1 would be better, Stalin said. Marshal Zhukov was wanted in Moscow for a parade on June 24, and would not return to Germany until June 28 or 30. Also, according to Stalin, "some of the districts of Berlin have not yet been cleared of mines, nor can such mine-clearing operations be finished until late June." But, of course, it was reparations, not "mines," of which Berlin was being cleared and the Soviets needed several more weeks to complete the process.

In spite of this, Stalin's request for postponement was accepted. President Truman directed the Joint Chiefs of Staff to instruct Eisenhower to begin the evacuation from the Soviet zone on July 1. The final details of the movement together with the arrangements for American access to Berlin were to be handled by General Eisenhower as Supreme Commander.[19]

In commenting later on these instructions, former President Truman has stated that:

> It was my own opinion that it would be silly if these arrangements were to lead to an isolated Berlin . . . to which we would have no access. I asked Stalin, with Churchill's backing, in my cable of June 14 for free access by air, road, and rail to Berlin . . . as part of the withdrawal of troops previously agreed to by Roosevelt, Churchill and Stalin.
>
> At my forthcoming meeting with Churchill and Stalin I intended to call for the setting up of a centralized Allied-controlled government. I was opposed to the breaking up of Germany into several Allied segments. . . . At no time did I believe that Ger-

many should be split into several rival territorial divisions or that its capital should become an island shut off from the rest of the country.* [20]

Prime Minister Churchill also emphasized the importance of access rights to Berlin in his message to Stalin on June 15.[21] "I also am ready," Churchill stated, "to issue instructions to Field Marshal Montgomery to make the necessary arrangements . . . for the similar withdrawal of British troops into their zones in Germany, for the simultaneous movement of Allied garrisons into Greater Berlin, and for the provision of free movement for British forces by air, rail, and road to and from the British zone to Berlin." [22]

In his reply to both Churchill and President Truman, however, Marshal Stalin made no reference to Allied access to Berlin, but the omission was not considered significant at the time; some in the West were led to believe that the matter of access was taken for granted.[23]

On June 25, in preparation for the Allied withdrawal, General Marshall informed Eisenhower of the importance President Truman attached to the question of access to Berlin. "In accordance with the President's message to Stalin," Marshall stated, arrangements for access should be made "simultaneously with arrangements for other adjustments." Marshall assumed that "appropriate Russian commanders have been instructed accordingly," and requested Major General John R. Deane, Chief of the U.S. Military Mission to Moscow, to check this out "with the Soviet Staff." [24]

Later that day, June 25, 1945, General Deane advised both Marshall and Eisenhower that, "I have requested General Antonov [Chief of the Russian General Staff] by letter to confirm fact that Soviet Commanders have been authorized to agree with American Commanders on freedom of access by road, rail, and air to Berlin . . . as directed in your . . . [message] of 25 June. Will meet with either Antonov or his representative today and hope to get an answer at that time."

The Russian military passed Deane's inquiry on to their political leaders in the Kremlin and later in the day, Andre Vyshinsky, then

---

* As has been noted (see Chapter II), the question of access to Berlin was considered both in Washington, and by the American delegation to the European Advisory Commission in London. For a variety of reasons, however, no specific assurance of Allied access to Berlin had been provided. Instead, the issue was to be handled as a purely military matter by the commanders once the hostilities were over.

Deputy Soviet Foreign Minister, told Ambassador Harriman that Zhukov had been authorized to discuss the matter of access with General Eisenhower. On June 27, two days later, General Antonov reported the same thing to General Deane and suggested that a meeting take place in Berlin on June 29. Deane relayed the message to General Marshall adding: "It is my opinion that when our representatives meet with Zhukov there will be little difficulty in arranging for free access for our troops in Berlin." [25]

On June 28, the day before the meeting with Zhukov, Eisenhower gave General Clay a summary of the American and British requirements for access to Berlin. Clay, who was to be the American representative at the meeting, was instructed to forward the requirements to Marshal Zhukov so that the Russians would be prepared to act on them the following day. The main features of these requirements were as follows:

> First, the unrestricted right to use two highways between Berlin and the Western zones, "including the right to repair and construct surfaces and bridges." These, if possible should be the autobahns Berlin-Magdeburg-Hanover and Berlin-Halle-Frankfurt.
>
> Second, the right to use three designated rail lines, including the maintenance of rights of way, and the right to use British and American trained rail crews and similarly supervised German civilians.
>
> Third, unrestricted air travel, including the right of fighter escort, between the American and British zones and the Staaken, Tempelhof and Gatow airfields in Berlin.
>
> Fourth, an agreement that all Allied traffic on authorized rights of way be free from border search or control by customs or military authorities.[26]

The meeting with Marshal Zhukov took place as scheduled in Berlin on June 29. Accompanying General Clay in the American delegation were Major General Floyd C. Parks, who had been designated the new commandant of the American sector in Berlin, and Robert Murphy, General Eisenhower's political adviser from the Department of State.

Great Britain was represented by Lieutenant General Sir Ronald Weeks. No French officers were present at the meeting since the location of the French sector in Berlin had not yet been agreed upon.

Marshal Zhukov, who was presiding, announced that the first item on the agenda was the withdrawal of American and British troops from Thuringia, Saxony and Saxony-Anhalt. According to General Clay's account, agreement was quickly reached. The evacuation would begin on July 1, and would be completed within four days.* Soviet troops would be allowed to follow the withdrawing Allied forces at intervals of not less than one kilometer; liaison representatives were to be exchanged between the various commanders along the front, Soviet reconnaissance parties would be permitted to enter the areas to be evacuated, and similar Allied parties would be allowed to proceed to Berlin.[27]

Having agreed to the arrangements for the Western withdrawal, the ensuing negotiations over access to Berlin became a great deal more difficult. Although he did not realize it at the time, General Clay was witnessing what Prime Minister Churchill had feared. In agreeing to the withdrawal of Allied troops from the Soviet zone, the West had played its high cards in Germany. As a result, Clay and Weeks now had to take what Zhukov offered and this, as it turned out, was not very much.

Zhukov informed the British and American generals that the Soviet Union considered access to Berlin as a privilege which they were granting the Allies, not as a right to which they were entitled. The Western demands which General Clay had given him the previous day, Zhukov said, were excessive. When Clay stated that the United States had not expected exclusive use of the facilities which he had mentioned but only the right of access over them, Zhukov remained adamant. He had instructions from Moscow, he said, which were explicit. The Allies could use one highway, that between Berlin and Hanover (through Helmstedt), one railroad, and one air corridor.** The air corridor, Zhukov said, might have two branches once it reached Magdeburg. One of these could continue on towards Hanover in the British zone while

---

* Previously, in tentative discussions between the Allied and Soviet commands, a nine-day period for the withdrawal had been agreed upon. General Clay reports that Zhukov "believed this much too long," and that he agreed with him.

Subsequently, there has been considerable speculation that the reason for the sudden Soviet reversal was due to a fear that the Western Allies would have that much more time to loot the areas from which they were withdrawing. See Frank Howley, *Berlin Command*, pp. 42–43; Field Marshal Montgomery, *Memoirs*, p. 344; Lucius D. Clay, *Decision in Germany*, p. 25.

** In his *Memoirs*, President Truman cites this as the autobahn "Hanau-Magdeburg-Berlin." Although this was the phrase used by Ambassador Murphy in his cable to the State Department, it is in error. The correct reading should be "Hanover-Magdeburg-Berlin." Cf. Harry S Truman, *Year of Decisions*, p. 307.

the other could veer in the direction of Frankfurt in the American zone. As for airfields in Berlin itself, the Russians stated that according to their maps, Gatow and Tempelhof were in the Western sectors and so the Allies were free to use them. Staaken was not and therefore was not available. This was the extent of Russia's offer, and Zhukov remained affable but could not be budged. He had orders from Moscow, he said, which he could not exceed.

Generals Clay and Weeks were now in an extremely unenviable position. As Lieutenant Generals they were acting only as the agents of their chiefs, General Eisenhower and Field Marshal Montgomery, respectively. To some extent, they undoubtedly felt obliged to bring home an agreement and were certainly not as free as their principals would have been to break off negotiations at this point. Also, they were clearly outranked. Zhukov was a Marshal of the Soviet Union, and Russia's greatest military hero. Neither Weeks nor Clay had been combat soldiers. While the question of relative rank probably would not have disturbed a trained civilian negotiator, it was a subtle consideration which could not help entering into the judgment of a professional soldier. It was a technique which the Russians were to follow repeatedly during the next several years of Allied dealings in Berlin.

In spite of the factors at work against him, General Clay at first declined to accept the Russian proposal and Weeks supported him. When Zhukov then said that the arrangement might be considered a temporary one and could be brought up later in the Control Council, Clay reluctantly agreed to accept it. In referring to the incident afterwards, General Clay stated: "Therefore Weeks and I accepted as a temporary arrangement the allocation of a main highway and rail line and two air corridors, reserving the right to reopen the question in the Allied Control Council. I must admit that we did not fully realize that the requirement of unanimous consent would enable a Soviet veto in the Allied Control Council to block all of our future efforts. . . ." [28]

As a result of General Clay's decision, the United States and Great Britain were to withdraw from the Soviet zone in return for only the most minimal Russian guarantees of access to Berlin. To General Clay's credit, he has courageously acknowledged his part in these proceedings. Writing in 1950 he stated:

I think now that I was mistaken in not . . . making free access to Berlin a condition to our withdrawal into our occupation zone. The import of the issue was recognized but I did not want an agreement in writing which established anything less than the right of unrestricted access. We were sincere in our desire to move into Berlin for the purpose of establishing quadripartite government which we hoped would develop better understanding and solve many problems. Also we had a large and combat-experienced army in Germany which at the moment prevented us from having any worries over the possibility of being blockaded there.[29]

"General Eisenhower," Clay continues, "had delegated full authority to me to conduct the negotiations and the responsibility for the decision was mine." Although General Clay discreetly did not mention it, perhaps he also was aware of the maxim of the military service which cautions that while authority may be delegated, responsibility never can.

The limited arrangements for access, to which Generals Clay and Weeks verbally agreed on June 29, were never recorded in an official document. As Clay has stated, "we did not wish to accept specific routes which might be interpreted as a denial of our right of access over all routes." There is considerable merit in General Clay's position. He—and his military and civilian superiors as well—thought it would be possible to work together amicably with the Soviet representatives in the Allied Control Council. By not putting what was considered a temporary agreement into writing, Clay felt that it would be easier to obtain revisions when the Control Council met.

As a result of the Clay-Weeks-Zhukov discussions, the armies of the United States and Great Britain began their withdrawal from the Soviet zone on July 1, 1945, followed by masses of refugees and others seeking safety from the Red Army. In the words of Winston Churchill, "Soviet Russia was established in the heart of Europe. This was a fateful milestone for mankind." [30]

At the time of the Western withdrawal, my wife, then a child of seven, was living with her family in Blankenburg/Harz, a mountain village in Saxony-Anhalt which was to be evacuated. She has since described the fear and dread with which the older people anticipated the coming of the Russian Army. It made an indelible impression upon her and can be appreciated, perhaps, only by those who have lived through a similar experience.

Simultaneously with the American evacuation of the Soviet zone, advance elements of the American Military Government sped towards Berlin. Colonel Frank Howley, who later succeeded General Parks as Commandant of the American sector in Berlin, has described the scene as it appeared to him at the time.

> On July 1, 1945, the road to Berlin was the highroad to Bedlam. It was packed with tanks, trucks, and other vehicles, Military Government people and troops, all hurrying toward the previously forbidden city. Russian officers . . . raced up and down our columns to see that we weren't escaping with plunder from the territory we had surrendered. . . .
> A disagreeable summer rain was pelting down when we finally straggled into Berlin late in the afternoon. The Russians had not allowed us to look over our sector before coming in, although that had been in the agreement, and none of us knew exactly where to go once we arrived. . . . As it was, hundreds of officers and men milled around, looking for places to stay in the ruins, and most of them, in Class A uniforms, wound up sleeping in the rain.[31]

Howley and his military government detachment fared only slightly better. They had brought their field gear with them and in the absence of any accommodations, spent the night camped in the Grunewald, Berlin's forest-like city park. As Howley recalls, "I pulled up my vehicles in a protective circle, as in the old covered-wagon days on the prairie, and posted guards."

The following day Howley and General Parks visited the Russian commandant in Berlin, Colonel General Gorbatov, to arrange for the take-over of the American sector.* Both parties agreed that July 4, then two days away, was a suitable date. Early on the morning of the fourth, the leading elements of the American 2nd Armored Division arrived in Berlin. The 2nd Armored Division, which was part of

---

* At this point it is well to distinguish between the sector commandants in Berlin and the Commanders-in-Chief of each of the Allied forces. The sector commandants were relatively junior "General Officers" and were usually several echelons below the Commanders-in-Chief in the chain of command. Their responsibilities extended only to the City of Berlin whereas the Commanders-in-Chief were responsible for all of Germany, including Berlin. Thus, General Gorbatov, a Colonel General, was the Russian sector Commandant in Berlin and was responsible to Marshal Zhukov who was the Russian Commander-in-Chief. Similarly, Major General Parks was the commander of the American sector in Berlin and likewise, was responsible for his actions to General Eisenhower, the American Commander-in-Chief.

Simpson's Ninth Army, had been sitting on the banks of the Elbe since April 11, a period of almost three months, waiting for the opportunity to push on to Berlin. When they arrived, a brief change-over ceremony was held, and General Bradley, who had flown to Berlin especially for the occasion, spoke briefly to the assembled troops. Flags were exchanged between the Russians and Americans, and elements of the Red Army passed in review.

Later that day as the Americans were preparing to take over their sector, Major General Parks received a note signed by Marshal Zhukov. In it, Zhukov stated that under the agreements Berlin was to be governed by an Allied Kommandatura composed of each of the four sector commandants.* Since the Kommandatura had not been established, Zhukov said, the American sector could not be turned over to the U.S. forces. This was another Soviet strategem but General Parks and his deputy, Colonel Howley, refused to be put off. In the absence of orders from American headquarters in Frankfurt, Parks took the initiative and instructed Howley to "go ahead as planned, but don't get into too much trouble. After all, the occupation is just beginning." [32]

At dawn the following morning Colonel Howley moved his military government personnel and borough commanders into each of the six boroughs of the American sector. In each of the six borough halls Howley's officers "requisitioned" space and raised the American flag. The German officials who were there were told that henceforth they would receive their instructions from the Americans. When the Russians awoke later in the day they were confronted with a *fait accompli*. After a brief protest, they acquiesced and withdrew, and according to General Clay, "we had learned our first lesson in how to obtain Russian consent." [33]

On July 7, General Clay and General Weeks again met with Marshal Zhukov to discuss occupation policy. The purpose of the meeting was to arrange for the permanent supply of food and fuel needed in Berlin

---

* Under the provisions of the Allied agreement on control machinery in Germany which had been signed by each of the four Commanders-in-Chief on June 5, the city of Berlin was to be governed jointly by "an Inter-Allied Governing Authority or Kommandatura." The Kommandatura was to operate under the direction of the Allied Control Council, and would have a technical staff to control the various organs of city government. Like the Control Council, its chairmanship would rotate on a monthly basis.

and to establish the quadripartite machinery for the city government. With little discussion, Generals Clay and Weeks accepted the Russian draft for the organization of the Kommandatura. At General Clay's suggestion, it was decided that the Kommandatura would hold its first meeting on the eleventh of July.

The second subject discussed, that of supplying food and fuel for Berlin, was not so easily resolved. Marshal Zhukov insisted that the Western powers would have to bring into Berlin the necessary food to support their individual sectors. Previously, all of Berlin had received its food from the surrounding countryside which was now under Soviet occupation. When Clay and Weeks protested and pointed this out, Zhukov stressed the severe food shortage which he said was then impending in the Soviet zone and in the Soviet Union itself. Moved by this argument, Generals Clay and Weeks accepted the responsibility for bringing in the necessary food to support the population of the Western sectors. "Weeks and I knew," Clay has written:

> . . . that there was a definite food shortage in both eastern Germany and the Soviet Union. Fighting between the ground forces in eastern Germany had gone on for a much longer period than in western Germany and was certain to have cut down its resources. We could not expect the ill-nourished Russians to eat less in order to feed Berlin. Therefore, subject to the establishment of a common ration in all sectors of Berlin and with the understanding that the Control Council when it was established would arrange for the exchange of food between all zones of occupation . . . I accepted the responsibility for bringing in the food necessary to support the population of the American sector.[34]

As a result of General Clay's decision, the Western Allies assumed the burden for supporting their sectors in Berlin, as well as for governing them. It is interesting to speculate how the situation in Berlin would have developed had the Russians been compelled to continue to provide the food and fuel for all of the sectors of Berlin. Presumably, the dependence of the Western sectors on the Western Allies (and the Western zones in Germany) would not have existed. Conversely, a blockade three years later which cut off the supplies from the Soviet zone might have been all the more serious. Likewise, had the responsibility for the feeding of the Western sectors of Berlin not been placed on the Western Allies, it is questionable whether the feeling of mutual dependence, which subsequently developed between Berlin and the West, would have flourished. In the absence of General Clay's decision, Berlin very definitely might have gone behind the Iron Curtain in 1945.

The four-power occupation in Berlin officially began when the Berlin Kommandatura held its first meeting on July 11. All four sector commandants were present. The United States was represented by Major General Floyd Parks and his deputy, Colonel Howley. Great Britain was represented by Major General Lewis Lyne and the Soviet Union by Colonel General Alexander V. Gorbatov. France, whose sector in Berlin had not yet been established, was represented by Brigadier General Geoffroi de Beauchesne.

In its first item of business, the Kommandatura, at Soviet insistence, agreed that all orders previously issued by the Russians would remain in effect until further notice. This was a serious mistake. All decisions of the Kommandatura had to be unanimous. Accordingly, it later became impossible to change many aspects of the Berlin city government which the Russians had imposed. Most important of these were the replacement of Soviet appointed officials in the Western sectors and the control of the city's police force. Political parties and labor unions also found it difficult to organize on an independent basis as a result of the Kommandatura's decision. As Colonel Howley later stated, "when we signed that document we acquiesced to Russian control of Berlin."

6

Blockade

On the afternoon of July 15, 1945, four days after the first meeting of the Allied Kommandatura, President of the United States Harry S Truman landed at Gatow airfield in Berlin. He had come to the former German capital to take part in the final wartime conference of the Big Three scheduled to begin at Potsdam the following day.

As a code name for the Potsdam Conference, Prime Minister Churchill had suggested the word TERMINAL. The war against Germany was over. The three Allied heads of government were meeting in a final gathering on conquered soil to survey the wreckage. To Mr. Churchill, and to Stalin and Truman who quickly agreed, the word TERMINAL would commemorate the end of the perilous journey which each nation had undertaken.

It quickly became apparent, however, that TERMINAL had an ironic significance. With the common enemy destroyed, the reason for the Allied coalition no longer existed. Like Hitler's Europe, the Grand Alliance was also at an end. The co-operation which had held firm throughout the war would not continue into the peace, and a time of mutual understanding yielded to a time of mutual distrust.

For Churchill himself, the Potsdam Conference also marked the end of his tenure as Great Britain's Prime Minister. Midway through its proceedings, the great Englishman was turned out of office by the British electorate. The courageous spirit who had rallied the Western world in the darkest days of 1940 no longer was thought fit to lead His Majesty's Government in the new world which was beginning.

As noted in the previous chapter, Prime Minister Churchill had sought to hold the Potsdam Conference more than a month before; at a time when American and British armies in Europe were at their greatest strength, when large areas of the Soviet zone were still in Allied hands and consequently, when the overall bargaining position of the West was exceedingly strong. His suggestion, however, had been rejected in Washington.

The major item on the agenda at Potsdam was Germany. Marshal Stalin arrived for the Conference determined not only to press the claim of the Soviet Union for crippling reparations but to effect major territorial revisions at Germany's expense as well. Great Britain arrived equally determined to halt Russia's westward expansion, hoping to create once more in Germany a viable buffer between East and West. The United States, caught in between, pursued the ideal of friendly accommodation, seeking compromise when possible and hoping through its sincerity to reach a lasting accord with the Communist regime.

The results of the Potsdam Conference relate more to the final settlement in Germany than to Berlin itself. Specifically, it was agreed that the economy of Germany would be decentralized, that her production would be rigidly controlled and that her development would be limited mainly to "agriculture and peaceful domestic industries." Politically, while local selfgovernment in Germany was to be encouraged, it was decided that supreme authority should remain vested in the Allied Control Council. The trials of those labeled major war criminals were to begin at the earliest possible date. Territorially, "pending the final determination of Poland's Western frontier," the provinces beyond the Oder-Neisse were turned over to Polish administration. East Prussia, as Stalin demanded, was divided between Poland and the Soviet Union. Last, and most onerous perhaps, the nine million German people living in the lands ceded to the various nations of Eastern Europe were to be cleared from those lands and transferred in an "orderly and humane manner" to the four occupied zones of Germany itself.[1]

While he was at Potsdam, President Truman participated in a modest ceremony in the courtyard of the American Headquarters in Zehlendorf marking the official raising of the American flag over Berlin. The date selected was July 20, 1945, the first anniversary of the abortive plot on Hitler's life, and the flag used was the one which had flown over the Capitol in Washington on December 7, 1941— the same flag previously raised over Rome, and later to be raised over Tokyo. The President made some brief, well chosen remarks on what General Clay remembers as an impressive occasion:

> While the soldier is schooled against emotion, I have never forgotten that short ceremony as our flag rose to the staff. When in later days anyone suggested the possibility of our departure from Berlin before, of our own choice, we left a free Berlin, I could not help thinking that no one who had seen our flag raised by right of victory but dedicated to the preservation of freedom and peace could possibly see it withdrawn until peace and freedom had been established.[2]

The following week, on July 26, the question of the French sector in Berlin finally was settled. At Yalta, Marshal Stalin had indicated he would not object to France joining in the occupation of Germany providing the territory France occupied came from that already designated for the Western powers. As we have seen, the French zone in Western Germany was established by splitting Baden-Wuerttemberg in the American zone and adding the Rhinish Palatinate and the Saar from the British. In the case of Berlin, however, the problem was more difficult, and when the Potsdam Conference assembled, the European Advisory Commission still had reached no solution. The difficulty was caused by American insistence that the French sector in Berlin should be made up of territory given jointly by all three powers, not just the United States and Great Britain alone. Since this was not in accordance with the decision of Stalin at Yalta, the Russians refused to agree. The issue was not resolved until July 26, midway through the Potsdam Conference, when the British announced that they would give the French two boroughs from their own sector in Berlin. This amounted to a splitting of the British sector while the American and Russian sectors remained the same and everyone quickly agreed.

Under this new arrangement, the Russians still had eight boroughs, the Americans six, the British now four, and the French two. Two weeks later, on August 12, 1945, the French officially took control of their two boroughs.*

With the French now installed in Berlin, the occupation regime was complete. The French representative to the Allied Kommandatura, General Geoffroi de Beauchesne, was admitted as a voting member and the task of governing the city went forward on a four-power basis.

At first, Western policy in Berlin was characterized by a desire to get along with the Russians at almost any price. The two earlier meetings of General Clay with Marshal Zhukov were indicative of the approach which was to be followed by Western occupation officials for more than a year. "We were going to get along with the Russians and we were quite willing to start off on their terms." Clay sums up the attitude as follows:

> Our government had accepted the principle of four-power control and we had determined on our part to try in every way to allay Soviet suspicion, to create the mutual understanding that might make it successful. It is possible that this desire to make a success of quadripartite government led us in the early months to take compromise positions which merely deferred the real issues. . . .[3]

In spite of Western attempts to be agreeable, difficulties soon arose. At first, these differences were not serious and many in the Allied occupation thought that they were only local aberrations. The Allies, for example, immediately had to deal with the original Communist appointees to the city government who had been selected by the Russians when they had Berlin to themselves. After the Western powers arrived, a number of these appointees continued to take their orders from the Soviet Military Administration. For this reason, the mayor of the borough of Steglitz in the American sector, and other

* Reinickendorf and Wedding, located in the northwestern part of the city. Interestingly, during the course of the negotiations over the French sector, one of the proposals put forward by the United States for the redivision of Berlin would have given the Russians the borough of Neukölln located adjacent to Tempelhof airfield. Had the proposal been accepted, it would have made the later airlift virtually impossible since the Russians easily could have obstructed the approach to Tempelhof simply by constructing a number of tall buildings in their sector. See W. Phillips Davison, *The Berlin Blockade* (Princeton: Princeton University Press, 1958), p. 31. Also see Mosely, *op. cit.*, pp. 601–2.

borough mayors in the French and British sectors, finally had to be removed from office.[4]

Similarly, in the borough of Schöneberg in the American sector, a majority of the government officials were known Communists and received their orders directly from the local secretary of the Communist Party. Colonel Frank Howley, the Deputy American Commandant, was certain that the local secretary's orders came from the Central Party Headquarters in East Berlin, but in keeping with the American policy to avoid an open split with the Russians, he did not expose the tie.[5] Ten of the borough officials were later arrested, however, and two were convicted and sentenced to five years imprisonment for interfering with local officers carrying out the orders of the American Military Government.[6]

Even with these occasional incidents four-power government in Berlin continued smoothly for almost a year. On November 30, 1945, the Allied Control Council officially approved an "Air Corridor Agreement" which clearly spelled out the rights of the Western Allies in the air corridors between Berlin and the Western zones. Significantly, this agreement is the only written accord ever concluded with the Soviet Union in which the right of Allied access was precisely defined. The detailed provisions of the agreement were negotiated at the "working level" by the four-power Allied Air Directorate located in Berlin. It was approved largely as a result of the persistence of the American Air Force personnel then engaged in flying into the isolated city. The fact that it was negotiated and approved suggests that had Generals Clay and Weeks shown a similar persistence earlier, other agreements on access could have been secured. Whether they would have been observed, of course, is another matter.*

The first really serious conflict between East and West in Berlin developed early in 1946 over a proposed reorganization of the city

* The Air Corridor Agreement authorized the Western powers three air corridors instead of the earlier two; each twenty miles wide, extending between Berlin and the cities of Hamburg, Hanover and Frankfurt. Flights through the corridors were to be unrestricted, and only minimal identification required (for safety purposes) from each aircraft upon entering the corridor. A four-power Air Safety Center was established in the American sector to handle the technical routing of planes through the corridors and to control their approach over Berlin. To simplify traffic patterns above the city, a special Berlin Control Zone was established. This zone extended twenty miles in every direction from the Allied Control Council building, and included all of the air space over the city up to an altitude of 10,000 feet.

government. A draft Constitution which allowed the Berliners the right to elect their own Mayor and many of the city officials was then in preparation. In anticipation of the election which was to follow the adoption of this Constitution, the Russians attempted to force a merger of the powerful Socialist party in Berlin (Social Democratic Party or SPD) with the local Communist party.

Traditionally, Berlin, the most highly industrialized city in Germany, has been a Socialist stronghold. The thousands of workers who flocked there following the industrial revolution voted Socialist in economic protest against the misery which then existed. In the times of Bismarck and the Kaiser, Berlin had been noted for its leftist leanings and during the Weimar Republic the city repeatedly delivered thumping majorities for the local SPD candidates. In 1946, the Russians hoped to capitalize on this tradition and form a joint Socialist-Communist party (Socialist Unity Party or SED) under Communist leadership.

Initially, there was every indication that the Russians would succeed. Otto Grotewohl, then chairman of the SPD in Berlin,* actively supported the merger. American and British military officials were apathetic, and most Berliners were far too busy fighting hunger and cold in the first postwar winter to be concerned with political maneuvers, especially when one of those doing the maneuvering was an occupying power.

Opposition to the merger did not solidify, in fact, until February 14, 1946, when a number of SPD officials from the various borough organizations in Berlin met informally in an unheated living room behind a textile shop. From this and subsequent meetings later in the month a determined few galvanized the party's membership into active opposition. Kurt Schumacher, the great postwar leader of the Socialist Party (SPD) in the Western zones of Germany, flew to Berlin and campaigned vigorously against the merger.

On March 1, at a meeting of the party's central committee, the rebellious delegates, over Grotewohl's strenuous objections, voted that the proposed merger could not take place without the approval of the entire membership of the party in a special election. Until this point the Western Allies had remained completely neutral. There had been no effort whatever to counterbalance the pressure from the

* Later, Prime Minister of the "German Democratic Republic."

Soviet authorities demanding merger. Colonel Howley has stated that even at the top level the American view on merger was divided.[7]

With a plebiscite suddenly in the offing, the West felt obliged to insure that the election was held in a democratic manner. To most in the Military Government, however, it was still a purely German affair and there was no direct intervention. On March 31, 1946, when the election was held, seventy-five percent of the registered SPD members in Berlin went to the polls. In the Western sectors, the vote ran approximately 19 to 2 against the merger. In the Soviet sector, no count was taken. Fearful of an impending defeat, the Russians closed the polls early, using the pretext of supposed "voting irregularities."

Having lost in their attempt to merge the Social Democrats with the Communist Party in the Western sectors,* the Soviets began to resist Allied efforts for city-wide elections in Berlin under the new Constitution. When the question arose in the Allied Kommandatura it was vetoed by the Soviet representative. The Western commandants then appealed the decision to the Allied Control Council, where, through the combined efforts of all three Western Commanders-in-Chief, Marshal Sokolovsky (Zhukov's successor) finally relented and October 20, 1946, was selected as the date for the election—the first free elections to be held in Berlin since 1933.[8]

With the elections agreed upon, the Soviets made every effort to win. During the campaign, the Communist Party (now the SED) distributed more propaganda in the city than the three non-Communist parties combined. Food and coal were given away by local SED officials and notebooks, "compliments of the SED," were presented to school children in every election district. In the Soviet sector itself, democratic parties were harassed, SPD meetings were prohibited, and voters were blatantly intimidated. The Western powers, although not intervening, did their best to insure that the Berliners would be allowed to vote unmolested, but this was not always an easy task.

The final election returns represented an overwhelming defeat for the Russians. Both the Soviet Union and its puppet party, the SED,

---

* In spite of their defeat in the Western sectors, however, the Russians went ahead and merged the SPD and the Communist Parties throughout their zone of Germany and in the East sector of Berlin. No referendum was held and no discussion was permitted. On April 21, the new Socialist Unity Party (SED) consisting of a rump element of the SPD and the Communists, was inaugurated throughout Soviet controlled territory.

were clearly repudiated. Even in the workers' boroughs of Neukölln and Wedding, where the infamous "rent barracks" of Berthold Brecht and Gerhart Hauptmann still stood and where Communist feeling traditionally ran high, the vote went against the SED. The city-wide results were as follows:

SPD (Social Democrats)	48.7%
CDU (Christian Democrats)	22.2%
SED (Communists)	19.8%
LPD (Liberal Democrats)	9.3%

Defeated at the polls, the Russians learned a simple lesson: the Berliners would never choose communism of their own free will. In spite of all the inducements which the Soviet regime had offered, the Socialist Unity Party (SED) had been vigorously rejected. As a result, Berlin would never have another city-wide election.

The city government which was installed in Berlin following the election in 1946 represented a coalition of all four parties. Dr. Otto Ostrowski of the SPD was chosen as Lord Mayor. At first, Ostrowski attempted to follow a middle course between East and West. Soon, however, Soviet pressure became too much and he agreed to sign an understanding with the Russians pledging his co-operation with the SED. When the news of Ostrowski's agreement was discovered, it was formally repudiated by an outraged city assembly in a vote of 85–20. The following week, Ostrowski resigned from office.

Following Ostrowski's resignation, Dr. Ernst Reuter (SPD) was elected as Lord Mayor by the city assembly. Reuter unquestionably was the leading anti-Communist in Berlin at that time. His political career began prior to the First World War. A Social Democrat, he had opposed the voting of war credits to the Kaiser in 1914. During the First World War he became a Communist, then broke with the party in 1922 to become one of the driving forces in the SPD during the Weimar Republic. He opposed Hitler's rise to power and spent the Nazi years in an enforced exile teaching politics and economics in Turkey. In 1946 he received permission to return to Berlin and became one of the leaders of the city's postwar Social Democratic Party.

The Communists never forgave Reuter's earlier apostasy in leaving the Party. Following his election as Lord Mayor, the Soviets exercised their veto in the Allied Kommandatura to prevent him from taking office. The city assembly stood its ground, however, and refused to elect anyone in Reuter's place. For the next eighteen months Ernst Reuter remained the duly elected Lord Mayor of Berlin although barred from office by the Russians. In the interim, the two Deputy Mayors of Berlin—Louise Schroeder of the SPD and Ferdinand Friedensburg of the CDU—temporarily filled the gap. Symbolically, the Lord Mayor's quarters in Berlin's City Hall remained vacant.

The political situation in Berlin was but one indication of the rapidly deteriorating façade of East-West co-operation. On February 9, 1946, Marshal Stalin in a major speech from the Kremlin stated that the world revolution of communism was still marching forward. Indeed, the Soviet Union already was trying to incorporate its zone of Germany into the cordon of satellite states it was creating in Eastern Europe. As a result of Russian pressure, political life in the Soviet zone soon lost all traces of its democratic and Western elements. Communist control at all echelons of government became a political fact of life. Walter Ulbricht, Wilhelm Pieck and Otto Grotewohl, the latter following his defection from the SPD, became the principal instruments through which Soviet policy was administered. The political right of local self-determination guaranteed to the German people by the Potsdam Protocol was studiously ignored.

Moreover, the Soviets effectively thwarted Allied efforts toward Germany's economic reconstruction. In December of 1945, Marshal Zhukov vetoed a proposal in the Allied Control Council to open all zonal boundaries within Germany to free travel and commerce. Later, when the Western powers requested the Soviet Union to place East zone production into a pool with that of the other zones in order to pay for essential German imports—an arrangement provided for at Potsdam—the Russians refused to comply.

By late 1946, in fact, it had become evident that the Soviet Union did not intend to co-operate in the joint government of Germany, and repeated Soviet vetoes had reduced the Allied Control Council to virtual impotence. On September 6, 1946, American Secretary of State James F. Byrnes, in a major foreign policy speech at Stuttgart, bluntly informed the Soviets that as a result of their actions the Allied Control Council was "neither governing Germany nor allowing Germany to govern itself." Accordingly, Secretary Byrnes said, the American and

British zones in Western Germany would be merged for economic purposes effective January 1, 1947.

Indeed, Soviet motives had become increasingly plain. "Peoples Governments" already had been established in Poland, Rumania, and Bulgaria; and Hungary would soon fall completely into the Soviet orbit. In Greece, the Russians were openly promoting civil war against the established government; Turkey was being pressed for concessions in the Dardanelles which would jeopardize her independence.

To the credit of the Western world, President Truman soon responded with the vigor which was to characterize the next six years of his Administration. Originally, Mr. Truman had backed the earlier Allied efforts toward accommodation with the Soviet Union. Such a course, he felt, might lead to a permanent understanding between East and West. This had been the policy of Franklin Delano Roosevelt, and he did not intend to abandon it until it was proven ineffective. It soon became apparent to him that this was the case, and that American "co-operation" could only be continued at the price of surrendering Europe to communism. Thereupon Mr. Truman, in March of 1947, in what later came to be known as the Truman Doctrine, moved to stop Soviet aggression in Greece and Turkey by extending military and economic assistance to those nations. Four months later, in a commencement speech at Harvard, Secretary of State George C. Marshall announced the beginning of a program of large scale American economic assistance to promote European recovery. In an offer tendered to East and West alike, Secretary Marshall offered massive financial aid to those European nations whose economies had been disrupted by the war. The American offer was gratefully accepted by the nations of Western Europe, but there was an enforced silence among those of the East.

In the fall of 1947, General Clay returned to Washington to take part in the discussions on Marshall Plan aid for Germany. There, he warned the President and the National Security Council of the rising tide of Soviet pressure in Germany, and of possible Russian efforts to force the Allies out of Berlin. Walter Bedell Smith, formerly Eisenhower's Chief of Staff at SHAEF and now U.S. Ambassador to Moscow, concurred in Clay's analysis.

Shortly after Clay's visit to Washington, the fifth session of the

Council of Foreign Ministers convened in London, and the question
of peace treaties with Austria and Germany headed the agenda. From
the beginning, Russian Foreign Minister Molotov demonstrated that
the Soviet Union would accept no agreement which would permit
German recovery. In their final communique at the close of the conference, the Western Foreign Ministers stated that a treaty on Germany could not be reached except "under conditions which would
not only enslave the German people but would seriously retard the
recovery of all Europe." Significantly, no arrangements were made
for a subsequent meeting.

As General Clay has recalled:

> I am sure that all of us present in London, recognized that, with
> the Council adjourned, we were now engaged in a competitive
> struggle, not with arms but with economic resources, with ideas
> and ideals. It was a struggle in which we desired no territory but
> were determined that others should not acquire further territory
> through the use of oppressive power, fear to dull the hearts, and
> distorted information to capture the minds of people powerless to
> resist. There could be no escape from the struggle. We could hope
> with some assurance that it would not lead to physical force. We
> knew not how long it would last or what turn it would take." [9]

But it did not take long for the West to find out. In January, the
Soviets imposed stringent curbs on civilian passenger traffic on interzonal trains in Germany. Shortly afterwards, and this time in direct
violation of the verbal agreement between General Clay and Marshal
Zhukov, Russian inspectors boarded American military trains and
insisted on the right to check the identity papers of individual passengers. General Clay responded by placing armed military guards
on the trains to bar the Soviets forcibly. Throughout February and
March, the game of political cat-and-mouse continued. Frequently
the Soviets would shuttle American military trains to a siding because
the American train commander refused to allow the Soviet inspectors
aboard. The trains usually were released after several hours of extended bargaining. [10]

At the same time, the Soviets began a concerted propaganda barrage in Germany against the Western powers. Western newspapers
and periodicals were confiscated and burned in the Soviet zone. On
February 17, 1948, Soviet military police seized all copies of Western

books at newstands and bookstores in East Berlin. News distribution agencies in the Soviet zone were placed under rigid Soviet control and only approved publications were allowed to be sold.

Soviet authorities also began to spread rumors that the Western Allies were leaving Berlin. Some of these were picked up and embellished by the more timid Military Government personnel in Berlin. The *New York Times* on October 12, 1947, reported: "It is a matter of common knowledge that many Military Government officials openly discuss the possibility of a three power withdrawal from this city." Needless to say, these discussions had a serious effect on the morale of the Western sectors.

Events in the Allied Control Council at this time likewise testified to the rising tension between East and West. On January 20, 1948, Marshal Sokolovsky demanded the immediate dissolution of the bizonal economic agreement between Great Britain and the United States which Secretary Byrnes had announced at Stuttgart more than a year before. At the following Council meeting on February 11, Sokolovsky accused the Western powers of seeking to include Germany in "a military and political Western bloc," a charge which General Clay hotly denied.

Elsewhere, the situation was also critical. On February 25, 1948, one more nation passed behind the Iron Curtain when the government of Czechoslovakia fell to the Communists in a carefully laid plot. On March 10, Jan Masaryk, the freedom-loving ex-Foreign Minister of Czechoslovakia, leaped to his death from the window of his apartment in Prague.

Shortly after the Czechoslovakia coup, General Clay advised Washington that something was about to happen in Germany. On March 5, he cabled:

For many months, based on logical analysis I have felt and held that war was unlikely for at least two years. Within the last few weeks, I have felt a subtle change in Soviet attitude which I cannot define but which now gives me a feeling that it may come with dramatic suddenness. I cannot support this change in my own thinking with any data or outward evidence in relationships other than to describe it as a feeling of a new tenseness in every Soviet individual with whom we have official relations. I am unable to submit any official report in the absence of supporting data but my feeling is real. You may advise the Chief of Staff

[General Bradley] of this for whatever it may be worth if you feel it advisable.[11]

In notifying Washington that something was up, General Clay was acting purely on his own initiative. The intelligence reports which he saw daily contained nothing to arouse suspicion, and on the surface, the water was still calm. This was one of the rare cases in recent American history when the responsible Commander on the spot has not only sensed something that the intelligence "experts" had overlooked but also dared to communicate this feeling to his superiors.

In Washington, Clay's telegram caused intense alarm.[12] As a result of Western demobilization immediately following the war, the military posture of the Allied camp was much like that of England and France in 1940. The United States was unable to send more than one additional division overseas without ordering a partial mobilization. Even then there was a serious question of where the transportation would come from. The atomic bomb remained the bulwark of Western defense but few gave serious consideration to its employment.

The concern which Clay's telegram caused in Washington put Allied forces in Germany on the alert, for the American Military Governor in the former Third Reich was not known for impetuous actions. Lieutenant General Lucius Dubignon Clay had come to Germany in April, 1945, as General Eisenhower's deputy for Military Government. Until then, he had spent most of the war in Washington, first as General Marshall's assistant for logistics (working under General Somervell), and then as deputy to James F. Byrnes in the Office of War Mobilization. On an earlier occasion in 1944, he had gone to Europe for several months to unsnarl a transportation bottleneck at the port of Cherbourg.

When he took over in Germany following the war, General Clay had little understanding either of the German people or of the Soviet Union. As a good soldier, he conscientiously followed the policy he had been given and earnestly endeavored to get along with the Russians. Political considerations were as alien to him as they were to Eisenhower and Marshall, and like many another career general, he was intolerant of dissent. But he was also a man of forthright courage and had the happy faculty of being able to recognize his own mistakes. As a result, Clay's opinion on Germany gradually changed. Slowly recognizing the need for Germany to recover industrially, he began to advocate American economic assistance. Reluctantly, he also had begun to question Soviet actions and motives. Of all those involved in the postwar occupation, General Clay could honestly say that he had tried to make four-power government a success. In 1947, when it became apparent that the Soviets were intent on wrecking the occupation, he reacted with the same determination which had characterized his earlier career. He had learned from experience how to get along with the Russians. Throughout the storms which were about to descend on Berlin, Clay remained a beacon light to the Western cause.

And in Berlin at this time the situation was steadily worsening. On March 10, 1948, Marshal Sokolovsky, in an attack which consumed the entire meeting of the Allied Control Council, castigated the Western powers as "intolerant of genuine democracy." At the following meeting on March 20, he launched into a similar tirade, and then the entire Soviet delegation rose as one and stalked from the conference room. With the exception of a fleeting moment the following year, they would not return.

Following Sokolovsky's walkout, Clay's plea for a firm stand created apprehension and doubt in Washington. On March 30, the Department of the Army summoned the General to a teleconference and requested his views on a proposal to withdraw American dependents from Berlin. Clay was opposed. Such a move, he said, would be politically disastrous: "Withdrawal of dependents from Berlin would create hysteria accompanied by rush of Germans to communism for safety. The condition would spread in Europe and would increase Communist political strength everywhere." [13]

The day after Clay's reply to Washington, Lieutenant General Dratvin, Deputy Soviet Military Governor for Germany, advised the American Military Government in Berlin that effective April 1, the Russians would check the identification of all passengers on military trains passing through their zone. Baggage and freight shipments would be subjected to a similar check. Should the Americans refuse, the trains would be halted at the zonal border.

Clay notified Washington immediately, and again he suggested a firm stand: "We cannot permit our military trains to be entered by representatives of other powers, and to do so would be inconsistent with the free and unrestricted right of access in Berlin which was the condition precedent to our evacuation of Saxony and Thuringia."

Clay proposed that a similar message be sent to the Soviet authorities and that a test train with a few armed guards be sent across the zonal border. Reluctantly, Washington agreed. Clay reports that he detected "some apprehension on the part of Secretary [of the Army Kenneth C.] Royall and his advisers that a firm stand . . . might develop incidents involving force which would lead to war." [14]

Clay replied to the Secretary that "weakness on our part would cost important prestige and that if war were desired by the Soviet government it would not be averted by weakness. I do not believe," Clay added, "this means war." When Clay had finished, Washington's answer was written by General of the Army Omar Bradley, not Secretary Royall. Unlike others in Washington, Bradley shared Clay's opinion. "Thanks muchly," he told Clay. "This has been an arduous day and *we* appreciate your co-operation." [15]

Meanwhile, in London, the British government already had decided on a show of force. "His Majesty's Government does not propose to stop running its military trains and will maintain armed guards on them, if necessary," a terse announcement from London stated.

On April 1, General Clay sent his test train with an armed guard detachment across the border. As had been feared, it was shuttled to a siding by the Soviets and left there. Several days later it withdrew under its own power.[16]

In Washington indecision now prevailed. On April 2, General Clay was again "invited" to a teleconference by the Pentagon. Pressures were rising at home, he was told, for the return of the American dependents. "Many responsible persons," Washington said, "believed it unthinkable that they should stay in Berlin." In effect, the Department of the Army was getting nervous and sought Clay's advice.

"I reported," Clay states, "that we could support the Americans in Berlin indefinitely with a very small airlift and that we should not evacuate our dependents. . . . Evacuation in face of Italian elections and European situation is to me almost unthinkable. Our women and children can take it, and they appreciate import. There are few here who have any thought of leaving unless required to do so." [17]

The day after Clay's cable, the Soviets closed the civilian freight lines into Berlin from Hamburg and Nuremberg. The following week, on April 9, the Soviets announced that all German freight trains on the one remaining rail line (Berlin-Helmstedt) would require individual clearances from the Soviet Military Authority. Twenty-four hours afterwards, Secretary of the Army Royall sought Clay's advice again. Was the General still sure that we should stay? The situation, according to Royall, was under constant discussion in Washington and, while the Army hadn't changed its position yet, it wanted to know Clay's views once more. In short, Clay was being asked if he still wanted to stick his neck out. The General's reply left little doubt. We should stay in Berlin, he said, "unless driven out by force."

> We have lost Czechoslovakia. Norway is threatened. We retreat from Berlin. When Berlin falls, western Germany will be next. If we mean . . . to hold Europe against Communism, we must not budge. We can take humiliation and pressure short of war in Berlin without losing face. If we withdraw, our position in Europe is threatened. If America does not understand this now, does not know that the issue is cast, then it never will and Communism will run rampant. I believe the future of democracy requires us to stay. . . .[18]

Clay's reply seemed to settle the question for the moment. Throughout April and May his "Little Airlift" continued to bring in supplies for the American personnel. Soviet pressure, however, continued to increase. Shortly after his message to Royall, American Signal Corps personnel who manned the communication lines between Berlin and the Western zones were expelled from Soviet territory. The East Berlin police force was incorporated into that of the Soviet zone on April 13. On April 20, restrictions were placed on barge traffic between Berlin and the West, and in May, additional documentation requirements were placed on all freight shipments.

In June the crisis rose to a climax. On June 10, Soviet representatives, attempting to remove locomotives and rolling stock from the American sector, were repulsed by armed military police, and the following day, all rail traffic between Berlin and West Germany was suspended. Two days later it was just as suddenly restored. On June 12, the Soviets closed the Berlin-Helmstedt autobahn to "repair" the Elbe River bridge. On the sixteenth, the Soviet Commandant walked out of the Kommandatura, and the split of the quadripartite control machinery was now complete. In addition to this the Communists had been undermining Allied currency, using a duplicate set of plates which had been given to the Russians in 1945. With these plates the Soviets had been able to print whatever quantity of occupation currency they desired, much of which was redeemable at face value by the United States Treasury. In the resulting wide-open money market, all Western financial assistance to Germany was being eaten up in an inflationary spiral. Accordingly, two days after the Soviets walked out of the Kommandatura, the United States, Great Britain and France announced a currency reform which would take place in the three Western zones of Germany. Berlin would not be affected.

The Soviets responded to the Western action by cutting all passenger traffic to Berlin and suspending all freight shipments out of Berlin except for the return of empty boxcars. This was followed on June 23 by a Soviet announcement of a currency reform of their own to be effective throughout the East zone and in all of Berlin. Later that same day, General Clay and the British Military Governor, General Sir Brian Robertson, acting on behalf of all three Western Allies, announced that the new West German currency would be introduced into the Western sectors of Berlin. To have allowed the new Soviet currency to be introduced into all of Berlin, they said, would mean turning the city over to the Russians.

The Soviets now had the excuse they were waiting for. At six A.M. the following day, June 24, 1948, all traffic to and from Berlin was severed. "Technical difficulties," the Russians announced, interfered with the normal service. Simultaneously with this action, the Soviets also announced that the flow of electric current could be expected in the Western sectors of Berlin only between eleven P.M. and one A.M.[19] With these announcements, the Berlin Blockade had begun.

For one day the fate of the city, and perhaps the fate of Western Europe, remained in the balance. Would the Western Allies evacuate Berlin? Whatever was to be decided, would have to be decided quickly. In the Western sectors the tension was slowly building to a peak. A Soviet radio bulletin announced that the water supply in West Berlin was about to fail. West Berlin housewives rushed to fill containers and were on the verge of really causing a breakdown when the American radio began broadcasting a reply. In a calculated gamble, the Berliners were told to use all the water they wanted.

"Give your baby a bath," they were told. "Plenty of water is available."
Once they were reassured, the demand subsided and a temporary
crisis was relieved.[20]

The larger crisis was still to be solved. What action should be taken?
For the United States, the decision that day was made by one man
—the man on the spot—Lieutenant General Lucius D. Clay. Because
he acted wisely and because he acted rapidly the situation was saved.

Earlier in the day, General Clay met with his military staff in Berlin
and found them divided. Some believed that the only sensible policy
for the United States was to withdraw. "If your hand is in the fire,"
one phrased it, "why not pull it out?" Others believed that the United
States had to stay. There was no agreed staff recommendation and no
consensus of opinion.

Acting on his own responsibility, General Clay then called for Ernst
Reuter, the debarred Lord Mayor of Berlin. Would the Berliners, he
asked Reuter, be able to hold out on the meagre supplies that could
be brought in by air? Could they last through the winter, if necessary?

Reuter replied without hesitation. The Berliners, he said, were prepared to fight for their liberties and would not give in. Willy Brandt,
who accompanied Reuter that day, reports that the Lord Mayor
"couldn't quite believe" that the city could be supplied by air. In
spite of this, said Brandt, Reuter answered immediately, "and he spoke
without any sharpness—'We shall in any case continue on our way.
Do what you are able to do; we shall do what we feel to be our
duty.'" According to Brandt, General Clay and his advisers "were
visibly impressed." [21]

For Lucius Clay the matter was settled. He called Lieutenant General Curtis LeMay at Wiesbaden and instructed him to mobilize all
the aircraft at his disposal and prepare to lift supplies into Berlin the
following day. "With air commanders of the stature of Curtis LeMay,"
Clay writes, "you have only to state what is wanted." The following
day, June 25, 1948, the Berlin Airlift became a reality. The first
American C–47's arrived at Tempelhof loaded with food.

Significantly, the decision to act in Berlin had been made by the
commander on the spot. His staff had been divided, Washington had
offered no encouragement, and the Allies, Great Britain and France,
were still pondering what to do. With very little more to guide him
than his own conscience and the opinion of a Socialist politician,

General Clay had resolved to begin the airlift. By so doing, he set in motion one of the great victories which the West was to achieve over communism.

As a matter of historical interest, at the very moment Clay was acting, the Pentagon was urging restraint. In a teleconference that day, the Department of the Army suggested to Clay that the introduction of Western currency in Berlin be slowed down if there was any possibility that it might worsen the situation. It was an assault to the rear which General Clay withstood. It was already too late, he told Washington, to halt the distribution of the new *marks*. The exchange was already underway.

Clay then exhorted the Department of the Army to stand firm in the crisis. "We do not expect armed conflict," he stated. "Our troops are in hand and can be trusted. We both [himself and General Robertson] realize the desire of our governments to avoid armed conflict. Nevertheless, we cannot be run over and a firm position always induces some risk."

He reminded Secretary Royall of the courageous resistance of the Berliners. "Every German leader . . . and thousands of Germans have courageously expressed their opposition to communism. We must not destroy their confidence by any indication of departure from Berlin."

As for the dependents, "I still do not believe that our dependents should be evacuated. Once again we have to sweat it out. . . . If the Soviets want war, it will not be because of the Berlin currency issue but because they believe this the right time." [22]

In Washington, Clay's stand was regarded with mixed emotions. The military departments feared that the Berlin confrontation could turn into a major war. Following a Cabinet meeting on Friday, June 25, Secretary of Defense James V. Forrestal, Secretary of the Army Royall, and Under Secretary of State Robert Lovett remained behind to discuss the Berlin situation with the President. They advised caution and restraint. The following day however President Truman came to Clay's support, and at the President's personal order, every available plane in the European Command was pressed into service and the airlift to Berlin put on a full-scale basis.[23]

Over the weekend, discussions continued at the Pentagon. On Sunday afternoon, an emergency meeting of the various Secretaries and service chiefs was held in Secretary Royall's office. Special studies of the crisis were ordered prepared for the President. Royall, Lovett, and Forrestal, it was also decided, would meet again with Mr. Truman on Monday, and once more they asked for Clay's advice.

In his diary entry of that day, Secretary Forrestal paints a grim picture of bureaucratic indecision. The comment of Walter Millis, editor of the *Forrestal Diaries*, is very much to the point:

> This entry is striking in a number of ways. Where, one is forced to ask, was all the elaborate machinery which had been set up to deal with such situations—the CIA, which was supposed to foresee and report the approach of crisis; the National Security Council, which was supposed to establish the governing policy?
>
> The Berlin crisis had been long in the making, [Millis continues,] but when it finally broke, the response was this *ad hoc* meeting at 4:00 P.M. on a Sunday afternoon in the Pentagon, which . . . incidentally overlooked the potentialities of the airlift.[24]

Whatever doubts the bureaucrats may have had were resolved the following day. The White House meeting had been set for 12:30 P.M. Under Secretary of State Lovett recounted the details of Sunday's conversation to the President. When he came to the specific question of whether to stay in Berlin, President Truman interrupted. There would be no discussion on that point, the President said. "The United States is going to stay. Period."

On hearing the President's statement, Secretary Royall incredulously inquired whether he had "thought through" the situation. Did the President realize that it might be necessary "to fight our way to Berlin"? Mr. Truman's reply settled the issue. We would have to deal with that situation when it developed, he said. "We are in Berlin by terms of an agreement and the Russians have no right to get us out by either direct or indirect pressures." There were no further questions.[25]

Two days later, on June 30, Great Britain announced her similar determination to remain in Berlin. Foreign Secretary Ernest Bevin, speaking before a crowded House of Commons, stated that the decision to remain in Berlin could lead to a grave situation. "Should such a situation arise, we shall have to ask the House to face it. His Majesty's Government and our Western Allies can see no alternative between that and surrender, and none of us can accept surrender."

As for the Berliners, he said, "we cannot abandon those stout-hearted Berlin democrats who are refusing to bow to Soviet pressure. The morale of the large Berlin population is excellent, and their determination to put up with any degree of privation rather than be surrendered to exclusive Russian domination must carry our fullest support." [26]

Sir Winston Churchill, then leader of His Majesty's Loyal Opposition, vigorously seconded Bevin's statement. With one exception, a Communist member, the House unanimously supported the government.

The following month General Clay returned to Washington to give President Truman a first-hand report.* At a meeting of the National Security Council on July 22, Clay stated that given enough planes, the United States could maintain its position in Berlin indefinitely. When Under Secretary of State Lovett asked him if he thought the Russians might try to block our airplanes, the General replied they would not do so unless they had decided to go to war. When Air Chief of Staff General Hoyt Vandenberg demurred from a further concentration of aircraft in Europe, the President overruled him and directed the Air Force "to furnish the fullest support possible to the problem of supplying Berlin." [27]

When the Council adjourned, President Truman requested General Clay to stay behind in his office for a further discussion. Together, they talked about Berlin and the Berliners and, as General Clay later recalled, "I left his office inspired by the understanding and confidence I received from him." [28]

---

* The decision to recall General Clay for consultations was an attempt by the President to illustrate his support for a firm stand in Berlin. Until this time, Clay had been carrying the ball alone and many in Berlin and West Germany once more had begun to wonder to what extent Washington was behind him. Clay reported this rising fear to Bradley, and the message was relayed to the President through Congressional channels. Mr. Truman's invitation to Clay was the result.

7

The City Is Split

THE DECISION OF GENERAL CLAY to begin the airlift settled temporarily the question of whether the United States would remain in Berlin. As we have seen, this decision was taken in the absence of a clear-cut directive from Washington. Even after the airlift began, there were many in Washington who thought that Berlin could not be defended. The Department of Defense agreed with the Army in considering the Allied position in the isolated city militarily unsound. The Air Staff in the Pentagon was similarly dubious and resisted for almost a month all efforts to increase the number of transport planes in Europe on the grounds that so great a concentration of Allied aircraft would be militarily unwise. It relented only when the Air Chief of Staff, General Hoyt Vandenberg, was specifically overruled by President Truman at the meeting of the National Security Council on July 22.

The military were not alone in questioning our decision to remain in Berlin. Secretary Marshall and many in the State Department likewise doubted whether the Allied position could, or even should, be maintained if the Soviets were serious in continuing the blockade. In addition to the strategic considerations, many felt that it wasn't fair to force the people of Berlin to go hungry and cold merely to maintain Western prestige. There were also those who felt that Berlin was not worth risking war in a showdown with the Soviet Union. Indeed, in the summer of 1948, Washington seemed more fearful of the risks than cognizant of the advantages of a firm stand in Berlin.

Fortunately for the West, President Truman was an exception. Like General Clay in Berlin, the President recognized that a time of crisis was a time for firm decision and a time for rapid action. Like General Clay, he was prepared to make that decision and to take the necessary action in the teeth of the conflicting and, indeed, the contrary opinions of his principal advisers. Had he not, had he temporized or engaged in the extensive deliberations which many sought to foist upon him, the position in Berlin very likely would have been lost.

In Berlin itself, when Ernst Reuter was asked by General Clay if the Berliners would resist, the intrepid Mayor cast his lot with the Allies and trusted in his ability to bring the city with him. At the moment when Reuter pledged himself to Clay, however, the Berliners themselves were still wavering between the fear that the Soviet blockade had induced, and their own desire for freedom. There was then no way for them to know whether the West would stay in Berlin or whether, under Soviet pressure, they would leave never to return. In this context, a moment's hesitation, even the slightest sign of indecision by the West, would have driven many to seek their peace with the East.

For Ernst Reuter, the road to resistance in 1948 had been a difficult one. When he arrived in Berlin after the war, Reuter shared the view of most of his colleagues in the Social Democratic Party that the city government should try to get along with all four occupying powers and not just the West alone. Throughout 1946 and 1947, he continued to believe that by co-operating with all four powers Berlin could serve as a bridge between East and West—as a pilot study which might lead to the eventual reunification of Germany.[1]

In a similar spirit, most of Berlin's other political leaders in 1947, and even into 1948, continued to oppose the economic integration of the Western zones in Germany, and the creation of a West German state. Such a state they feared would cause the Soviets to take further repressive measures in their own zone and would only widen the existing breach between East and West.

Only gradually did this opinion change, and among the leaders who brought about this change was Ernst Reuter. By the spring of 1948, he, like General Clay, had decided that the Soviets were intent not only on maintaining the division of Germany but on absorbing Berlin as well. The only way to prevent this, Reuter felt, would be for Berlin to tie her future firmly to that of the emerging West German government and to secure Western economic assistance.

To Reuter, the presence of the Western powers in Berlin ceased being a burden and became a guarantee of freedom. The greatest danger in the immediate future, as he saw it, was that under Soviet pressure the Allies might decide to withdraw. To prevent this, he and other SPD leaders, in early 1948, began the arduous process of convincing the people of Berlin that only through a complete acceptance of the Western occupation could their liberty be insured.

Until the airlift began, the Western powers gave Reuter little support. To many in the Allied military occupation it was still the Germans, not the Russians, who were the principal danger to peace. When the Soviets had utilized their veto in the Kommandatura to keep Reuter from becoming mayor, the United States, Great Britain and France had quietly acquiesced. But in spite of this, Reuter continued his efforts to arouse both the Berliners and the occupation authorities to the dangers they faced. "A struggle for Berlin is going on," Reuter wrote in April, 1948. "It may be that the Berliners will not be able to determine the final decision in this struggle, but without them Berlin would have been written off long ago. The fact that it cannot any longer be written off today, is certainly due to the efforts of freedom loving Berliners." [2]

As the creeping Soviet blockade tightened around Berlin in March and April of 1948, very few of the city's political leaders continued to believe that the Russians would allow a peaceful reunification of Germany. The greatest problem for Reuter therefore became whether the West would stand firm. Had Washington offered any appreciable compromise to the Soviets in the spring of 1948, Reuter and the other Berliners who had spoken out for resistance would have had the ground cut from under them.

The events in Berlin immediately preceding the airlift illustrate the difficulty which Reuter and his associates in the city government faced. On June 18, the Western powers ordered the currency reform which was to take place in their zones of Western Germany but not Berlin. Four days later, on the evening of June 22, Berlin's acting mayor, Louise Schroeder, and deputy mayor Dr. Ferdinand Friedensburg were summoned to the City Hall by the Soviet liaison officer to the city government, Major Vladimir Otschkin. Major Otschkin informed Louise Schroeder and Friedensburg that on the following day, June 23, a new Soviet currency reform would go into effect throughout the Soviet zone and would include the entire city of Berlin. He then handed them an order to that effect signed by Marshal Sokolovsky.

Although the Soviet currency move had been anticipated, the Western powers were little agreed how it should be met. Later in the evening, when they received the details of the Soviet order from Frau Schroeder, Generals Clay and Robertson * proposed a second currency reform of their own. General Koenig, the French Military Governor, was not in Berlin at the time and his deputy, General Noiret, refused to accept the proposal.** When General Clay persisted and said that the United States and Britain would act anyway, the French still declined to participate. Only after the Western currency order was in its final stages of preparation early the next morning did the French agree to participate. Even then, they advised Clay and Robertson (in writing) that they were acting only because they had been forced to and that they still were not in sympathy with the move.[3]

Under the provisions of the Western currency order, the Western sectors of Berlin would convert to their own currency (i.e., the new West German currency with a "B" superimposed) simultaneously with the conversion in the Soviet sector. The two currencies would then circulate together throughout the city and would be interchangeable at par. In General Clay's words, to have accepted the Soviet currency (*Ostmarks*) as the sole currency of the Western sector would mean that henceforth "we would be guests in Berlin." [4]

One of the results of the rival currency orders was that the Soviet

---

* General Sir Brian Robertson, the British Military Governor.
** Because of the initial difficulty over the French sector in Berlin (see Chapter VI) French occupation headquarters for Germany had been established at Baden-Baden. Later, when the somewhat smaller French sector was finally agreed to, General De Gaulle considered it an affront and declined to move French headquarters to Berlin. As a result, the French Military Governor for Germany continued to sit in Baden-Baden while his counterparts were in Berlin. He came to Berlin for official meetings of the Control Council but otherwise was represented there by his deputy.

occupation authorities in Berlin were given a splendid pretext to intimidate the city government. When the city assembly attempted to convene on the afternoon of June 23 to take final action on the conflicting reforms, the way to the City Hall was blocked by several thousand Communist demonstrators. Berlin's historic City Hall was located in what had been the downtown area of the city and was now in the Soviet sector. The East sector police made no effort to control the demonstrators and the assembly members had to get through the mob as best they could.

While the mob milled outside City Hall, other demonstrators entered the building and took over the assembly chamber and gallery. Here, they refused to allow the meeting to begin and withdrew only when signaled to do so by the several Communist (SED) delegates who were members of the assembly. When the meeting finally began, the city assembly defied the Communist mob and, in a courageous demonstration of spirit, voted that Marshal Sokolovsky's currency order would apply only to the Soviet sector and not to the entire city.

Afterwards, when the assembly members filed out of the building, they were brutally set upon by Communist thugs. One SPD assemblywoman, Jeanette Wolff, who formerly had been imprisoned by the Nazis, was critically injured. Once more, the East sector police refused to intervene, and a police official who later escorted several of the delegates safely out of the building was discharged the following day by order of the Soviet Military Government.[5]

The courageous behavior of the members of the city assembly in the face of the Communist mob did much to rally the people of the Western sectors to resistance. The following day, when the Soviets instituted the total blockade, a mass meeting of 80,000 citizens heard Ernst Reuter and Franz Neumann, the local SPD chairman, attack the Communist action. According to Neumann: "More than ever the eyes of the world are focused on Berlin. Yesterday the Communists Grotewohl and Pieck, following the model of Hitler and the example of Prague, tried to seize power in Berlin by terror. But they miscalculated . . . Berlin will remain free, it will never become Communist."

In the principal speech that day Ernst Reuter accused the Russians of trying to use "the look of hunger and the specter of economic blockade to achieve that which they were not able to attain with raw violence in front of City Hall." When acting mayor Louise Schroeder escorted a limping assemblywoman Jeanette Wolff to the platform, they were given a tumultuous ovation. Neumann closed the meeting with an appeal to the world to come to Berlin's assistance.[6]

When the airlift began the following day, most Berliners were still uncertain whether the West would remain. Phillips Davison, in his definitive work on the blockade,* has described the uncertainty which the rival currency measures created among many West Berliners. Should they also convert some of their money to *Ostmarks* as a precaution against Allied withdrawal? And what about their own existence? How would they themselves be able to survive in the face of the Russian blockade?

Then, as doubt increased, as people wondered what would happen and what course the Allies would take, the roar of the planes which General Clay had ordered could be heard overhead. Suddenly, the airlift became a vivid demonstration to the Berliners that the United States intended to remain. As the number of planes increased, so did the confidence of the Western sectors. By the first week in July, there was a widespread conviction among the Berliners that the city could be held.[7]

The Allies, however, were not so sure. Two days after the airlift began General Robertson wrote Marshal Sokolovsky to suggest a meeting on lifting the blockade in return for the acceptance of Soviet currency in the Western sectors. According to General Clay, both he and General Koenig were opposed to the meeting but "the British appeared to want agreement so badly that they believed it possible of attainment." Washington left the decision whether to attend up to Clay, who reluctantly agreed.[8]

The meeting with Sokolovsky took place at Russian headquarters in Potsdam on July 3. When General Robertson mentioned the blockade and indicated a Western desire to compromise on the currency issue, Sokolovsky interrupted. The "technical difficulties," he said, would continue until the West gave up its plans for a West German government. As General Clay reports it, Sokolovsky did not even refer to the currency matter. "It was evident," states Clay, "that he was confident we would be forced to leave Berlin and that he was enjoying

* W. Phillips Davison, *The Berlin Blockade* (Princeton: Princeton University Press, 1958).

the situation. We were not. We had nothing further to gain from the the conference so we left after a very brief discussion. . . ." [9]

The break-up of the meeting with Sokolovsky was reported to the three Allied capitals, and after some intramural sparring in which the United States suggested taking the issue immediately to the UN, it was decided that the next round of negotiations would be conducted in Moscow. Accordingly, on July 6, U.S. Ambassador Walter Bedell Smith, and his British and French colleagues, called at the Kremlin and demanded that the blockade be lifted immediately. Like Sokolovsky, however, Moscow was in no mood for compromise and the Western demand was ignored.

Meanwhile, in Berlin, the firm stand taken by General Clay was already having its effect. Tensions there had relaxed surprisingly; the Berliners now felt assured that the West was going to stand fast. What few local incidents the Russians attempted were countered promptly by Western military authorities and as a result, the Soviets had become extremely cautious. On July 10, four days after the Allied ambassadors had called on the Kremlin, General Clay reported this change to Washington and suggested that the West now try to break the blockade by decisive action. According to Clay:

> The care with which the Russians avoided measures which would have been resisted with force had convinced me that the Soviet Government did not want war although it believed that the Western Allies would yield much of their position rather than risk war. . . . I reported this conviction . . . suggesting that we advise the Soviet representatives in Germany that under our rights to be in Berlin we proposed on a specific date to move an armed convoy which would be equipped with the engineering material to overcome the technical difficulties which the Soviet representatives appeared unable to solve. . . .
> In my view the chances of such a convoy being met by force with subsequent developments of hostilities were small. I was confident that it would get through to Berlin and that the highway blockade would be ended. . . .[10]

In Washington, General Clay's suggestion was turned down. Four days later, Moscow replied to the West's diplomatic demand that the blockade be lifted by announcing that Russia would discuss the situation in Berlin only as a part of the overall German question.

Until such "all-German" talks began, Moscow said, the blockade would continue. Clearly, the Kremlin had raised its demands in Germany and was waiting for the West to give in.

As a result of Moscow's reply, the Allies themselves now fell to bickering and the next two weeks were spent in ironing out individual Western differences. In particular, both France and Great Britain were a great deal more anxious to compromise and meet the Soviet demands than was the United States. Washington by this time was beginning to share Clay's opinion and therefore resisted any headlong dash toward concessions.

On July 19, General Clay again requested permission to send an armored column to Berlin and once more was turned down. Clay's insight into the situation, however, is worth quoting. Said Clay:

> I feel that the world is now facing the most vital issue that has developed since Hitler placed his political aggression underway. In fact the Soviet government has a greater strength under its immediate control than Hitler had to carry out his purpose. Under the circumstances which exist today, only we can assert world leadership. Only we have the strength to halt this aggressive policy here and now. It may be too late the next time. I am sure that determined action will bring it to a halt now without war. It can be stopped only if we assume some risk.[11]

The day after Clay's message, the Soviets resumed the offensive in Berlin and began a determined effort to undermine the city's morale. Food, including fresh fruits and vegetables, they announced, henceforth would be available in East Berlin for all those from the West who wanted it. All the West Berliners would have to do would be to come to the East sector and fill out a registration form. They could pay in East marks—then worth only one third a West mark—for their purchases.

The Soviet offer caused immediate alarm in West Berlin. Were enough people to accept it, the morale of the city would be seriously weakened.

As it turned out, there was little reason to be disturbed. For most Berliners the Soviet food offer was an opportunity to demonstrate their faith in the Western cause. By not taking advantage of it they could show their neighbors and the Allies alike that they were doing their share in the city's defense. In the first three weeks after the Soviet plan was announced, less than one percent of the more than two million people in the Western sectors had succumbed to it. In the entire eleven months of the blockade, including even the dreary winter months of December and January, the number of people from West Berlin who registered in the East totaled less than 85,000 (3.2 percent).[12]

By July 30, Allied differences on Berlin had been settled and the three Western ambassadors returned to the Kremlin. This time they requested a personal interview with Marshal Stalin and the meeting was arranged for 9 P.M. on the evening of August 2. When the meeting took place, Stalin appeared more open to argument than his subordinates had been. After initially questioning the integration of the three Western zones in Germany, Stalin indicated that he might be willing to lift the blockade provided the Allies agreed to accept Soviet currency in Berlin. Unlike his subordinates, Stalin no longer insisted that the settlement be made contingent on solving the overall problem of Germany.[13]

The negotiations in Moscow continued throughout the month of August. The West stood firm on West German integration but were willing to concede part of the issue in Berlin. The airlift had not yet been proven and there was a great deal of pressure, particularly from France and Great Britain, to reach a negotiated agreement that would lift the blockade.

On August 30, a modified settlement was reached. The Western powers agreed to recognize the East mark as the sole currency in Berlin and in return, the Soviets agreed to lift the blockade. The four military governors were to carry out the agreement and Stalin orally agreed that the West could share in the control of the new currency. Stalin's promise, however, was not incorporated into the instructions which were then sent to the four military governors.

In Berlin, news of the Moscow Agreement caused widespread apprehension. General Clay was concerned because Stalin's remarks about currency control had not been included in the final directive. He also feared the effect that returning the negotiations to Berlin might have on the city's morale. "I could see no reason to hope," Clay states, "that the military governors would be able to succeed in view of their previous failure. . . . I felt certain that the Soviet Foreign Office had no intention of really permitting quadripartite control [of

East German currency] and that our acceptance of ambiguous word-ing just to obtain an agreed directive would lead nowhere." [14]

When the four military governors met the following day, Clay stole the march on the Russians and insisted that before any agreement could be put into effect, the arrangements for controlling the East German currency would have to be nailed down. Doubtless, Clay's earlier experience in negotiating with the Soviets helped prompt this stand. Perhaps more important, however, was his belief that the air-lift would succeed and that compromise would not be necessary. Therefore, by insisting on his own terms for effective control before considering the implementation of the Moscow Agreement, General Clay was exerting a veto over the whole proceeding.*

Marshal Sokolovsky, on his part, was also in no hurry to press for an agreement since the Russians were convinced that the airlift would soon fail. Accordingly, he refused to expand the scope of the Mos-cow directive to include Stalin's comments and even demanded cer-tain added provisions which would insure Soviet control of civilian air traffic into Berlin. On these points the negotiations quickly broke down. When Clay questioned Sokolovsky's additional demands and once more insisted on the right to share in the control of the Soviet currency, Washington supported him. As Clay has suggested, an agree-ment on currency without effective provisions for Western control would have made a mockery of Berlin's resistance. Had the Moscow Agreement been implemented without such a provision, financial con-trol of Berlin would have been handed over to the Russians. Since the blockade had been begun in the first place because the West had refused to agree to the introduction of the Soviet currency on June 23, an acceptance of it at this point would have amounted to a virtual surrender. Thus, by now insisting on a firm agreement regarding con-trol of the Eastern currency, Clay doomed the negotiations from the start.

The failure of the Berlin negotiations greatly disheartened those in the West who feared that the airlift would not succeed, and this feel-ing existed in Washington as well as in London and Paris. At a meet-ing of the National Security Council on September 9, Secretary of

---

* In General Clay's own words, "our insistence in Berlin that the final agreement reflect [Stalin's] comment led in large part to the breakdown of negotiations." Lucius D. Clay, *Decision in Germany*, p. 370.

State Marshall said that in spite of the airlift, time was on the side of the Russians in Berlin.[15] Ambassador Bedell Smith in Moscow also thought that Berlin was an indefensible position and should be disposed of as soon as possible.[16] The Western planners at this time, of course, grossly under-estimated the effectiveness of the airlift and the determination of the Berliners to resist, both of which were nearly scuttled in the desire of the Allied capitals for agreement. A later Rand Corporation research study of these negotiations concludes as follows:

> . . . the West, particularly the United States, seems frequently to have misinterpreted Soviet signals. American newspapermen, and also those professionally concerned with the conduct of U.S. foreign policy, tended to greet each affable expression or minor concession by the Soviets as an indication of a basic change in Soviet foreign policy, without asking whether this affability might have some other meaning. This tendency precluded a full and sober assessment of what the Soviets were really trying to accomplish, and it also inhibited any long-term measures by which to offset Communist pressure.[17]

Following the break-up of the negotiations in Berlin, the Western powers returned to the regular diplomatic channels. On September 14, the Western ambassadors presented Stalin with an *aide-mémoire* placing the blame for failure of the Berlin talks on Marshal Sokolovsky's refusal to agree on a suitable method for currency control. The Soviets replied on September 18, blaming the West for failure and pointing out (correctly) that the matter of four-power currency control had not been contained in the original August 30th Moscow directive.[18] Four days later the West replied in identical notes delivered to the Kremlin restating their position and asking the Soviet Union to remove the blockade before negotiations were continued.

In Berlin, meanwhile, the Soviets intensified their efforts to gain control of the city government. On August 26, just four days before the Moscow accord was completed, five thousand Communist demonstrators stormed a meeting of the city assembly in City Hall. The following week, while the military governors were still in conference, two more demonstrations were held before City Hall. On September 3, just after the negotiations broke down, the Russian Commandant in Berlin announced that he could no longer guarantee order in front of City Hall, and a meeting of the city assembly scheduled for that day was then canceled by the delegates themselves.

On September 6, when the assembly attempted to meet once more, Communist toughs again stormed the building and Soviet sector police obligingly made no effort to interfere. Forty-six policemen who had gone over from the Western sectors to preserve order proved unable to cope with the situation.* The assemblymen were driven out of the building and fled to the West where they reconvened later that afternoon. At the second meeting, according to Colonel Frank Howley, the U.S. Commandant, the assemblymen had no chairs or desks but were able to conduct their business nonetheless. They voted to establish their permanent meeting place in West Berlin, and the old Berlin City Hall in the Soviet sector was officially abandoned as the seat of the city government.[19]

The action of the Soviets on September 6, forcing the city government out of East Berlin, was protested on September 9 by a mass meeting of Berliners in front of the blackened ruins of the Reichstag (located in the British sector near the Brandenburg Gate). Over three hundred thousand Berliners stood in a drizzling rain that day to hear Ernst Reuter and Franz Neumann condemn the Soviet action. Following the rally, part of the crowd marched into the nearby Soviet sector, where several youths climbed to the top of the Brandenburg Gate and tore down the Russian flag which was flying there. When others in the crowd began to burn the flag, Russian guards stationed at the nearby Soviet War Memorial rushed to recover it. Almost be-

---

* The fate of these forty-six policemen provides an interesting footnote to Russian faithlessness. When it became obvious that they would not be able to control the Communist mob, the policemen had sought shelter in the offices of the American, British, and French liaison groups which were located in the City Hall. The Soviet sector police then forced their way into the United States Liaison Office and at pistol point seized twenty of the West Berlin policemen. The British and French liaison officers thereupon refused to open their doors to the East sector police and for two days the other West Berlin policemen remained there, unable to leave.

Meanwhile, General Koenig, the French Military Governor, obtained a promise from Marshal Sokolovsky that the policemen would be allowed to leave unmolested. General Ganeval, the French Commandant in Berlin, received a similar guarantee from the Soviet Commandant, General Kotikov.

As a result of these assurances, the West Berlin policemen emerged from their sanctuary and prepared to board a French military vehicle which had been sent to take them back to the Western sectors. As soon as they left the building, however, they were arrested by East sector police and imprisoned. Three were subsequently sentenced to long prison terms. See Howley, Berlin Command, pp. 215–17.

fore anyone was aware of what was happening the Russians fired into the crowd, killing at least two and injuring others. The British Deputy Provost Marshal then courageously jumped in front of the Russian soldiers and ordered them to cease firing. Had it not been for his action, a bloodbath would have ensued.[20] But British military police worked frantically to restore order and by evening the crowd had been dispersed. The action of the Russian soldiers, however, ended any hope of compromise in Berlin.

Shortly afterward, the Russians gave up their efforts to intimidate the city government and began instead to incorporate East Berlin into the Soviet zone. Up until this point, all of the bureaus of the city government, except for the police, had carried on a precarious city-wide operation. By the end of September, however, Russian authorities had removed all non-Communist personnel chiefs from the borough administrations of the eight boroughs comprising the Soviet sector. By October 10, over one thousand other borough officials had been dismissed in East Berlin, and by the end of the month the total had risen to two thousand.[21]

At the same time, the various agencies of the city government, reacting to the pressure which the Russians were exerting, laboriously began to move their departments from East Berlin to the Western sectors. Since most of these offices had been located in the eastern part of the city since the time of the Hohenzollerns, this was a lengthy process and one accomplished only with the greatest difficulty. The Soviets, however, made little effort to interfere and by the middle of November virtually all of the city offices had been transferred.

While the Russians were acting to complete the division within the city, the Western powers were moving to bring the Berlin question before the United Nations. After an initial Allied request, the UN Security Council agreed to place the matter on its agenda. On October 19, the three Western delegates, Dr. Philip Jessup for the United States, Sir Alexander Cadogan for Great Britain, and Alexandre Parodi for France, presented the Allied case. Three days later, on October 22, the six remaining member nations of the Security Council who were not involved in the Berlin dispute suggested a resolution aimed toward settlement. Under its provisions, all traffic restrictions imposed on Berlin were to be raised immediately, four-power talks between the military governors were to be resumed on the currency question, and the Council of Foreign Ministers would reconvene for further discussions on the subject of Germany. These recommendations were vetoed by Andre Vyshinsky, the Soviet delegate to the Security Council, on October 25.

In spite of the Soviet veto, the six "neutral" nations on the Security Council continued their efforts toward settlement. Simultaneous with their efforts, Trygve Lie, the UN Secretary General, sought to arrange a solution through informal discussion between the principals themselves. But Lie's offer was declined by the West since its acceptance would have constituted a willingness to negotiate with the Russians while the blockade was still in effect. Instead, the Western powers encouraged the "neutrals" to continue their independent efforts. A committee of experts was then set up by the "neutrals" to consider the technical details involved in Berlin. Heading the committee of experts was Dr. Gunnar Myrdal of Sweden, who at that time was Executive Secretary of the United Nations Economic Commission for Europe.

In preparing its recommendations, the committee attempted to implement the Moscow Agreement calling for Soviet currency in Berlin, and therefore soon antagonized the West, especially the United States. When the Committee finally submitted its proposals for settlement in December, the United States refused to accept them. According to an American UN official, the Committee "took the 'neutralist' position that East and West were equally to blame for the situation in Berlin, and they were always trying to shove East marks down our throat." [22]

President Truman, who was determined not to yield in Berlin at any price, was equally critical of the Committee's proposals. According to the President:

> Our reactions to these proposals were that our experience with the Russians impelled us to reject any plan that provided for four power operation. We had learned that the Russians would usually agree in principle but would rarely perform in practice. We wanted a settlement, but we could not accept a settlement that would put the people of Berlin at the mercy of the Soviets and their German Communist hirelings. [23]

While the UN negotiations were in progress, the Russians continued their efforts to complete the separation of the Soviet and Western sectors. On November 15, the Soviet Military Administration unilaterally dismissed the chiefs of each of the various city departments. The Allied Commandants responded in each case with an announcement that the Soviet order was invalid in the Western sectors and that the incumbents would remain in office. The Soviets then appointed their own division chiefs for the Eastern sector and announced that the old department heads were holding office illegally. Two weeks later, on November 30, 1948, the Soviets convened what they termed an "extraordinary session of the city assembly" in East Berlin. This meeting, however, was attended not by the regularly elected city representatives but by 1,500 carefully selected Communist functionaries. Fritz Ebert, Jr., son of the first President of the Weimar Republic, was elected (there was no opposition) *Oberbürgermeister* of Greater Berlin and a new city executive body was appointed. As a result of the Soviet action, Berlin now for the first time had two city governments: the one which had been duly elected by the people of Berlin and which continued to meet in the Western sectors, and the rump government installed by the Russians which assumed control in the East.

Five days after the Soviets had installed their puppet government in office, free elections were held in the Western sectors. The residents of East Berlin were prohibited by the Russians from participating. In spite of heavy pressure from the Communist Party (SED) to stay away from the polls, 86.3 percent of those who were eligible in West Berlin turned out to vote. It was the first election held in Berlin since the blockade had begun and the results were a crushing defeat for the Soviets. Ernst Reuter was overwhelmingly elected Lord Mayor, and this time was not prevented from taking office by a Soviet veto. When the out-going city assembly met two days after the election, Reuter was temporarily installed in office pending the meeting of the new assembly in January. The final tabulation of the election results was as follows:

SPD (Social Democratic Party)	64.5%
CDU (Christian Democratic Party)	19.4%
LDP (Liberal Democratic Party)	16.1%

Two weeks after the election had taken place, the Allied Kommandatura in Berlin was reorganized on a three-power basis. The Russians were tendered an invitation to return whenever they wished but in the interim, the three Western Commandants said they would govern in West Berlin without them.

The reorganization of the Allied Kommandatura represented the climax in Soviet efforts to split Berlin's government. The effect of the move was administrative rather than juridical, however, and the joint four-power status of Berlin remained unchanged. The Kommandatura, it should be remembered, was a creation of the military authorities to aid in the governing of Berlin and had been established in July of 1945, after the Allied sectors had been taken over from the Russians. The four-power status of the city rested on the political agreements which had been concluded while the war was still in progress. Accordingly, except for simplifying the administrative set-up in the Western sectors, the reorganization of the Kommandatura had no outward effect on life in Berlin. Free movement between the sectors continued unimpeded and all other occupation agreements remained in effect.

But still, the splitting of the city government represented the high point of Soviet recalcitrance in Berlin. Unquestionably, one of the major reasons for this recalcitrance was the Russian belief that the airlift would soon fail. Winter was reaching its height in Berlin and the Soviets were not only sure that the Allies would be unable to bring in enough fuel by air to keep the city from freezing, but that flying itself would soon be seriously curtailed.

In many respects the Soviets were very nearly right. The thick ground fog which accompanies winter in Berlin halted airlift operations on several occasions for about a week at a time. In November, planes were able to fly on only fifteen out of thirty days and conditions did not improve materially in December. By January, an acute shortage of coal had developed in Berlin with scarcely one week's supply remaining on hand. At this point, with the Russians still gambling on failure, Generals Clay and Howley * took a calculated risk. With a thirty-day supply of food still on hand, food was cut from the airlift in favor of coal. Within a few days, the supply of coal in the city had been brought up to a three-week supply, with food stocks reduced to about the same level. At this point, the weather broke and Allied aircraft were able to fly every day from then on. The winter

* Colonel Howley was promoted to Brigadier General in December, 1948.

had been defeated and the Soviets now had to recognize that the blockade had failed.*

The success of the airlift naturally had a great deal to do with reinforcing Western diplomatic resolve not to give in. Just as the Berliners didn't want to let the airlift down, a feeling began to develop in the West that it in turn could not let the Berliners down. On October 27, 1948, General Clay had reported to Washington that the airlift was capable of supplying Berlin indefinitely. As President Truman has recorded it, General Clay "placed before us an account not only of the technical achievement of the airlift but also of the effect our action in Berlin had had on the German people. They had closed ranks and applied themselves to the task of reconstruction with new vigor. It had turned them sharply against communism. Germany, which had been waiting passively to see where it should cast its lot for the future, was veering toward the cause of the Western nations." [24]

In his *Memoirs*, Trygve Lie notes that as the success of the airlift increased, the less ready the Western powers were to make concessions. In particular, he mentions the case of Ambassador Jessup who visited Berlin in October and saw the airlift in operation. From that time onward, according to Lie, Jessup was convinced that the West would be able to hold out.[25]

By the end of January, with the success of the airlift demonstrated, the United States repudiated the Moscow Agreement entirely and announced that the West mark would remain the currency in West Berlin until a unified government was restored on a workable basis. This decision represented a decisive victory for Clay and Howley, as well as for those in Washington who had advocated a strong line from the beginning.

In Germany meanwhile the pressure of the West's counter-blockade was also beginning to be felt. When the blockade first began, Generals Clay and Robertson had ordered all shipments of goods between West Berlin and the Soviet zone halted. On July 8, reparation

---

* In June, 1948, when the airlift first began, scarcely more than three hundred tons of supplies had been brought into Berlin during each 24-hour period. Military government officials estimated 4,000 tons as the minimum necessary to sustain the city's existence and 8,000 tons as essential to sustain its economy. In January the daily average of supplies brought into Berlin rose to 5,500 tons. By March, the 8,000-ton daily figure had been exceeded and on April 12, 1949, almost 13,000 tons were brought into Berlin in one 24-hour period.

deliveries to the Soviet Union from the Western zones were also suspended and on September 13, the shipment of all goods produced in the American and British zones to the Russian zone was prohibited. Thereafter, the counter-blockade was gradually tightened until soon only a small trickle of goods was arriving in eastern Germany from the West. Since most of East Germany's manufactured goods at this time came from the West, the counter-blockade now began to hurt the Soviet Union more than the blockade of Berlin was hurting the Allies.

By the end of January, 1949, it had become apparent to the Russians that the West was not going to withdraw from Berlin, nor yield to any settlement short of an outright lifting of the blockade. The Russians therefore began to seek a way out and on January 31, 1949, Stalin granted an interview in Moscow to Kingsbury Smith of the International News Service. Smith's questions to Stalin were submitted before hand in writing and the Kremlin made public Stalin's replies.

One of the questions asked dealt with Berlin. In his answer, Stalin indicated that he might be willing to lift the blockade regardless of the outcome of the currency problem. Smith's question and Stalin's reply were as follows:

> *Question:* If the governments of the United States of America, the United Kingdom and France agreed to postpone the establishment of a separate West German state, pending a meeting of the Council of Foreign Ministers to consider the German problem as a whole, would the Government of the U.S.S.R. be prepared to remove the restrictions which the Soviet authorities have imposed on communications between Berlin and the Western zones of Germany?

> *Answer:* Provided the United States of America, Great Britain, and France observe the conditions set forth [above], the Soviet Government sees no obstacles to lifting transport restrictions, on the understanding, however, that transport and trade restrictions introduced by the three powers should be lifted simultaneously.

Stalin's answer caused little jubilation in the West. There was no intention at that time of delaying the formation of the West German government, and Smith's question had been prefaced on this condition. But in the State Department, Stalin's reply was considered with great care. President Truman reports how he and Secretary of State Dean Acheson studied Stalin's answer during one of Acheson's regularly scheduled visits to the White House. According to the President, "we noticed that for the first time since June, 1948, the Berlin blockade was not tied to the currency matter in the Russian statement. Acheson suggested, and I approved, that we instruct Jessup to find out from the Russian delegation at the U.N. if this had been intentional." [26]

Accordingly, on February 15, 1949, Philip Jessup asked his counterpart, Jacob Malik, whether this omission by Stalin had been accidental. One month later, on March 15, Malik replied that the omission was "not accidental."

Following Malik's reply negotiations went ahead rapidly. Jessup asked Malik whether the Soviet Union would be willing to lift the blockade to allow a meeting of the Council of Foreign Ministers to take place. On March 21, Malik replied that if a definite date were set for the Foreign Ministers' meeting, then restrictions on transportation could be lifted reciprocally by both East and West prior to the meeting.

From that point on, the Malik–Jessup conversations were conducted in the greatest secrecy. Not even General Clay was informed that they were in progress. The month of April was consumed largely with completing the final arrangements of the agreement and on May 5, an official statement announcing the end of the blockade effective May 12 was released simultaneously in London, Paris, Washington and Moscow. According to the communique:

> The Governments of France, the Union of Soviet Socialist Republics, the United Kingdom, and the United States have reached the following agreement:
>
> 1. All the restrictions imposed since March 1, 1948, by the Government of the Union of Soviet Socialist Republics on communications, transportation, and trade between Berlin and the Western zones of Germany and between the Eastern zone and the Western zones will be removed on May 12, 1949.
> 2. All the restrictions imposed since March 1, 1948, by the Governments of France, the United Kingdom, and the United States, or any one of them, on communications, transportation, and trade between Berlin and the Eastern zone and between the Western and Eastern zones of Germany will also be removed on May 12, 1949.
> 3. Eleven days subsequent to the removal of the restrictions

referred to in paragraphs one and two, namely, on May 23, 1949, a meeting of the Council of Foreign Ministers will be convened in Paris to consider questions relating to Germany and problems arising out of the situation in Berlin, including also the question of currency in Berlin.

In effect, the Soviets had agreed to lift the blockade without extracting any concessions from the West in return. The firm stand by General Clay was vindicated, and Russia had been forced to acknowledge its defeat.

When the barriers across the highways and rail lines into Berlin finally were lifted at midnight May 11, 1949, Berlin was a city of wild rejoicing. Everyone who could headed for the autobahn to greet the first trucks as they arrived. Similar ceremonies were held along the rail lines when the first flower-bedecked locomotives came in early the following morning. May 12 itself was declared a city holiday, schools were dismissed after a brief lesson on the airlift, and a special commemorative meeting of the city assembly was held which was attended by all three Western military governors and all of the major political leaders of western Germany.

When Mayor Reuter rose to address the assembly he spoke of the forty-eight American and British pilots who had lost their lives in air crashes during the blockade. As he spoke, all those present rose to their feet in a moment of tribute. Franz Neumann, chairman of the SPD, then read the names of the airmen who had been killed and introduced a resolution that the plaza in front of Tempelhof airfield be renamed *Platz der Luftbrücke* (Plaza of the Airlift) in honor of them. The resolution was passed unanimously.[27]

Reuter concluded the meeting of the city assembly with a ringing tribute to the man who had made the airlift possible:

> In our great demonstrations in the summer of the past year, we called on the world for help. The world heard our cry. We are happy to have here in our midst as a guest the man who, together with his two colleagues, took the initiative in organizing the airlift in the summer of last year. The memory of General Clay will never fade in Berlin. We know for what we have to thank this man [prolonged stormy applause] and we take advantage of this hour in which he bids farewell to Berlin to say that we will never forget what he has done for us.

8

Recovery
(1949-1958)

THREE DAYS AFTER THE BLOCKADE was lifted General Lucius D. Clay returned to America. In his four years in Berlin he had seen Germany rise from the depths of defeat and find its place among the free people of the world. He had seen the beginnings of its economic recovery and the revival of its democratic traditions. He had seen the wave of Communist expansion halted and the tide of victory turn toward the West. Now, with the Communist pressure removed, he was going home, and on the day before he left, he took an unprecedented step. As the American Military Governor for Germany he wanted to pay his respect to the German people, and he did it with a gesture they would understand. Casting precedent aside, he paid a personal visit to Mayor Reuter in the Mayor's own office in West Berlin's City Hall.

The following day when General Clay left from Tempelhof, over a quarter of a million Berliners were there to see him go. Two days later in Washington he addressed both the United States Senate and the House of Representatives. To the House, Clay said that in Berlin the spirit and soul of the German people had been reborn; to the Senate, that the rule of law had been restored.[1]

131

Two weeks after General Clay's departure, the Council of Foreign Ministers convened in Paris. The Paris meeting had been one of Russia's conditions for lifting the blockade and the principal item to be discussed was the question of Germany. The session lasted twenty-nine days, and when it adjourned, settlement was no closer than when it began.

In their final communique, issued on June 20, the four Foreign Ministers (Acheson, Bevin, Schuman, and Vyshinsky) acknowledged that they had been unable to reach an agreement. They did say however that they would continue their efforts and that a future meeting would be arranged.

The communique also stated that the occupation officials in Germany would consult on a quadripartite basis to restore transportation between East and West, to expand trade, and to improve economic relations.

As for Berlin, the Foreign Ministers agreed that the May 4th Declaration lifting the blockade would remain in effect. Specifically:

> (5) The Governments of France, the Union of Soviet Socialist Republics, the United Kingdom and the United States agree that the New York Agreement of 4th May, 1949, shall be maintained. Moreover, . . . in order to improve and supplement this and other arrangements and agreements as regards the movement of persons and goods and communications between the Eastern zone and the Western zones and between the zones and Berlin, . . . the Occupation Authorities, each in his own zone, will have an obligation to take the measures necessary to insure the normal functioning and utilization of rail, water and road transport for such movement of persons and goods, and such communications by post, telephone, and telegraph.[2]

The result of the Paris meeting was to reaffirm Allied rights in Berlin. By agreeing to remove its earlier restrictions, the Soviet Union once more recognized these rights, and the right of Western access as well. Russia had lost her fight to force the Allies out of Berlin and, as with the ebb and flow of the tide, Communist pressure now receded.

Indeed, the Russians had lost more than the fight in Berlin. With the departure of General Clay, the Allied military administration of Germany ended. General Clay was succeeded by a civilian, John J. McCloy, who was to serve as U.S. High Commissioner instead of Military Governor. Throughout Germany military government officials were replaced with civilian administrators and the occupation took on a tone of recovery.

More important, the Soviet pressure on Berlin had hastened the formation of a West German government. One of the major reasons for the blockade (if not the major reason) had been to prevent the political merger of the three Western zones. Had it not been for Western determination in Berlin, the Soviets very likely would have succeeded. Allied withdrawal from Berlin in 1948, would have signalled a new shift in the balance of power in Europe. In its aftermath, few Germans would have dared oppose the Russian behemoth. The West persevered, however, and on May 8, 1949—just four days before the blockade was lifted—the Basic Law of the German Federal Republic was officially proclaimed.

The creation of the West German government had been a difficult process. In addition to Communist opposition, the Allies themselves were at first somewhat skeptical, and it was not until April of 1948, that France agreed to join the preliminary talks.[3] Within Germany itself, opposition during the early stages had been pronounced. The Social Democrats in particular opposed the formation of a new nation which would include only part of Germany. Had Communist intentions not been so clearly demonstrated by the blockade, it is quite likely that the opposition of the Germans themselves would have prevented a West German government from coming into existence. As it was, the Russians could not have picked a better method to insure its formation. The heroic stand of the Berliners, and especially of the SPD's own Ernst Reuter, soon converted what opposition there had been.

On September 1, 1948, ten weeks after the blockade began, a special "Parliamentary Council" of German leaders from the three Allied zones convened in Bonn to draft a provisional constitution. The members of the Parliamentary Council had been elected by each of the local parliaments throughout western Germany. Dr. Konrad Adenauer, the venerable ex-mayor of Cologne, was chosen as the Council's chairman.*

---

* An account of these first proceedings, probably apocryphal, relates how Dr. Adenauer arrived at the first meeting, saw the seat belonging to the chairman vacant and took it. Being the oldest member present, he supposedly assumed that the seat at the head of the table was intended for him.

By January of 1949, the draft of the Parliamentary Council was finished.* Bowing to the wish for a united Germany, however, the delegates called the resulting document a "Basic Law" rather than a Constitution. A Constitution, they felt, could only be drafted when German reunification became a reality.

As adopted, the Basic Law contained 146 Articles and provided the legal basis for the political merger of the eleven states (*Länder*) which at that time comprised the Western zones. In the words of the Preamble, the Federal Republic was created: "Conscious of its responsibility before God and mankind, filled with resolve to preserve its national and political unity and to serve world peace as an equal partner in a united Europe." [4]

The new government of the Federal Republic was parliamentary in type, resembling most other European democracies. Executive authority was vested in a Chancellor elected by the lower house (Bundestag) of parliament. The Bundestag itself would be composed of 402 members, each of whom would be elected by the people for a term of four years. The upper house of parliament, or Bundesrat, was to be composed of representatives appointed by the governments of each of the eleven states comprising the Federal Republic, who were to serve for an indefinite term at the pleasure of the state which they represented. The concurrence of both houses was required for the passage of all legislation. The Federal President, who was the official head of state, like the heads of state of most continental nations, was largely a ceremonial official with little actual power.

On May 10, 1949, the Rhineland town of Bonn was chosen as the provisional capital of the new government. The first elections took place three months later, and seventy-nine percent of those eligible in West Germany went to the polls, returning a Bundestag divided among five principal parties and numerous smaller ones.**

---

* On February 16, 1949, the initial draft of the Basic Law was presented to the three military governors. March and April of 1949, were spent ironing out minor differences and on April 25, in a special meeting at Frankfurt, Generals Clay, Robertson and Koenig informally gave their consent. On May 8, the Basic Law was officially adopted by the Parliamentary Council, and on May 12, the day on which the blockade was lifted, the governments of France, Great Britain, and the United States tendered their formal approval.
** The largest party, the CDU (Christian Democratic Union), received thirty-one percent of the vote cast and obtained 139 seats. The SPD became the second largest party in the Federal Republic with 131 seats followed by the Free Democrats with 52 seats, the German Party with 17 seats and the Communists (SED) with 15.

On September 7, the new Parliament met in Bonn and five days later Professor Theodor Heuss, noted Tübingen professor and outspoken critic of the Nazi regime, was elected Federal President. Three days afterwards, on September 15, the seventy-three-year-old Konrad Adenauer was elected Chancellor.

The following week, on September 21, 1949, the Federal Republic of Germany formally came into being. The three Allied High Commissioners promulgated a new Occupation Statute and terminated the military occupation. On the same day, the High Commissioners officially received Chancellor Adenauer and the members of his new government in a special ceremony in the Petersberg Hotel overlooking the Rhine just outside Bonn. (The Petersberg Hotel had been the residence of the British delegation during the fateful 1938 meeting between Neville Chamberlain and Adolph Hitler at Bad Godesberg.)

In a moving speech, Chancellor Adenauer expressed his gratitude to the Commissioners for the help which the Allies had given Germany during the military occupation. The Chancellor then shook hands with each of the High Commissioners and afterwards presented his cabinet. But the cabinet did not shake hands. They were appointees of the Chancellor, not the Allies, and *der Alte* wanted to make this point clear.[5]

The status of Berlin under the West German Basic Law is unique. The members of the Parliamentary Council originally proposed that Berlin should be included as a state (*Land*) within the Federal Republic. The Allies took exception to this proposal, however, since Berlin was still under four-power occupation. The French especially were hesitant about the inclusion of Berlin in the new West German government, but more because of fear of a united Germany than because of the city's four-power status.

On November 22, 1948, while the negotiations over the Basic Law were still in progress, General Clay advised Washington of this difficulty. After detailing several other areas of conflict with the French, Clay stated:

> I am even more concerned with the French comment that the participation of the representatives of Berlin at Bonn is threatening the political reconstruction of western Germany. We have told the French that if quadripartite government exists in Berlin at the

time that the constitution is approved, we will have to disapprove Berlin participation in western German government. *On the other hand, if Berlin is then a split city, it must be supported by western Germany.* Careful attention must be given under the conditions which the constitution is approved to including Berlin in western German government. The French do not really want a united Germany with Berlin as the capital. Our policy calls for a united Germany. Any act on our part which would indicate that we oppose a united Germany would lessen greatly our influence in western Germany.[6] [Italics added.]

When the initial draft of the Basic Law was presented to the military governors three months later, Berlin was included as one of the states of the Federal Republic. Since the blockade was then still in effect, there was some doubt whether the four-power status of Berlin would continue. Also, the Social Democrats were extremely desirous of uniting Berlin with the Federal Republic. Berlin was one of the traditional centers of SPD strength in Germany and the Socialists wanted its votes in the new German government. It can be assumed that the Christian Democrats were somewhat less enthusiastic about Berlin's inclusion, although for political reasons they supported it vigorously.[7]

Had the blockade continued or had the West decided to end the fiction of four-power occupation in Berlin, it is conceivable that the former German capital would have been included as a full member state of the Federal Republic. On May 8, 1949, when the Parliamentary Council formally ratified the Basic Law, the provisions regarding Berlin were still included.* [8] But when the Allied military governors formally approved the Basic Law four days later, specific exception was taken to these provisions. In a letter to Dr. Adenauer, the military governers stated:

* Specifically, these articles provide:

Article 23
For the time being, the Basic Law shall apply in the territory of the *Länder* Baden, Bavaria, Bremen, Greater Berlin, Hamburg, Hesse, Lower Saxony, North Rhine-Westphalia, Rhineland-Palatinate, Schleswig-Holstein, Wuerttemberg-Baden and Wuerttemberg-Hohenzollern. It shall be put into force for others parts of Germany on their accession.

Article 144
(2) Insofar as restrictions are imposed on the application of the Basic Law to one of the *Länder* enumerated in Article 23, . . . or to a part of one of these *Länder* enumerated, that *land* or a part of the *land* shall have the right, . . . to send representatives to the *Bundestag* and . . . to the *Bundesrat*.

A third reservation [of the Western powers] concerns the participation of Greater Berlin in the Federation. We interpret the effect of Articles 23 and 144(2) of the Basic Law as constituting acceptance of our previous request that while Berlin may not be accorded voting membership in the *Bundestag* or *Bundesrat* nor be governed by the Federation she may, nevertheless, designate a small number of representatives to attend the meetings of those legislative bodies.[9]

Thus, while Berlin was recognized by the Basic Law as a state of the Federal Republic, the action of the military governors in taking exception to these provisions prevented her from becoming a full-fledged member. One month later, when the Berlin city assembly officially requested the Commandants of the Western sectors to remove this restriction, their request was refused. Accordingly, when the Federal Republic officially came into being on September 21, the representatives from Berlin were present in Bonn in an advisory capacity only.[10]

Today, Berlin's position is much the same. It is still technically under four-power occupation although according to the Basic Law of the German Federal Republic it is also a *Land* of West Germany. Only the Allied reservation of May 13, 1949, keeps these provisions of the Basic Law from being applicable. Laws passed by the Federal Assembly in Bonn are applicable to Berlin when they are approved by the Berlin city assembly. In practice, laws passed in Bonn which are intended to affect Berlin contain a special "Berlin clause" which provides that the city shall put the particular law into effect within thirty days. The action of the Berlin assembly is then a formality.[11]

Except for the fact that it has remained under *de jure* Allied occupation, the development of self-government in Berlin has proceeded concurrently with that of West Germany. On August 29, 1950, a new Constitution for Berlin was approved by the three Western Commandants which granted the Berliners virtual independence.* Two

---

* Under the 1950 Constitution, the city government in Berlin consists of a Lord Mayor, a Deputy Lord Mayor, a Senate (*Senat*) of 13 senators, and a City Assembly of 133 members. The City Assembly is directly elected by the people and in turn elects the mayors and the *Senat*. The *Senat*, in practice, is an executive body rather than a deliberative one, and each senator is charged with the administration of some facet of city government (*e.g.*, transportation, finance, education, etc.). Since Berlin is also an unofficial *Land* of the Federal Republic, the Lord Mayor of Berlin also serves as a type of Prime Minister for the city, and the

years later, on May 26, 1952, when the occupation of West Germany finally ended, the ties between Berlin and the Federal Republic were strengthened considerably. In a letter to Chancellor Adenauer, the three Western High Commissioners advised him that they would co-operate with the Federal Republic as much as possible in the city's political and economic development. Shortly afterward, the Western Commandants officially waived their right to review the actions of the city assembly.[12]

In contrast to her political recovery, Berlin's economic recovery proceeded slowly. The ten months of the blockade prevented all but the most essential commerce from taking place. Food and fuel took priority on the incoming aircraft, and without raw materials Berlin's industries stood idle. Even after the blockade was lifted Berlin con-tinued to lag far behind its West German competitors. There were several reasons for this.

First, situated one hundred and ten miles within the Soviet zone, Berlin was deprived of its normal commercial contacts with the sur-rounding area. Its trade, by necessity, was conducted with the West, from which it was geographically isolated. Aside from the added trans-portation costs, this remoteness in itself seriously hindered a thriv-ing economy.

Second, because of the blockade, Berlin was unable to take advan-tage of the currency revision in mid-1948 that restored a stable deutsche mark. Whereas in West Germany the new currency meant that business and industry could begin to plan for the future without fear of a ruinous inflation, the blockade prevented similar plans from being carried out in Berlin. Accordingly, West Germany gained an extremely important one-year head start in putting the sound currency to work.

Third, and directly related to the first two reasons, Berlin was plagued by a mountainous unemployment problem. Before the war, Berlin was not only the capital of the German state but the center of Germany's business and commerce as well. Thousands of people

---

city assembly as its House of Representatives, but there is little added respon-sibility as a result.

[The Hanseatic cities of Bremen and Hamburg also occupy this type of dual status, being both states of the Federal Republic and cities as well. In the United States, the same would be true should Washington, D.C., be admitted to the Union as a sovereign state.]

were employed there as white-collar officials and clerks in the head offices of Germany's banking, insurance and industrial combines, and thousands more in government. When the war ended, all this was over. The government was dissolved and most of the major commercial organizations moved their headquarters to West Germany. As a result, Berlin's immense army of clerks and officials were left without a means of livelihood. While the city's industrial workers could be reemployed quite easily, these could not.

Paradoxically, the blockade itself eased Berlin's immediate unemployment problem by putting large numbers of people to work unloading and distributing supplies. The construction of Tegel airfield alone employed over 20,000 persons. When the blockade ended these temporary jobs also ended, and the number of unemployed in Berlin by mid-1949 exceeded 400,000.

In addition, Berlin's postwar population was no longer young and vigorous. Over twenty-five percent were pensioners. Persons older than sixty far outnumbered those under twenty, and men between the ages of twenty-five and forty were only one-third as numerous as before the war.

Thus, even though the airlift had succeeded, Berlin's economic plight was desperate. Money was urgently needed to begin the process of reconstruction. On July 30, the city government petitioned the Western Commandants to include Berlin in the Marshall Plan. Two weeks later American High Commissioner McCloy announced that 55 million deutsche marks ($13 million) would be made available to Berlin immediately for the construction of electric generating facilities. And on December 15, 1949, a three-year Marshall Plan agreement was signed in Bonn authorizing Berlin 95 million marks ($24 million) in economic assistance. Fifty million of the ninety-five million were to be spent for housing and small industries; forty million for heavy industry, and five million for public communication systems.[13]

With these infusions, Berlin gradually began to recover. Rubble removal was stepped up to a two-shift per day basis, and priority for employment was given to those supporting families. Construction also resumed on an accelerated basis and by the mid-1950's amounted to more than 250 million dollars annually. The value of Berlin's total exports rose from three million dollars in 1950 to thirty million in 1954, and production returned to almost seventy percent of its prewar

level. The number of jobless was reduced to 268,000 in 1952, and 158,-
000 in 1954. By 1959, unemployment was virtually unknown.

As Berlin's industrial capacity increased, so did the prosperity of
its commercial establishments. Stores again were well stocked; hotels
and restaurants began to thrive; neon lights went on at night, and
the *Kurfürstendamm* and *Tauentzien* once more became alive with
shoppers and tourists.

But Berlin's recovery was still a tenuous one. Its lifeline to West
Germany stretched 110 miles through the Soviet zone and was sus-
ceptible at every point to interruption and control by Communist authorities. Even after the Allied airlift ended, a "commercial airlift"
of ninety to a hundred planes continued flying products out of Berlin which, if carried overland, might have been seized under various
pretexts by the East. A so-called "creeping blockade" applied inter-
mittently by the Soviets over the years further hampered efforts toward recovery. While the Communist measures have never seriously
interfered with the commercial life of Berlin for an extended period,
they have had considerable nuisance value in keeping the Berliners
aware of their precarious existence.

An example of this intermittent harassment occurred on July 8, 1949,
less than three weeks after the Paris Conference of Foreign Ministers,
when the Soviet authorities closed down all of the crossing points
between their zone and the West for a period of seven days. No excuse was given, and facilities were not restored until a formal protest
was lodged by the Western Commandants on July 12.[14]

In January of 1950, the assault on commercial traffic between West
Germany and Berlin was resumed. Trucks traveling the Berlin-Helmstedt autobahn were subjected to prolonged searches and those carrying scrap metal were denied passage. Allied protests brought only occasional relief, and truck traffic to Berlin did not return to normal
until the nineteenth of February.[15]

For two days in July, 1950, electricity into West Berlin from the
power plants located in the East was interrupted. On September 21,
the East German authorities cut the flow of current completely. The
generator which had been constructed in West Berlin with Marshall
Plan funds then took over the supply of the three Western sectors
permanently. Two days later, on September 23, Soviet authorities

blocked barge traffic into West Berlin, and did not restore it until October 5.[16]

In 1951, the Communist harassment continued. Following the expiration of a trade agreement between East and West Germany on August 2, 1951, Soviet authorities imposed what amounted to a prohibitive road tax on all autobahn traffic to Berlin. This tax was not reduced until the signing of a new trade pact on September 20, 1951.

In May of 1952, Russian authorities denied passage to all American and British military vehicles on the Helmstedt autobahn for one week. This was the first interference with Allied traffic since the blockade had been lifted in 1949. The Soviet ban against Allied vehicles was followed on May 27, 1952 (the date of West Germany's admission to the European Defense Community), with the total closure of the borders surrounding West Berlin and the cutting of all telephone communications between West Berlin and both East Berlin and East Germany. Although the border was reopened later that month following Allied protests, direct telephone connections were never resumed.

Also in 1952, an American hospital plane was buzzed by two Soviet MIG–15 fighters when it strayed slightly from the air corridor in heavy weather. The following year, a British Lincoln bomber was shot down by MIG fighters over the Elbe River just outside the Hamburg corridor with the loss of all on board.

In spite of such pressure, perhaps to some extent because of it, the Berliners did not waver in their resistance to communism. On October 24, 1950, to commemorate this resistance, the American people presented to Berlin the Freedom Bell—a replica of the Liberty Bell and inscribed after the fashion of Abraham Lincoln: "That this world under God may have a new birth of freedom." The day the Freedom Bell was unveiled in Berlin was a day of rejoicing. General Clay returned from America to make the dedication, and his reception was a moving testament to the place he occupies in the hearts of the Berliners. From all over the city they came to welcome him; almost half a million crowded into the plaza and streets in front of the *Schöneberger Rathaus* for the ceremony. Children were let out of school to attend, and many persons from the East also came over.

For those from the East it was an especially memorable day. Life under the puppet regime of Walter Ulbricht was bleak beyond description. Shortly after the splitting of the city government in 1948, a system of Communist house and street wardens, much like that of the Nazis, had been established in East Berlin. On April 25, 1949, all land and private houses in East Berlin were expropriated. This was followed on May 1, by a governmental order seizing all banks and insurance companies. On May 30, the East German People's Council formally proclaimed a constitution for the so-called "German Democratic Republic," and on October 7, 1949, the regime officially came into existence.

In April of 1950, when the Berlin city assembly requested free citywide elections, the East refused to take part. When the request was repeated again in 1951 by Mayor Reuter, the East German government again declined, calling the proposed elections "uninteresting parish contests." [17] The following April, a special UN Commission investigating the possibility of all-German elections was denied admission to East Berlin.

In addition to the lack of political liberty, the economic plight of the average citizen in the so-called "workers and peasants state" of East Germany was disastrous. A pound of butter—when it was available—cost 10 marks ($2.50); a pound of meat, 12 marks ($3.00); a pound of coffee, 75 marks ($18.75). Shoes were three times as expensive in the East as in West Germany, and new clothes were virtually unobtainable.

Private enterprise in the Soviet zone was quickly liquidated by the Ulbricht regime. At the end of 1950, less than nine percent of the basic industry of East Germany was privately owned, and by 1958, the figure had sunk to less than four percent. Retail trade, which previously had been all independently owned, was less than fifty percent private in 1950, and less than twenty-five percent in 1958.[18]

In agriculture, the situation in East Germany was chaotic. In 1945, when the Soviet occupation began, all land holdings over 247 acres had been expropriated. Collectivization began in 1952, and was completed in the spring of 1960. Today, eighteen years after the war, East Germany still produces less agriculturally than it did in 1939, and food shortages are still very much of a problem.

One of the immediate results of the attempts to collectivize East German agriculture in 1952 was a pronounced increase in the number of refugees leaving the Soviet zone. To halt it, the Ulbricht regime began the construction of a 100-meter "death strip" along the West German frontier, and evacuated all families living along the border who were not "politically reliable." At the same time, the number of crossing points from East to West Berlin was reduced from 227 to less than a hundred. Armed policemen were placed at the remaining crossing points, and everyone (other than Allied personnel) traveling between the two sectors was forced to submit to rigorous customs checks.

In spite of the East German security measures, over 20,000 persons fled the Communist Workers' Paradise in September. The trend continued throughout the year, and the month of January, 1953, brought no respite. By February the monthly total of refugees was exceeding 30,000, and on the second day of March, 1953, more than 6,000 persons reported in West Berlin to ask for asylum.

Stalin's death on March 6, 1953, caused a brief relaxation in Communist terror, but the exodus continued unabated. Over 58,000 persons—an all time monthly record—fled the "German Democratic Republic" that month. During April and May the figures remained at about the same level, and a feeling of extreme tenseness now gripped the Soviet zone.

On May 14, 1953, the Central Committee of the Communist Party in East Germany proposed a ten percent increase in individual production quotas. When the measures were put into effect the following month, reaction was bitter. In East Berlin, the workers on the gigantic Stalin Allee housing project held a dramatic protest meeting. On June 16, a delegation of over 300 from the project marched to the East German House of Ministries on *Leipzigerstr.* (the former headquarters of Hermann Goering's *Luftwaffen Ministerium*).

As the marchers made their way through the city, other workers joined them, and by the time they arrived at *Leipzigerstr.* the crowd numbered over 5,000. The East German police made no effort to interfere with the demonstrators, and the Communist functionaries who tried to explain the new quotas were shouted down. The rest of the day was spent in organizing other protest rallies throughout East Berlin, and by nightfall a full-fledged revolt was in the making.

The following morning, June 17, 1953, East German workers and Soviet tanks clashed repeatedly in East Berlin. A crowd of 50,000 East Berliners stormed through the Brandenburg Gate and tore down the

Red flag flying above it. For a fleeting moment, freedom seemed to reign in East Germany.

But the revolt was doomed by Russian intervention. By the evening of June 17, it was over. In the next several days the uprising in East Berlin spread throughout East Germany but there, as in Berlin, it was also put down by the bayonets of the Red Army.

On June 18, Mayor Ernst Reuter, speaking over the radio from West Berlin, eloquently delivered its epitaph:

> A people cannot be held in submission in the long run, with martial law and bayonets and tanks; and it would be terrible if the graves, which are already deep enough, should be made deeper. . . .
>
> What I saw today at the Potsdamer Platz of these wastes, this dead, empty city, reminded me of my first impression at the end of 1946 in that terrible winter when I first returned to Berlin and saw the Tiergarten. A man's heart could have stopped, and it could stop today as we see this city murdered by the forces of history in which we have all been torn.
>
> We renew our appeal to the entire world; the world must finally understand and I hope must admit that the Germans are a people who know the worth of freedom. . . .[19]

Less than four months later this stirring German leader, Professor Ernst Reuter, Lord Mayor of Berlin, was dead. The Berlin radio at half-hour intervals on the afternoon and evening of September 27, 1953, announced that the Lord Mayor had died of heart failure earlier that day. To the Berliners, the departure of a great friend and leader brought profound grief. They remembered that the previous year at Christmas time Ernst Reuter had asked them to place lighted candles in their windows as a greeting to their loved ones who were missing —to those still held prisoner in Russia. And now, on Reuter's death, to express their grief once more, windows all over Berlin again were filled with candles. It was a spontaneous demonstration of the place which Ernst Reuter held in the hearts and minds of his people.

To Reuter's friend, Willy Brandt, as he walked home from the Mayor's house that day, "those innumerable, flickering little flames . . . looked like innumerable glittering tears. The Berliner wept wherever he received the news . . . a whole city was mourning for its dead leader; the people were moved as many Americans were when, in April of 1945, President Roosevelt left them forever."[20]

With Reuter's death Berlin was plunged momentarily into a period of despair. The coalition of Social Democrats, Christian Democrats and Free Democrats which he had fashioned during the blockade fell apart. Dr. Walter Schreiber of the CDU, who had been Deputy Mayor under Reuter, became Lord Mayor, but his political sympathies belonged, it seemed, to an era long past. The Social Democratic Party, the largest and most powerful party in Berlin, left the government coalition, and without its support the city government was frustrated.

The times themselves following Reuter's death also were troubled. The inability of the Western powers to take positive measures following the June 17th uprising still rankled. The courageous people of East Berlin who had dared to take revolution into their own hands had been ignored—left alone, it seemed, to fight the military might of the Red Army. The East German regime, despised and hated though it was, had been allowed to keep itself in power, while the West confined itself to anguished hand-wringing and paper protests.

In Berlin itself, the immediate Allied reaction on June 17 had been to dissociate from the revolt. In their first public announcement the three Western Commandants denied their complicity in the uprising. Only later was the Soviet action in putting it down formally protested.[21] For many in West Berlin who had suffered through the blockade, it seemed that the Allies were resting on their laurels. At a time when East Germany was in turmoil, when guidance and direction from Moscow were crippled as a result of Stalin's death, many thought the West should have acted (at least diplomatically) to seek an overall settlement in Germany.

As a result of the inability of the Western powers to intervene, the Soviets were given a free hand to restore the power of the satrapal Ulbricht regime. Over ten thousand persons were arrested in the Soviet zone for complicity in the uprising. Although most were later released, sixteen were sentenced to death by a Soviet military court.[22] For many people in the East, the lesson of the revolt was a tragic one. There now seemed no alternative but to get along with the Communists as best they could. If there was to be salvation, it would have to come from without.

In West Berlin and West Germany the immediate response to the East German uprising was similar to that of the Western powers. A feeling of helplessness gripped everyone. On July 1, 1953, the West

German Bundestag declared that henceforth the seventeenth of June would be celebrated as a national holiday—the Day of German Unity. In West Berlin, the broad extension of the *Unter den Linden* leading into the Brandenburg Gate was renamed the *Strasse of the Seventeenth of June* in commemoration of the revolt. In the East, the workers on the Stalin Allee project succeeded in their immediate aim of reducing production quotas but only for two months, and in August the quotas were raised again to their former level.

In January of 1954, six months after the East Berlin revolt, a new effort was made to reach a settlement in Germany. Following preliminary consultations in the UN, the Seventh Session of the Council of Foreign Ministers convened in Berlin on January 25. Indicative of the growing rift between East and West, the site of the meetings alternated daily between the Allied Control Council in the American sector and the Russian Embassy. The Conference itself produced little in the way of tangible results. Western proposals for free all-German elections were rejected out of hand by Soviet Foreign Minister Molotov, and when the conference adjourned on February 20, agreement on Germany was still in the far distant future.

One month later, on March 25, 1954, the Soviet Union announced that it was granting the puppet East German regime "full sovereignty." The Soviet pronouncement was followed on April 8, by a joint Western declaration refusing to recognize the Soviet action.

> The three governments, [according to the Allied statement,] . . . will continue to regard the Soviet Union as the responsible power for the Soviet zone of Germany. These governments do not recognize the sovereignty of the East German regime which is not based on free elections, and do not intend to deal with it as a government. They believe that this attitude will be shared by other states, who, like themselves, will continue to recognize the Government of the Federal Republic as the only freely elected and legally constituted government in Germany.[23]

In a partial reply to the Soviet efforts to create a separate and "sovereign" East German state, the Federal Parliament, in a symbolic gesture of German unity, convened in Berlin on July 17, 1954, and reelected the benign Dr. Heuss as Federal President for a second term. Heuss's election was followed by the passage of a joint resolution proclaiming Berlin as the natural capital of German political life, and calling for eventual German reunification.

Three months later the first elections were held in West Berlin since the end of the blockade. The Social Democrats, who had not yet recovered from the loss of Ernst Reuter, remained the largest single party in Berlin, but lost almost 20 percent of its former strength to the CDU, which was then coasting on a wave of Adenauer popularity. The Communist (SED) Party entered the lists once more, after having sat out the 1948 elections, but received less than 3 percent of the total vote. Professor Otto Suhr of the Social Democrats was elected Lord Mayor and a coalition government returned to power. With the unusually high figure of 91.8 percent of the electorate voting, the results were as follows:

SPD	684,906	(44.6%) =	69 seats
CDU	467,117	(30.4%) =	44 seats
FDP	197,204	(12.8%) =	19 seats
Small parties	145,291	(9.5%) =	—
SED	41,345	(2.7%) =	—

The following year, 1955, saw a brief thaw in East-West relations. Following the signing of the Austrian Peace Treaty in May, the first postwar Summit Conference between the Big Four heads of government convened in Geneva in early July. Nikita Khrushchev, who had recently come to power in Russia following the overthrow of Georgi Malenkov, seemed willing to reach a settlement in Germany. In a final directive to their Foreign Ministers, the Big Four agreed that the reunification of Germany was to be carried out by means of free elections, and that the settlement of the "German question" was to be achieved "in conformity with the natural interests of the German people and the interests of European security."

But the "Spirit of Geneva" was shortlived. On September 20, the Soviet Union granted full diplomatic recognition to the East German regime and gave East Germany the right to control all traffic to and from Berlin, except for that of the Allied forces.[24]

The Western powers replied to the Soviet action the following week by announcing that they would continue to hold the Soviet Union responsible for the fulfillment of all previous agreements regarding

Berlin. The three Western Foreign Ministers meeting in Washington
also reaffirmed "that the Federal Republic of Germany is the only
German Government freely and legitimately constituted and therefore entitled to speak for Germany as the representative of the German people. . . . These three governments do not recognize the
East German regime nor the existence of a state in the Soviet
zone." * 25

The following year, on October 23, 1956, news of the Hungarian
Revolution broke over Berlin with a sudden fury, and with it rose the
star of another Berliner who in a short time was to fall heir to the
mantle of Ernst Reuter. In the Budapest massacre the Berliners were
witnessing another revolt of free people violently suppressed by the
armed might of the Red Army, and memories of the East Berlin uprising rapidly revived. As on June 17, 1953, indignation combined with
helplessness raised the temper of the city to a fever pitch. A mass protest rally was organized in front of the *Schöneberger Rathaus* on the
evening of November 4. By this time it had become obvious that the
West would not intervene, and the 100,000 Berliners who assembled
there that evening were in an ugly mood. Both Franz Neumann and
Ernst Lemmer, leaders respectively of Berlin's SPD and CDU, were
hissed and booed when they tried to speak. They were followed by a
speaker who was not even on the program—the relatively obscure
forty-three-year-old President of Berlin's city assembly, Willy Brandt.

The early life of Brandt is well known.[26] He was born out of wedlock
in Lübeck on December 18, 1913. His father was never known to
him. His early name, "Herbert Framm," was taken from his mother's

---

* Following the Western announcement, the Soviet Union stated that Allied access to Berlin would not be affected. According to the Kremlin:

> As for control over the movement between the German Federal Republic and
> West Berlin of military personnel and freight of garrisons of the U.S.A., Great
> Britain, and France, quartered in Berlin, in negotiations between the Govern-
> ments of the U.S.S.R. and the German Democratic Republic, it was stipulated
> that this control would henceforth be carried out by the command of the
> Soviet Military forces in Germany temporarily until the achievement of a suitable
> agreement.
> It is self-understood that, in concluding the above mentioned treaty, the
> Governments of the Soviet Union and the German Democratic Republic took
> into consideration the obligations which both have under existing international
> agreements relating to Germany as a whole.

U.S. Congress, Senate, *Documents on Germany, 1944–1959*, Committee Print,
Committee on Foreign Relations (Washington: Government Printing Office, 1959),
pp. 159–60.

family and he grew up in the most modest circumstances. He took part in early Socialist causes in Germany; fought the storm troopers and the *Stahlhelm;* fled when the Nazis came to power in the early 'Thirties; and fought with the loyalists in the Spanish Civil War. Afterward he went to Norway, became a Norwegian citizen, joined the resistance and according to some, fought against the Germans during the Nazi invasion in 1940.

In 1946, Brandt returned to Berlin as press attaché to the Norwegian Military Mission, and carried the rank of Major in the Norwegian Army. At the end of 1947, he renounced his Norwegian citizenship and applied for renaturalization in Germany. A friend of both Ernst Reuter and Kurt Schumacher, Brandt became head of the SPD's liaison office in Berlin which dealt directly with the Allied Military Government. In 1949, following the departure of the Allied High Commissioners from Berlin to West Germany, he was chosen as one of Berlin's eight representatives to the Bundestag in Bonn. Later that year he became the local SPD chairman in the borough of Wilmersdorf. In 1950, he was elected to the city assembly, and became its president in 1955. In both 1952 and 1954, he ran against Franz Neumann for the SPD party chairmanship in Berlin, but was defeated on both occasions.

Now, on the evening of November 4, as he began to address the Budapest demonstrators, Brandt quickly found a responsive chord. Instead of encouraging a march into East Berlin as many wanted, he volunteered to lead the crowd to the Memorial for the Victims of Stalinism located on the *Steinplatz* in the British sector. Most of the demonstrators followed Brandt and the others drifted off. When they reached the *Steinplatz,* Brandt concluded the march with a short speech and then led in the singing of the sentimental German folksong *"Ich hatt' einen Kameraden."*

As the meeting was breaking up, word was brought to Brandt that another group of demonstrators with torches in hand were marching to the Brandenburg Gate. The West Berlin police, he was told, were trying to contain the marchers but the situation was critical. Brandt, and his wife Ruth, then jumped into a car and rushed toward the Gate. Already a formation of the East German Peoples Police and Russian tanks were drawn up beyond it on the *Unter den Linden,* and an armed clash seemed in the offing.

On the way to the Brandenburg Gate, Brandt and his wife passed another column of marchers in the *Tiergarten*. Here the police also were having a difficult time and Brandt stopped, grabbed a microphone from a damaged police car and spoke to the crowd. According to his own later account, the pressure on the West Berlin police cordon slackened. Again the song, *"Ich hatt' einen Kameraden,"* and the marchers dispersed.

At the Brandenburg Gate the situation was still critical. West Berlin police president Johannes Stumm had succeeded partially in restoring order, but there was still danger that the situation would get out of hand. Brandt spoke to the demonstrators from atop an automobile. "Then," he states, "I placed myself at the head of another procession, a smaller one this time, and led it away from the Brandenburg Gate, past the Russian War Memorial, situated on West Berlin territory. Here I asked the people to sing defiantly the German national anthem. In political situations it is useful to remember that my German countrymen are fond of singing." [27]

With the singing of the *"Deutschland Lied,"* the demonstration was over, and what could have been a very nasty incident had been averted. In October of the following year, on the death of Professor Suhr, Willy Brandt was elected Lord Mayor of Berlin.

9

The First Ultimatum

IN 1957 EAST-WEST RELATIONS continued to deteriorate. The Soviet Union was reaping the whirlwind as a result of its intervention in Hungary, and everywhere behind the Iron Curtain police pressure was intensified. In East Germany, following a rigorous crackdown against sympathizers of the Hungarian Revolution, the Ulbricht regime stepped up its drive for academic conformity—students and grammar school pupils were forbidden to travel West, and intellectual discussion of political issues came under stringent state control. Yet, as Western opinion decried the increased Communist terror, the tide of world fortune changed with dramatic suddenness. On October 4, 1957, from a launching pad in Central Siberia, the first earth satellite (Sputnik) hurtled skyward and began encircling the globe. One month later, on November 3, Sputnik II was successfully launched and carried with it the world's first space passenger, a two year old dog named Laika. The Soviet space triumphs were merely an outward indication of the changing balance of scientific power. Behind them rested years of solid growth of Soviet technology—technology which was equally applicable to the development of intercontinental ballistic missiles, or explosive devices of megaton capacity.

News of the great Russian achievements was greeted in the West with a mixture of shock and despair. Although Presidential Assistant Sherman Adams and United States Secretary of Defense Charles E. Wilson discounted the Soviet breakthrough as an attempt to score points in a non-existent basketball game in outer space, the more perceptive military authorities and the public at large regarded the event as a serious challenge to the security of the democratic world. The reality of the missile gap was quickly brought home and the complacency of the early 'Fifties yielded to an overriding feeling of anxiety and concern. The public press was filled with appeals for greater American efforts, for more rigorous education, and for increased military expenditures.

As the clamor for action mounted in the West, the Soviet Union recognized that their success had triggered an unwanted reaction. Accordingly, the Kremlin increased its propaganda advocating peaceful coexistence and on December 10, 1957, one week before a scheduled NATO conference in Paris, Nikolai Bulganin, then Chairman of the Soviet Council of Ministers, wrote a personal letter to President Eisenhower decrying Western concern and suggesting an early meeting at the Summit.

"I am addressing this letter to you," Bulganin wrote, "in order to share with you certain thoughts regarding the international situation which is developing at the present time." The Soviet Government, he said, had reviewed the world picture and could not but note "that at the initiative of the United States of America and Great Britain, measures are now being developed the purpose of which is a sharp intensification of the military preparations of the NATO members, and that specific plans are being considered in connection with the forthcoming session of the NATO Council. . . .

"I must frankly say to you, Mr. President, that the reaction of certain circles in your country and in certain other NATO countries regarding the recent accomplishments of the U.S.S.R. in the scientific and technical field, and regarding the launching . . . of the Soviet artificial earth satellites in particular, appears to us a great mistake."

The launching of artificial earth satellites, Bulganin said, "bears witness to the great achievements of the U.S.S.R., both in the field of

peaceful scientific research and in the field of military technology."
As if to belie Western fears, however, he then added that the Soviet
Union sought only peace. According to Bulganin, "the U.S.S.R. has
insisted and still insists that neither ballistic missiles nor hydrogen
and atomic bombs should ever be used for purposes of destruction. . . . The Soviet Union has no intention of attacking either the
U.S.A. or any other country. It is calling for agreement and for peaceful coexistence. The same position is held by many states, including
the Chinese Peoples' Republic and other Socialist countries."

Bulganin continued his message with an attack on the Western
policy of equipping NATO forces in Europe with tactical nuclear
weapons and, particularly, of equipping West German forces with
such weapons.

> Military circles in the West are attempting to implant the idea that
> the so-called "tactical" atomic weapons are not very different from
> conventional types of weapons and that their use would not entail
> as destructive results as that of atomic and hydrogen bombs. One
> cannot fail to see that such reasoning, designed to mislead public
> opinion, constitutes a dangerous attempt to justify preparation for
> unleasing an atomic war. . . . One likewise cannot fail to take into
> account, for example, the fact that the placing of nuclear weapons
> at the disposal of the Federal Republic of Germany may set in
> motion such forces in Europe and entail such consequences as
> even the NATO members may not contemplate.

Bulganin said that it was now necessary to recognize that capitalist
and socialist states exist side by side. "None of us can fail to take into
account," he said, "the fact that any attempts to change this situation
by external force, and to upset the status quo, or any attempts to impose any territorial changes, would lead to catastrophic consequences."

The Soviet Premier then concluded with a direct plea for a face-to-
face confrontation.

> A consciousness of the gravity of the present situation, [he
> said,] prompts us to address to you, Mr. President, an appeal to
> undertake joint efforts to put an end to the "cold war," to terminate
> the armaments race, and to enter resolutely upon the path of
> peaceful coexistence.
> Attaching great importance to personal contacts between states-
> men, which facilitate finding a common point of view on important
> international problems, we, for our part, would be prepared to

come to an agreement on a personal meeting of state leaders to discuss both the problems mentioned in this letter and other problems. The participants in the meeting could agree upon these other subjects that might need to be discussed.[1]

Bulganin's letter was received stoically in the West. Russian failure to implement the Geneva Agreement * calling for discussions on German reunification based on free elections led most responsible Western statesmen to discount Moscow's new overtures toward peaceful coexistence. At the first session of the NATO heads of government on December 16, 1957, President Eisenhower castigated Soviet refusal to agree to all-German elections and announced a new United States space program soon to be put into effect.

Significantly, and although Bulganin had not mentioned it in his letter, President Eisenhower referred to Berlin and exhorted the NATO nations to stand firm. "I cannot let this occasion pass," he said, "without recalling our common concern over the status of Berlin. The clear rights there of the Western powers must be maintained. Any sign of Western weakness at this forward position could be misinterpreted with grevous consequences." [2]

The following month, in his State of the Union address delivered on January 9, President Eisenhower said that the United States was not taking the Russian achievements lightly. The entire message dealt with the subject of peace and security, and the President offered a special eight-point program designed to regain American scientific and military leadership. From the tenor of his remarks, it was clear that the United States was responding to the Soviet challenge with vigor.[3]

The next day, when asked at a news conference about Bulganin's letter and whether a new Summit meeting was likely, Secretary of State John Foster Dulles replied that some positive evidence of Soviet good faith would have to be furnished first.

> The most realistic and encouraging act would be the carrying out of some of the prior agreements that have been made and most particularly I would say the agreement which was arrived at at the last Summit meeting with the Soviets. There it was stated that the Four Powers recognize their common responsibility for the German problem and the reunification of Germany and agree that Germany shall be reunified by free elections. That agreement was

* Concluded at the 1955 Geneva Conference by Eisenhower, Eden, Bulganin, and French Premier Edgar Faure. (See previous chapter.)

the principal product of the Geneva Summit meeting. Since then the Soviet Union has taken the position that it had no further responsibility for the reunification of Germany and that in any event that reunification by free elections was not an acceptable method. Now that certainly throws doubt upon the worth-whileness of these meetings.[4]

Two days later, on January 12, President Eisenhower formally replied to Bulganin's letter. After deploring Soviet failure to carry out the Geneva Agreement, the President echoed Dulles' remarks regarding the Summit. Personal contacts between statesmen, Eisenhower told Bulganin, were of value "but meetings between us do not automatically produce good results. Preparatory work, with good will on both sides, is a prerequisite to success." The President then suggested a meeting of Foreign Ministers to complete the preliminary details and to ascertain whether "such a top-level meeting would . . . hold good hope of advancing the cause of peace." Upon the successful conclusion of the Foreign Ministers' talks, Eisenhower said, a Summit Conference could then take place.[5]

But it readily became apparent that the Russians were not interested in negotiating seriously about world problems and had suggested the Summit meeting primarily for the propaganda value. Also, with both the space and missile races running in their favor, the Russians felt no obligation to carry out the provisions of the Geneva Agreement regarding free all-German elections—an event which they knew would spell the end of communism in the Soviet zone.*

Accordingly, President Eisenhower's offer for preliminary negotiations was spurned and for the next several months the Russians increased world tensions by a steady cannonade of invective accusing the West of preventing a Summit. Taking advantage of their new-found scientific superiority, the Communists combined their propaganda attack with a concerted effort to weaken Western military forces in Central Europe, and particularly, in Western Germany.

* At the Conference of Foreign Ministers subsequent to the Geneva Summit, Mr. Molotov made this explicit. In his words, "It has been suggested here that a plan should be adopted for All-German elections. . . . As I have already shown, such a plan ignores the real conditions in Germany, inasmuch as the question of holding such elections has not yet matured. Such a mechanical merging of the two parts of Germany through so-called free elections, held, moreover, in the presence of foreign troops as envisaged in the Eden plan, might result in the violation of the vital interests of the working people of the German Democratic Republic, and we cannot agree to that." *Pravda*, November 9, 1955.

On February 14, 1958, the Polish Foreign Ministry formally presented to the American Ambassador in Warsaw, Mr. Jacob Beam, the Rapacki Plan for the establishment of a neutralized zone in Central Europe.* Under the Rapacki Plan, both East and West would agree not to station nuclear weapons in Germany, Czechoslovakia or Poland. Since the major Western missile capability at this time was based on the medium range weapons then located in West Germany, acceptance of the Rapacki Plan would have given the Communists a decided strategic advantage. Also, if it were put into effect, West Germany, and indeed, all Western Europe, would have been left in an extremely vulnerable position for an invasion by the ground forces of the Russian Army. Although the Polish plan was given little serious consideration by the Administration, the East made considerable propaganda mileage out of their trumpeted desire to "lessen tensions." Even in the West, many were lulled by this supposed sign of Communist reasonableness.

Two weeks later, on February 28, Russian Foreign Minister Andrei Gromyko repeated the Soviet demand for a Summit in an *aide-mémoire* to U.S. Ambassador Llewellyn Thompson in Moscow. The Soviet note announced the willingness of Russia to agree to a prior conference of Foreign Ministers but insisted that such a session should be "strictly limited" to organizational matters.

As for Germany, the Soviet note spelled out Russia's latest position. Reunification, if it was to come, would have to come through the efforts of the *two* German governments and not through free elections. The very subject of reunification, in fact, was no longer considered a fit subject for Summit discussion. According to the Soviet note, "the question of unification of the German Democratic Republic and the Federal German Republic into one state, wholly relating to the competence of these two German states, cannot be the subject of consideration at a forthcoming conference at the summit." [6]

In effect, the Soviet Union was officially washing its hands of German reunification and was advancing once more to tighten its grip on Central Europe. Henceforth, as we shall see, Russia moved adroitly to consolidate its position in the eastern part of Germany and, if pos-

* The contents of the Polish note outlining the Rapacki Plan can be found in *Department of State Bulletin*, May 19, 1958, pp. 822–23.

sible, to take Berlin in the process. The train of events set in motion by Western resistance to the blockade in 1948 had been reversed and the Kremlin was now riding a wave of solid scientific achievement.

Bulganin's formal reply to President Eisenhower three days later made the Russian position crystal clear:

> I should like to remind you, [the erstwhile Soviet Premier stated,] that in our proposals of January 8th there was a direct statement concerning the willingness of the Soviet Government also to discuss, by mutual agreement, such additional constructive proposals contributing to a termination of the "cold war" as might be presented by the other participants in the meeting. However, this does not mean that we can agree to discuss matters that are in the sphere of internal affairs of other states, the consideration of which could have no results other than a still further aggravation of the relation between states. Precisely in this category belong such matters as the situation in the countries of Eastern Europe and the unification into a single state of the German Democratic Republic and the Federal Republic of Germany. . . . The problem of uniting the GDR and the FRG into a single state . . . cannot, as the Soviet Government has already stated repeatedly, be the subject of discussion at the forthcoming summit conference.[7]

In Berlin itself, with the beginning of 1958, the relative increase in Communist military and scientific power was reflected directly in the increased harassment to which the Western garrisons were now subjected. On January 15, three days after President Eisenhower's reply to Premier Bulganin declining a meeting at the Summit without prior preparation, Soviet military authorities detained all American military trains on the run between Berlin and West Germany claiming that "new documentary procedures" had gone into effect.[8] Three days later, Mrs. Barksdale Hamlett, wife of Major General Barksdale Hamlett, Commandant of the American sector, was detained by East German police for three hours while shopping in East Berlin. A formal American protest was rejected on February 4 by the Soviet Commandant in East Berlin on the grounds that it was a matter between the United States and the "sovereign" German Democratic Republic.

Similar petty incidents along the sector border continued to plague Allied authorities in Berlin for the next several months as the Russians attempted to force more and more direct contact between East German officials and the West in the hope of gaining a greater degree of *de facto* recognition for their puppet regime.[9]

The Soviets also kept up their pressure for a Summit, hoping thereby to force the West into a position of compromise. Indeed, the Kremlin had nothing to lose. If the Western powers continued to insist on sufficient prior preparations to make a Summit conference meaningful, the Communists could keep on shouting that the West had no desire to "lessen tensions." If the West should agree to a meeting, then an even greater propaganda gain would have been made and the West, in effect, would have consented to Russia's refusal to carry out the Geneva Agreement. On March 24, a second *aide-mémoire* was handed to Ambassador Thompson in Moscow, once more proclaiming the Soviet desire for the peaceful settling of world problems—on Soviet terms. With a pointed reference to the recent gains in Soviet technology, the Russian note announced that "considerable time has elapsed since the Geneva Conference and the international situation has changed substantially. That is why the Soviet Government has proposed that a new approach should be made to the solution of pressing international problems." [10]

At a press conference in Washington the following day, Secretary of State Dulles reaffirmed the existing American position towards negotiations at the Summit. When asked about the Russian note, Dulles replied:

> Now, as you know, President Eisenhower has made perfectly clear that he wants to have a Summit Meeting if there is any reasonable chance of reaching substantial agreements which will ease the international situation and make peace more likely.
>
> But it's more and more apparent, and has been revealed I think by this exchange of correspondence, that the Soviets are demanding a very high political price as a condition to having such a meeting, and the question is whether there is enough hope out of such a meeting to justify paying the political price which the Soviets seem to be exacting.[11]

The West responded to the Soviet *aide-mémoire* the following week with a note recommending that a Summit meeting be held, providing sufficient preparatory work was done beforehand to at least "bring out the possibilities of agreement." For this purpose, exchanges through diplomatic channels beginning in Moscow during the latter half of April were suggested after which a meeting of the four Foreign Ministers could be held. "The Foreign Ministers, assuming they have concluded the preparatory work to their satisfaction, would reach agreement on the date and place of the Summit meeting and decide on its composition." [12]

The Soviet government did not reply to the Allied note. Instead, on May 5, Foreign Minister Gromyko advised the Western ambassadors in Moscow of those matters which the Soviet Union proposed to consider at the Summit. No mention was made of a prior meeting of Foreign Ministers and the question of German reunification was specifically excluded. The items which Russia agreed to discuss at the Summit were all designed to weaken the Western position in Europe— specifically: the creation of a denuclearized zone in Germany, the "liquidation of foreign military bases in foreign territories," a reduction in the number of foreign troops stationed in Germany, and, as a kicker, the signing of a nonaggression pact between NATO and the Warsaw Pact. [13]

Two weeks later, on May 23, the Communists stepped up their pressure in Berlin. East sector police tightened customs controls along the West Berlin border and all civilian traffic crossing the boundary was halted and subjected to a rigorous inspection before being allowed to proceed. The new measures were necessary, the East German regime announced, to halt the smuggling of butter and other scarce commodities into West Berlin. [14]

The West formally replied to Gromyko's note of May 5 by submitting its own list of terms for discussion. The Allies gave primary emphasis to the question of Germany and the implementation of the Geneva Agreement. As both Dulles and Eisenhower had made clear, the Soviet refusal to allow free all-German elections and the reunification of Germany as a result of these elections was making the road to the Summit extremely rocky. [15]

On June 11, Nikita Khrushchev, who had succeeded Bulganin as Soviet Premier during the latter part of February, wrote to President Eisenhower expressing Russian concern over what he termed "Western delay" in agreeing to a Summit. Khrushchev was particularly critical of Western insistence that German reunification be discussed. This insistence, he said, could only be considered as "proof of an intention to bury in its very embryo state the conference with the participation of the heads of Government." [16]

Interestingly, Khrushchev gives a revealing picture in his letter, of the Soviet attitude toward international guarantees:

> It is a known fact, that guarantees are usually given by a strong state (or states) to a weak state. In this connection the basic premise is the inequality of strength, and a strong state determines the conditions with respect to the weak state. A state to which guarantees are given is made dependent on the state which gives these guarantees. History contains many examples where a state that had given guarantees violated its obligations and thereby created a situation where there was no way out for the state to which the guarantees had been given. [17]

Following Khrushchev's letter, the attitude of Soviet officials in Berlin became more belligerent. On Monday, June 23, a 54-vehicle American convoy bound from Berlin to West Germany was denied entrance to the East German autobahn at the Soviet Babelsberg checkpoint. The American vehicles were part of the advance party of the 2nd Battle Group, Sixth Infantry, which is stationed in Berlin, and were en route to the Hohenfels training area near Nuremberg.* When the American convoy commander, Major Cecil R. Dansby, presented the required documentation to the Russian control officer, he was blandly informed it was insufficient. Henceforth, he was told, the Soviet Union would require a complete manifest of each vehicle and would insist on checking the identity papers of each individual. In accordance with his orders, Major Dansby refused to comply and returned with the convoy to the American sector. The following evening it left by rail using the standard documentation. [18]

The Soviet action in denying passage to the motor convoy was a deliberate attempt to expand the documentation requirements then existing for Allied movements between Berlin and West Germany. The Russian Military Authority in East Berlin had been informed of the battle group's move several days before it was to take place—a standard procedure—and had deliberately chosen to make an issue of the crossing. In so doing, it was closely following Moscow's new line of increasing pressure on the West.

* Because of the limited training areas in Berlin, the Allied garrisons there have regularly gone to West Germany for several weeks each year for sustained field training exercises.

Two weeks later, President Eisenhower replied to Khrushchev's letter. Like Khrushchev, the President betrayed a tone of annoyance.

I was frankly surprised by your letter of June 11, [Eisenhower said.] You complain about delay in preparation for a Summit meeting precisely at the moment when the Western powers have submitted a proposal for a serious and effective procedure for conducting these preparations. This refutes the allegation contained in your letter that the three Western powers are creating obstacles and impeding progress toward a Summit meeting. . . . In spite of the arbitrary action of the Soviet Government and its apparent unwillingness to negotiate seriously on concrete points at issue, the Western powers do not propose to abandon hope or to relax their efforts to seek solutions of the major outstanding problems.[19]

Already, however, East-West relations were in serious disrepair, and the Berlin episode was only one example. In Lebanon, Soviet agents took advantage of internal pressures threatening to topple the democratic government of President Chamoun. In Tripoli, Communist agitators led a series of riots designed to force a closing of the nearby Wheelus Air Base operated by the United States Air Force.

On July 15, the Soviet Foreign Ministry presented a new note to Ambassador Thompson in which the West was directly accused of whipping up the armaments race and fanning the flames of war. Attached to the belligerent Soviet note was a typical Russian gimmick— a "Draft Treaty on Friendship and Cooperation" containing the usual Communist provisions for the withdrawal of Western troops from Germany and the liquidation of "foreign" military bases. Significantly, the Soviets now made no request for a meeting at the Summit.[20]

The following day, President Eisenhower, yielding to a plea from President Chamoun of Lebanon, ordered United States Marines to Beirut to help the Lebanese government defend its position.[21] The President's action was greeted in Berlin by corresponding military alerts, first by the Soviets, then by the Allies. Russian tanks encircled the Western sectors as they had done following the Hungarian uprising in 1956. The American garrison was placed on a full state of combat readiness, and armored vehicles of the Berlin Command took up strategic positions throughout the city.

Two weeks later, East German Peoples Police (*Volkspolizei*) invaded the isolated American enclave of Steinstuecken in West Berlin and, using Gestapo tactics, began searching buildings and questioning residents reportedly in search of deserters from the East German army. The formal protest lodged by the American Sector Commander, Major General Barksdale Hamlett, was rejected by the Soviets on August 12. Hamlett was told once more to direct his objections to the "sovereign" German Democratic Republic.[22]

Throughout the months of September and October the diplomatic fusillade between East and West continued. A note from the Soviet Foreign Ministry on September 18 recommended a four-power commission to consider a German peace treaty and a meeting of East and West German delegates to discuss a "confederation" between the two. No request for a Summit conference was included and no mention made of the Geneva Agreement.[23]

On September 30, the American government rejected talks between East and West Germany until a government had been created in the Soviet zone which "truly reflects the will of the German people." "The regime established in the Soviet zone of Germany," the American note stated, "does not represent the will of the people of eastern Germany. It is rightly regarded by the people of all parts of Germany as a regime imposed by a foreign power and maintained in power by foreign forces. Since this regime has no mandate from the people it purports to speak for, it would violate any genuine concern for the interests of the German people to allow such a regime to participate in any discussions involving their future government." [24]

Following the American statement, the puppet East German regime itself got into the act. On October 29, Walter Ulbricht, then First Secretary of the East German Socialist Unity Party (SED), charged that the presence of Allied forces in Berlin was illegal. According to Ulbricht, Berlin belonged to the German Democratic Republic; and with patent disregard for the relevant four-power agreements, Ulbricht stated that "when various zones of occupation were created, Berlin was not made a fifth zone. It remained part of the Soviet zone of Germany."

In a dispatch from Bonn that same day, *New York Times* correspondent Sydney Gruson reported that "Herr Ulbricht's statement was interpreted here as signaling a new East German effort to exert pressure on West Berlin. . . . Nothing drastic or dramatic was expected from the Communists immediately. But it was noted here [in Bonn] that they had been trying to build a legal case for their claim to Berlin for almost a year." [25]

The following week John Foster Dulles took notice of the increasing Communist pressure on Berlin at a State Department press conference:

> Q.—Mr. Secretary, East German Communists have begun to say repeatedly that West Berlin belongs to East Germany and have begun to compare it to Quemoy. Do you see any potential danger in this kind of propaganda campaign?

> A.—No. I see no danger in it, because, as I pointed out, we are most solemnly committed to hold West Berlin, if need be by military force. That is a very solemn and formal three-power commitment to which the United States stands bound. I think as long as we stand firm there, and the Communists know we will stand firm, that there is no danger to West Berlin.[26]

Less than a week later, on November 10, 1958, at a meeting at the Polish Embassy in Moscow honoring the state visit of Wladyslaw Gomulka, the real Soviet attack on Berlin began. Speaking to the assembled guests, Nikita Khrushchev announced that the Soviet Union was determined to end the Allied occupation of Berlin. "The imperialists have turned the German question into an abiding source of international tension," Khrushchev said. "The ruling circles of Western Germany are doing everything to whip up military passions against the German Democratic Republic, against the Polish People's Republic, against all the socialist countries."

Khrushchev then launched into a heated attack against "Western militarism" and bluntly accused the United States, Britain, and France of violating the protocols of the Potsdam Agreement regarding German rearmament:

> What then is left of the Potsdam Agreement? One thing in effect: the so-called four-power status of Berlin, that is, a position in which the three western powers—the United States, Britain, and France—have the possibility of lording it in Western Berlin, turning that part of the city, which is the capital of the German Democratic Republic, into some kind of state within a state and, profiting by this, conducting subversive activities from Western Berlin

against the German Democratic Republic, against the Soviet Union and the other Warsaw Treaty countries.

Let the United States, France, and Britain themselves build their relations with the German Democratic Republic, let them reach agreement with it themselves if they are interested in any questions concerning Berlin. . . . They have violated the Potsdam Agreement repeatedly and with impunity, while we remain loyal to it as if nothing had changed. We have every reason to set ourselves free from obligations under the Potsdam Agreement, obligations which have outlived themselves and which the western powers are clinging to, and to pursue with regard to Berlin a policy that would spring from the interests of the Warsaw Treaty.[27]

For two weeks Khrushchev's charges went unanswered. Then, on November 26, Secretary of State Dulles replied during the course of one of his regular press conferences. When asked for his opinion as to why the Berlin question was reactivated at this time, Dulles responded as follows:

I was not surprised by it at all. I think that the Soviet Union and the Chinese Communists—what Khrushchev calls "the International Communist Movement"—is disposed periodically to try to probe in different areas of the world to develop, if possible, weak spots; to develop, if possible, differences. . . . The effort is, I think, periodically to try to find out whether they are up against firmness and strength and unity. If they find that, then I think the probing will cease.

✿   ✿   ✿

Q.—Mr. Secretary, last week late there was considerable evidence that on Saturday the Soviet Government would make its promised proposals about the status in Berlin and perhaps East Germany. The Soviet Government did not do so. Do you have any intimation as to how quickly it may act in this matter or why it did not act on Saturday?

A.—Well, somebody suggested to me that perhaps Mr. Khrushchev had submitted his idea to his legal advisers and that they had raised some questions which had caused a pause. Because the fact of the matter is . . . that he had based his case upon alleged breach of the Potsdam Agreement.

Now, the rights and status of the Allies in Berlin and the responsibilities and obligation of the Soviet Union do not in any way whatsoever derive from the Potsdam Agreements. . . . Therefore to say that because the Potsdam Agreements have been violated the Soviet Union is relieved of obligations which it assumed explicitly some four years later [under the New York and Paris Agreements of 1949 lifting the blockade] seems to be a *non sequitur,* to put it mildly.* [28]

The following day, November 27, 1958, the storm broke. In separate notes to the United States, Great Britain, and France, the Soviet Union demanded that the occupation of Berlin be terminated and that West Berlin be converted into a demilitarized free city. Six months, said the Russians, should be sufficient. If the West had not accepted its proposals within that time, then the Kremlin would conclude its own agreement with East Germany and end the occupation regardless.

As in June of 1948, the Russians once more were trying to force the West from Berlin. Unlike 1948, however, Moscow took no action. Instead, it merely announced what it intended to do and waited for the West to respond. But as surely as Stalin had imposed the Blockade, a new Berlin Crisis was at hand.

Khrushchev's note of November 27, 1958, is the formal beginning of the present deadlock in Berlin. As we have seen, the roots of the Russian note lie in the earlier gains of Soviet technology and, most particularly, in the successful launching of Soviet space satellites the year before. In the following paragraphs, the Russian message is reprinted in detail. No editorial comment is injected except for an occasional change to *italics* to emphasize a particular passage. For the most part, the document speaks for itself:

---

* As noted previously (see Chapter VI), the provisions of the Potsdam Agreement related to the overall settlement in Germany and not to Berlin. Indeed, the final Protocol of the Potsdam Conference did not mention Berlin except to refer to it (in one instance—Paragraph I, 4, (II), D) as the seat of the Allied Control Council.

Thus, as Dulles points out, Allied rights in the former German capital do not derive from the Potsdam Agreement but from the Protocols drafted earlier in the European Advisory Commission—Protocols which were ratified at Yalta (see Chapter II)—and from the agreements lifting the blockade in 1949 (see Chapter VII). Accordingly, in basing his case on the Potsdam Agreement, Khrushchev had chosen the wrong pact.

Also, since Khrushchev incorrectly based the Soviet case on the Potsdam Agreement, he is equally wrong in assuming that the agreements on Berlin were temporary and have "expired." The protocols drafted by the EAC—and ratified by Roosevelt, Churchill and Stalin—contained no time limit and clearly were to remain in effect until the Allies were able to agree on a suitable successor arrangement. By harping on the Potsdam Agreement, Khrushchev, who patently knew better, had imparted a slight tone of unreality to his attack which indeed, may have been intentional. As the subsequent Soviet note of November 27 will show, he wriggled out of this predicament nicely.

FROM THE SOVIET FOREIGN MINISTRY *
November 27, 1958

The government of the Union of Soviet Socialist Republics addresses the Government of the United States of America as one of the signatory powers of the Potsdam Agreement on the urgent question of the status of Berlin.

The problem of Berlin, which is situated in the center of the German Democratic Republic but the western part of which is cut off from the GDR as a result of foreign occupation deeply affects not only the national interests of the German people but also the interests of all nations desirous of establishing lasting peace in Europe.** Here in the historic capital of Germany two worlds are in direct contact and at every turn there tower the barricades of the "cold war." A situation of constant friction and tension has prevailed for many years in this city, which is divided into two parts. Berlin, which witnessed the greatest triumph of the joint struggle of our countries against Fascist aggression, has now become a dangerous center of contradiction between the Great Powers, allies in the last war. Its role in the relations between the Powers may be compared to a smoldering fuse that has been connected to a powder keg. Incidents arising here, even if they seem to be of local significance, may, in an atmosphere of heated passions, suspicion, and mutual apprehensions, cause a conflagration which will be difficult to extinguish. . . .

HISTORY OF OPPOSITION TO HITLER

To assess correctly the real importance of the Berlin problem confronting us today and to determine the existing possibilities for normalizing the situation in Berlin it is necessary to recall the development of the policy of the Powers parties to the anti-Hitler coalition with respect to Germany.

It is common knowledge that the USA, as well as Great Britain and France, by no means immediately came to the conclusion that it was essential to establish cooperation with the Soviet Union for

---

* Italics and passage headings added throughout.

** Here Khrushchev is implanting the idea that West Berlin belongs to East Germany. He refers to "the Western part" of Berlin as being "cut off from the GDR as a result of foreign occupation." The implications of this argument, as subsequent passages will make clear, is that the Soviet Union is trying to restore a "normal" situation in Berlin by ending the "foreign" occupation. Of course, this overlooks entirely that the East German regime—the so-called German Democratic Republic—is in itself an abnormal creation and retains its power in Germany only because of the bayonets of the Red Army.

the purpose of counteracting Hitlerite aggression, although the Soviet Union constantly indicated its readiness to do so. In the capitals of the Western states opposite tendencies prevailed for a long time and they became especially marked in the period of the Munich deal with Hitler. Entertaining the hope of controlling German militarism and pushing it eastward, the governments of the Western Powers tolerated and encouraged the policy of black-mail and threats pursued by Hitler and acts of direct aggression by Hitlerite Germany and its ally, Fascist Italy, against a number of peace-loving states.

It was only when Fascist Germany, upsetting the shortsighted calculations of the inspirers of Munich, turned against the Western Powers, when Hitler's army started moving westward, crushing Denmark, Norway, Belgium, and the Netherlands, and toppling France, that the governments of the USA and Great Britain had no alternative but to admit their miscalculations and embark upon the path of organizing, jointly with the Soviet Union, resistance to Fascist Germany, Italy and Japan. . . .*

When the peoples were celebrating victory over Hitlerite Germany a conference of the heads of government of the Soviet Union, the USA and Great Britain was held in Potsdam in order to work out a joint policy with respect to postwar Germany. . . . The entire content of this agreement was directed toward creating conditions precluding the possibility of yet another attack by Germany against peace-loving states, toward preventing German militarists from unleashing another world war so that Germany, having abandoned forever the mirage of a policy of conquest, might make a firm start on the road to peaceful development.

. . . However, further developments deviated a great deal from

---

* The above rewriting of the history of the early opposition to Hitler is one of the literary highlights of the Soviet message. In preparing it, the Soviet Foreign Ministry seems to have overlooked that from 1930 to 1933 the Soviet Union, through its international apparatus of the Comintern, directed the German Communist Party to collaborate with the Nazis in undermining the German Weimar Republic, leading directly to Hitler's rise to power. That during the period 1933–1939 the Soviet Union concluded no less than twelve commercial treaties with Nazi Germany materially assisting in the buildup of Hitler's military power. That on August 23, 1939, the Soviet Union backed away from negotiations then in progress with Great Britain and France in Moscow regarding an anti-Hitler pact, and concluded the notorious Molotov-Ribbentrop Agreement which set the stage for the subsequent invasion of Poland. That in spite of repeated warnings from the Western powers, particularly Great Britain, of an impending German attack, the Soviet Government continued to provide vast quantities of raw materials to Nazi Germany until the very date that Hitler's armies marched across the Russian frontier on June 22, 1941. And finally, that in April, 1941, the Soviet Union signed a joint neutrality pact with Japan, thereby clearing the way for the Japanese attack on Pearl Harbor on December 7, 1941.

the direction mapped out at Potsdam. Relations between the USSR and the Three Western Powers kept deteriorating. Mutual distrust and suspicion kept growing and have now developed into unfriendly relations.

THE POLICIES OF WINSTON CHURCHILL

The policy of the Western Powers was increasingly influenced by forces obsessed with hatred for Socialist and Communist ideas but which concealed during the war their hostile designs against the Soviet Union. As a result, the course was set in the West toward the utmost aggravation of the ideological struggle headed by aggressive leaders, opponents of the peaceful coexistence of states. The signal for this was given to the United States and to other Western countries by W. Churchill in his notorious Fulton speech in March 1946.*

The conflict between the two ideologies—a struggle of minds and convictions—in itself could not have been particularly detrimental to relations between states. The ideological struggle has never abated and it will continue so long as there are different views on the structure of society. But, unfortunately, the pronouncements of W. Churchilll and those who share his views influenced the minds of other Western statesmen, which had the most regrettable consequences. Governmental bodies and the armed forces joined in the ideological struggle that blazed forth. The results are universally known. Instead of developing cooperation between the major Great Powers, the world was split into opposing military alignments and competition began in the manufacture and stockpiling of atomic and hydrogen weapons. . . .

ALLEGED WESTERN VIOLATIONS OF THE POTSDAM AGREEMENT

A particularly drastic change in relations between the USA, as well as Britain and France, and the Soviet Union occurred when those powers shifted to pursuing a policy in Germany that ran counter to the Potsdam Agreement. The first violation of the Potsdam Agreement was the refusal by the governments of the USA, Great Britain, and France to honor their commitments under the aforesaid agreement regarding the transfer to the Soviet Union of the agreed amount of industrial equipment from West Germany,

---

* The Soviet accusations against the West, and particularly against Sir Winston Churchill, ignore the fact that Sir Winston's Fulton speech came four weeks after the Moscow speech of Premier Stalin delivered on February 9, 1946, announcing that the wartime alliance had ended and that the world revolution of communism was to be resumed.

in partial compensation for the destruction and damage inflicted upon the national economy of the USSR by the aggression of Hitlerite Germany.

But the matter did not end there. With every passing year the governments of the USA and Great Britain drifted farther and farther away from the principles underlying the Potsdam Agreement. The same road was followed by France which, although it acceded to the Potsdam Agreement later, cannot, of course, disdain its share of the responsibility for carrying out this agreement.*

MILITARISM IN WEST GERMANY

Having embarked upon the restoration of the military and economic potential of West Germany, the Western Powers revived and strengthened the very forces that had forged Hitler's war machine. Had the Western Powers honored the Potsdam Agreement they would have prevented the German militarists from regaining their positions, checked revanche tendencies, and not permitted Germany to create an army and an industry manufacturing the means of destruction. . . .

It is evident that the bitter lessons of the murderous war have been lost on certain Western statesmen, who are once again dragging out the notorious Munich policy of inciting German militarism against the Soviet Union, their recent comrade in arms.**

* Reparations deliveries to the Soviet Union from the Western zones of Germany were not halted until July 8, 1948, two weeks after the imposition of the Berlin Blockade and six weeks after the Russians had walked out of the Allied Control Council—the organization set up explicitly by the Potsdam Agreement for governing Germany. But even before reparations deliveries to the Soviet Union were halted, Russia had milked the Western zones for over two billion dollars worth of materials and the Soviet zone for eight times that figure. Also, and though Khrushchev studiously refrains from mentioning it, reparations deliveries to the Soviet Union were made contingent by the Potsdam Agreement upon "exchange for an equivalent value of food, coal, potash, zinc, timber, clay products, petroleum products, and such other commodities as may be agreed upon" which were to be furnished by the Soviets to the West. Items, it need not be added, which were never delivered by Russia in spite of having received reparations from the Western zones for over three years.

It should also be noted that here Khrushchev is still basing his case on the Potsdam Agreement which, as has been indicated, did not refer to the occupation of Berlin but to occupation policy for Germany as a whole. But in mentioning the Potsdam Agreement, Khrushchev declines to list those elements which are still in effect and from which Russia continues to benefit. Among these are the temporary recognition of the Oder-Neisse line as Germany's eastern frontier, the division of East Prussia between Russia and Poland, the delivery of a sizable portion of the German merchant marine to the Soviet Union, and the recognition of the "Polish Provisional Government of National Unity" (Communist) as the legal Polish Government.

** As is well known, the rearmament of West Germany began only after the Soviet

The Peaceful Aims of East Germany

. . . Whereas in West Germany, whose development was directed by the United States, Britain, and France, a government took office the representatives of which do not conceal their hatred for the Soviet Union and often openly advertise the similarity of their aspirations to the plans of the Hitlerite aggressors, in East Germany a government was formed which has irrevocably broken with Germany's aggressive past. State and public affairs in the German Democratic Republic are governed by a constitution fully in keeping with the principles of the Potsdam Agreement and the finest progressive traditions of the German nation. The rule of monopolies and Junkers has been abolished forever in the GDR. Nazism has been eradicated and a number of other social and economic reforms have been carried out, which have destroyed the basis for a revival of militarism and have made the German Democratic Republic an important factor of peace in Europe. . . .

The Soviet Union Stands for Nonintervention

There is only one conclusion to be drawn from the foregoing: The Potsdam Agreement has been grossly violated by the Western Powers. It is like the trunk of a tree, once mighty and fruitful, but now cut down with its heart taken out. The lofty goals for which the Potsdam Agreement was concluded have long since been renounced by the Western Powers, and what they are actually doing in Germany is diametrically opposed to what the Potsdam Agreement had envisaged. The crux of the matter is not, of course, that the social and political systems of the GDR and the FRG are basically different. The Soviet Government considers that the solution of the question of social structure of both German States is the concern of the Germans themselves. *The Soviet Union stands for complete noninterference in the internal affairs of the German people or in those of any other people.**

. . . The recent elections for the People's Chamber and local

---

Union demonstrated its intention of dominating Western Europe, and indeed the entire free world. At first, rearmament was strongly opposed in West Germany and was accepted reluctantly after the Soviets had created a 100,000 man "People's Police in Barracks" in East Germany, and had sponsored the invasion of South Korea. Even today the West German Bundeswehr is numerically inferior to the forces under arms in the Soviet zone—a fact even more significant when one considers that the Soviet zone has only one-fourth as many people as West Germany.

* East Berlin, June 17, 1953?? Budapest, October 23, 1956??

bodies of the German Democratic Republic are yet another striking indication that the population of the GDR unanimously sup-
ports the policy of its Government, which is aimed at preserving
peace and reuniting Germany on a peaceful and democratic basis,
and is fully determined to defend its Socialist gains. . . .

BERLIN

Actually, of all the Allied agreements on Germany, only one is
being carried out today. It is the agreement on the so-called quadripartite status of Berlin.* On the basis of that status, the Three
Western Powers are ruling the roost in West Berlin, turning it into
a kind of state within a state and using it as a center from which
to pursue subversive activity against the GDR, the Soviet Union,
and the other parties to the Warsaw Treaty. The United States,
Great Britain and France are freely communicating with West
Berlin through lines of communication passing through the territory and airspace of the German Democratic Republic, which they
do not even want to recognize.

The governments of the Three Powers are seeking to keep in
force the long obsolete part of the wartime agreements that governed the occupation of Germany and entitled them in the past to
stay in Berlin. At the same time, as stated above, the Western
Powers have grossly violated the Four-Power agreements, including the Potsdam Agreement, which is the most concentrated expression of the obligations of the powers with respect to Germany.
Moreover, the Four-Power agreements on the occupation of Germany, which the governments of the USA, Great Britain, and
France invoke in support of their rights in West Berlin, were approved by the Potsdam Agreement or adopted for its implementation. In other words, the Three Powers are demanding, for their
own sake, the preservation of the occupation privileges based on
those Four-Power agreements, which they themselves have violated.

If the USA, Great Britain and France are indeed staying in Berlin by virtue of the right stemming from the aforementioned international agreements and, primarily, from the Potsdam Agreement,
this implies their duty to abide by these agreements. Those who
have grossly violated these agreements have lost the right to main-

---

* Here Khrushchev moves away from the idea that Allied rights in Berlin are
based on the Potsdam Agreement—i.e., away from the stand he took at the
Polish Embassy on November 10, and which Dulles referred to as a "*non-
sequitur.*" Khrushchev's method of doing so, as illustrated in the next paragraph,
is extremely clever and indicates the adeptness of the Soviets at bending words
(and agreements) to suit their purpose.

tain their occupation regime in Berlin or any other part of Germany. . . .

It is well known that the conventional way to put an end to occupation is for the parties that were at war to conclude a peace treaty offering the defeated country the conditions necessary for the re-establishment of normal life.

The fact that Germany still has no peace treaty is the fault primarily of the governments of the USA, Britain, and France, which have never seemed to be in sympathy with the idea of drafting such a treaty. It is known that the governments of the Three Powers reacted negatively to every approach the Soviet Government has made to them regarding the preparation of a peace treaty with Germany.*

. . . The result is a veritable vicious circle: The U.S. Government is objecting to the drafting of a German peace treaty by referring to the absence of a united German state while at the same time hampering the reunification of Germany by rejecting the only real possibility of solving this problem through agreement between the two German states.

Is it not because the Western Powers would like to prolong indefinitely their privileges in West Germany and the occupation regime in West Berlin that they take the position on the question of drafting a peace treaty? It is becoming increasingly clear that such is the actual state of affairs.

Allied Agreements no Longer Binding

An obviously absurd situation has thus arisen, in which the Soviet Union seems to be supporting and maintaining favorable conditions for the Western Powers in their activities against the Soviet Union and its Allies under the Warsaw Treaty.

It is obvious that the Soviet Union, just as other parties to the Warsaw Treaty, cannot tolerate such a situation any longer. For the occupation regime in West Berlin to continue would be tantamount to recognizing something like a privileged position of the NATO countries, for which there is, of course, no reason whatsoever.

. . . It should be clear for anybody with common sense that

---

* The West, of course, has not refused to sign a peace treaty with Germany and repeatedly has suggested methods for completing such a document based on free elections. But the Soviets have insisted that a peace treaty must be signed with "both" German states and not as a result of free elections—a proposal which the Western powers have declined because, as Dulles points out, the East German regime does not reflect the will of the German people—the people to whom all four Allies have an obligation as a result of the defeat of Nazism.

the Soviet Union cannot maintain a situation in West Berlin that is detrimental to its lawful interests, its security, and the security of other Socialist countries. It would be well to bear in mind that the Soviet Union is not a Jordan or an Iran and will never tolerate any methods of pressure upon it for the purpose of imposing conditions advantageous to the opposing NATO military bloc. But this is precisely what the Western Powers are trying to get the Soviet Union to endorse in their attempts to retain their rights of occupants in West Berlin.

Can the Soviet Union disregard all these facts, which affect the vital security interests of the Soviet Union, of its ally—the German Democratic Republic—and of all the member states of the Warsaw Defense Treaty? Of course not! The Soviet Government can no longer consider itself bound by that part of the Allied agreements on Germany that has assumed an inequitable character and is being used for the purpose of maintaining the occupation regime in West Berlin and interfering in the internal affairs of the GDR.

In this connection, the Government of the USSR hereby notifies the United States Government that the Soviet Union regards as null and void the "Protocol of the Agreement between the Governments of the Union of Soviet Socialist Republics, the United States of America, and the United Kingdom on the zones of occupation in Germany and on the administration of Greater Berlin," of September 12, 1944, and the related supplementary agreements, including the agreement on the control machinery in Germany, concluded between the governments of the USSR, the USA, Great Britain, and France on May 1, 1945, i.e., the agreements that were intended to be in effect during the first years after the capitulation of Germany.

NEGOTIATIONS WITH THE GDR WILL BEGIN

Pursuant to the foregoing and proceeding from the principle of respect for the sovereignty of the German Democratic Republic, the Soviet Government will enter into negotiations with the Government of the GDR at an appropriate time with a view to transferring to the German Democratic Republic the functions temporarily performed by the Soviet authorities by virtue of the above-mentioned Allied agreements and under the agreement between the USSR and the GDR of September 20, 1955. The best way to solve the Berlin problem would undoubtedly be to adopt a decision based on the enforcement of the Potsdam Agreement on Germany. But this is possible only in the event that the three Western Powers return to a policy in German Affairs that would be pursued jointly with the USSR and in conformity with the spirit and principles of the Potsdam Agreement. In the present circumstances this would mean the withdrawal of the Federal Republic of Germany from NATO with the simultaneous withdrawal of the German Democratic Republic from the Warsaw Treaty, and an agreement whereby in accordance with the principles of the Potsdam Agreement, neither of the two German states would have armed forces except those needed to maintain law and order at home and guard the frontiers.

Soviet Union Seeks no Annexation

. . . Some ill-wishers of the Soviet Union may of course try to interpret the position of the Soviet Government in the question of the occupation regime in Berlin as the striving for some sort of annexation. It goes without saying that such an interpretation has nothing in common with reality. The Soviet Union, just as other Socialist states, has no territorial claims. In its policy, it is firmly guided by the principle of condemning annexation, i.e., the seizure of foreign territories and forced annexation of foreign peoples. This principle was proclaimed by Lenin, the founder of the Soviet state, as far back as the first days of Soviet power in Russia.

The USSR does not seek any conquests. All it wants is to put an end to the abnormal and dangerous situation that has developed in Berlin because of the continued occupation of its western sectors by the USA, Great Britain and France.*

The Soviet Solution

Essentially speaking, the only interest the United States, Great Britain and France have in West Berlin consists in using this "front line city," as it is vociferously called in the West, as a vantage point from which to carry on hostile activities against the socialist countries. The Western powers gain nothing else from their stay in Berlin as occupants. The ending of the illegal occupation of West Berlin would cause no harm whatever, either to the United States or to Great Britain or France. It would, on the other hand, sub-

---

* The above paragraphs should be read in light of Soviet actions in Poland in 1939, in Finland in 1939–40, and in the Baltic states, Bessarabia and East Prussia immediately following the war. The key phrase in this section is Khrushchev's definition of annexation, "i.e., the seizure of *foreign* territories." As subsequent paragraphs will show, the Soviet Union does not consider West Berlin as "foreign" territory but as legitimately belonging to the German Democratic Republic. Accordingly, for the East German regime to later absorb it would not be "annexation" in the Marxist sense.

stantially improve the international atmosphere in Europe and set peoples' minds at rest in all countries.

Of course, the most correct and natural way to solve the problem would be for the western part of Berlin, *now actually detached from the GDR*, to be reunited with its eastern part and for Berlin to become a unified city within that state in whose territory it is situated.

ECONOMIC GUARANTEE TO WEST BERLIN

However, the Soviet Government, taking into account the present unrealistic policy of the USA as well as of Great Britain and France with respect to the German Democratic Republic, cannot but foresee the difficulties the Western powers have in contributing to such a solution of the Berlin problem. At the same time, it is guided by the concern that the process of liquidating the occupation regime may not involve any painful break in the established way of life of the West Berlin population.

. . . The Soviet Government considers that when the foreign occupation is ended the population of West Berlin must be granted the right to have whatever way of life it wishes for itself. If the inhabitants of West Berlin desire to preserve the present way of life based on private capitalistic ownership, that is up to them. The USSR, for its part, would respect any choice of the West Berliners in this matter.*

FREE CITY PROPOSAL

In view of all these considerations, the Soviet Government on its part would consider it possible to solve the West Berlin question at the present time by the conversion of West Berlin into an independent political unit—a free city, without any state, including both existing German states, interfering in its life. Specifically, it might be possible to agree that the territory of the free city be demilitarized and that no armed forces be contained therein. The free city, West Berlin, could have its own government and run its own economic, administrative, and other affairs.

The Four Powers which shared in the administration of Berlin after the war could, as well as both of the German states, undertake to respect the status of West Berlin as a free city. . . .**

---

* But what about Ulbricht and the GDR—the country of which, according to Khrushchev, West Berlin is a part?

** Acceptance of this provision, of course, would mean the introduction of the Red Army into West Berlin, and a concommitant curtailment of its freedom and independence. In addition, if the Soviets were able to establish themselves in

For its part, the Soviet Government would have no objection to the United Nations also sharing, in one way or other, in observing the free-city status of West Berlin.

NECESSITY FOR AGREEMENTS WITH THE GDR

It is obvious that, considering the specific position of West Berlin, which lies within the territory of the GDR and is cut off from the outside world, the question would arise of some kind of arrangement with the German Democratic Republic concerning guarantees of unhindered communications between the free city and the outside world—both to the East and to the West—with the object of free movement of passenger and freight traffic. In its turn West Berlin would undertake not to permit on its territory any hostile subversive activity directed against the GDR or any other state.*

FREE CITY A CONCESSION

Naturally, it would also be realized that the GDR's agreement to set up *on its territory* such an independent political organism as a free city of West Berlin would be a concession, a definite sacrifice on the part of the GDR for the sake of strengthening peace in Europe, and for the sake of the national interest of the German people as a whole.

THE THREAT OF UNILATERAL ACTION

The Soviet Government, guided by a desire to normalize the situation in Berlin in the interest of European peace and in the interest of a peaceful and independent development of Germany, has resolved to effect measures on its part designed to liquidate the occupation regime in Berlin. It hopes that the Government of the USA will show a proper understanding of these motives and make a realistic approach to the Berlin question.

. . . In case this proposal is not acceptable to the government

---

West Berlin, many Berliners, for safety alone, would be forced to make their peace with the East. Many also, seeing the handwriting on the wall, would turn to communism for their own well being.

* An arrangement of this sort would entitle the Soviets, who would now have authority in West Berlin, to prohibit any form of life there which they might deem "hostile" or "subversive." Certainly included in this category would be an uncensored press, a free radio, and the right of free assembly. Indeed, Khrushchev has made it clear that West Berlin as a free and independent city would not exist.

of the USA then there will no longer remain any topic for negotiations between the former occupying powers on the Berlin question.

THE ULTIMATUM

The Soviet Government seeks to have the necessary change in Berlin's situation take place in a cold atmosphere, without haste and unnecessary friction, with maximum possible consideration for the interests of the parties concerned. Obviously, a certain period of time will be necessary for the powers which occupied Germany after the defeat of Hitler's Wehrmacht to agree on proclaiming West Berlin a free city, provided, naturally, that the Western powers display due interest in this proposal.

. . . *In view of this, the Soviet Government proposes to make no changes in the present procedure for military traffic of the USA, Great Britain, and France from West Berlin to the FRG for half a year.* It regards such a period as fully sufficient to provide a sound basis for the solution of the questions connected with the change in Berlin's situation and to prevent a possibility of any complications, provided, naturally, that the governments of the Western powers do not deliberately seek such complications. During the above-mentioned period the parties will have an opportunity to prove in practice their desire to ease international tension by settling the Berlin question.

If the above mentioned period is not utilized to reach an adequate agreement, the Soviet Union will then carry out the planned measures through an agreement with the GDR. It is envisaged that the German Democratic Republic, like any other independent state, must fully deal with questions concerning its space, i.e., exercise its sovereignty on land, on water, and in the air. At the same time, there will terminate all contacts still maintained between the representatives of the armed forces and other officials of the Soviet Union in Germany and corresponding representatives of the armed forces and other officials of the USA, Great Britain, and France in questions pertaining to Berlin.

ONLY MADMEN . . .

The Government of the Soviet Union would like to hope that the problem of normalizing the situation in Berlin, which life itself raises before our states as a natural necessity, will in any case be solved in accordance with considerations of statesmenship, the interests of peace between peoples, without the unnecessary nervous strain and intensification of a "cold war."

Methods of blackmail and reckless threats of force will be least of all appropriate in solving such a problem as the Berlin question. Such methods will not help solve a single question, but can only bring the situation to the danger point. But only madmen can go to the length of unleashing another world war over the preservation of privileges of occupiers in West Berlin. If such madmen should really appear, there is no doubt that strait jackets can be found for them. If the statesmen responsible for the policy of the Western powers are guided by feelings of hatred for communism and the socialist countries in their approach to the Berlin question as well as other international problems, no good will come out of it.*

Sweetness and Light

The Soviet Government believes that it would be sensible to recognize the situation prevailing in the world and to create normal relations for the coexistence of all states, to develop international trade, to build relations between our countries on the basis of the well known principles of mutual respect for one another's sovereignty and territorial integrity, non-aggression, non-interference in one another's internal affairs, equality and mutual benefit.

The Soviet Union and its people and government are sincerely striving for the restoration of good relations with the United States of America, relations based on trust, which are quite feasible as shown by the experience in the joint struggle against the Hitlerite aggressors, and which in peacetime would hold out to our countries nothing but the advantages of mutually enriched spiritual and material cooperation between our peoples, and to all other people the blessings of a tranquil life under conditions of an enduring peace.[29]

. ——— .

The implications of the Soviet note are clear. Russia had decided to force the Western powers from Berlin—to incorporate the city's West-

---

* This is very similar to the argument advanced against the stopping of Hitler's march into the Rhineland in 1936, into Austria and Czechoslovakia in 1938, and into Poland in 1939. "Why fight for Danzig?"

All dictators seem to be able to credit their own position with sanity and anyone who would oppose them with madness. Thus, just as it would have been "madness" according to Hitler for Britain and France to have gone to war in 1936 to prevent him from going into the Rhineland, so would it be madness for the Western powers to oppose Khrushchev, and fight for Berlin in 1958.

ern sectors into the GDR—and, buttressed by the achievement of Soviet technology, had selected this time to begin. But Khrushchev's thrust was varied. First he accused the Western powers of seeking to perpetuate a state of war with Germany by clinging to out-dated occupation agreements. Then he charged the West with violating these very agreements; of no longer deserving the rights of occupiers, and of seeking to use their position in Germany to disrupt the "normal" order of things in the "Socialist camp." Thus, while he himself was attempting to change the situation—attempting to annex West Berlin and deny its citizens the freedom they presently enjoy—it was the West that was blamed for revanchist aspirations and for menacing the peace of Europe.

From this characterization, Khrushchev moved on to the postwar development of Germany; to the creation of what he termed the Hitlerite state of the Federal Republic and the new and "democratic" regime in East Germany which had "irrevocably broken with Germany's aggressive past." Clearly, this was an attempt to gain sympathy and support for the tyrannical Ulbricht state from those perhaps unfamiliar with the Berlin question, from the emerging nations of Asia and Africa, from the neutrals and the uncommitted.

The ruse of a "free city" which Khrushchev suggested was in line with this attempt. By making Soviet demands outwardly palatable, the West would be hard put to explain their objections. Unlike the blockade, which had cast the Russians in the role of aggressors, the Soviet note of November 27 placed the West on the defensive—placed the Allies in the position of explaining why they were against the Soviet proposals, and why, as Khrushchev would have it, they were against ending the remnants of World War II.

Khrushchev's "free city," of course, would have been free from nothing save freedom itself. The introduction of Soviet forces to West Berlin territory, combined with the prohibition of what the Communists termed "subversive" activity there, would have meant the end of the city's independent existence.

And after giving the West an undisguised ultimatum of six months, Khrushchev labeled any so foolish to oppose his plan as madmen for whom strait jackets could be found. Only madmen, he said, would risk world war for the preservation of their privileges as occupiers. But now Khrushchev was talking to the West and not to the neutrals; to those who felt an accommodation with Russia was possible, and to those who shrank back from the necessity of halting aggression in its infancy. To be sure, it was not for their rights as occupiers that the West would fight in Berlin, but for the freedom of the two and a half million people who composed the Western sectors and who for the past thirteen years had devoted themselves to the cause of freedom. But this was a point Khrushchev sought to obscure, and by making it look as though the West opposed his plan just to perpetuate their rights as occupiers the Soviet leader was preempting the moral justification for Western resistance.

Last, but certainly not least, Khrushchev also sought to gain a greater degree of recognition for the puppet East German regime and the Soviet henchmen who controlled it. By continually referring to the GDR as though it was a sovereign state, indeed, by insisting that the West would have to deal with it, and that Berlin was a part of it, Khrushchev was endeavoring to have the world recognize what he considered an accomplished fact. Namely, that the sixteen million of people of East Germany had no voice other than that of Walter Ulbricht.

10

Negotiations under Pressure

(November 1958—August 1959)

THE SOVIET NOTE CAUSED the usual gastronomical reaction among the Western powers, who cautiously withheld comment while trying hard to digest its contents. It had been ten years since the last major Soviet drive on Berlin and therefore it took some time for the significance of the Russian ultimatum to register. The Allies viewed Berlin as merely a part of the overall German question and accordingly, were not prepared at first for the specific nature of the Kremlin's demands. But in Berlin and West Germany, the Soviet announcement caused intense alarm and people anxiously waited to see what course the Allies would take.

The Berliners were not reassured by the first soundings emanating from Washington and London on the evening of November 27. Given the belligerent and insulting tone of the Soviet note, it would not have been out of place for the Western powers to have summarily dismissed it. Indeed, the fact that this wasn't done was viewed in many quarters as a partial Western concession.

Instead of dismissing it, the State Department in Washington issued a brief announcement that they had received and were studying the

Russian message. Fortunately, the tone of the State Department announcement was firm:

> The United States, [it said,] along with Britain and France, is solemnly committed to the security of the Western sectors of Berlin. Two and a quarter million West Berliners in reliance thereon, have convincingly and courageously demonstrated the good fruits of freedom.
>
> Another consideration is that the United States will not acquiesce in a unilateral repudiation by the Soviet Union of its obligations and responsibilities . . . in relation to Berlin. Neither will it enter into any agreement with the Soviet Union which . . . would have the end result of abandoning the people of West Berlin to hostile domination.[1]

The State Department reply was personally drafted by Secretary Dulles. President Eisenhower, who was then vacationing in Augusta, withheld comment "pending receipt of an official translation of the Kremlin message." [2]

Dismay in West Germany at the lack of a more positive American response was accentuated by Secretary Dulles' comment in a press conference the day before, that if the Russians insisted on turning control of the routes to Berlin over to the Ulbricht regime, the United States might agree to deal with the East Germans as "agents" of the Soviet Union.

> Q.—Mr. Secretary, what if, despite this responsibility, the Soviets go ahead and turn over to the East German authorities the check points on the autobahn . . . would we deal with the East German officials who would man these check points . . . ?
>
> A.—Well, we would certainly not deal with them in any way which involved our acceptance of the East German regime as a substitute for the Soviet Union.
>
> Q.—Does that mean that we might deal with them as agents of the Soviet Union?
>
> A.—We might, yes. . . . It all depends upon the details of just how they act and how they function. . . .[3]

When seen in their full context, however, Dulles' remarks are not as compromising as they at first appeared. The Western press unfortunately had played up the Secretary's answer to this particular question and virtually ignored other and, indeed, much firmer statements which he had made during the course of the interview. Specifically, Dulles had been asked whether the U.S. had ruled out the use of force should the East Germans attempt to block our access to Berlin and he had replied: "We have not ruled out any of our rights at all including the use of force if necessary."

But since Dulles' latter remarks had not been emphasized in the news, the American response to the Soviet note on November 27 seemed dishearteningly cautious. As in June of 1948, once the average Berliner heard about the Russian demand, he doubted whether the West would remain. Persons from all over the city began calling up their American acquaintances to find out if the United States was planning to leave. Reflecting the city's anxiety, Governing Mayor Willy Brandt issued a nervous statement reminding the world that Berlin was only a part of the larger conflict between East and West —that Berlin was the result, not the cause, of the friction between communism and democracy. Indeed, Brandt's statement betrayed the fear common to most Berliners at the time that a deal might be made with the Russians at their expense. "There is no isolated solution of the Berlin question," the Mayor said. "If there is to be a contribution made toward relaxation of tension . . . then it is not a matter of the Berlin question but of overcoming the division of Germany."

"Now particularly the people of Berlin," he continued, "has trust in its friends throughout the world. In the coming weeks it is a matter not only of the fate of our city but of the German people." [4]

Ernst Lemmer, party leader of the CDU in Berlin, sounded a note of defiance. "We will never permit ourselves to be converted," he said, "into a No Man's Land in the heart of Germany and Europe." From Bonn, Chancellor Konrad Adenauer added his voice to those calling for a firm stand and stated that "everything would be done to preserve the status of Berlin." [5]

In London, on the other hand, reaction to the Soviet note was noticeably weak. A *New York Times* dispatch by Walter H. Waggoner reported that "a sense of relief seemed evident in Foreign Office quarters, where the note was regarded as more moderate than might have been expected." The six-month respite in Khrushchev's proposal, he said, was regarded by responsible opinion as "a promising aspect." [6]

Unofficial opinion in Great Britain was a great deal more critical of the Soviet note, however. The London *Times* in a lead editorial condemned the Russian ultimatum as "the opening move in a very long and tough tussle of wills." "Clearly enough," it continued, "the prospect is in many ways as serious . . . as it was over ten years ago when Stalin was planning to blockade Berlin." In Paris, French Information Minister Jacques Soustelle attacked the Soviet note but declined further comment until its full text had been received by the French government.[7]

By November 28, the seriousness of the Soviet note was apparent in the West. Following continued reports of the tension which had been aroused in Berlin, Secretary of State Dulles journeyed from his offices in Foggy Bottom across the Potomac to the Pentagon where he conferred with Secretary of Defense Neil McElroy for more than an hour.[8] Vice President Nixon, then in London, denounced the Soviet proposal in vigorous terms. The *New York Times,* reflecting perhaps the Administration's position, was beside itself with indignation. "The history of diplomacy," it stated editorially, "knows many tendentious and self-serving documents, but there is surely none among them so arrogant and insolent, so cynical and so full of distortions and barefaced lies as the latest Soviet note on Berlin." [9]

The Communists by this time were keeping up a steady pressure on the West, stressing simultaneously the reasonableness of the Soviet proposals and the consequences which might result from their rejection. At his press conference on November 27 announcing the Russian plan for Berlin, Premier Khrushchev had worn a gold dove of peace on his lapel to emphasize, as he put it, "the peaceful nature of Soviet intentions." The conference itself had lasted ninety minutes and Khrushchev's manner had been friendly to the point of comradery. He wisecracked to newsmen that the Soviet Union at last had embarked on the road to peace, and bantered good-naturedly during the question and answer period when asked about specific passages. Significantly, throughout the entire ninety-minute session Khrushchev not once referred to any of the advisers who accompanied him nor did he use any notes. His answers frequently paraphrased or quoted the ultimatum exactly, and indeed, convinced many of those who were present that he had written it himself.[10]

On November 29, Walter Ulbricht added the basso to Khrushchev's tenor. For two days now the East German press had trumpeted the news that Moscow's ultimatum was a Communist victory. When asked by a Western correspondent in East Berlin what would happen if the Allies chose to answer the Soviet proposals with an airlift, Ulbricht replied that such a move "would be considered a military threat" to East Germany and would be answered accordingly.[11]

But Ulbricht's tin horn was the exception. Having struck up the music once more in Berlin, most Russian spokesmen responded with harmonious tones. A Soviet Embassy official in East Berlin stated that the six-month time limit for proposed negotiations was not "rigid." According to a report quoted by the West German News Agency, the Russian official implied "that the Soviet Union might delay the transfer of its Berlin responsibilities to the East German Government if the negotiations showed any hope of success." [12]

Likewise, at an Albanian Embassy reception in Moscow on November 29, Khrushchev himself made much the same comment. No text of Khrushchev's impromptu remarks was kept, but the agreed gist was that Russia would not act unilaterally to alter Berlin's status in six months, providing East-West talks had begun within that time.[13]

Khrushchev's pleas for parley however fooled no one in the U.S., and the official American position continued to harden. On November 30, Secretary Dulles visited President Eisenhower in Augusta, and upon leaving, read a short statement to the press emphasizing American determination. The statement was deliberately terse—its terseness, in fact, had an extremely reassuring quality. "The President reiterated," Dulles said, "our government's firm purpose that the United States will not enter into any arrangement or embark on any course of conduct which will have the effect of abandoning the responsibilities which the United States, with Great Britain and France, has formally assumed for the freedom and security of the people of West Berlin." [14] Dulles' announcement was a way of advising the world that the United States intended to stand firm.

In Berlin itself the United States also took decisive steps to underline its determination to remain. On the same date as Dulles' visit to Augusta, General Henry I. Hodes, Commander-in-Chief of the United States Army in Europe, arrived in Berlin on a special inspection. Hodes' visit was a none too subtle reminder to the Communists that the Allied position in the isolated city was supported by more than the 11,000 men of the Western garrison. It also reemphasized to the Berliners that the United States was militarily prepared to defend its position in Berlin with whatever force was necessary. Hodes' visit was widely publicized in the West Berlin press and his arrival just three days after the Soviet ultimatum did much to buttress the morale of the Western sectors. He stated emphatically that the United States was going to stay in Berlin and insisted, as General Clay had earlier, that "no dependents of servicemen have been evacuated and none are going to be." [15] Following General Hodes' assurances, everyone in Berlin, Allied as well as German, breathed an audible sigh of relief. Mayor Brandt said that the people of the city now knew they would not be forsaken, and in the American colony, mothers and housewives once more went about their business with a smile on their lips, firmly aware of their role in the city's defense.

There were also indications that by this time official British thinking had also hardened. In an interview on the American television program, "Meet the Press," Iain MacLeod, Minister of Labor in the Macmillan Cabinet, stated positively that Great Britain intended to stay in Berlin. "Just because someone twitches the strings," he said, "doesn't necessarily mean that we should dance. It should be made quite clear that we have our rights in Berlin—that we intend to stay there." [16]

And while the West was fortifying its position, the East German regime kept up its steady propaganda barrage designed to shake Berlin's morale. Elections were due to take place in the Western sectors on Sunday, December 7, and the Communists clearly hoped to capitalize on the fear which the Soviet ultimatum had produced. Already there had been a noted economic reaction in West Berlin following the Russian announcement. Between six and seven million dollars in personal savings had been withdrawn from the banks and nervous housewives had begun to stock up on non-perishable items like coffee and sugar from their neighborhood grocer.

On December 1, Lothar Bolz, Foreign Minister of the puppet East German state, attempted to add further to the Berliners' feeling of insecurity by announcing that the Allied occupation agreements no longer were valid. Speaking before a widely publicized political rally in East Berlin, Bolz stated that as a result of the Soviet note "no agreements exist between the Soviet Union and the Western powers." Berlin, he said, "was a part of the Soviet occupation zone of

Germany and today is a part of the German Democratic Republic." [17]

Bolz's statement was an ill-concealed effort to influence the coming election. An increased vote for the Communists (Socialist Unity Party, or SED), who were still recognized in West Berlin, would be interpreted throughout the world as an endorsement of the Russian proposals. Accordingly, the day after Bolz's attack, Chancellor Adenauer, recognizing the gravity of the situation, paid one of his rare visits to Berlin to add his weight to the Western cause. In one of his equally rare displays of non-partisanship, the Chancellor advised the Berliners that more important than a vote for the CDU * was a vote against the Communists. Together with the SPD's Willy Brandt, Adenauer toured the city to remind the voters of the peril they faced. Even the working class boroughs of Neukölln and Wedding, where *der Alte* had never been popular, this time gave the pair a tumultuous welcome. Speaking later at his departure, again in the company of Mayor Brandt, Adenauer stated that although "the clouds have darkened over this city . . . we shall not be frightened." [18]

As a result of the combined efforts of Adenauer and Brandt, the election that took place in Berlin the following Sunday decisively answered Ulbricht and Bolz. Over 93.1 percent of the registered electorate of almost two million went to the polls in the largest turnout for a free election in German history. The city's eighteen hundred and sixty polling places were jammed throughout the day. As soon as the first returns began coming in that evening it was apparent that the Communists had been overwhelmingly defeated. The SPD of Mayor Brandt received over 52 percent of the total votes cast. Adenauer's Christian Democrats followed with 37 percent, the Free Democrats with 6 percent, and the German Party with 3 percent. The SED, which in 1954 had polled almost 4 percent, now received less than 2 percent—a total of 31,520 votes out of the more than 1,700,000 ballots that were cast.

While the counting was still under way, Ernst Lemmer, the Berlin leader of the CDU, pledged his support to Mayor Brandt for another four years. Two days later Brandt was reelected Mayor by the city assembly in a record vote of 127–1. The Communist assault had caused the city to close ranks and a unanimity prevailed which had not been seen in Berlin since the days of Ernst Reuter. When Willy Brandt now

* Christian Democratic Union.

spoke, the world could be sure that he was speaking for all the Berliners.[19]

In Washington the results of the Berlin election were greeted with jubilation. According to State Department Press Officer Lincoln White:

> The West Berlin elections give a clear evidence of the sentiments of the free people of West Berlin with reference to Soviet proposals to transform the area into a so-called free city. The decisive defeat of the Socialist Unity Party should give some idea as to the amount of trust the people of West Berlin are willing to place in Soviet proposals regarding their future.[20]

On December 10, three days after the West Berlin elections, President Eisenhower held his first press conference since the Russian note had arrived. He devoted his opening remarks to Berlin and emphasized that the Western powers would stand firm. The occupation agreements, the President said, had "given the West not only the right but the duty of preserving the peaceful and free existence" of their sectors and he intended to see that that duty was carried out. He spoke admiringly of the results of the Berlin election, and said that the United States would not let the Berliners down.[21] His words, understandably, were received with rejoicing in Berlin.

Three days later Secretary of State Dulles left Washington for a session of the NATO Council scheduled to meet in Paris on December 15. Dulles left for Paris from a hospital bed at the Walter Reed Medical Center in Washington where he had been under treatment since December 5, with what was then diagnosed as "a nonmalignant inflammatory condition in the lower colon." In spite of his illness, the Secretary was determined to add his prestige to the Western meeting.

On December 14, Dulles met with the Foreign Ministers of Great Britain, France, and West Germany * and heard Mayor Brandt present a summary of the existing situation in Berlin. Following the meeting, the Foreign Ministers issued a statement which for the first time since November 27 unequivocally placed all four governments on record against the Soviet proposal. For Dulles, the announcement marked a deliberate effort to dissociate himself from his earlier remark about East Germans acting as "agents" for the Soviet Union on the access routes to Berlin.

* Selwyn Lloyd, Couve de Murville, and Heinrich von Brentano.

According to the communique, the Foreign Ministers "reaffirmed the determination of their governments to maintain their position and their rights with respect to Berlin including the right of free access." Unilateral repudiation by the Soviet Government of its obligations in respect to these rights, or the substitution of East German officials for the Soviet Union "insofar as those rights are concerned," the Foreign Ministers said, was unacceptable.[22]

Two days later, the NATO Council issued a formal declaration on Berlin specifically upholding the Foreign Ministers' pronouncement. "The Council," it stated, "fully associates itself with the views expressed [by the Foreign Ministers] in their statement of 14th December. . . . The demands expressed by the Soviet Government have created a serious situation which must be faced with determination." [23]

Indeed, the NATO Council devoted most of its time to the question of Berlin. The firm line advocated by Dulles and Brandt was explicitly endorsed and the member states agreed that a solution in Berlin could only be achieved "in the framework of an agreement on Germany as a whole." The door to negotiations with Russia was left open, but it was stressed that these negotiations should center on German reunification based on free elections.

The final NATO communique issued two days later stated that after "a comprehensive survey of the international situation and particularly of the events in Berlin," the Council "make clear their resolution not to yield to threats. Their unanimous view was expressed in the Council's Declaration of 16 December." [24]

Two days after the adjournment of the NATO Council, the State Department in Washington issued a press release on the legal aspects of the Berlin situation. This release presents in detail the factual legal basis for the Western position in Berlin. Its provisions are still applicable to Allied rights in the isolated city and represent the most complete restatement of the legal points involved which has been issued since 1945. In it, the Department specifically objected to the claim of the Soviet Union to end unilaterally the right of occupation belonging individually to each of the four wartime Allies. "The United States," it said, "considers that the agreements denounced by the Soviet Union are in full force and effect, that the Soviet Union remains fully responsible for discharging the obligations which it assumed under

the agreements, and that the attempts by the Soviet Union to undermine the rights of the United States to be in Berlin and to have access
thereto are in violation of international law."

As to the specific legal questions involved, the release stated:

> The legal dispute of the United States Government with the
> Soviet Government involves fundamental questions of interna-
> tional law. Among them are the respective rights acquired by the
> occupying authorities in Germany at the conclusion of World
> War II and the status of those rights pending a final peace settle-
> ment with Germany; the question of whether a nation may uni-
> laterally abrogate without cause international agreements to which
> it is a party in order to divest itself of responsibilities which it has
> voluntarily assumed; and what is the effect of a unilateral re-
> nunciation of jointly shared rights of military occupation by one
> of the occupants.*

After treating the historical development of the situation in Berlin,
the Department stated that Allied rights "do not depend in any respect upon the sufferance or acquiescence of the Soviet Union. Those
rights derive from the total defeat of the Third Reich and the subsequent assumption of supreme authority. . . . This defeat and assumption of authority, were carried out as joint undertakings in which
the participants were deemed to have equal standing." Accordingly,
"the rights of each occupying power exist independently. . . . The
right of each power to be in occupation of Berlin is of the same standing as the right of each power to be in occupation of its zone."

Also, "the rights of the three Western powers to free access to Berlin . . . is of the same stature as the right of occupation itself. The
Soviet Union did not bestow upon the Western powers rights of access
to Berlin. It accepted its zone subject to those rights of access. If this
were not true . . . then, for example, the United States would now
be free to require the Soviet Union to withdraw from the portion of
the Soviet Zone originally occupied by American forces. . . ."

Thus, "inasmuch as the rights of occupation and of access do not
stem from the Soviet Union, the Soviets are without any authority
to repeal those rights by denunciation of agreements or by purported
transfer of control over them to third parties. The Soviet Union can-

---

* I.e., How does a renunciation by one of the occupiers affect the rights of the
others.

not affect the rights by declaring agreements null and void because the rights exist independently of the Soviet Union. . . ."

As for the specific legal point at issue, i.e., whether the Soviet Union could unilaterally void the occupation agreement, the State Department said that since the agreement was a "multi-lateral agreement" and rested on the consent of other parties, the Soviet Union was powerless to terminate it singlehandedly:

> In the absence of agreement by the other parties to terminate the agreement, or in the absence of a specified duration in the agreement itself, the question of termination must be justified in terms of international law. International law does not recognize any right of unilateral denunciation under such circumstances.

The analysis concluded by stating that "there can be no legal or moral doubt of the right of the United States to maintain its right of occupation in Berlin and its corollary right of access thereto and that efforts of the Soviet Union to assail and interfere with those rights are in violation of international law." [25]

By acting to clarify the legal status of the Western powers in Berlin, the State Department was paving the way for the formal Western reply to the Soviet note which was soon to come. Meanwhile, in Berlin, the Western garrisons stepped up their preparations to guard against a Communist attempt to seize power through a "popular" coup. During the third week in December, Major General Barksdale Hamlett, the Commandant of the American sector, met with the officers of the Berlin Command to review the situation. Hamlett emphasized that the United States was going to stay in Berlin and ordered detailed plans prepared to contain any possible East German demonstration. The Allied command knew that any contemplated East German move would probably be launched on a weekend or holiday. With the Christmas season approaching, Hamlett wanted to take no chances. He imposed a rigorous curfew and placed the garrison on a standby alert.

Two weeks later, on December 31, 1958, the formal Western reply to the Soviet message of November 27, was announced. The three Western Ambassadors in Moscow presented the answer of their governments simultaneously to the Kremlin and, except for the formal greetings, the messages were identical. The Allied messages began by pointing out the historical fallacies of the Soviet note and particularly, the attempts to portray the Western powers as supporters of Hitler. These attempts, the Allies said, were "in sharp contrast to the actual facts."

Referring to the withdrawal of the Allied forces in 1945 from what was to be the territory of the Soviet zone, the U.S. note stated that:

> . . . the Soviet Union has directly and through its puppet regime —the so-called German Democratic Republic—consolidated its hold over the large areas which the Western Allies relinquished to it. It now demands that the Western Allies should relinquish the positions in Berlin which in effect were the *quid pro quo*.
>
> The three Western Powers are in Berlin as occupying powers and they are not prepared to relinquish the rights which they acquired through victory just as they assume the Soviet Union is not willing now to restore to the occupancy of the Western Powers the positions which they had won in Mecklenburg, Saxony, Thuringia and Anhalt and which, under the agreements of 1944 and 1945, they turned over for occupation by the Soviet Union.
>
> The agreements made by the Four Powers cannot be considered obsolete because the Soviet Union has already obtained the full advantage therefrom and now wishes to deprive the other parties of their compensating advantages. These agreements are binding upon all of the signatories so long as they have not been replaced by others following free negotiations.
>
> . . . The Government of the United States will continue to hold the Soviet Government directly responsible for the discharge of its obligations undertaken with respect to Berlin under existing agreements. As the Soviet Government knows, the French, British, and United States Governments have the right to maintain garrisons in their sectors of Berlin and to have free access thereto. . . . The Government of the United States will not accept a unilateral repudiation on the part of the Soviet Government of its obligations in respect of that freedom of access. Nor will it accept the substitution of the regime which the Soviet Government refers to as the German Democratic Republic for the Soviet Government in this respect.

The Western replies also exposed the Soviet charge that the Allied garrisons in Berlin constituted a threat to the "Socialist camp."

> The forces of the three Western Powers in Berlin number about ten thousand men. The Soviet Government, on the other hand, is said to maintain some three hundred and fifty thousand troops in

Eastern Germany, while the regime which the Soviet Government refers to as the German Democratic Republic is understood also to maintain over two hundred thousand men under arms. In these circumstances, the fear that the Western troops in Berlin may "inflict harm" appears to be wholly unfounded. If Berlin has become a focus of international tension, it is because the Soviet Government has deliberately threatened to disturb the existing arrangements at present in force there, arrangements to which the Soviet Government is itself a party.

The Western note ended on an air of resolution. The Soviet proposals for "a so-called 'free city' of West Berlin" were termed unacceptable as were any proposals "which would have the effect of jeopardizing the freedom and security of the two million people of West Berlin." The Kremlin was advised that the West was prepared to begin negotiations on the overall question of Germany—of which Berlin was a part—but that such negotiations could not take place under threat of an ultimatum.[26]

On January 10, the Soviet Union replied to the Western note. Along with its reply the Russian government included a draft peace treaty for Germany. The Soviet treaty was an obvious propaganda gimmick designed to impress the "neutrals" and contained the usual pro-Communist provisions: recognition of "the two existing" German states, withdrawal of foreign troops from German soil, and the permanent recognition of the Oder-Neisse frontier. The Soviet note itself contained little new and for the most part was a rehash of the November 27th polemic. Russia threatened once more to "divest itself of the functions being carried out in relation to Berlin" and to sign a separate agreement with the East German regime. "Summing up what has been said," the note concluded, "the Soviet Government, besides the proposal about the calling of a peace conference, proposes also to discuss with interested states the question of Berlin. If, however, the Western powers consider it expedient before the calling of a peace conference preliminarily to exchange opinions with the Soviet Union about the content of a peace treaty, then the Soviet Government will be agreeable to that." In such a case, the Soviets said, it would be necessary to insure appropriate East and West German participation.[27]

Thus, very subtly, the Soviets were taking the West up on the offer to parley. Communist demands, however, remained undiminished and by now insisting upon East German participation, the Russians were adroitly moving to extract what amounted to a *de facto* recognition for their zonal puppets from the Western powers. The offensive launched by Khrushchev on November 27, was already bearing fruit. If the West would now agree to inviting the Ulbricht regime to a forthcoming conference, a considerable gain would have been made. Western refusal to recognize East Germany, it should be remembered, was not based simply on dislike for its Government but on the fact that Germany, as a previously occupied nation, was a responsibility of all four victorious powers. Under the terms of the occupation agreement (Potsdam), self-government was to be encouraged in all of Germany until such time as a peace treaty could be concluded. Since the regime of the Soviet zone is an affront to the very concept of self-government, and, indeed, since to recognize it would be tantamount to recognizing the division of Germany, the Western powers consistently refused to do so.

At a press conference three days later, Secretary of State Dulles reviewed the American position toward German reunification. Dulles' statement represents a summary of the prevailing Western sentiment at the time and is highly significant. The exchange was as follows:

Q.—Mr. Secretary, what's your reaction . . . to the Soviet proposal of last weekend for a peace conference to draft a new peace treaty for Germany?

A.—That proposal highlights what I just referred to as the two different philosophies about dealing with Germany. The Soviet Union has consistently believed that Germany should be isolated, segregated, to a large extent demilitarized and neutralized and separated from close association with the neighboring countries.

We don't believe that is a sound approach to the problem. On the contrary we take the view that Germany and the German people are too great, vigorous and vital a people to be dealt with in that way . . . We believe the future is best served by encouraging the closest possible relations between Germany and other Western European countries which are peace-loving [so] that independent, aggressive, nationalist action by Germany becomes as a practical matter impossible. . . .

Q.—Mr. Secretary, when you said the Soviet plan for Germany is "stupid" because it wouldn't work, in what sense did you mean it wouldn't work? . . .

A.—I believe that if you try to isolate and segregate a great people like the Germans in the center of Europe that they will become a restive and dangerous force . . . I don't think that you can put the Germans within the kind of a smothering blanket that the Soviet Union has in mind and expect it to hold. That, in a way, was the approach of the Treaty of Versailles, and it just didn't work. And I don't think it will work again. I think that a so-called "neutralized" and largely demilitarized Germany, attempted to be demilitarized in the center of Europe, is just something that won't work, and that, instead of trying to isolate Germany the best way is to tie Germany in.

Now that is the basic thesis of Adenauer. I believe that Adenauer's claim to greatness rests upon his effort to assure that Germany will not again follow the path which Germany followed in 1914 and again in 1939. He is the one who has invented, you might say, this solution, and I believe it is the most practical and sound solution for those who really want to end for all time the kind of danger that has come from Germany in the past.[28]

Simultaneously with the Soviet note, Russian spokesmen began to drop more hints that their earlier six-month ultimatum might be postponed. During a whirlwind unofficial visit to the United States in the first half of January, Deputy Soviet Premier Anastas Mikoyan repeatedly implied that the previous six-month ultimatum related only to the beginning of talks—not to the settlement of the dispute. Upon his return to Moscow, Mikoyan stated the same thing from the Kremlin in a formal press interview on January 24. "There is nothing unusual or abnormal about a deadline for the talks," he said. "The main thing in our proposal is not the six-month deadline but the proposal to have talks. If the talks are concluded in the spirit of finding a settlement . . . then of course negotiations could be prolonged for a few days or even a few months." [29]

Indeed, the rising crescendo of Russian requests for negotiations tended to obscure the fact that the original difficulty over Germany had been created by Soviet intransigence in carrying out the Geneva Agreement calling for free elections. Accordingly, the week after Mikoyan's statement, Secretary Dulles attempted to set the record straight:

Never yet has the Soviet Union, [Dulles told the House Foreign Affairs Committee,] made any proposal designed to promote ending the "cold war." There is, I know, always the temptation to grasp at a formula of words which might seem to end the continuing strains, the burdens, the risks, to which we are now subjected. But the Soviet proposals constitute not remedies but drugs which would numb us to the real danger which will then become greater than ever. . . . It would be reckless to be intimidated, or lured, into measures which far from ending the present danger would merely increase it.[30]

Five days after Dulles addressed the House committee, an incident occurred at the Marienborn checkpoint on the Berlin autobahn which seemed to underline the Secretary's remarks. At 1:05 P.M. on February 2, Soviet military authorities at Marienborn refused to allow an American military convoy to pass through the Soviet control point into West Germany. The four two-and-one-half ton trucks which were on a regular supply run between Berlin and West Germany had cleared the Russian checkpoint at the Berlin end of the autobahn without difficulty four hours before. But when they arrived at the other end, Soviet authorities, in clear violation of existing agreements, insisted on boarding the trucks and making a personal inspection of their cargo. Pursuant to his orders, the American convoy commander, Corporal Richard C. Masiero, refused to allow the Russians to do so. For over two days the American vehicles were kept impounded while Corporal Masiero and the four drivers under his command held their ground. Even when a full colonel of the Soviet Army had demanded to inspect the cargo, he had been politely refused by the steadfast Masiero.

When it was learned in Berlin that the vehicles were being detained at Marienborn (Checkpoint Alfa), the American command lodged an immediate protest with Russian military authorities in East Berlin. This produced no results. The following day, the headquarters of the United States Army in Europe, at Heidelberg, filed a similar protest with Russian headquarters in Potsdam. Again the request was refused and the Soviets declined to allow the trucks to proceed. By this time, of course, the incident at Checkpoint Alfa had become a matter of major importance. The Soviets were at their usual game attempting to curtail Western rights bit by bit and although their demand to board the American trucks may have seemed of little consequence, it was a dangerous precedent which could be extended to every vehicle on the Berlin access routes.

In Washington, the seriousness of the action at Checkpoint Alfa was appreciated immediately. After the two protests from the military authorities had gone unanswered, the Department of State wired an official protest to the American Embassy in Moscow. This was presented to the Kremlin on February 4, at 3:30 P.M. At approximately the same time, President Eisenhower announced the protest to a specially called press conference at the White House. The Soviet action, he said, was a clear violation of existing agreements and the United States demanded that the vehicles be allowed to proceed immediately.* 31

Three and one-half hours after the American note was delivered in Moscow the convoy was released. The vehicles were not inspected and Western firmness had made its point. The ease with which President Kennedy was able to reinforce the Berlin garrison in August, 1961, was in no small measure due to the determination displayed on this occasion by the five American enlisted men who had refused to allow their vehicles to be searched.

Simultaneously with the incident at Checkpoint Alfa, Secretary of State Dulles departed from Washington on a tour of the major West European capitals. His purpose was to consult at first hand with America's Allies on the larger Berlin crisis and, if possible, to formulate a common Western policy. It has been suggested that one of the reasons for the incident at Checkpoint Alfa was a Soviet desire to impress Paris and London with the precariousness of the Berlin lifeline on the eve of Dulles' departure.32 If anything, it had the opposite effect. When Dulles returned to Washington on February 9, he made the strongest pronouncement on Berlin by an American official since Khrushchev's ultimatum had been received. The United States and its Allies, Dulles said, would hold their position in Berlin by force if necessary. "We do not accept the substitution of East Ger-

---

* Five months before when the Russians had detained two U.S. Army trucks at the Berlin end of the autobahn (Checkpoint Bravo), Major General Hamlett had ordered a full alert of the American garrison and gave the Soviets a one-hour ultimatum to release the vehicles. While waiting for the Soviets to respond, Hamlett moved a detachment of tanks into position next to the Soviet checkpoint with orders to go in and get the trucks if the Soviets refused. As soon as the tanks appeared the Russians backed down and the vehicles were allowed to return to the American sector unmolested.

Since there were no American units stationed near the West German end of the autobahn (Checkpoint Alfa), the same maneuver could not be repeated when Masiero's party was held up.

mans for the Soviet Union in its responsibilities toward Berlin and its obligations to us. We are resolved that our position in, and access to, West Berlin shall be preserved. We are in general agreement as to the procedure we shall follow if physical means are employed to interfere with our rights in this respect. . . ."[33]

Immediately following his statement, and a short conversation at the White House with President Eisenhower, Mr. Dulles went to the Walter Reed Hospital in Washington. Although the Secretary remained in close touch with the State Department, his health was failing rapidly. Under Secretary Christian Herter, who took over most of Dulles' duties, was unable to duplicate the firm guidance which Dulles had given to the Western cause and, as a result, Allied steadfastness over Berlin began to diminish noticeably.

But for a time, Dulles remained in control. One week after he entered the hospital the United States formally advised the Soviet Union that it was prepared to discuss the issue of Germany "in all its aspects and implications" at the level of Foreign Ministers.[34] The tone of the American note was firm and represented no compromise from the position which the Administration had announced even before Khrushchev's ultimatum. The Russians were told that the Western powers intended to uphold their rights in Berlin "by all appropriate means" and that the Soviet demands constituted a major danger to world peace. In short, the Communists were being given an invitation to talk but were being told beforehand of those issues on which the West would not yield.

On March 2, the Soviet Union replied to the American note. Moscow said it still preferred a meeting of statesmen "at the highest level." The road to negotiations at the level of Foreign Ministers was a long one. "If the governments of the Western powers are not yet ready to take part in a summit conference, however, then the Soviet Union considers that . . . there could be convoked a conference of the Ministers of Foreign Affairs." Both German states, according to the Soviet Union, should be represented. The meeting should take place in a neutral location, preferably Vienna or Geneva, and April would be an appropriate time.[35] In effect, Russia was pushing as hard as ever for negotiations to begin. By suggesting the date of April, the Kremlin was insuring that their six-month ultimatum—at least insofar as it related to the beginning of negotiations—would be complied with.

Five days after the Soviet note arrived in Washington, Premier Khrushchev journeyed to East Germany to address what was euphemistically described by the Communists at the "Ninth All-German Workers Conference" in Leipzig. As this would be Khrushchev's first venture into the so-called German Democratic Republic since the new crisis had begun, his speech was eagerly awaited for the hints it might give about the future course of Soviet policy. Characteristically, Khrushchev attempted to satisfy East and West alike. To the East Germans he held out the branch of communal work with the Soviet Union toward the inevitable victory of Leninism. But to Ulbricht's undoubted discomfiture, Khrushchev counseled patience. "Do not hurry," he said. "The wind does not blow in your face. . . . The conditions are not ripe as yet for a new scheme of things. . . . As the saying goes, each fruit has its season." [36]

Two days later, on March 9, Khrushchev spoke in East Berlin. Once more he cautioned that delay was necessary, although this time his tone was more menacing. "The signing of a peace treaty," he said, "would mean the solution of the West Berlin question, which as part of Greater Berlin forms part of the territory of the German Democratic Republic." By referring to West Berlin as a part of the GDR, Khrushchev was reminding his listeners that the situation there—at least as Russia saw it—was a temporary one.[37]

But Khrushchev's words also reminded the West of the dangers still lurking in Berlin. These dangers, of course, were traceable directly to the historic policy of the Soviet Government—a policy described by President Eisenhower one week later as being "no less than world domination." The President made these remarks in a nationwide television address to the American people. According to the President (and here he was quoting Secretary Dulles), the Soviets sought to achieve this purpose by gaining power "in each of the many areas which had been afflicted by war, so that in the end the United States . . . would be isolated and closely encircled."

"The current Berlin effort of the Soviets falls within the pattern of this basic purpose," the President continued:

> The first instance of unusual pressure, clearly evidencing these purposes, came in 1948 when the Communists imposed a blockade to force the protecting Western troops out of Berlin and to starve the people of that city into submission.

That plan failed. A free people and a dramatic airlift broke the back of the scheme.

In the end the Communists abandoned the blockade and concluded an agreement in 1949 with the Western Powers, reconfirming our right of unrestricted access.

Then, last November, the Soviets announced that they intended to repudiate these solemn obligations. They once more appear to be living by the Communist formula that "Promises are like pie crusts, made to be broken." . . .

The Soviet threat has since been repeated several times, accompanied by various and changing suggestions for dealing with the status of the city. Their proposals have included a vague offer to make the Western part of Berlin—though not the Eastern part, which the Soviets control—a so-called free city.

We have no intention of forgetting our own rights or of deserting a free people, [the President said.] Soviet rulers should remember that free men have, before this, died for so-called "scraps of paper" which represented duty and honor and freedom.

The shirking of our responsibilities would solve no problems for us. . . . One result would be to undermine the mutual confidence upon which our entire system of collective security is founded. . . . The second choice which the Soviets have compelled us to face, is the possibility of war.

Certainly, the American and Western peoples do not want war. . . . But all history has taught us the grim lesson that no nation has ever been successful in avoiding the terrors of war by refusing to defend its rights—by attempting to placate aggression.

The risk of war is minimized if we stand firm. War would become more likely if we gave way and encouraged a rule of terrorism rather than a rule of law and order. . . . We cannot try to purchase peace by forsaking two million free people of Berlin. . . . We must not, by weakness or irresolution, increase the risk of war. Finally, we cannot merely for the sake of demonstrating so-called "flexibility" accept any agreement or arrangement which would undermine the security of the United States and its Allies.[38]

Ten days after the President spoke, the Department of State delivered a note in Moscow acknowledging Russian willingness to negotiate at the level of Foreign Ministers and specifically suggesting that such a conference be held in Geneva beginning on May 11. The Soviet Union, which had now realized its immediate objective, quickly announced its acceptance.[39]

The day following, as if to demonstrate to the world that the impending negotiations did not mean that the West intended to yield its position in Berlin, the United States dispatched a high flying C–130 Lockheed Hercules along the air corridor into Berlin. As soon as the flight plan of the C–130, which called for an altitude of 25,000 feet, was given to the Air Safety Center in Berlin the Soviet representative lodged a vigorous protest. According to the Soviets, the maximum altitude permissible in the air corridors was 10,000 feet although clearly there was no such agreement. The Russian protest was ignored by the U.S., and the flight to and from Berlin was made at 25,000 feet as scheduled.

According to State Department Press Officer Lincoln White, the United States intended to "continue to fly planes into Berlin at above 10,000 feet when that was the normal operating altitude." A formal Soviet protest which was delivered in Washington on April 4, was denied by the State Department the following week. "The United States government," the American reply stated, "rejects the Soviet contention that flights above 10,000 feet are precluded by regulations covering flights in the corridors. . . . The Government of the Soviet Union, having itself put into service aircraft (such as the TU–104) technical characteristics of which require flight at higher altitudes than those formerly in use, will appreciate the influence of such factors on operating altitudes of United States aircraft." [40]

On April 4, 1959, the same date the Russian protest over the first flight of the C–130 into Berlin was received in Washington, President Eisenhower again reasserted our determination to hold fast in Berlin. Speaking at the Gettysburg College convocation in Gettysburg, Pennsylvania, the President once more pointed to the pitfalls of irresolution and compromise. Against the background of the continuing Communist conspiracy to gain world domination, he said, the sacrifice of the two million free people of West Berlin would be unthinkable. "The course of appeasement," he continued, "is not only dishonorable, it is the most dangerous one we could pursue. The world paid a high price for the lesson of Munich, but it has learned the lesson well. We have learned, too, that the costs of defending freedom— of defending America—must be paid in many forms and in many places. They are assessed in all parts of the world—in Berlin, Viet-

Nam, in the Middle East, here at home. But wherever they occur, in whatever form they appear, they are first and last a proper charge against the national security of the United States. . . ." [41]

On April 15, less than two weeks after the President's speech at Gettysburg, John Foster Dulles resigned as American Secretary of State. In the negotiations that were soon to commence in Geneva his presence would be sorely missed. Secretary Herter, who succeeded him, had neither the confidence of the President, nor the same moralistic fervor of Dulles in combating the tide of Communist expansion. As a result, the Western powers now began to waver perceptibly in the defense of Berlin and the Soviet Union came near to realizing its goal of a neutralized "free city." Indicative of the slackening Western determination, a scheduled flight of another C–130 aircraft into Berlin was canceled just one week after Dulles' resignation due to what was officially described in Washington as "British timidity." [42]

The Geneva Conference convened as scheduled on May 11, 1959. To some extent, the decision to hold the conference represented a concession to the Soviet Union. Without explicitly removing their ultimatum of November 27, the Russians had forced the West into negotiations intended to alter the status of Berlin. The opening of the Geneva Conference boded ill for the West for other reasons as well. In addition to the confusion resulting from the resignation of Secretary Dulles, the Western camp was now in serious disarray as to how the Soviet threat should be met. As in 1948, London in particular advocated a position of compromise and tended to view every Soviet pronouncement as an indication of Russian good faith. Large bodies of opinion both in the United States and Great Britain ignored the original Soviet ultimatum and blamed West German rearmament and the militant anti-communism of Chancellor Konrad Adenauer as principal causes of the crisis in Berlin. [43]

In the United States Senate, Senators William Fulbright and Mike Mansfield kept up a steady fusillade against the Administration position of standing firm against the Communist threat. On March 16, Mr. Fulbright lashed out violently at the policy of Secretary Dulles and indorsed immediate negotiations with the Soviet Union announcing that he saw "no virtue in maintaining the *status quo*." The day prior to that, Senator Mansfield, appearing on the CBS television program "Face the Nation," recommended that because of the present crisis the United States should evacuate all military dependents from Berlin. The effect of such a move, as General Clay had pointed out eleven years before, would have been a total collapse of Western morale. Yet Mansfield continued carping and on April 8, just one week before Dulles' resignation, advised a banquet of the New York University Alumni Association in New York that the West should seriously consider a compromise in Berlin, and that "firmness is not an end in itself." [44] While Dulles was in the hospital, in fact, both Fulbright and Mansfield had kept up a steady flow of invective against the ailing Secretary and demanded that his resignation be tendered immediately.

Besides the disarray in the Western camp, the Geneva Conference of Foreign Ministers also marked the introduction into world councils of the puppet regime of the "German Democratic Republic." This in itself was a substantial gain for the Soviet Union—a gain which Dulles most certainly would have resisted—and for the first several days of the Conference the attention of the entire world was directed to the ensuing discussions as to how these Soviet satraps would be seated. Although they were subsequently placed at an adjoining table to that of the Big Four Foreign Ministers, the fact remained that the East Germans were present at the conference and were being consulted just as though they were a properly recognized national government.

On May 14, three days after the conference began, the Western Foreign Ministers (Herter, Selwyn Lloyd and Couve de Murville) introduced a package plan for solving the Berlin crisis by tying it to eventual German reunification. Considering the seeming confusion which then prevailed in the Western camp, the plan was not a bad one. It was a four-phase measure calling first for the reunification of Berlin and then proceeding gradually to a reunification of all of Germany. Whether it represented a legitimate Western proposal or whether it was intended as a starting point from which to begin concessions is open to conjecture.

In the first phase of the Allied proposal, East and West Berlin would be unified under free elections held under quadripartite or United Nations supervision. As a result of these elections a city council would be formed for all of Berlin which would then govern it as the first step toward German unification.

Phase two called for a mixed committee consisting of twenty-five members from West Germany and ten from East Germany to draft an election law for all-German elections. Under stage three, all-German elections for a General Assembly would then be held and, following their election, the General Assembly would draft a constitution for Germany. Stage four of the Western plan called for the formation of an all-German government under the constitution drafted by the General Assembly and the conclusion of a peace treaty with that government.

As soon as it was introduced, the Western proposal was summarily rejected by Soviet Foreign Minister Andrei Gromyko. One month later, following a harrowing period of fruitless negotiations, the Soviet Union presented their own set of proposals for Berlin. These extended the occupation period of the Western powers for one year but demanded onerous concessions in return. Among these, the Western powers would reduce the size of their forces in West Berlin to "symbolic contingents"; "hostile propaganda against the GDR and other Socialist countries" from West Berlin would be stopped; all organizations engaged in "espionage and subversive activities against the GDR, the USSR, and other Socialist countries" in West Berlin would be "liquidated"; and the Western powers would agree not to erect atomic or missile installations in West Berlin. During the one-year time limit which the Soviets proposed, an all-German committee would be set up on an equal basis between East and West Germany to formulate an agreement on German reunification and a final peace treaty. If agreement was not reached within one year, the Soviet Union would conclude a separate peace treaty with the GDR and negotiations regarding Berlin would go forward from that point.[45]

The Russian proposals were immediately dismissed by Secretary Herter. But unfortunately, the urge to compromise now seemed to take hold of the Western delegations and for the next two months an aura of concession enshrouded Geneva. With the death of John Foster Dulles on May 26, the determination of the Allied negotiators sagged noticeably. Prodded by British Foreign Secretary Selwyn Lloyd, Herter and Couve de Murville joined in offering a second set of Western proposals on June 16, which, if accepted, would have made the Allied position in Berlin untenable.

Under the new proposals the Allies agreed to consider a reduction of the size of the Western garrisons and to establish a four-power commission designed to eliminate "subversion and espionage" in both parts of Berlin.[46] This last item was extremely defensive in nature and would have curtailed the operation of such Western agencies as the RIAS broadcasting station in West Berlin, and probably all the free newspapers as well. It would have also amounted to the introduction of Soviet personnel in an official capacity into the Western sectors and would have been a serious setback for the Allied cause. The Western proposal also made no mention of Allied rights of occupation—a fact which could have been used by the Communists to deny the existence of these rights later on.

Announcement of the Western proposals caused a near panic in West Berlin. Mayor Brandt and Chancellor Adenauer barely managed to conceal their open hostility, and Allied unity was now dangerously close to foundering on the rocks of compromise.* In spite of the German protests, however, the Western proposals were presented in much the same form three days later when both East and West agreed to present a summary of their positions. Following the introduction of these summaries, the conferees had agreed to recess for a period of three weeks.

But instead of being a summary of its position, the Western proposals presented on June 19, represented even greater concessions. Under these proposals the West agreed to:

a. The limitation of the Western garrison to 11,000 men.

b. The understanding that they would be armed only with conventional (non-atomic) weapons.

c. Consideration of a reduction in the size of the garrison "if developments in the situation permit."

d. East German control of the access routes to Berlin but with recognition of the right of "continued free access."

e. A curb on propaganda and intelligence activities "in both parts of Berlin." [47]

---

* On May 9, 1962, Mayor Brandt advised the author that he considered the Western proposals made at Geneva the weakest ever put forward by the Allies —weaker even than the American plan on access presented by Secretary Rusk in his conversations with Soviet Ambassador Dobrynin in April, 1962. (See Chapter XIV.)

The final Soviet proposals submitted before the recess were not significantly different from the Western set. Gromyko, in presenting the Russian proposals, in fact, was extremely conciliatory in manner and indicated that the Soviet Union was most pleased with the progress it had made. "On the basis of the exchange of views held so far," he stated, "the Soviet government believes that it is quite possible to find an acceptable basis for agreement on the Berlin question and on the question of an all-German committee."

Gromyko began his presentation by announcing that the Russian government no longer considered the time element "of major importance nor principle." He would suggest an eighteen-month interim period in Berlin, he said, but this should not be considered a stumbling block. As for Berlin itself during the interim period, Gromyko suggested:

a. The reduction of the occupation forces to symbolic contingents;

b. the termination of subversive activities in West Berlin;

c. non-location in West Berlin of atomic and rocket weapons.

During the time limit, whatever it happened to be, an all-German committee would consider the problems of reunification and the writing of a German peace treaty. If no agreement was reached by the all-German Committee, then the Big Four would resume consideration of the Berlin problem based on the situation as it existed at that time.[48]

The only difference between the Russian and Western proposals, it should be noted, dealt with the time limit as to the new status of Berlin, and Gromyko himself had declared that this was a matter of little importance. Both sets of proposals called for the reduction of the Allied garrisons and the curtailment of "subversive activities," and the West had abandoned its proposals for German reunification based on free elections. Thus, less than eight months after the original Soviet ultimatum, Russia was on the verge of seeing its demands realized. The East German regime already had been partially recognized by its attendance at the conference and now a substantive gain in Berlin itself was about to be made.

The day after the Communist and Western proposals were presented the conference recessed. When it convened again on July 13.

the West had had a chance to subject its position to closer scrutiny. As a result, a harder line began to emerge. On July 25, Secretary Herter visited West Berlin to participate in renaming one of the city's streets in honor of the late John Foster Dulles. While there, he conferred with Mayor Brandt and Major General Barksdale Hamlett, the Commandant of the American Sector. The principal argument that day was made by Hamlett. He advised the Secretary that from a military standpoint it would be impossible to guarantee the territorial integrity of West Berlin should the garrison be reduced from its present level. Eleven thousand men, Hamlett said, was the bare minimum with which the safety of the city could be assured from Communist inspired rioters who might try to seize control in West Berlin through public disorder.

General Hamlett's argument impressed the Secretary. When the final Western proposals were presented at Geneva three days later, all mention of a reduction in the size of the Allied garrison had been deleted. Secretary Herter, in fact, had been visibly impressed by his reception in Berlin. In addition to the brilliant presentation made by Hamlett, the Secretary had been subjected to one of Berlin's moving public demonstrations. Everywhere the Secretary had gone during his brief stay he had been cheered by great masses of Berliners. He was able to see at first hand the importance of a free Berlin to the Western cause and to realize the tragic results which would follow from its surrender. He also learned of Berlin's role in the fight for freedom —of the hope it meant to those behind the Iron Curtain—and, like many another statesman who had flown into Berlin during the blockade, he departed deeply moved by what he had seen. As he boarded his plane, he assured the Berliners "that the United States will not forget its responsibilities toward Berlin." [49]

But in spite of the favorable impression made on Secretary Herter by his visit to Berlin, the final Allied proposals presented to the Geneva Conference still came dangerously close to effectively ending the free existence of West Berlin. Although no mention was made in these proposals of a reduction in the size of the Western garrison, the earlier proposals made on June 19 remained the same. These included the use of East Germans as "agents" for the Soviet Union on the routes of access into Berlin, and the curtailment of all propaganda and intelligence activities. In addition, the final Western proposals also included a provision limiting the agreement on Berlin to a five-year duration. This would clearly have redounded to the advantage of the Soviet Union by giving the Western occupation a decidedly temporary appearance.

The final Soviet proposals were a repeat of their earlier recommendations. The Western powers, over muffled British protest, announced that the Russian proposals remained unacceptable as a basis for negotiations, and the conference adjourned on August 5, without having reached an agreement. The final days between the submission of the Western and Soviet plans on July 28, and the adjournment, however, was an extremely critical period for the West. Had Gromyko accepted the final Western proposals, West Berlin's hope of survival would have been destroyed. Mayor Brandt, in fact, hurried to Geneva as soon as the Western proposals were announced to caution against them. Fortunately for the West, by this time the strategists of the Kremlin were interested in other matters.

11

The Tale of Three Summits

(Camp David—Paris—Vienna)

ALTHOUGH THE WEST HAD PROPOSED major concessions at Geneva, the Soviet Union chose not to accept them. In the closing days of the conference, their reason for not doing so became clear. Nikita Khrushchev was going to America. During early July the Soviet Premier had been contacted by President Eisenhower and officially tendered an invitation. Khrushchev had quickly accepted and now, with a meeting of this kind in the offing, there was little incentive for the Soviet delegation in Geneva to accept the so-called "final" Western proposal of July 28. Indeed, there was good reason for the Russians to believe that in the personal confrontations between the two leaders, an even more advantageous arrangement on Berlin might be secured. The Soviet Union therefore spurned the last Western offer at the meeting of Foreign Ministers and embarked on the road to the Summit.

In retrospect, President Eisenhower's invitation to Khrushchev must be regarded as a major diplomatic triumph. As noted in the previous chapter, the West was on the verge of making extremely serious concessions at Geneva. By suddenly granting the Russians the meeting at the Summit which they had so long desired, the rationale behind the Geneva negotiations disappeared. The crippling Western proposals were thereby preempted and the Allied position in Berlin temporarily secured. Although admittedly this may not have been the reason for the initial invitation to Khrushchev, it is clear that this was the result.

The formal announcement of Premier Khrushchev's visit to the United States was made simultaneously in Washington and Moscow on August 3. In Washington, President Eisenhower himself broke the news. According to the President, Khrushchev would arrive on September 15, tour the country for ten days and then return to Washington for a two-day conference on world affairs.[1]

Khrushchev's itinerary went exactly as planned. He arrived at Andrews Air Base outside Washington on September 15, and thereafter followed ten of the most exciting days in the memory of the American public as the ruler of the Soviet Union freely toured the length and breadth of the United States. On September 25, Nikita Khrushchev was back in Washington. And although his visit had averted a major diplomatic rout at Geneva, it was not without its drawbacks. His ten days of barnstorming across the country had created many illusions that his intentions were innocent. His repeated praise of "peaceful coexistence" had convinced many others that a thaw in the cold war was at hand. His perpetual friendliness and buoyancy further encouraged those who sought accommodation at any price.

The two days of conferences between Premier Khrushchev and President Eisenhower were conducted at the President's Camp David retreat situated in the Maryland mountains overlooking the peaceful Catoctin River. Khrushchev arrived there by helicopter in the late afternoon of September 25, and was met as he landed by President Eisenhower. The two immediately began a series of discussions and, according to Press Secretary James Hagerty, the talks revolved around a general consideration of world affairs. The discussions held on the following day, Saturday, September 26, 1959, were devoted primarily to Germany and Berlin. For almost the entire day and evening on Saturday the two world leaders were closeted on this issue.[2]

When the talks concluded, an agreement of sorts had been reached. In return for Khrushchev's withdrawal of the earlier Soviet ultimatum, the President agreed to reopen negotiations on Berlin in a Big Four Summit Conference the following year. The communique ending the Camp David meeting announced the President's part of the bargain, and on his return to Moscow, Nikita Khrushchev said that the future discussions would be subjected to no fixed time limit provided the West entered the negotiations in good faith.[3]

The Camp David accord has been criticized in the West from both sides. Some have objected that the President, perhaps unintentionally, misled Khrushchev into believing that the West might agree to a solution somewhat along Soviet lines at the forthcoming Summit. Others have objected that in agreeing to discuss the Berlin problem at all at the Summit, President Eisenhower was going too far to accommodate the Russians. But the fact remains that the Camp David agreement succeeded in gaining a much needed breathing period for the West and at least temporarily put the lid on further Western concessions. As a result of the relaxation achieved, the West was able to restudy the possible consequences of the Geneva proposals and thus discard them by the time the negotiations resumed.

Yet, although the Camp David meeting did introduce a brief period of calm—at least insofar as direct Soviet assaults on the position of the West in Berlin was concerned—it marked no relaxation in Soviet efforts to undermine the freedom of West Berlin by others means. The most effective of these means was by referring to the situation in Berlin as the abnormal result of the Second World War. By trumpeting this idea, the Soviets were implanting the thought that the situation in Berlin needed changing. If this belief could be nourished, a substantial erosion of the Western position would have been made.

According to the Russians, the best way to end the "abnormality" of West Berlin would be to conclude a peace treaty. Naturally, since there were two German states, two separate treaties would have to be signed. Khrushchev, in fact, lost no opportunity to hammer this point home. During a question and answer period at the National Press Club in Washington on the day following the Camp David discussions, the Soviet Chairman stated: "As day follows night, so peace follows war, and therefore peace should be signed, and since there is no united Germany we think that peace should be signed with the two German states. I see no other way toward that end. . . ."[4]

Later that afternoon Khrushchev expressed much the same sentiment in a nationwide television broadcast to the American people. His remarks left no doubt that instead of the reunification of Germany, Russia actually sought the recognition of a divided Germany and the complete assimilation of its eastern portion into the Soviet bloc. "It is well known," Khrushchev said, "that there are today in reality two German states and each of them is living its own way. Neither one German state or the other is willing to give up its social system." Accordingly, he suggested, "would it not be best to conclude a peace treaty with both German states without any further procrastination and thereby stamp out the sparks among the embers before they have a chance to kindle a new conflagration?"

As for Berlin, Khrushchev said that "the conclusion of a peace treaty would also extinguish the sparks smoldering in West Berlin and would thereby create a normal situation there." [5] Already Russia's insistence on changing the status of Berlin had convinced many in the West that Khrushchev was right when he referred to the situation in Berlin as abnormal. But the real abnormality, as the late Secretary Dulles had pointed out frequently, was not the situation in Berlin but the division of Germany. With Dulles gone, however, Western spokesmen seldom mentioned this, and the field was left to the Russians almost by default; Khrushchev's charges went unrebutted, and more and more the West came to look on its position in Berlin as something that needed to be changed.

Even in the highest places it was obvious that Khrushchev's tactics had struck home. Indeed, President Eisenhower himself was soon referring to the situation in West Berlin as abnormal. The President's remark occurred at a highly publicized press conference immediately following Khrushchev's visit.

The President's off-hand comment necessitated the issuance of a formal statement immediately afterwards by Press Secretary Hagerty clarifying what the President had meant. The original question, and Mr. Eisenhower's reply, are as follows:

> Q.—Mr. President, when we move into these new negotiations on Berlin, could you tell us whether we will be guided by the same standards and principles that we had before, namely, that any solution must guarantee Allied rights there, and protect the freedom of the West Berliners?

> A.—I can't guarantee anything of this kind for the simple reason, I don't know what kind of solution may finally prove acceptable, as I say, but you must start off with this. *The situation is abnormal.* It was brought about by a truce, a military truce, after

the end of the war, an armistice, and it put strangely a few—or a number of free people in a very awkward position.[6]

Needless to say, President Eisenhower's answer caused intense concern throughout the Western camp. Was the United States preparing to make a deal with Russia at free Berlin's expense? From the President's answer one certainly could think so. Hagerty's statement following the press conference attempted to set the record straight, but considerable damage already had been done. "The President," Hagerty announced, "of course did not mean that the freedom of the people of West Berlin is going to be abandoned or that Allied rights are going to be surrendered by any unilateral action. What he was referring to was that he could not now give in detail the ultimate solution to the Berlin question."

"Any agreement," Hagerty continued, "must be acceptable to the people of the area, including those most concerned—the people of West Berlin and the Federal Republic of Germany." [7]

But the President's statement still left a good deal of doubt, and so the following week Secretary of State Christian Herter reaffirmed American determination to stand fast in Berlin. United States policy, he said, was based on the idea that American forces would remain in Berlin until Germany was reunified. "That is the position we have taken, and we see no reason to move away from it." [8]

The effect of Mr. Eisenhower's statement was felt in Moscow as well as in Western Europe and when combined with the impressions which Khrushchev had formed at Camp David, caused the Communists also to have their doubts about Western firmness. As a result, the East resumed its probing operations in Berlin, seeking to test Allied response. For the most part, this testing was now done by the puppet East German regime of Walter Ulbricht. Indeed, while the Russians outwardly attempted to fulfill the conditions of Camp David, their East German henchmen began a series of harassing actions against the Allied garrison in Berlin designed not only to increase the pressure on the Western powers but to shake the confidence of the Berliners as well.

The first of the East German probing actions came on October 6, 1959, during the celebration commemorating the founding of the so-called "German Democratic Republic." To recognize the occasion, the

East German regime placed flags of the GDR over each of the S-Bahn (elevated) stations in West Berlin.* When West Berlin police attempted to remove the flags they were assaulted by mobs of Communist toughs especially brought over from East Berlin for just such an eventuality. Six policemen were critically injured, and although the flags were removed, they were all replaced that evening.

The following day, Mayor Brandt met with the three Western Commandants and requested permission to remove the flags with whatever force was necessary. The people, he said, were aroused and a failure to act would be interpreted as a sign of weakness. Specifically, Brandt requested the Commandants to order out Berlin's special riot police (Force B) which, like the riot police in most continental capitals, is equipped with heavy infantry weapons and would have been ideally suited for removing the flags.

But the Commandants were not convinced. General Hamlett, the American Commandant, was out of Berlin at the time, and in his absence, his British colleague, General Sir Rohan Delacombe, carried the day. Mayor Brandt left the meeting disheartened but determined to comply with Allied policy. The riot police were not ordered out and the East German flags remaining flying for the duration of the celebration.

The following month, the East Germans threatened to raise the flags once more but this time the West was better prepared. General Hamlett was now back in Berlin and was determined that October's fiasco would not be repeated. The occasion for the new flag raising was the coming celebration of the 1917 Bolshevik Revolution—a celebration due to begin on November 6. The East Germans had widely trumpeted their intentions to raise the flags once more and in response the three Allied Commandants met in special session on October 29. This time Hamlett and General Jean LaComme, the French Commandant, convinced Delacombe that the only way to meet the Communist threat was to advise the Russians that any attempt to hoist the East German flags in West Berlin would be met by force. Reluctantly, Delacombe agreed and a joint Allied note to this effect was then transmitted to Soviet military headquarters in East Berlin.[9]

---

* The original occupation agreements in Berlin had given the Soviets control of all railroad facilities within the city. The S-Bahn system was a part of these facilities and was turned over by the Soviets to the East German regime in 1949.

Washington, which was also aroused over the implications of the East German flag raising, notified the Soviet Union the following day that American troops were prepared to take whatever "security requirements" might be necessary in West Berlin to prevent the East German flags from being flown. Immediately after the American statement, the French Foreign Ministry in Paris announced that France "formally associated itself" with the United States position.

On November 3, three days before the celebration was to begin, General Hamlett paid a personal call on Major General Zaharov, his counterpart in East Berlin, to inform him once more that the United States was prepared to act. Later that afternoon Hamlett called a meeting of the senior American officers in Berlin in which he reviewed the situation and his conversation with Zaharov as well. "I told him," Hamlett stated, "that if the flags were put up, the West Berlin police would take them down. If the police couldn't do it, then we would." Hamlett said he was alerting the entire command and that all units were to be prepared to take whatever action was necessary.

The following afternoon, *Neues Deutschland,* the official East Berlin newspaper, reported with seeming disdain that "we do not assume that the flags will be hoisted." [10] The East German flags which already had been distributed to each of the S-Bahn stations in West Berlin were placed under lock and key by the Communist functionaries in each station and were returned surreptitiously to East Berlin that evening—a precaution lest any be raised the following day by an overzealous disciple. The tough stand of Brandt and Hamlett thus was vindicated; when confronted by a show of Western determination, the Communists had backed down.

Shortly after the second flag incident had been resolved, the Western Big Four met in Paris. By this time the West had had an opportunity to study the Geneva proposals in greater detail and to realize their full effect. Under the gentle prodding of Chancellor Adenauer, the Allied heads of government therefore agreed that they would no longer consider themselves bound by the so-called "final" Western proposal of July 28—the proposal calling for turning control of access to Berlin over to the East Germans and for the elimination of the so-called "irritants." Instead, it was decided that any future negotiations over Berlin would have to start from the beginning.[11]

Three weeks later, speaking before the West Berlin city assembly,

Chancellor Adenauer reassured the Berliners that the West would make no "deal" with Russia at the city's expense. According to the Chancellor, "any change in Berlin would be a change for the worse . . . and nothing could be worse or more mistaken than to begin again where one left off in Geneva. All the Western proposals on Berlin," Adenauer said, "are no longer existent since the Soviet Union rejected them."

And while the West reviewed its position, the East likewise was taking stock of the situation. Although the Camp David agreement was not specifically repudiated, ominous voices were now raised in the Communist camp threatening a separate peace treaty with East Germany. At the meeting of the Warsaw Pact signatories in Moscow on February 4, the West was pointedly warned against attempting to delay a settlement in Berlin. Any procrastination, the Communists said, would lead to a separate treaty with East Germany, and the solution of "the question of West Berlin" on this basis. Specifically, the Warsaw members stated:

> If the efforts toward the conclusion of a peace treaty with both German states do not meet with support and if the solution of this question comes up against attempts at procrastination, the states represented at the present conference will have no alternative but to conclude a peace treaty with the German Democratic Republic . . . and to solve on this basis the question of West Berlin as well.[12]

Five days after the Warsaw Pact meeting adjourned, Nikita Khrushchev himself threatened a separate treaty with East Germany. Speaking at a reception at the Italian Embassy in Moscow, Khrushchev repeated the Communist liturgy that a settlement of the West Berlin question "brooked no delay." Still anxious for the promised Summit, however, the Soviet leader carefully avoided mention of a specific deadline.

By now reviving the question of Berlin, the Soviets were preparing their position for these very Summit negotiations. Indeed, Khrushchev's remarks at the Italian Embassy marked the beginning of a long distance snipping campaign which kept up until the Summit began. Realizing perhaps what was happening, Secretary Herter issued an immediate reply to Khrushchev. Any unilateral action to alter the status of Berlin, Herter announced from Washington, "would be a very serious thing." Such an action, he said, would be in clear violation of the Camp David agreement.[13]

Just as the Communists were oiling their weapons for the Summit, the West likewise began to buttress its position. The following week, Secretary Herter repeated the earlier Western proposal for reunification of Germany based on a popular plebiscite. Nikita Khrushchev replied on February 29; speaking from Jakarta, Indonesia, the Soviet Premier said that such a proposal would be a clear "interference in German internal affairs." If a suitable agreement on Germany were not reached, Khrushchev declared, the Soviet Union would "be forced to sign a treaty with the German Democratic Republic." Should this be the case, "all consequences of World War II in the German Democratic Republic will cease to exist, including the question of Berlin, which is situated on the territory of the German Democratic Republic."

Simultaneously with the long-distance sparring which was now going on between Khrushchev and the West, East German authorities stepped up their harassment of the Allied forces in Berlin. On February 3, the Ulbricht regime announced that henceforth the Allied military missions in Potsdam would be accredited to the GDR rather than the Soviet Union.

The Allied military missions in Potsdam had been established shortly after the end of the war ostensibly to facilitate communications between the Soviet and Western commands. Each of the three Western powers employed about twenty officers and men in their missions and the Soviet Union had three similar missions in West Germany.* The size and composition of each of the three Soviet missions corresponded exactly to the opposite Western mission at Potsdam.

Although the stated purpose of these missions was to facilitate communications, in reality each operated as an officially sanctioned intelligence service, watching "the other side." Since this was a two-way street, the Western powers and the Soviets carefully duplicated one another as to restrictions and prohibitions. Each mission was generally free to travel throughout the area of the other command, and this was a major means of collecting information.

Accordingly, the East German action on February 3 announcing that the missions would now be accredited to the "German Demo-

---

* One in each of the former Allied zones, i.e., a mission in Baden-Baden to the French, one in Buende with the British, and one in Frankfurt with the Americans.

cratic Republic" was very significant. To have acquiesced to the East German announcement would have constituted a virtual recognition of the Ulbricht regime. Indeed, the East Germans had supported their announcement by issuing new passes to each of the Western missions which clearly stated that the issuing authority was the German Democratic Republic. The old passes which had been issued by the Russians, the East Germans said, were no longer valid.

The United States and France immediately objected. The passes furnished by the East Germans, they said, were unacceptable and if the Soviet Union was not prepared to continue issuing the passes in the normal manner, then the West would have no alternative but to withdraw their missions from the Soviet zone. This, they added, would mean that the Soviet missions in West Germany would also have to be closed.

For several weeks the Russians stood firm. Either the Allies would accept the East German passes or none at all. But on February 25, the situation suddenly changed. The French, under De Gaulle, now among Berlin's strongest defenders, took affairs into their own hands and restricted the Soviet mission in Baden-Baden to its headquarters pending the issuance of new passes for the French mission in Potsdam. Two weeks later the United States and Great Britain followed suit. Immediately following the American action, the State Department in Washington announced that the Russians were "not improving the atmosphere in advance of the forthcoming Summit."

With the onus now placed directly upon them, the Soviets relented. On March 14, they announced that the passes issued by the East German regime would be withdrawn. "Ruled by the wish not to worsen the attitude in the relations between the great powers especially prior to the Summit conference," the Kremlin said, "the Soviet Union has ordered its commander not to change the former valid passes of the American, British, and French military missions in Potsdam for the time being." The following day, the restrictions which had been imposed on the Soviet missions by the Western powers were also withdrawn.[14]

There were other reasons as well why the Communists decided to withdraw the East German passes. On February 29, the United States had announced that the high altitude flights of C-130 aircraft into Berlin would soon be resumed. For the Russians this was a very serious matter. As was to be demonstrated shortly, high flying air-craft are of major strategic importance in gathering otherwise un-obtainable intelligence data; although this was never mentioned by the Russians in their protests over the C–130 flights into Berlin, they were clearly disturbed by the prospect. Indeed, the East German pass demands seemed of little importance in contrast.

The American announcement about the resumption of the C–130 flights was heartily approved in both Bonn and Paris. In London, however, the British Government hung back. Such a course, they contended, would upset the delicate balance of East–West relations. The British protests over the resumption of the C–130 flights were vehement and even erupted into the House of Commons, where the Government bench did little to conceal its distaste for the American move. Accordingly, on March 9, and before the flights could take place, Washington yielded to the British pressure rather than face an open break in Allied ranks. Speaking at a press conference that day, Secretary Herter said that President Eisenhower, while still re-serving the right to make such flights, found "no operational necessity" for doing so at the present time.[15]

The fact that the United States had been willing to make the high altitude flights made its point with the Russians, however, and five days later Communist pressure on the Potsdam missions was withdrawn. Clearly, a *quid pro quo* had been achieved.

Shortly after Secretary Herter's announcement canceling the C–130 flights, Konrad Adenauer was in Washington. In spite of the *quid pro quo* the Chancellor made no secret of the fact that he felt that the West had backed down.[16] Indeed, *der Alte* was profoundly worried at this time about the total course of Allied policy toward Berlin, and espe-cially, about preparations for the forthcoming Summit. Accordingly, in his private discussions with the President, Adenauer stressed that the Berlin question should not be negotiated at the coming Paris meeting except within the context of the overall problem of German reunifica-tion. A separate deal on West Berlin, he indicated, would give rise to a feeling among the Berliners that they were being forsaken—being treated differently from the other members of the NATO community. The result, Adenauer said, would be tragedy for the Western alliance.

The Chancellor's arguments met with only limited success. The joint communique issued at the close of the conversations reaffirmed merely that no deal would be made with the Soviets about Berlin which did not reflect the sentiment of the Berliners. No connection was made, however, between the Berlin problem and the larger problem of German reunification—the tie advocated for so long not only by Adenauer, but by Dulles and, indeed, by Acheson as well.[17]

A study of this period prepared by Dr. Hans Speier cites a report appearing in a responsible West German newspaper, the *Süddeutsche Zeitung*, that Chancellor Adenauer had serious doubts during these discussions about American firmness.[18] In fact, the day after the discussions ended, *der Alte* proposed that a plebiscite be held in West Berlin prior to the Summit to inform the Western statesmen how the Berliners felt. Since the feeling of the Berliners was already well known, no action was ever taken on the Chancellor's proposal. But the fact that it was made, and made by a statesman of Adenauer's rank, effectively reminded the Western powers of German concern.

Perhaps sensing the uncertainty in the West, on March 25, Nikita Khrushchev, then on a state visit to France, returned to the offensive and announced that a separate Soviet treaty with East Germany would end the occupation status of Berlin. As soon as Khrushchev spoke, Washington issued an immediate rebuttal. "There is no substance whatever to the contention voiced by Mr. Khrushchev," the State Department said, that a separate peace treaty would "alter Western rights and responsibilities." [19]

Khrushchev appeared undaunted by the State Department's answer and three weeks later again threatened a separate peace treaty with the GDR. Speaking at Baku, in the Caucasus, he repeated once more that if the forthcoming Summit talks were not fruitful, the Soviet Union would end the occupation in West Berlin on its own terms. According to Khrushchev, and here again he was attempting to plant a seed of doubt in the West, West Berlin was on the territory of the GDR and therefore once a peace treaty was concluded, the presence of Allied forces there would then be illegal.

It was evident, however, that Adenauer's visit to Washington had served its purpose. Five days before Khrushchev spoke, American Under Secretary of State C. Douglas Dillon officially put the Kremlin on notice that the United States was not prepared to surrender any of its substantive rights in Berlin. In the strongest statement made by any Adminisration official since the death of Secretary Dulles, Dillon told the closing session of an AFL-CIO conference in New York that come what may, Berlin would not be sacrificed. "No nation," the Secretary said, "could preserve its faith in collective security if we permitted the courageous people of West Berlin to be sold into slavery." Acknowledging that the problem in Berlin could be solved only by the reunification of Germany—the point Adenauer had stressed—Dillon carefully qualified the type of interim solution which the United States would accept. "We are determined to maintain our presence in Berlin and to preserve its ties with the Federal Republic," he said. "We will not accept any arrangement which might become the first step toward the abandonment of West Berlin or the extinguishing of freedom in that part of Germany which is a free, peaceful, and democratic member of the world community."

Several days later, President Eisenhower explicitly endorsed Mr. Dillon's remarks. Appearing at a press conference on April 27, the President stated that the Administration position at the forthcoming Summit had been completely covered in Dillon's speech. "The point is," Mr. Eisenhower said, "we are not going to give up the juridical rights that we have." [20]

As the American position on Berlin stiffened, an incident occurred on May 1, which rendered further negotiations virtually impossible. At exactly 5:36 A.M. that day, an American intelligence pilot, Francis Gary Powers of Pound, Virginia, was forced down over Soviet territory. As is now well known, Powers was flying a highly classified reconnaissance aircraft (U-2) engaged in aerial surveillance activities. His equipment was captured virtually intact by the Russians, and although Nikita Khrushchev and other top Soviet officials had known of the U-2 activities for some years,[21] the forcing down of Powers' aircraft was transformed by the Soviet Union into a major diplomatic incident. Two weeks later, when Khrushchev arrived in Paris for the opening of the Summit Conference, he announced that the meeting could not be held except under humiliating conditions. President Eisenhower, he said, would have to apologize publicly for the U-2 flight, and all those in the American Government who had had a hand in it would have to be dismissed.

Khrushchev knew these demands could not be fulfilled. Indeed, it seems clear that the U-2 incident was simply seized upon by the Russians as a pretext for breaking off the conference. The public statements of the American government in the previous two months, and particularly that of Under Secretary Dillon, had convinced the Soviets that their demands on Berlin would not be fulfilled. With an American presidential campaign then in the offing, why not wait six or eight months until the new Administration had taken office?

Not surprisingly, this is exactly what Khrushchev proposed. The Summit, he said, was not being canceled but only postponed until a more suitable occasion. Following Khrushchev's remarks, a Soviet spokesman at the Russian Embassy in Paris took great care to announce that the Soviet Union would make no unilateral move regarding a peace treaty with East Germany.[22] Three days later, Khrushchev himself said much the same thing in East Berlin. In short, the Soviet Union was willing to seize on the U-2 incident to interrupt negotiations at the Summit when it seemed likely that their demands would not be met. But they were not prepared to use the flight as a pretext for terminating negotiations entirely. Without doubt, the Russians expected to gain their prize in Berlin and were willing to wait once more for it to ripen. In the meantime, the East German puppet regime could continue its war of nerves.

By not using the U-2 episode as an excuse for consummating a separate peace treaty with East Germany, it is conceivable that the Soviet Union was attempting to lull Western suspicions and restore an outward international calm. The efficiency of the U-2 flights—judged from the material captured by the Soviets—undoubtedly caused many in the Kremlin to have second thoughts regarding Russia's military position vis-a-vis the West. As a result, Khrushchev did not press his diplomatic advantage and for the next six months Moscow scrupulously refrained from issuing any announcement about Berlin threatening the Western position.

Also, it is not improbable that Khrushchev's earlier threat to sign a separate treaty with the Ulbricht regime was merely a tactical maneuver designed to intimidate the West into further concessions. Such a treaty, if concluded, would have put the East Germans in a direct position of responsibility toward the West and would have made them legally liable—at least in Communist eyes—for relations with the Western powers. If this were done, then the "German Democratic Republic's" effectiveness as a ploy (or stalking horse) would be destroyed immediately and Ulbricht himself would thenceforth be entrusted with *de jure* Communist control over Western access to Berlin. There is no reason to believe that the Kremlin desired either of these possibilities.

First, it was far better from Moscow's point of view to use the East Germans as puppets to harass the West. If they went too far, they could always be disowned without involving the Soviet Union in any significant risk. Second, with official Communist responsibility for Western access in Ulbricht's hands, the East Germans might precipitate a crisis with the West leading directly to war. Certainly the Russians would prefer to keep this responsibility to themselves.[23]

Khrushchev's speech in East Berlin immediately following the Paris Summit left little doubt that this was what the Soviet Union had in mind. "We are realists and shall never follow an adventurous policy," he said. "In this situation, time is required." According to Khrushchev:

> We would like to believe that a summit conference will be held in six or eight months. Under these circumstances, it makes sense to wait still a little longer and try through the joint efforts of all four victorious powers to find a solution to the long since ripe question of the signing of a peace treaty with the two German states. . . . What is fallen from the wagon is lost.

Clearly, the Kremlin had decided to wait. Russia would take no unilateral action herself. The Western powers would not be pushed directly in Berlin, and the threat of a separate treaty with the so-called GDR would be shelved. But while the Russians waited, the East Germans, with tacit Soviet approval, stepped up their campaign to incorporate West Berlin, and at first, these efforts were directed against the ties binding the Western sectors to the Federal Republic.

The first incident in this new East German offensive arose over a proposed meeting of the West German Bundestag in Berlin, scheduled for July. Following the election of President Heuss in Berlin in 1954, the Bundestag had regularly opened its annual session with a one week symbolic meeting in the isolated city. Since the beginning of the Berlin crisis in 1958, however, the Russians had attacked these sessions as provocative. Now, in the summer of 1960, the East Germans vigorously took up the cry. Such a move this year, said Ulbricht, would be an assault against the sovereignty of the GDR and would jeopardize the temporary occupation status which he claimed West Berlin enjoyed.

But unlike previous Bundestag sessions, the West this time met the

East German attack in utter disarray. Within the Federal Republic opinion was bitterly divided between the CDU, which counseled caution, and the SPD of Mayor Brandt, which advocated holding the meeting in Berlin regardless of the Communist threat. The United States, which under Dulles had supported the meetings vigorously, now washed its hands of the matter, saying it was a problem for the Germans themselves to decide. France and Great Britain made it no secret that they opposed the meeting and, as a result, the Bundestag session was canceled.

The next East German move against Berlin occurred at the end of August. During the first four days of September each year the various West German refugee organizations (representing mainly those persons displaced from their homes by the advancing Red Army in 1945) have held an annual convention honoring "Homeland Day." In 1960, this ceremony was to be held in West Berlin. But on August 30, two days before the convention was to begin, the East German regime announced that passage to Berlin through the Soviet zone would be barred to all West Germans who intended to take part in these activities. The ban, they said, would remain in effect until midnight on Sunday, September 4.

The East German announcement was in clear violation of the 1949 accord that had lifted the blockade and guaranteed free access between West Berlin and the Federal Republic. A *New York Times* dispatch from Berlin on the day following the East German announcement described the restrictions as "the most stringent Communist interference with Western rights of free access to West Berlin . . . since the Berlin blockade of 1948–49." [24]

The East German move, it should be noted, did not affect Allied traffic and was aimed at only one particular group—a group whose purposes clearly ran counter to those of the GDR. Before the East German announcement had been made, certain elements of the Western press, especially in Britain and France, had been critical of holding the refugee meeting in Berlin. [25] Thus, by now moving against the meeting, the East Germans once more had chosen an issue on which the West was divided. By establishing their right to deny passage to Berlin to one group, however, the Communists were establishing their right to deny passage to all groups. If the East could make the ban stick, another slice of Western "salami" in Berlin would have disappeared, and as Mayor Brandt warned the West, the whole sausage would soon be gone, slice by slice.

The East German attack, as it turned out, was two-pronged. Simultaneously with the ban on travel to West Berlin, the Ulbricht regime also prohibited entry into East Berlin to all West Germans without a special pass issued by East Berlin authorities. On August 31, following a meeting with Mayor Brandt, the three Western Commandants dispatched a formal protest over both actions to Major General Zaharov, the Soviet Commandant in East Berlin. The East German travel ban was countered the following day by the organization of a "baby airlift" from Hanover which flew into Berlin anyone who had been denied passage by road. The West did nothing about the partial closing of the East Berlin border, however, and the East German regime scored another uncontested tactical victory.

Immediately after the East German measures went into effect, Allied spokesmen in Berlin attributed the East German moves to previous Western indecision. "Encouraged by Western hesitation to sanction the symbolic annual session of the West German Parliament in Berlin," the *New York Times* stated, "the East German puppet regime is now trying to put Western mettle to a further test. . . . The real purpose is, of course, to isolate West Berlin, to discourage West Berlin's political and economic development by constant threats against its lifeline and thereby make it wither on the vine." [26]

As the Ulbricht regime had announced, the restrictions remained in effect until midnight, September 4, then they were lifted without incident. Thus, without direct involvement, the Soviet Union witnessed the East Germans effecting one more curtailment of the Western position. The right of unimpeded Western access to Berlin had been effectively challenged and, perhaps even more significant, the "German Democratic Republic" had usurped the authority to curtail freedom of movement within the city itself.

As a result of their success, the East Germans continued their efforts. The day after the travel bans were lifted, GDR authorities halted twenty-three barges bound from Hamburg to West Berlin. According to East zone authorities, the barges carried too much weight for the water level of the canals. After three days of fruitless negotiations the

West yielded and reloaded the barges. There were few in Berlin who did not remember, however, that the 1948–49 Communist blockade had begun with a similar interruption of barge traffic.[27]

On September 8, less than one week after the earlier travel bans had been lifted, the East German regime announced that the restrictions on the entry of West Germans into East Berlin would be reimposed on a permanent basis. As has been noted, the West had not countered this restriction when it had first been imposed. The East Germans undoubtedly were encouraged by this and were willing to gamble that the West once more would not interfere. At an emergency session of the city council, Mayor Brandt prophetically warned that "we haven't yet reached the climax of the new crisis." Although the Western powers protested the East German action to the Soviet Union (the Soviets still had not answered the original protest filed on August 31), the East German restrictions were not eased. Where free circulation within all of Berlin formerly had been guaranteed to everyone, the West Germans now were singled out for special treatment. Entry into East Berlin was denied them except at the four crossing points where special passes were given out. A dangerous precedent was being set—again without significant Western reaction. The formal Western protest was rejected by the Soviet Union one week later with the curt statement that the GDR "has full responsibility for the territory under its control."[28]

On September 13, the same day that the Soviets rejected the Western protest, the East German regime resumed the attack. Passports issued by the Federal Republic to the citizens of West Berlin, they announced, would no longer be valid for travel through the Soviet zone. Shortly afterwards, Czechoslovakia and Poland announced that they too would not recognize West German passports for the Berliners. Once more the Soviet Union stood by and watched with satisfaction. To informed observers in Berlin at the time, the evidence seemed clear that Khrushchev had given the Ulbricht regime a free hand to go as far as it could in eroding Western rights in Berlin short of an actual showdown.

Five days after the passport announcement, the East Germans denied entry into East Berlin to the Apostolic Nuncio in Germany, Archbishop Corrado Bafile. In spite of the fact that the Archbishop was the official diplomatic representative of the Vatican—indeed, probably because of it—he was barred by East German border guards from attending services in the Soviet sector. The Communist action marked the first time that a foreigner equipped with proper identification had been denied free movement within the city. A Western protest was rejected by the Russians and three days later, on September 21, the GDR formally announced that all diplomats accredited in Bonn would have to receive "legal permission" before entering East Berlin. Thus, once again Ulbricht had moved from the particular to the general—from the Papal Nuncio to all diplomats. Thus, once again, another slice of Western sausage had disappeared in Berlin.

But now the West was ready to act—or at least, almost ready to act. The day after the East German announcement, American Ambassador to West Germany Walter Dowling drove through the Brandenburg Gate into East Berlin. Dowling's car was marked with American license plates and flew a large American flag on the fender. As it crossed the boundary it was stopped by East German People's Police. The Ambassador was told that he would have to turn around; that he could not proceed into East Berlin. Dowling replied that he was in Berlin as head of the American mission and was entitled to free access to all parts of the city. The East German officer demanded to see the Ambassador's identification and the Ambassador unwittingly produced it. As soon as he had done so the car was waved on.[29] By showing his identification papers to the East German border guards, Dowling inadvertently had recognized the right of the East zone authorities to control the movement of Allied personnel into East Berlin. Thus, in spite of the fact that his visit to East Berlin refuted the East German claim to be able to deny entrance to the Soviet sector to Allied diplomats, another precedent had been set. The following day, the official East German News Agency (ADN) announced that the diplomatic representatives of the United States, Great Britain, and France would not be denied access to East Berlin providing they showed their identity papers to the East German police on duty. In other words, they could enter East Berlin as long as the East Germans were granted the right to inspect these papers.[30]

Encouraged by their success, the East quickly pressed its advantage. On September 26, in supposed reaction to a rally being held near the sector boundary by the evangelist Billy Graham, the GDR announced the temporary closing of the East Berlin border. Although the closure lasted less than a day, the Communists clearly were testing Allied response. Mayor Brandt lost no time in warning the West accordingly.[31]

By now, Berlin public sentiment was indignant at Western inaction. In Bonn, where the situation was better understood—and where the voice of the Berliners carried more weight—the Adenauer Government began to speculate publicly on the rupture of all economic ties with the Soviet zone. The trade pact between the two areas was due to expire on December 31, and Chancellor Adenauer's spokesmen now lost no opportunity to remind the East that it would not be extended in the face of further Communist encroachments. The West German reaction served its purpose. Almost overnight the situation in Berlin eased and for the next three months the GDR attempted no further moves against Western rights. Indeed, many of the measures previously invoked were now relaxed. The GDR made no further attempts to restrict movement into East Berlin and Western diplomats were allowed to pass uninspected.

But during the year 1960, the Communists had made significant gains in Berlin. First, the Ulbricht regime had demonstrated the right to interrupt the flow of travel to Berlin from West Germany by road, rail, and water. Second, it had succeeded in curtailing free circulation within the city, establishing in the process the right to control entry into East Berlin, including entry even for accredited diplomatic officials. Third, it had successfully made a point of differentiating between West Berliners and West Germans both in the passport issue and over entrance into East Berlin, thereby encouraging the idea that Berlin was separate and distinct from the Federal Republic. In addition, the GDR had intimidated the Western powers by forcing the cancellation of the meeting of the Bundestag in West Berlin and, perhaps most important, had successfully sealed the border between East and West Berlin for almost twenty-four hours. To each of these actions Allied response had been negligible. A serious erosion of the Western position in Berlin thus had resulted and the Communists had been given numerous precedents on which to base their future action.

And as the year 1960 drew to a close, so did the Eisenhower Administration. The new President for whom Khrushchev professed to be waiting soon would assume office. Whether Khrushchev expected a change of policy on Berlin from the new administration is a moot point. Little, of course, was known of Senator Kennedy's views on the former German capital. During the second of the great TV debates with Vice

President Nixon, both candidates had been asked whether they would take military action to defend Berlin. Mr. Kennedy's answer, which is quoted below in full, could hardly have been reassuring to the Kremlin.

SENATOR KENNEDY: Mr. McGee [Dale McGee, N.B.C. News], we have a contractual right to be in Berlin coming out of the conversations at Potsdam and of World War II that has been reinforced by direct commitments of the President of the United States.

It's been reinforced by a number of other nations under NATO. I've stated on a number of occasions that the United States must meet its commitments in Berlin. It is a commitment that we have to meet if we are going to protect the security of Western Europe, and therefore on this question I don't think that there is any doubt in the mind of any American. I hope there is not any doubt in the mind of any member of the community of West Berlin.

I'm sure there isn't any doubt in the mind of the Russians.

We will meet our commitments to maintain the freedom and independence of West Berlin.[32]

Three months later, on January 20, 1961, John F. Kennedy was inaugurated thirty-fifth President of the United States. Although in his inaugural address he mentioned no area specifically, his tone again was of resolution and determination. Europe and the free world were heartened. Chancellor Adenauer and Mayor Brandt were warm in their praise of the new American President.

There was also reason to feel that the Berlin problem might have eased; that a standoff there had been achieved. Since the end of the Paris Conference the Soviet Union had made no move against the Western position. The Ulbricht regime—when faced with the threat of a trade embargo—had retreated from their sausage-slicing tactics of the previous autumn and now scrupulously avoided interfering with Western rights. Indeed, the show of Western firmness symbolized by the U-2 flight in May and the threatened trade embargo of October seemed to have removed Berlin from among the major world trouble spots. The first news conferences held by President Kennedy and Secretary of State Dean Rusk confirmed this. Neither spoke of Berlin when mentioning the major problem areas; Secretary Rusk specifically stated that the pressure on Berlin had eased.[33]

With this background of easing tensions, President Kennedy dispatched a personal note to Premier Khrushchev on February 22. Although both the President and Secretary Rusk had earlier expressed a distaste for "Summit diplomacy," Washington freely acknowledged that the note to Khrushchev contained a proposal for just such a meeting. The decision to dispatch the letter to Khrushchev came after two weeks of intensive discussions at the White House among the President's key foreign policy advisers. Taking part in these discussions were three previous Ambassadors to the Soviet Union; Charles Bohlen, George Kennan and Averell Harriman; the current American Ambassador, Llewellyn Thompson; Secretary Rusk, and other members of the President's personal directorate. When the discussions were over, it had been decided that a meeting between Mr. Kennedy and Premier Khrushchev might serve to reduce the chances of Russian miscalculation of American intent. Nothing was to be negotiated at such a meeting but a face to face confrontation, it was felt, would "clear the air" and pave the way for the resumption of "normal" U.S.-Soviet relations. Accordingly, on his return to Moscow in late February, Ambassador Thompson carried with him the President's message which he subsequently delivered to Premier Khrushchev in the Siberian industrial city of Novosibirsk on March 9.[34]

Simultaneous with the President's message to Khrushchev, Administration spokesmen began a series of public statements designed to answer Russian questions about Berlin. During a stop-off in the isolated city on March 8, Averell Harriman, the President's roving Ambassador, announced that the new Administration did not consider itself committed to any discussions on Berlin which had been conducted under President Eisenhower. "All discussions on Berlin," Harriman said, "must begin from the start." Specifically, Harriman's comment was an attempt to inform the Soviets that the final concessionary proposals offered at Geneva in July, 1959, were no longer valid. Two days later, State Department spokesman Lincoln White clarified this explicitly. The United States, he said, was "no longer bound" by the Geneva proposals and all negotiations with the Soviet Union will have to start from scratch, "not from August 5, 1959." Significantly, White added that the size of the American garrison in Berlin would not be cut. "I would like to state unequivocally," he said, "that the United States has no intention of reducing its garrison in West Berlin."[35]

Thus, although the Russians had witnessed a new Administration come to power in America, they were unable to discern any change in

American policy toward Berlin. If anything, the new Democratic Administration, if judged by its public statements, was taking an even firmer stand on Berlin than had the previous one. Khrushchev had been tendered an invitation to meet at the Summit but at the same time was put on notice as to what the West would not yield. Its rights in Berlin were among these.

For almost two months after the receipt of Kennedy's invitation, Khrushchev remained silent. Clearly, the Kremlin wanted no part of a Summit meeting with an Administration so positively committed, so determined to maintain its position and so outwardly successful—or at least, so outwardly untarnished by the events of the day. The Warsaw Pact nations, meeting in Moscow on March 28 and 29, 1961, made no reference to the President's message. Germany was mentioned but only in connection with purported rearmament activities. The threat of a separate treaty with the Ulbricht regime was not repeated.[36]

During the month of April, however, the fortune of world politics turned against the United States and, of course, against the Kennedy Administration. The ill-fated landing in the Bay of Pigs combined with the deteriorating Western position in Laos quickly diminished the luster of the new American government. American foreign policy had suffered decisive setbacks; in both Cuba and Laos, the Administration had been guilty of talking firmly and acting timidly. Confronted with these American failures, the Soviet Union now took the initiative.

On May 4, the Kremlin advised the American Embassy in Moscow that Mr. Khrushchev "still was willing" to meet with President Kennedy "if Mr. Kennedy was interested." The United States advised the Kremlin that an official U.S. reply would be made before May 20. Two weeks later, on May 16, Soviet Ambassador Menshikov called at the White House to deliver Khrushchev's formal answer to the President's letter. Over two months had elapsed since Khrushchev had received it and the world situation had changed considerably.

Three days after Menshikov's call at the White House, it was officially announced that a Kennedy–Khrushchev meeting would take place. The site would be Vienna and the dates June 3 and 4—immediately following the President's already scheduled visit to France. The announcement of the meeting, issued simultaneously by Washington and Moscow, stressed that the two leaders did not plan to negotiate but only to meet and discuss their positions.

Coming as it did with virtually no diplomatic preparation and on top of Administration failures in Laos and Cuba, the mere fact that the Vienna Conference was being held represented a tactical victory for the Soviet Union. Instead of talking from a position of strength, President Kennedy was reduced to speaking from a background of failure. While his four day stop-over in Paris served admirably to renew Western ties with De Gaulle, the two days spent in Vienna turned into a diplomatic rout.

Before his arrival in Vienna, President Kennedy joined General De Gaulle in espousing their joint determination to defend Berlin by whatever means were necessary. The public statements made in Paris were replete with professions of firmness. It is therefore all the more remarkable that the Vienna encounter was used by Khrushchev for once more regaining the initiative in Berlin. The tough talk of Paris, seen in the context of Laos and Cuba, evidently failed to impress the Soviet leader.

The first meeting of President Kennedy and Premier Khrushchev in Vienna was devoted to Laos and disarmament. The following day, June 4, 1961, Berlin and Germany were discussed. At the onset of the second day's discussions Premier Khrushchev presented Mr. Kennedy with an *aide-mémoire* defining the Soviet position. But the Soviet note was more than merely a statement of policy. Khrushchev had used it—and the Vienna Conference—to begin a new Soviet assault on the free status of West Berlin.

Basically, the Russian *aide-mémoire* of June 4 repeated the original Soviet note of November 27, 1958, and brought it up to date. It threatened a separate treaty with the regime of the Soviet zone, demanded a demilitarized status for West Berlin, and prescribed a new time limit. Indeed, the Soviet *aide-mémoire* was far more specific than the original note of November 27 had been. Detailed treaty arrangements with Germany were suggested and, if the United States was "not prepared" to sign an agreement with the GDR, the Soviets suggested two treaties —"with both or with one German state at its discretion." According to the Russians, "these treaties do not have to have identical texts but must contain the same provisions on the major questions of a peace settlement."

As for Berlin, the conclusion of a peace treaty, the Soviets said, would "normalize" the situation there by converting it into a demilitarized free city.

. . . as the Soviet Government sees it, West Berlin must be strictly neutral. It must not be tolerated, of course, that West Berlin be used further as a base for provocative hostile activity against the USSR, the German Democratic Republic or any other state or that it continue to remain a dangerous seat of tension and international conflict.

To guarantee the "neutrality" of West Berlin, Khrushchev proposed that "token contingents" of the four Allies, including the Soviet Union, be stationed there.

In perhaps the most significant part of the note, the Soviets demanded that both German states meet together and "explore the possibilities of agreement" within six months. This, of course, would mean the end of German reunification based on free elections and represented a further effort by the Soviets to legitimize their puppet regime in East Germany. The six-month time limit suggested by the Russians also marked a repudiation of the Camp David agreement and the imposition of a new ultimatum.

The international climate had changed substantially since Paris, and Khrushchev was once more on the offensive. The *aide-mémoire* concluded with an undisguised threat:

> If the United States does not show an understanding of the necessity for concluding a peace treaty, we shall have to sign a peace treaty . . . not with all states but only with those that want to sign it.
> The peace treaty will specifically record the status of West Berlin as a free city and the Soviet Union . . . will strictly observe it. In addition, measures will be taken to see that this status is also respected by the other countries. At the same time this will also mean the liquidation of the occupation regime in West Berlin with all the resulting consequences. Specifically, the questions of using land, water, and air communications across the territory of the German Democratic Republic will have to be settled in no other way than through appropriate agreements with the German Democratic Republic.

Confronted with the new Soviet assault, President Kennedy sought to hold his ground. The final communique issued at the close of the second day's conference stressed only that the meeting had provided a useful exchange of views. The fact that the President and Khrushchev had met was held up as a sign of encouragement. The Soviet *aide-*

mémoire was not mentioned and the world was not yet apprised that the third Soviet attack on Berlin had begun.

Immediately upon his return to the United States, President Kennedy reported to the American people on the results of the Vienna meeting. In the President's words, "it was a very sober two days." The advantages of the conferences were admittedly vague and related to the supposedly reduced possibilities of misjudgment. "No spectacular progress was either achieved or pretended. . . . [but] at least the chances of a dangerous misjudgment on either side should now be less, and at least the men on whose decisions the peace, in part, depends have agreed to remain in contact." [37]

According to President Kennedy: "Our most somber talks were on the subject of Berlin. I made it clear to Mr. Khrushchev that the security of Western Europe and therefore our own security are deeply involved in our presence and our access rights to West Berlin, that those rights are based on law not on sufferance; and that we are determined to maintain those rights at any risk and thus our obligation to the people of West Berlin and their right to choose their own future. . . . We and our Allies cannot abandon our obligations to the people of West Berlin."

Thus, if Khrushchev had used the Vienna meeting to launch another attack on West Berlin, President Kennedy had used it to emphasize to the Soviet leader the risks which such a policy involved. But the supposed advantages arising from the resumption of diplomatic contact at the highest level can be quickly dismissed. Khrushchev simply had assessed the tide of world events to be running in his favor and had used the Vienna Conference to pursue his advantage. Like Hitler at Munich, he had used it to impress on the West the risks of opposing his policy and the dangers of total war. Indeed, he had imparted a caution to Western policy where previously none had existed—a caution unfortunately reminiscent of Neville Chamberlain in 1938. The only results of the so-called "resumption of contact at the highest level," in fact, were a decided worsening of U.S.–Soviet relations, a concomitant increase in defense expenditures, and an accelerated deterioration of the situation in Berlin. Once more the Kremlin had played the game of Summit diplomacy to its own advantage.

12

From Vienna to August 13

FOLLOWING THE DISCLOSURE of the American U–2 activities and the rupture of the Paris Summit, the Russians scrupulously refrained from making further demands on Berlin. Once the threat of economic sanctions had been applied, the Soviet stooges in East Germany likewise had remained silent. But at Vienna the Communist offensive began once more. With the presentation of the Soviet *aide-mémoire* to President Kennedy, the Berlin Crisis resumed with an intensity not equalled since the original Russian ultimatum of three years before. John F. Kennedy had gone to Vienna to convince Khrushchev of American greatness and determination. He left shaken by new Soviet demands and belligerence; in the President's own words, the effect was "sobering."

Premier Khrushchev wasted little time in adding new fuel to the fire. The day after his return to Moscow the Soviet Union dispatched seething notes to the four Western powers protesting a forthcoming meeting of the West German Bundesrat in Berlin. According to the Soviet note, the meeting, which was scheduled for June 16, constituted an "unlawful interference of authorities of the Federal Republic of Germany in the affairs of West Berlin and its use for the organization of international provocation endangering peace and tranquility in the heart of Europe."

The United States quickly denounced the unfounded Soviet charges. State Department spokesman Lincoln White said that this Government considered the meeting of the Bundesrat in Berlin neither provocative nor "in any way inconsistent with the special status of Berlin. . . . We continue to find it difficult to understand," White stated, "how the routine meeting of a free, democratic parliament can, by any stretch of the imagination, be characterized as a 'new, major provocation against the Soviet Union.'" [1]

But second thoughts quickly arose over White's statement. Both London and Paris were still dubious about West German parliamentary sessions in Berlin and Chancellor Adenauer tended to agree. Even in the United States powerful voices within the Administration could be heard questioning the wisdom of such a move. Accordingly, two days later in Bonn, Bundesrat President Franz Meyers announced that the Berlin meeting "which had been tentatively scheduled for Friday," would be canceled. [2]

The Soviet notes protesting the Bundesrat meeting were dispatched on June 8. On June 10, the Soviet news agency Tass released the text of the *aide-mémoire* which had been presented to President Kennedy in Vienna because of "inexact" and "distorted" versions of the note which had appeared in the Western press.

The State Department interpreted this as another sign that the Russians intended "to stir up as much trouble as possible over Berlin during the coming months." Immediately following the Vienna Conference, in fact, Dean Rusk had told the NATO Council that one way of judging Soviet intent would be to see whether Moscow published the memorandum or kept it secret. If they kept it secret, then the document would undoubtedly be meant for serious bargaining. If it were published, Rusk said, it would indicate that it had been prepared for "propaganda purposes" and meant the beginning of a new Soviet offensive. [3]

The publication of the Soviet *aide-mémoire* was received in Europe much as Rusk had suggested. No discernible split was evident in Allied ranks and, if anything, the principal powers drew closer together awaiting the new Communist onslaught. London and Paris both announced that the Soviet demands for a peace treaty and a demilitarized free city of West Berlin were unacceptable as a basis for negotiation. In Hanover, Chancellor Konrad Adenauer, speaking before an election rally of an estimated 300,000 persons, demanded the right of "self-determination and freedom for all of Germany." In Berlin itself, Mayor Brandt warned that the West "must not accept unilateral Soviet steps leading to a repetition of the disastrous Munich agreement of 1938 that led to Czechoslovakia's downfall." [4]

As was foreseen, the publication of the *aide-mémoire* marked the beginning of the new Soviet offensive. On June 15, five days after its release, Nikita Khrushchev, in an unprecedented television report to the Soviet people, stated that "the conclusion of a peace treaty with Germany cannot be postponed any longer; *a peaceful settlement in Europe must be attained this year.* . . . Should certain countries refuse to take part in the negotiations on the conclusion of a peace treaty . . . we shall sign it with the German Democratic Republic alone."

In marked contrast to the firm, and indeed, tough statements by President Kennedy regarding Berlin, Khrushchev hid his "shaft of iron" between repeated avowals of peaceful intent. Unlike the West, Khrushchev sought not to convince the world of firmness but rather to cloak the demands of aggression in the language of peace. Already, in fact, Soviet arguments for a German peace treaty and a demilitarized "free city" of West Berlin were making serious inroads among the neutral and uncommitted nations. Many of these were only faintly aware of the issues in Berlin and Khrushchev's constant championing of peace and peace treaties caused large blocs in Asia and Africa to identify Russia as the country seeking to solve the Berlin Crisis and the Western powers—the age old colonialists—as those blocking the way.

This superficial reasoning obscured the origin of the crisis in the first place and Khrushchev lost no opportunity to encourage it. In his speech to the Russian people he played this line to the hilt. "Every person," he said, "if not deprived of common sense, understands that the signing of a peace treaty is the road toward improving relations between states. The refusal to sign a peace treaty and the perpetuation of the occupation regime in West Berlin are directed at continuing the cold war, and who can say where lies the borderline between a cold war and a war in the full sense of the word?"

The conclusion of Khrushchev's television address offers an interesting insight into the Communist view of world politics. "Our talks with President Kennedy," the Soviet leader said, "revealed the fact that we understand the peaceful coexistence of states differently. The President's idea is to build up some sort of dam against the peoples' movements."

> Naturally this is an absolutely wrong concept and we cannot agree with it. It is in no one's power to halt the peoples' wish for freedom. All regimes which are built on the oppression and exploitation of peoples are unstable and cannot exist forever. . . .
>
> The changing of the social and political life of society is an inevitable process. It does not depend on agreement between statesmen.
>
> It is impossible to erect an obstacle in the path of the peoples' movement to progress, to a better life. This has been proven by the entire course of human development. At one time there existed slavery; it was replaced by feudalism, and then its place was taken by capitalism. One system replaced another because the new system was more progressive.
>
> . . . A class struggle is under way in the capitalist countries. The people are fighting against their oppressors, against reactionary regimes. It is impossible to regulate these processes by agreement. He who would like to reach an agreement on this question would only show that he does not understand history, does not understand the laws of the development of society.

The day before Khrushchev spoke, there was further evidence that the United States was having serious second thoughts about its position in Berlin. The Kennedy Administration, which took office so determined to arrest the decline of American prestige, began to waver perceptibly under the burdens of responsibility and to shrink back from the risks of a firm policy. In the absence of vigorous Presidential leadership the sceptre fell to other hands; on June 14, Senate Majority Leader Mike Mansfield, who previously had advocated compromise in Berlin, once more addressed to the United States Senate his plan for converting Berlin into a demilitarized free city. The present American policy, Mansfield stated, "carries the ultimate implication of American willingness to pledge the lives and fortunes of every man, woman, and child in the nation to Berlin's defense." The Montana Democrat, evidently unprepared to face this eventuality, suggested a so-called "third way" between the U.S. and Russian positions which would turn the city over to the already hard pressed United Nations.[5]

Although Mansfield's speech was immediately denounced by Republican Senators Jacob Javits (N.Y.) and Hugh Scott (Pa.), and although President Kennedy soon took pains to dissociate himself from Mansfield, the fact that Mike Mansfield was Senate Majority Leader led many—and especially many in Europe—to question whether his speech had not been an Administration trial balloon. Its delivery on the eve of Khrushchev's major television report hardly sustained American firm intentions.

The day following Mansfield's speech, and several hours before Premier Khrushchev was to address the Russian people, Walter Ulbricht held an extremely informative press conference in East Berlin. Once more Ulbricht was playing the heavy to the Kremlin's virtuoso, leaving little doubt what the Communists meant by a "free city" in West Berlin. When that came about, Ulbricht said, the refugee camps would be shut down and RIAS and all other "irritants" to the East German regime would be liquidated. Emigration from the Peoples' Republic would then be halted and only those who "obtained permission" would be allowed to leave.[6]

Also, according to Ulbricht, when a peace treaty with the Soviet Union had been signed, communications to Berlin would be controlled by the GDR. When asked if this would mean that Tempelhof airport in West Berlin would be closed down, Ulbricht responded that "perhaps the airport will close itself down. . . . Think of the West Berliners. Today they are constantly disturbed by the noise of aircraft and they are exposed to the danger—as happened in Munich *—of aircraft crashing into buildings."

But in spite of the statements by Ulbricht and Khrushchev describing their aims in Berlin, the Senate debate on firmness continued. On June 20, in a tone reminiscent of an earlier Senator from Montana, prewar isolationist Burton K. Wheeler, Mike Mansfield once more criticized American determination to remain in Berlin. Unless the United States was willing to change its approach, the majority leader said, "we shall find ourselves in pursuit of the last car of a train that is al-

---

* This refers to a crash by an American C–53 in downtown Munich at Christmas time, 1960, killing over 100 persons.

ways pulling away from us." Again, since it was the leader of the President's party in the Senate who was speaking, his words brought little assurance to America's allies and, indeed, did even less to convince the Kremlin that the Kennedy Administration was prepared to fight for Berlin.

Already, in fact, serious doubts were arising in Europe as to American determination. In London, where official policy on Berlin had hardened considerably since the promotion of Lord Home to Foreign Minister, Government opinion was reported concerned lest Russia underestimate Western determination.[7] A *New York Times* dispatch dated the same day as Mansfield's remarks to the Senate reported that in London's view, the major crisis in Berlin was due to the fact "that Premier Khrushchev does not take seriously the West's intention to support their rights in Berlin under pressure." France likewise now began to advocate a firm stand on Berlin and during the first part of July, President De Gaulle grandly reminded visitors to the Elysee Palace— including U.S. Ambassador James Gavin—of the perils of negotiating with the Communists from a position of weakness.[8]

Thus, in the month following the Vienna Conference the center of Western determination to remain in Berlin shifted precariously from Washington to Europe. President Kennedy had gone to Vienna to convince Khrushchev of Western resolve, but now, in the face of Khrushchev's ever increasing attacks, he was singularly silent about combating Russia's latest demands, and hesitated to exert the leadership which was so sorely needed. To some extent, Mr. Kennedy's hesitancy undoubtedly stemmed from the failure of our intervention in Cuba. The Administration leaders (and President Kennedy particularly) were well aware that the Democratic Party had been identified in numerous public opinion polls before the election as "the war party." With the Cuban fiasco manifestly lending credence to this label, the Administration now was doubly cautious to take any stand which could be termed belligerent.

Also, following Vienna, President Kennedy himself—perhaps for the first time—realized the risks that a firm stand in Berlin entailed. With his profound sense of history, he recoiled before the spectre of nuclear war and the possible charge of future generations that perhaps because of his youth he had precipitated the global holocaust his predecessors had avoided. His closest advisers report that the President was literally

stunned by his meeting with Khrushchev. *Time* magazine, in selecting
Mr. Kennedy as the "Man of the Year" for 1961, states that the period
after Vienna was "the most critical so far in the personal and political
life of John Kennedy." According to *Time*, "the President became
moody, withdrawn, often fell into deep thought in the midst of festive
occasions with family and friends." Supposedly, he sat up late in the
White House brooding about the dangers of war.

Mr. Paul B. Fay, Assistant Secretary of the Navy and an old wartime
friend of the President, reports that during this period he was called
on the telephone by Mr. Kennedy and asked whether he had built his
bomb shelter.

"No," Fay says he replied, "I built a swimming pool." "You made a
mistake," the President said. "And he was dead serious," Fay adds.*

Khrushchev himself was aware of the change that Vienna had
wrought in the President and remarked in his television speech of
June 15, "I have the impression that President Kennedy understands
the great responsibility that lies with the governments of two such
powerful states . . . I should like to hope that the awareness of this
responsibility will remain in the future." 9

In the absence of the President's firmness, United States policy was
stuck on dead center. No effective American counter was offered to
the Russian propaganda offensive and the Soviet attack continued to
mount in intensity.

On June 21, less than one week from the date of his nationwide television and radio appearance, Nikita Khrushchev spoke once more on
the German situation. The occasion was the twentieth anniversary of
the invasion of Russia by Hitler in 1941, and Khrushchev lost no opportunity to identify the present West German government with Hitler's policies. Khrushchev's assault was another attempt to create dissension in the West—another attempt to fan the embers of anti-German
sentiment—and once more pictured the Soviet Union as the real cham-
pion of peace seeking to end the vestiges of World War II.

"Today," said Khrushchev, "I should like to warn those who, like
Chancellor Adenauer, call for 'standing firm' . . . in reply to the Soviet
Union's peaceful proposals. On more than one occasion we reminded

---

* This conversation was reported by Fay to William Manchester, then doing a
feature piece on the President which later appeared in the April, 1962, issue of
Holiday.

the leaders of the Federal Republic of Germany about the merits of reason. Is it possible, gentlemen, that you have forgotten the inglorious experience of your predecessors and would like to repeat it?"

After briefly describing the advances in Soviet military strength during the past twenty years, Khrushchev castigated the West German Chancellor for his "noisy rantings." "It goes without saying," Khrushchev said, "that some unreasonable person may commit suicide. His relations will weep over him, but humanity will not suffer from that. But when statesmen invested with high authority are playing with fire . . . at stake are not only their lives but also the destiny of their peoples. By dragging West Germany into an adventure, you are pushing the people of your country toward suicide."

In contrast to his attack on Adenauer, Khrushchev notably omitted any criticism of other Western leaders. For Mike Mansfield, in fact, he had the highest praise. Said Khrushchev:

> On the question of West Berlin the governments of the United States, Britain and France adhere to the positions of yesterday. Even Western political leaders have to admit this. Mansfield, the Democratic majority leader in the United States Senate, declared in his speech of June 14th, 1961, that he could not agree with the position of the Kennedy Administration. . . . He stressed that it is not courageous to stand stubbornly on untenable positions but it is better to seek agreement with other parties concerned on a businesslike basis. This is a current approach and we can only welcome it.

Khrushchev interlarded his attacks on West Germany with repeated appeals to the neutral nations and further avowals of peaceful intent. Again he announced his intention of concluding a peace treaty—"this question is not only ripe but overripe"—and repeated the Soviet pledge to solve the problem in Berlin "at the end of this year." [10]

Reaction to Khrushchev's speech in Washington was noncommittal. The United States made no effort either to reaffirm its ties to Berlin or to combat Khrushchev's open appeal to the "uncommitted" nations. The attack on West Germany and Konrad Adenauer went virtually unanswered, and Secretary of State Rusk, at a press conference shortly afterward, refused to concede that Khrushchev's threat to sign a separate treaty before the end of the year constituted an ultimatum. The strongest statement Rusk could muster, in fact, was that Khrushchev's speech "must be a keen disappointment to those who seek to advance the cause of peace." The Secretary pointedly disagreed with a newsman who referred to the situation in Berlin as the most serious threat to the West since "the beginning of the cold war period" and stated that he "did not want to use superlatives" in discussing the matter.

The following day, U.S. officials held a lengthy three-hour session at the White House to review American policy. This was to be the first of many such sessions over the next two months and the beginning of many publicly announced "reviews of defense posture." The outcome, on this occasion, was for the Administration to disclaim any defense build-up "at the present time" and to plead for calm in meeting the Russian threat.[11] Because of the implication that something is amiss, a method less likely to inspire public confidence than an announced policy review at the White House has yet to be devised. London, Paris, Bonn and Berlin all now wondered about the future course of the United States and were perplexed that this, of all times, should be selected by the American government to reconsider Administration policy.

The next several days of June passed without incident. On June 27, the Executive Council of the AFL-CIO attempted to put some steel into American resolve and condemned the Mansfield proposals for converting Berlin into a "free city" as a sure method of surrendering the city to communism. But their efforts were of little avail, and the following day Nikita Khrushchev returned to the charge. The West was in disarray and the Kremlin knew it. American leadership—needed so vitally in a time of crisis—now was totally lacking.

The occasion for Khrushchev's new outburst was a meeting in Moscow honoring Soviet-Vietnamese friendship. Again Khrushchev singled out West Germany for his attack. The other Western powers escaped only with a warning of Soviet strength and a threat not to interfere in the affairs of the GDR. "If certain Western Powers do not wish to respect the sovereignty of the German Democratic Republic and if, for this reason, they believe they have the right to resort to force, it is the right of a highwayman, and prayers will not save anyone from him. A highwayman can be beaten off only with a stick."

Once more Khrushchev paid special attention to those in the West who sought compromise. "There are quite a few sober voices in the

West," he said, "speaking in favor of the peaceful solution of the German problem with due regard for the obtaining situation in Europe." Perhaps in deference to these "sober voices" Khrushchev repeated his proposals for a free West Berlin with "international guarantees" and assured the West that there would be no blockade. Of course, he added, since the lines of access all went through the German Democratic Republic, an "agreement with the government of this state" would have to be made.

Thus, for the third time in two weeks, and for the fifth time after his first meeting with President Kennedy, Nikita Khrushchev was attacking the status quo in Berlin. But unlike his assaults in previous years which had united the West, this time Khrushchev found dissension and hesitation. The European Allies—Great Britain, France, and West Germany—remained determined but the United States, under the hazards of a new Administration, seemed unable to get its bearings and declined to take positive action. In Bonn, Paris, and even London, cries of anguish at American procrastination already could be heard. Speaking to the House of Commons shortly after Khrushchev's speech to the Vietnamese, Prime Minister Harold Macmillan made little effort to conceal his distress at Washington's inaction. The policy of Her Majesty's Government, he told the Commons, was that no proposal regarding Berlin or Germany could be considered which did not include a "provision for German reunification."

Except for Macmillan's statement, however, Khrushchev's assaults went largely unanswered. At his press conference on June 28, President Kennedy even declined to discuss the Berlin issue until he received a report on the crisis from a special committee under Dean Acheson.

Even after the Acheson report was presented (June 28), the Administration seemed uncertain how to proceed in Berlin. Daily newspaper accounts emanating from Washington during the first few weeks of July are full of conflicting stories leaked by unidentified "high level officials" stating that first this and then that course would be followed. Official statements from the American Government, however, were conspicuous by their absence. An *ad hoc* meeting of the President, Secretary Rusk, Secretary of Defense Robert McNamara and General Maxwell Taylor at Hyannis Port on July 8, decided only that the nation's military strength should be "re-examined" in view of the present crisis.[12]

Significantly, the Hyannis Port consultations of the Administration were interrupted by an announcement that Premier Khrushchev was again at the rostrum. The occasion this time was a Kremlin reception for graduating students of the Soviet Union's military academies; as usual, the German Federal Republic and Chancellor Adenauer were the major targets of Khrushchev's attack, but now, Macmillan and De Gaulle were also singled out for criticism—the former for his "firm" remarks, the latter for announcing the return of one division from Algeria to Europe. The arguments for a peace treaty with "both German states" were repeated by Khrushchev and the security of a "free city" of West Berlin was again guaranteed.

But the most important part of Khrushchev's speech dealt with Soviet defense policy. Citing a three-billion dollar increase in the defense budget requested by President Kennedy in "his recent messages to Congress," Khrushchev announced a whopping twenty-five percent increase in Russian military spending. He naturally did not mention that President Kennedy's "recent messages" took place in March—well before the Vienna Conference—and that the three-billion dollar increase amounted to only 7.5 percent of the American budget. Said Khrushchev: "In view of the growing military budgets of the NATO countries, the Soviet Government has passed a decision to increase defense spending in the current year by 3.144 billion rubles, thereby raising the total military expenditures in 1961 to 12.399 billion rubles."

Also, the proposed reduction of the armed forces planned for this year, Khrushchev said, would not take place. But "these are forced measures," he assured his listeners. "We are taking them, due to the emergency circumstances, because we cannot neglect the interests of the Soviet people's security." [13]

Khrushchev's speech to the military academy graduates was the sixth time since Vienna that Russia had brought pressure on Berlin and the United States had yet to answer the original Soviet *aide-mémoire*. But while Washington waited, Berlin's other protectors were busy. On July 12, President De Gaulle added his voice to Macmillan's and Adenauer's in decrying the latest Soviet offensive. Majestically, the President of the Fifth Republic put aside any idea that the Russians would succeed in changing the status of the former German capital. "Here are the Russians," he told France, "renewing their claim to settle unilaterally the fate of Berlin. . . . I state, once again, that there is no chance that that will be accepted." [14]

As De Gaulle spoke, rumblings were still being heard from the other Western European capitals at American delay in coming to grips with the Berlin problem. London especially was reported dissatisfied. The British government was more than sensitive to the charges of appeasement which previously had been leveled at it and now sought to allay any suspicion of "softness." At the same time—and perhaps with a good deal of justification—the British began to decry previous Western reliance exclusively on the rights of occupation in Berlin. Instead, the Macmillan Government suggested that the West should take the diplomatic offensive and charge Russia with unilaterally attempting to change the map of Central Europe.

Accepting the British position would have restored the initiative to the Allies. Russia would become the aggressor attempting to stifle the liberties of the two and a half million West Berliners, rather than the "peacemaker" seeking to end the "remnants" of the Second World War. According to the British, the reliance on sixteen-year-old occupation rights was a poor choice of weapons. War, if necessary, could be waged over the arbitrary surrender of East Germans and West Berliners to communism but not over the foreclosure of legalistic "rights." [15]

In spite of the British suggestion, however, the days continued to go by without a positive statement from America. A *New York Times* dispatch from London on July 14, reported intense anger in British governmental circles at the American refusal to speak out on Berlin. "The most frequent complaint" heard in London, said the *Times,* "is over the delay in the formation of a strong United States policy on Berlin." [16]

Indeed, by mid-July Washington had become extremely sensitive to the charges of procrastination emanating from Western Europe. But instead of acting boldly, the response once more was one of documented leaks to favorite reporters and officially stimulated rumors. For three successive days beginning on July 15, the *New York Times* carried front page stories describing how the situation in Berlin was being given "very careful consideration." In each case the source of the report was attributed to anonymous "high officials."

Arthur Krock, the venerable sage of the *Times* editorial page, was moved to remark that "this deluge of ink and air" could only serve to dilute whatever official statements were transmitted to Khrushchev. It was not responsible statesmanship, Krock said, to allow the delay in a reply to Moscow "to be punctuated with a succession of statements, inspired leaks, and huffs and puffs about what forceful things the United States is ultimately 'going to do.'" Should Khrushchev miscalculate American intent in Berlin, "this purely rhetorical flexing of our muscles will bear considerable responsibility." [17]

Krock, an earlier supporter of the President, minced few words in criticizing the Administration's procrastination. Indeed, his remarks are extremely revealing in describing the effect which the six-week moratorium on American action had had. "The last few days," according to Krock, "supplied a good example of the contrast between saying much and doing little that weakens world confidence in the capacity of a nation to decide what to do and the will then to move decisively. . . . And for this very reason, the brave talk by and for the Kennedy Administration has come to comparable climaxes before. The United States is being increasingly criticized as a big talker and a smaller doer." [18]

When at long last the American reply to the original Soviet *aide-mémoire* was delivered in Moscow on July 17—six weeks after the original Soviet demands had been handed President Kennedy at Vienna—there was little cause for jubilation. In most respects, the American note was a thinly veiled plea for compromise and caused only further alarm in Western Europe. With a clear reference to the concessionary proposals made at Geneva (proposals which the Administration had rejected before Vienna), the U.S. reply stated:

> That the United States is not wedded to one particular arrangement for Berlin is demonstrated by the all-Berlin solution which was proposed at Geneva in 1959. It has accepted the possibility of practical arrangements intended to improve the present situation in Berlin until such time as an over-all solution of the German problem can be achieved.[19]

Since the Geneva proposals had been disowned explicitly by Washington in March, their being mentioned again at this time was extremely significant and, needless to say, sent shivers down the spines of many who had been counting on vigorous American leadership.

The American note also had its firmer passages but these were more than outweighed by the reference to Geneva. After making the plea for negotiations, the U.S. reply went on to attack each of the Communist arguments for a separate treaty, to plead the case of self-determination, and to restate the legal basis of the Western position. In defer-

ence to British sentiments it also pointed out that the United States
was not insisting upon "the maintenance of its legal rights" in Berlin
merely because of a desire to perpetuate its presence there but because "the freedom of the people of West Berlin depends upon those
rights."

The note defended the German Federal Republic for consistently
taking "significant steps to integrate itself firmly and peacefully into
the Western European community," and roundly criticized Soviet
policy of obstructing reunification. The "so-called 'German Democratic
Republic,' which is not freely chosen," was particularly condemned
for being purely "an instrument of Soviet foreign policy."

The signing of a separate treaty, the U.S. note concluded, would
be without legal foundation and could have "unforeseeable consequences." "Should the U.S.S.R. make unilateral moves in its German
policy, . . . the NATO countries could only interpret such moves as
a purposeful threat to their national interests." This reference was
vague and ambiguous, however, and after six weeks of anticipation,
the U.S. reply fell considerably short of the response that had been
expected. From its tenor, it was obvious that the hesitancy to adopt
a firm, no-compromise stand continued to prevail in Washington.[20]

A press conference held by President Kennedy two days later went
a good deal further toward defining the United States position. Again,
however, the President pointedly omitted the all-out commitment to
Berlin which many in Europe thought was necessary. The most significant portion of Mr. Kennedy's statement was directed at the neutral
and uncommitted peoples; with great care the President effectively
exposed the Communist myth of a free city. "A city," he said, "does
not become free merely by calling it a 'free city.' For a city or a people to be free requires that they be given the opportunity, without
economic, political, or police pressure, to make their own choice and
to live their own lives. The people of West Berlin today have that
freedom. It is the objective of our policy that they shall continue to
have it." [21]

The week following the President's press conference, the East German government, no doubt encouraged by the reluctance of the United
States to meet the Soviet assault head-on, announced that upon the
conclusion of a peace treaty all "foreign aircraft" would have to get
"permission" before crossing its territory. The East German announce-

ment was a clear threat to Allied access into Berlin but again the Communist move went unanswered. Instead, on July 23, Secretary of State Rusk said that the United States would consider taking the Berlin issue to the United Nations "if it develops into a situation of high tension." Rusk's announcement was greeted with considerable misgiving in Paris and Bonn where sentiment for the UN was not running particularly high at this time and served to point up once more the differences in the West. According to Rusk, a UN debate on Berlin would discredit the Russian position among the neutral nations and would "be a very heavy price" for Khrushchev to pay since "he has made it clear that he has some political ambitions" in this part of the world.[22]

On July 25, two days after Rusk's statement regarding the UN, and as the situation in Berlin continued to deteriorate, President Kennedy broke the secrecy which had enshrouded Administration planning and, in a suddenly scheduled nationwide television speech, advised the world of the moves America intended to take. The seven-week delay since Khrushchev's original Vienna eruption, however, seriously vitiated the President's new avowals of firmness. Soviet Ambassador to the United States ("Smiling Mike") Menshikov had made the remark at a Washington cocktail party only the week before that he thought the West was bluffing. Since Soviet diplomats are generally well primed before talking, Menshikov's statement is highly revealing.

In many respects, President Kennedy's speech on July 25 was as firm as any made on the Berlin crisis since 1958. Not only did he emphasize American determination to remain in Berlin but he also outlined a positive program of defense measures which the United States was undertaking to support its position. After referring to West Berlin as "the great testing place of Western courage," the President waxed eloquent about its defense: "I hear it said that West Berlin is militarily untenable. And so was Bastogne. And so, in fact, was Stalingrad. Any dangerous spot is tenable if men—brave men—make it so."

Mr. Kennedy then reviewed the military measures which the Administration intended to take. "Our primary purpose is neither propaganda nor provocation—but preparation," he said. "We intend to have a wider choice than humiliation or all-out nuclear action." The following day, the President announced, he would ask the Congress for an additional $3,249,000,000 for the armed forces. Half of the total sum ($1.8 billion) would be spent for conventional weapons and equipment. All three services would be increased and draft calls would be "doubled and tripled" in the coming months. Certain Reserve and Air National Guard units would be called to active duty and airlift and sealift capacities would be expanded. The deactivation of the B–47 bombers of the Strategic Air Force was to be delayed, and Civil Defense expenditures would be increased by $207 million.

The President then pledged a diplomatic offensive to reduce the crisis. According to Mr. Kennedy, "our peacetime military posture is traditionally defensive; but our diplomatic posture need not be. Our response to the Berlin crisis will not be merely military or negative. It will be more than merely standing firm." Negotiations, he said, were welcome. In words once more reminiscent of Geneva, the President then stated:

> We have previously indicated our readiness to remove any actual irritants in West Berlin, but the freedom of that city is not negotiable. . . . We recognize the Soviet Union's historical concerns about their security in central and eastern Europe after a series of ravaging invasions, and we believe arrangements can be worked out which will help to meet those concerns . . .[23]

To many in NATO, these remarks sounded frightfully close to an appeal for "disengagement" and the end of the Atlantic Community. Indeed, they seriously counter-balanced the President's stirring appeal for resistance and clearly reflected the sentiments espoused earlier by Majority Leader Mansfield.

Also, in referring to Berlin in his speech, Mr. Kennedy each time had used the phrase "West Berlin," indicating, it would seem, that the United States was concerned only with its rights in the Western sectors. This too caused anxiety in Europe since by saying it was West Berlin that we would defend, the President implied we were not concerned with East Berlin; to declare one aspect of a problem non-negotiable, is tantamount to declaring other aspects negotiable.

Following the President's speech the U.S. military authorities moved to put the nation on a sounder defense footing. The size of the draft pool was doubled to 100,000 men and on August 1, the Air Force alerted 71 Air Reserve units for possible activation. The American defense measures, however, seemed to have little effect in Berlin. Possibly the Communists were heartened by the President's emphasis on "West Berlin." On August 1, the East German regime announced that new air regulations had been placed in effect by the GDR and that all "radio equipped" aircraft would have to register with a recently established East German Air Safety Center. Although the Western powers ignored the Communist demand the situation in Berlin was becoming dangerously tense.

Two days later the Soviet Union replied to Washington's note of July 17. For the most part the Russians repeated their previous arguments. They attacked the United States position as "trite and unconvincing," referred to West Germany again as a nation of "rampant revanchist passions," and repeated the threat of a separate peace treaty with East Germany.

Interestingly, the American stress on protecting the freedom of the Berliners—the argument previously advocated by London—must have rankled the Russians considerably because a large portion of the Soviet note was devoted to attacking it. This was the only new point, in fact, in the entire 5,000-word document. Said Moscow:

> "The commitments" with regard to West Berlin to which the United States Government refers were born not of the joint struggle of the peoples of the Soviet Union, the United States and other states against Hitler Germany. They are the consequence of another war imposed on the peoples—the cold war.
>
> Thus it appears that the United States would like to base the right to the presence of its troops in West Berlin [not] on the agreements signed together with the Soviet Union, but on the "commitments" with regard to that city—on the agreements concluded without the Soviet Union and against it. The Soviet Government cannot and will never recognize as legitimate such a contradictory position. . . . The right of military occupation is the only basis for the presence of the Western Powers in West Berlin.[24]

American reaction to Moscow's reply was ambivalent and once more reflected the split in Washington. While President Kennedy was able to tell a visiting group of labor leaders at the White House that no change in the Soviet position could be noted, Adlai Stevenson, who also had just seen the President, described the Russian note as "more conciliatory than earlier communications," holding out the hope of later negotiations.[25] And although it had been less than a week since he had vigorously moved to improve America's defense readiness, President Kennedy once more began to waver before the threat of nuclear war. The reason for this renewed hesitancy lay in the dire reports the President had received from disarmament adviser John J. McCloy following the latter's three-day meeting with Nikita Khrushchev at Sochi.* According to Mr. McCloy, Khrushchev had been incensed at the President's July 25th message and had said that the new American military measures constituted an unjustified affront to the Soviet Union, dangerously enhancing the possibilities of total war.

Though Khrushchev's outburst was not significantly different from what he had been saying publicly since Vienna, it evidently made a deep impression on Washington. Perhaps sensing this, the Soviet Union thereupon stepped up its campaign against Berlin and with the dispatch of Moscow's note of August 3, the final Communist drive began.

Simultaneously with the arrival of the Soviet note in Washington, the tenth meeting of the heads of government of the Warsaw Pact convened in Moscow. At this meeting Nikita Khrushchev yielded to the entreaties of Walter Ulbricht and approved the closing of the border in East Berlin. The communique, which was released at the conclusion of the conference on August 6, ambiguously stated that the participants had agreed that the question of "the normalization . . . of the situation in West Berlin is long ripe for solution and brooks no delay. . . ." According to the text: "The meeting instructed the appropriate competent bodies to prepare all necessary foreign political and economic measures ensuring the conclusion of a German peace treaty and observance of its provisions, including those provisions which refer to West Berlin as a free city."

At the same time that the Warsaw Pact leaders were meeting in Moscow, the Foreign Ministers of the United States, Britain, France and West Germany began a series of conferences in Paris designed

* John J. McCloy had gone to Moscow on July 17, to participate in a series of bilateral disarmament sessions with Soviet Deputy Foreign Minister Valerin Zorin. Immediately following President Kennedy's speech on July 25, he was summoned to Khrushchev's Black Sea retreat near Sochi for a series of personal conferences. McCloy reported the contents of these sessions to President Kennedy at Hyannis Port by cable on July 27, and was recalled by the President to make a personal report immediately afterward. (See *New York Times*, July 26–August 1, 1961.)

to patch up whatever differences had arisen in the Western alliance. From all outward indications it was clear that the Communist pressure on Berlin was not going to abate in the near future, and the Western position already was showing dangerous signs of stress. In particular, the United States now seemed to favor negotiations with the East, while Paris and Bonn held back. The outcome of the conference resulted in a partial victory for the continental position. De Gaulle, obstinate and irascible, firmly blocked the retreat of the Anglo-American powers and, according to a Gaullist spokesman at the Quai d'Orsay, it was decided by the conference that "a calm reliance on the status quo will serve to emphasize the fact that the war tension is created solely by Mr. Khrushchev." [26]

But although the Paris conference restored an outward unity, it also revealed a significant difference in approach to the German question between Secretary Rusk and his two great predecessors, Dean Acheson and John Foster Dulles. Unlike Acheson and Dulles, Rusk appeared ready to offer certain concessions to Russia in Central Europe in return for what was euphemistically called "the proper guarantees." To the West Germans, this smelled of a deal at their expense and they were quick to insist on a veto in all such conversations. "Reliable" reports appearing in the Western press at the time of the Paris meeting, in fact, made no secret of the differences between Rusk and the German government. An inspired leak appearing in the *New York Times* on August 7, described with an unconcealed smugness how Dean Rusk had delivered some "blunt talk" to the West Germans to the effect that "some hitherto forbidden subjects would have to be examined if the Berlin crisis worsened." The *Times* went on to explain how Rusk was referring to the "possibility of recognition" of the Oder-Neisse line, *de facto* recognition of the Ulbricht regime, and the inclusion of the GDR in subsequent negotiations.[27] Thus, in spite of President Kennedy's tough talk, the Administration still was not prepared to join its Allies in forcibly confronting the Communists over Berlin. There is little reason to believe that Rusk's "blunt talk" sat well in Europe and it certainly did little to cement the Western alliance at a time when Soviet pressure was growing ever stronger.

Indeed, while the Western Foreign Ministers were squabbling in Paris, and shortly after the adjournment of the Warsaw Pact conclave, Nikita Khrushchev adroitly began laying down a smoke screen to

cloak the impending East German moves. On the evening of August
7, immediately following the safe return to earth of Soviet Cosmonaut
Gherman Titov, Chairman Khrushchev delivered another fire and
brimstone sermon to the Russian people over a nationwide television
and radio hookup.

With the success of Titov's flight certain to impress his listeners,
Khrushchev unabashedly waved the spectre of all-out nuclear war at
the West. Although he was careful to leave the impression that it
was really the United States that was threatening war, he missed no
opportunity to recount the horrors of a global conflagration. Khrushchev's address was by far the most belligerent speech made on
Berlin since the crisis had been reactivated at Vienna, and clearly
presaged the violent storm which was soon to come.

Just to be sure that his message was properly understood in the
West, this time "military hysteria" in America shared equal billing
with the "orgy of revanchist passions" in West Germany as the principal cause of the cold war. The idea of a limited war over Berlin
was immediately dismissed by Khrushchev since a clash "between
the two giants . . . would quickly develop into a thermo-nuclear conflict with neither side ready to admit defeat without having used all
weapons, including the most destructive ones."

In effect, Khrushchev was warning the West against intervention
in Berlin to halt the impending border closure and the more he talked,
the greater his threats became. War would come home to the American people, he said, with a fury not seen "since the days of their own
Civil War." Not only would the territorial United States be crushed
but American military bases throughout the world also would be
rendered harmless. America's Allies would suffer a similar fate. "Any
state used as a springboard for an attack on the Socialist camp will
experience the full devastating power of our blow." It was a terrible
picture that Khrushchev was painting, and he continued without respite. War was almost at hand, he hinted. The Soviet people must be
on their guard!

And to remind the West of the dangers of intervention, Khrushchev
dwelt at length on the need for self-control and the perils of "an act
of madness." He told of an incident in World War II when a confused
Soviet general had committed suicide before his very eyes. "This
tragedy occurred," Khrushchev said, "because the man was thoroughly

unnerved. He no longer knew what he was doing and lost his self-control." It was not a direct analogy, the Chairman continued, but some people in the West are losing their self-possession and self-control. In the story, he said, it was only one man who perished. "But under present conditions, were some Western leaders to act recklessly and push the world into a new war, such a suicidal act would spell death to millions upon millions of people."

The German peace treaty was also discussed. This time, however, Khrushchev surprisingly adopted the position that he was for it because he had no choice. He was being forced into it by the Western powers. Was this an attempt to justify himself before world opinion for the act which the Warsaw Treaty meeting had just approved? In Khrushchev's words:

> What would happen if the German peace treaty were put off for several more years? It would mean giving in to the forces of aggression, retreating under their pressure. Such a position would still further encourage NATO and the Bonn Government to form more and more military divisions in West Germany . . . to convert West Germany into the main force for unleashing a new world war.
>
> There are those who might say: "But is it at all necessary to sign a peace treaty with Germany now? Why not wait another two or three years or even longer? Perhaps that would eliminate tension, remove the danger of war."

Khrushchev replied to his invisible interrogator in the negative. "This line of action is impossible," he said, and the reasons he gave are extremely interesting. "Were we to renounce the signing of a peace treaty," the Western powers "would regard this as a strategic breakthrough and would at once broaden the range of their demands. They would demand liquidation of the socialist system in the German Democratic Republic; try to annex the lands restored to Poland and Czechoslovakia under the Potsdam Agreement; and finally, attempt the abolition of the socialist system in all countries of the socialist camp." [28]

Surely Khrushchev did not believe this and his reasons for now espousing such a theory help to explain why the Berlin crisis was suddenly revived at Vienna after having remained dormant for almost a year. The reasons, perhaps, are two.

First, by the summer of 1961, Khrushchev had reason to believe that the balance of world power had shifted to the Communist camp. The Kennedy Administration certainly had not distinguished itself in the handling of Laos and Cuba, and the public statements of the new American government bore little resemblance to its actions once the chips were down. Indeed, it would have been possible to conclude that the United States no longer had the will to back up its global commitments. Add to this the continued Soviet successes in the space race; additional Russian gains in the field of nuclear and rocket weapons; the Communist view of the emergence of the new and independent states in Africa as a defeat for "imperialism," and a likely reason is at hand.

Second, and perhaps more important, was the desperate plight of the East German regime in the summer of 1961. The escape hatch in Berlin was draining off hundreds of thousands of the most productive citizens of the GDR each year. Since 1945, the entire population of the Soviet zone had suffered a net loss of over two million. Agriculture, following the forced 100 percent collectivization in 1960, was unable to produce enough to insure an adequate food supply throughout the zone, and serious shortages of such staples as potatoes, milk and butter were constantly being felt. The Communist functionaries throughout East Germany were being openly criticized by workers and farmers for the first time in years, and production levels in all phases of the economy were falling far short of the established quotas.[29] On top of this, the regime was being undermined daily by the thousands of East Germans who had been able to visit West Berlin and compare the accomplishments there with the privations and shortages at home. The disrupting influence represented by an open West Berlin so near at hand made it impossible for the Communists to consolidate their power in East Germany.

By June of 1961, in fact, the Ulbricht regime was near collapse. If something were not done, and not done quickly, a new 17th of June would be at hand. For this reason, the situation in West Berlin had to be "normalized" and to achieve this, the pressure for the peace treaty was resumed. The Vienna *aide-mémoire* and the subsequent attacks on the position of the Western powers in Berlin were therefore tactical moves to relieve the internal pressure on the Ulbricht regime—tactical moves, it should be noted, buttressed by the weight of Soviet achievement and encouraged by earlier American failure.

The desperate position of the East German regime was not unknown in the West. The daily refugee figures combined with the latest intelligence reports from the satellite states more than confirmed the precarious state of affairs in the GDR. At his press conference on June 15, Walter Ulbricht himself indicated that the steady flow of refugees was playing hob with the zone's economy and, as noted earlier, that the reception centers in West Berlin would have to be closed.[30] In talks with Soviet bloc diplomats later in June, Ulbricht also stated that he wanted to bar East Germans from entering West Berlin. Ulbricht's remarks were reported extensively in the Western press. A *New York Times* dispatch went so far as to state that according to reliable sources, "Herr Ulbricht is determined to make his move sometime this summer." [31]

Significantly, the resumption of the Berlin offensive at Vienna served only to intensify the crisis in the GDR. The East Germans, accustomed by years of practice to reading the signs of Communist intent, quickly foresaw in the renewed attack on Berlin the impending attempt to close the frontier. As a result, a near-panic spread throughout the zone and the flight of refugees soon reached record proportions.

Messages coming out of East Germany in June and July carried fresh news of the worsening internal situation. The official Communist newspaper in Leipzig, the *Leipziger Volkszeitung*, carried reports of housewives expressing their anger "in very irritated terms" at the increasing shortages of potatoes, vegetables, milk and butter. Other zonal newspapers reported evidence of a war scare gripping the East German people. Hoarding was frequently blamed for shortages of consumer goods. *Neues Deutschland*, the main organ of the East German government, said that the popular mood was such that Party officials frequently had not dared mention the "Communist Peace Plan" in public gatherings. Workers at the Henningsdorf Steel Works outside East Berlin booed and heckled Communist officials at a propaganda meeting, and East German farmers were specifically warned by the Party not to attempt any breakup of the collective farms.[32]

Perhaps in deference to the growing unrest, other Communist failures were partially acknowledged in the East zone's controlled press. Construction program shortcomings were openly discussed and the district of Frankfurt/Oder was accused of "inexcusable failure" in

completing only 22 percent of its projected quota. Certain portions
of the consumer goods industry were frankly reported at only one-
third their goal. Scattered criticism of the regime itself was also oc-
casionally published, probably in the hope that an official outlet would
release some of the pressure that was building up. The Magdeburg
newspaper *Volksstimme,* for example, published a letter in July from
a reader denouncing the idea of a separate Soviet treaty with East
Germany.[33]

To head off the impending crisis, Ulbricht moved quickly during
the months of June and July to sever the ties between East and West
Berlin. While Khrushchev thundered at the Western powers, the East
German regime, in what was obviously a testing action, began a systematic program to restrict communication within the city. During the
closing weeks of June local Communist Party officials visited the homes
of the 60,000 East sector residents who worked in West Berlin advising them to find jobs elsewhere. On July 3, *Neues Deutschland* carried forecasts of punitive measures soon to be taken against these
"border crossers." In a three-hour speech to the East German Assembly
(*Volkskammer*) on July 6, Party chief Ulbricht demanded that the
disrupting influence of West Berlin come to an end. The following
day East Berlin city officials announced that an earlier law requiring
persons working in the West to register with Communist authorities
would be rigorously enforced. Violators, they said, would be evicted
from their houses. Since there is no private ownership of real prop-
erty in East Berlin, this was a relatively easy threat to implement.

On July 11, less than a week after the registration law went into
full effect, the East Berlin government announced that henceforth,
persons still working in the West would not be allowed to purchase
major consumer goods in the East. Among such items were automo-
biles, motorcycles, television sets, refrigerators and washing machines.
The restrictive measures of July 11 were followed on July 14 by a
barrage of announcements in the East Berlin press citing incidents
of smuggling and illicit activities being conducted across the East-
West border. The butter shortage, in fact, was blamed on "profiteers"
who were carrying the precious item over to West Berlin and selling
it there for a higher price.

Thus, by the middle of July, Western officials in Berlin knew that
an attempted sealing of the border was imminent. The total of refugees

was mounting daily and virtually each one brought with him stories of the impending Communist action. Refugees crowding into the Marienfelde reception center on July 16 and 17, brought actual details of the border closure plans given to them by local Communist Party officials. Most said they were coming to get out while the "getting" was still good.[34]

Surprisingly, however, no action was taken at this time by Allied authorities in Berlin to arrest the East in their attempts to interfere with the freedom of movement throughout the city. The right to live and work in any part of Berlin had long been one of the recognized corollaries of four-power control, yet no occupation voice was raised during June or July to protest the new Communist measures. When the GDR had taken similar measures the previous autumn, the threat of economic sanctions quickly brought them to heel. Now, however, no one even suggested such a step. Also, a determined Western protest at this point—even an oral protest—would have given the Communists cause to pause. But the West declined to take such action and Ulbricht continued to nibble at Allied rights unopposed.

And while the West stood by, the refugee exodus grew even greater. Accordingly, during the latter part of July, the East German regime began to take more positive steps to cut the ties between East and West Berlin. On July 22, rigorous curbs were placed on passenger rail traffic into East Berlin from the surrounding countryside. On July 26, the Ulbricht government went even further and announced that anyone detected trying to flee from the GDR would be subject to two years imprisonment. The crime: "flight from the German Peoples Republic." In spite of these restrictions, however, the total of refugees for July was 30,444—the highest figure for any month since June, 1953.[35]

The increased flight of refugees gave Ulbricht more reason than ever to seek rapid closing of the East Berlin border. On July 30, he was given a major assist from an unexpected quarter. Appearing on a nationwide television show in the United States, Senator William Fulbright, Chairman of the Senate Foreign Relations Committee, stated categorically that he felt Ulbricht would be perfectly justified in sealing the sector boundary. Fulbright added that he didn't understand why the action hadn't been taken already.

According to the *New York Times*, Fulbright was asked whether he "would be willing to accept any concessions on the part of the West" which would close the escape hatch for refugees in Berlin. As mouths fell open all over the world, Fulbright answered:

> I think that that might certainly be a negotiable point. The truth of the matter is, I think, the Russians have the power to close it in any case. I mean you are not giving up very much because I believe that next week if they chose to close their borders they could, without violating any treaty.
> I don't understand why the East Germans don't close their border because I think they have a right to close it. So why is this a great concession? [36]

Two days after Fulbright spoke the East German Ministry of Health officially requested the government to suspend all travel between East and West Germany, including West Berlin, because of what it contended was a polio epidemic then raging in West Germany. With complete seriousness the Health Ministry suggested that West Germany's other neighbors were about to do likewise and that such a move was necessary to insure the well-being of the GDR.

The following day, East Berlin border guards were increased sixfold at all crossing points and "border crossers" were subjected to rigorous questioning and delay—many even had their identity cards taken away.

Immediately after the East German restrictions were imposed, the West Berlin government met in emergency session. Mayor Brandt, who, unlike Fulbright, was well aware of the violations and possible implications of the measures against the "border crossers," criticized them in no uncertain terms. The *Tagesspiegel*, an independent West Berlin daily, wrote with noticeable alarm that, "it is incomprehensible why thus far the West has failed to reply to the numerous measures that Pankow has taken in violation of the rights of free movement throughout Berlin. . . ." The West Berlin *Morgenpost*, a paper noticeably close to Mayor Brandt, pointed out with a direct reference to Fulbright that freedom of movement in the city concerned not only the Germans but also the Allies since this freedom was guaranteed by the four occupying powers.* At Brandt's request, the three Allied

---

* Freedom of movement through Berlin was explicitly agreed to by General Clay and Marshal Zhukov at their meeting on July 7, 1945, in which the actual occupation arrangements for Berlin were decided upon. See Lucius Clay, *Decision in Germany*, p. 29.

Commandants met on August 3, and after conferring with the embattled Mayor, dispatched a formal protest to the Soviet Commander, Colonel A. I. Solovyev, in East Berlin. Signed by Major General Albert Watson, II, the American Commander, the Allied protest "noted with concern" the recent East German restrictions. These restrictions it said were simply attempts "to intimidate people into giving up their work in the Western sectors."

The Allied protest was the first formal action taken by the Western powers in Berlin since the East German measures to restrict the flow of traffic began in June. To a large degree it reflected the influence of the West Berliners, which was finally brought to bear on the occupation officials by Mayor Brandt. The Allied protest is particularly significant since it presents in no uncertain terms the violations to the four-power status of Berlin which the Communists were committing. Although Fulbright may or may not have been aware of these, the Communists certainly were. According to the note:

> . . . the principle of freedom of movement is basic to the agreements regarding Berlin, which are binding on the four powers responsible for this city. In addition, in the agreement of June 20, 1949, the four powers pledged themselves to promote the normalization of life in Berlin and facilitate the movement of persons between Berlin and the rest of Germany. . . .
>
> The measures recently announced in the Soviet area of responsibility are clearly inconsistent with these agreements. They are also clearly objectionable on humanitarian grounds. They are bound to cause a deterioration in the atmosphere in Berlin.
>
> I therefore request you to give your attention to this situation and to bring about without delay the termination of the restrictive measures which affect the working population of Berlin.[37]

The Allied protest was ignored. The East German regime acknowledged it on August 4, by announcing that all persons still working in West Berlin would have to pay their rent in West marks. Since the "border crossers" received only part of their salary in West marks this was another serious step. A West Berlin government spokesman perceptively remarked that the East sector authorities were evidently trying to force the Berlin issue to a showdown.[38]

Once more Ulbricht's measures against the "border crossers" pushed the number of refugees even higher. Over five thousand registered at Marienfelde between August 6 and 8. Outside Berlin, Western authorities viewed the increased exodus with alarm. West German officials publicly voiced their fears that "Middle Germany" might soon be depopulated. American and British spokesmen stated that an explosive situation similar to that of June, 1953, was being created in the Soviet zone.

The refugee problem was discussed in great detail at the Foreign Ministers' meeting in Paris which has previously been referred to. Little secret was made of the fact that the Foreign Ministers deplored the mounting tension which the exodus was creating. German Foreign Minister Heinrich von Brentano presented Secretary Rusk with a letter setting forth the "concern" of the Adenauer government over "the implications of the refugee situation" and, while it would perhaps be too much to say that the Western Foreign Ministers were as eager as Ulbricht to shut off the increased flow of refugees, they certainly looked on it with considerable misgiving.

The Paris meeting, it should be remembered, was widely heralded as a "working session" designed to formulate detailed contingency plans for an emergency in Berlin. Accordingly, it is not at all unlikely that the possible courses of Western action in the event of a Communist border closure were also discussed. Indeed, since the Berlin issue at that moment virtually centered on the refugee problem, one would almost have to conclude that contingency plans for just this situation were not only discussed but were agreed upon. Were this not the case, then the Foreign Ministers would have been neglecting to provide for the most likely future occurrence.

But to the undoubted discomfiture of the Foreign Ministers, West Berlin's Willy Brandt continued to rock the boat. On August 7, speaking for his two and a half million Berliners, Brandt warned against any "tension easing" deal at the expense of Berlin. Sensing perhaps the feeling then prevalent in Paris, Brandt stated that "the city should not be split and the right of people to move freely in the city should be maintained." Brandt's words, however, had little effect and merely emphasized the possibilities then being considered.

On the same day that Brandt spoke, Nikita Khrushchev also delivered his rocket rattling television speech warning the West against intervention in Berlin. The following day the flight of the refugees reached even greater proportions. Over seventeen hundred registered in the first 24-hour period immediately afterward. All of those now coming reported that they felt Khrushchev's speech presaged an immediate closing of the escape route.

Two other significant events occurred on August 8. In Paris, the NATO Council gave its formal approval to the contingency plans prepared by the four Foreign Ministers. In Washington, Senator Hubert H. Humphrey, assistant Senate majority leader, reported to newsmen on the White House steps that the situation in East Germany was more critical at the present time than that in West Berlin. According to Humphrey, "the shoring up of East Germany and the precise demarcation of the Communist empire are at this moment far more important to Moscow than West Berlin." [39] Humphrey, who had just come from a weekly meeting with the President, was undoubtedly reflecting Administration sentiment. Accordingly, the decision of the NATO Council in Paris this same day takes on added significance. Surely, a set of contingency plans prepared for Berlin would not overlook the most possible contingency—in this case the "precise demarcation of the Communist empire"—a contingency which could only be accomplished by sealing the border in East Berlin.

Dispatches from Washington the following day tend to bear out Humphrey. The Administration was reliably reported to be considering that the possibility of an uprising in East Germany was "the most dangerous aspect" of the Berlin crisis. Such an uprising it was feared "would force the Soviet Union, West Germany, and the United States to make hasty decisions about military intervention." These decisions, in turn, could easily trigger a third world war.[40]

On August 10, President Kennedy himself commented as to the seriousness of the refugee problem. At his regular news conference, Mr. Kennedy was asked whether the United States had any policy about the refugees coming into West Berlin from East Germany. Questioned specifically about Fulbright's proposal for an East German closing of the border, the President indicated that the Administration had washed its hands of the problem. He pointedly made no reference to the right of free movement in Berlin and carefully avoided contradicting Fulbright's remarks. Indeed, the impression is unmistakable that the United States government considered the refugee problem a purely East German affair and would make no move should the East Germans act to solve it. The question and Mr. Kennedy's answer are as follows:

Q.—Mr. President, some members of your Administration and others have pointedly expressed concern that the continued large flight of East German refugees to the West might result in an act of violence. Senator Fulbright has suggested that the border might be closed. Could you give us your assessment of the danger, and could you tell us whether this government has any policy regarding the encouragement or discouragement of these German refugees moving West?

A.—No, I don't think we have attempted to encourage or discourage the movement of refugees, in answer to the last part of your question.

Of course, we're concerned about the situation in Eastern Germany and, really, in Eastern Europe. There has been a tremendous passage from East to West, which, I know, is a matter of concern to the Communists, because this tremendous speed-up of people leaving the Communist system to come to the West and freedom, of course, is a rather illuminating evidence of the comparative values of free life in an open society and those in a closed society under a Communist system.

In answer to your question, however, the United States Government does not attempt to encourage or discourage the movement of refugees. And I know of no plans to do so.[41]

By August 10, there were further indications that the Communists intended to act in Berlin. Ivan S. Konev, Marshal of the Soviet Union, hero of the Second World War, former Commander of the forces of the Warsaw Pact and Deputy Minister of Defense, was called out of retirement to head the Soviet army in East Germany. The significance of this move is about the same as if General Douglas MacArthur should be recalled to command American forces in South Korea.

In East Berlin itself, Walter Ulbricht, who had just returned from the Warsaw Pact meeting in Moscow, once more demanded that the refugee traffic come to a halt. Speaking at the Oberspree Cable Plant, Ulbricht said that it was the duty of every citizen of the GDR "to make an end once and for all to the man-trade" between East and West Berlin. Ulbricht, of course, was now using the phenomenon of the refugee migration as a justification for what he had sought in the first place—the closing of the border to West Berlin.

Thus, the eight weeks from Vienna to the early days of August had seen several things happen. Khrushchev, as perhaps he had expected, rallied the West to the defense of West Berlin by his attacks. At the same time, these attacks made the fear of a third world war all the greater in the West and the desire to avoid it all the stronger. But now, as a result of Khrushchev's attacks, the flow of refugees from East Germany into West Berlin had reached record proportions. In the resulting tension the possibility of a popular uprising in the GDR was feared imminent. Such an occurrence clearly could trigger the nuclear war which the West now sought desperately to avoid. To reduce this possibility it was therefore necessary to reduce the tension within the GDR. Since this could only be done by sealing the border, the West was put in the uncomfortable position of either acquiescing to such a move or else taking active steps to prevent it. The latter alternative, of course, would only aggravate the situation and make the possibility of an uprising all the more probable. Accordingly, one can only conclude that the West was prepared to accept a closure of the border as the price for reducing the threat of war. Indeed, during the latter part of July and early August, the Western powers had been exceptionally careful to identify their position in the former German capital only with its western sectors. "West Berlin" and not "Berlin" was what the West had decided to defend.

The actual Communist move to close the border on August 13 could have caught the West by no more than tactical surprise. Since no immediate action was taken to interfere with this move, one is forced once again to conclude that the West was prepared to accept the closure as the price of preventing a revolutionary spark from setting off what the Kennedy Administration thought could lead to World War III. As the events of August 13, indicated, however, this decision was not shared by everyone in Berlin. Mayor Brandt, especially, must be excluded from any complicity in this decision. Indeed, as subsequent events indicate, the decision to acquiesce to the border closure may have been as ill-considered as the decisions which put Berlin behind the Iron Curtain in the first place.

But, of course, the Communists were not as yet aware of the Western decision and on August 11, the East German Volkskammer met in special session. The announced purposes of the meeting were to consider the measures to be taken preparatory to concluding a peace treaty and to stop the flow of refugees. In closed session, Ulbricht advised the members of what had transpired at the Warsaw Pact meeting in Moscow. Afterwards, Deputy Premier Willy Stoph spoke for over an hour on the refugee question. As reported in the East German press, Stoph said that the regime was "no longer willing to look on without taking any action." The subsequent public announcement of the proceedings stated that the Volkskammer approved unanimously "the measures taken" by the regime to check the flight of refugees from East Berlin. There was no mention of what these measures might be.[42]

When told of the East German action, Willy Brandt prophetically remarked that it was like the "enabling bill" passed by the Reichstag giving dictatorial powers to Adolph Hitler. Once more, however, the Mayor's words went virtually unnoticed.

13

The Wall

IN THE EARLY MORNING of August 13, 1961, the long awaited Communist move to halt the flow of refugees into West Berlin finally began. At several minutes past midnight the East German News Agency (ADN) published a communique from the countries of the Warsaw Pact officially requesting the government of the German Democratic Republic (GDR) to take the necessary action to "establish order" along the border to West Berlin. The communique, together with the requested action, both had been arranged at the meeting of the Warsaw Pact leaders ten days before in Moscow.

The communique itself was a long one. It left little doubt why the measures were being taken and what would be their intended effect. "The present situation regarding the traffic on the borders of West Berlin," the communique began, was being used by the NATO powers for "undermining the GDR's economy." Unstable elements in East Germany were being made to leave their homeland through deceit, bribery, and blackmail. "This subversive activity inflicts damage not only on the German Democratic Republic but also affects the interests of other countries of the Socialist camp."

"In the face of the aggressive aspirations of the reactionary forces of the FRG [Federal Republic of Germany] and its NATO allies, the Warsaw Treaty member states cannot but take necessary measures for insuring their security, and primarily the security of the German Democratic Republic. . . ."

Accordingly, "the Governments of the Warsaw Treaty member states address the People's Chamber and the Government of the GDR . . . with a proposal to establish such an order on the borders of West Berlin which would securely block the way for the subversive activity against the Socialist camp. . . ."

Great pains were taken by the Communists to show that West Berlin itself was not being affected. The impending action was made to appear as though only the trouble in East Germany was being isolated. The rights of the Western Allies—or better, those rights for which the West had said they would fight—were carefully excepted. The right of Western access explicitly was not to be interfered with: "It goes without saying, that these measures must not affect the existing order of traffic and control on the ways of communication between West Berlin and West Germany."

The announcement of the Warsaw Pact concluded by stating that the measures being invoked along the East Berlin border would disappear only when a peace settlement with Germany had been achieved. The "present abnormal situation" in West Berlin would then be settled on that basis.[1]

Published alongside the Warsaw Pact communique was a decree of the East German government putting the control measures into effect. According to the East German announcement, "such control is to be introduced on the borders of the German Democratic Republic, including the border with the Western sectors of Greater Berlin, which is usually introduced along the borders of every sovereign state." Citizens of the GDR "may cross these borders only with special permission."

Like the Warsaw communique, the East German announcement went to great length to reassure the West that the right of access would not be interfered with. "This decree in no way revises former decisions on transit between West Berlin and West Germany via the German Democratic Republic." The rights of "citizens of other states" to visit the capital of the GDR would also not be affected. West

Berliners would be permitted to cross the border at specified points upon presentation of a West Berlin identity card.[2] The East German decree was accompanied by an order from the East Berlin city government barring all East Berliners from holding jobs in West Berlin.[3]

The decrees were put into effect immediately. At thirty-five minutes after midnight (7:35 P.M. Saturday, Washington time), armored cars of the East German People's Army rolled into the *Potsdamer Platz* in the center of Berlin—the crossing point where the American, British, and Soviet sectors all joined together. Other military units appeared at the Brandenburg Gate, at *Friedrichstrasse,* and at each of the other 80 crossing points between East and West Berlin. By 2:30 A.M. the entire twenty-eight mile border separating the Soviet sector from the three Western sectors had been sealed. A force reliably estimated as one fully motorized division of the East German Army heavily supported by People's Police and Communist factory militia (*Betriebskampfgruppen*) was deployed along it in tactical formation. Double strands of barbed wire and other light obstacles were emplaced. Of the eighty crossing points into East Berlin, only thirteen remained.

The East German action in Berlin was supported throughout the Soviet zone with extensive troop movements. The Soviet Army in East Germany, now under Marshal Konev, moved out of their *kasernen* shortly after midnight and took up tactical positions throughout the countryside. East German and Soviet armor filled the roads and highways in a calculated show of force designed to cow any feeling of popular resistance. An estimated force of two Soviet divisions lined the border between the Western sectors of Berlin and East Germany proper. As one East German official subsequently commented, the lesson of June 17, 1953, had been learned. The appearance of armed might was much more effective in putting down a revolt before it began rather than afterwards.

The significance of the East German action in closing the sector border was not immediately apparent to American military headquarters in West Berlin. Indeed, Allied authorities had long expected Communist measures to shut off the stream of refugees.[4] When the Communist moves were announced, it was therefore assumed that the border closure was a purely East German affair and that the strength of the Western position was not being affected. The East

German moves themselves had been cleverly cloaked in the language of the communique. Brigadier General Frederick O. Hartel, the Commanding General of the Berlin Command, advised a correspondent of the *New York Times* in the early hours following the border closure that "all responsibility for controlling traffic from East to West Berlin" belonged to the German police. He said that he did not anticipate taking any action and had not received any instructions to the contrary from Washington.[5]

It was only later in the day, after much prodding from Mayor Brandt, that Allied headquarters fully realized the significance of the East German action. By that time, of course, the border closure had been in effect for almost eighteen hours.*

General Hartel, it perhaps should be noted, had been in Berlin for less than six weeks when the East German action of August 13 occurred; his superior, Major General Albert Watson, II, the Commander of the American sector, for less than three months. Before coming to Berlin, Hartel had been stationed at the Pentagon in the Office of the Secretary of Defense. There, he had been closely connected with the Administration's contingency planning and his assignment to Berlin was a direct result of this experience. Accordingly, when he said that the traffic from East to West Berlin was a responsibility of the German police and not his, he was undoubtedly repeating official Washington sentiment.

Western contingency plans, it should also be remembered,** had in all probability encompassed the Communist closure of the East Berlin border. For several months reports of an imminent sealing of the frontier had been trickling out of East Germany. The recent statements of Western leaders, not to mention those of Ulbricht and the East German press, all pointed to this very possibility. The meeting of the Western Foreign Ministers held in Paris only a week before, held for the specific purpose of preparing plans for emergency action in Berlin, discussed the border closure in considerable detail. Thus, on the morning of August 13, when the American troop commander in

---

* Interestingly, when RIAS (Radio in the American Sector) broadcast its first bulletin of the Communist border closure at 4 A.M. Sunday morning, an editor removed the recorded song that was to follow the news. The song was entitled "Let's Do like the Swallows Do" and it was feared by the station's USIA personnel that its playing might be taken as a signal by listeners in the East to fly from their homes. (See *New York Times*, August 16, 1961.)

** See previous chapter.

Berlin did not voice any alarm at the East German action, much less suggest any counter measures, it can only be assumed that he followed the prescribed Allied response. In other words, the Western powers were prepared to see the East Germans close the border in East Berlin without contesting the point. Had another course of action been provided for, certainly the Berlin Command would have taken it.

In Washington, the immediate news of the East German move to seal the frontier was received virtually without comment. It was only seven o'clock Saturday evening in Washington when the Warsaw communique was published, and well before ten o'clock when the border closure had been completed. The State Department on Saturday evening, however, declined all comment. It was not even reported whether Secretary Rusk or President Kennedy had been informed, something which certainly would have been announced had the situation been thought critical.

Ironically, the only person in Washington who was willing to comment Saturday night was Senator William Fulbright, Chairman of the Senate Foreign Relations Committee. Smitten by the response which his earlier television remarks about the closing of the border had had,* Fulbright made a remarkable turn about. "It has been my understanding," the Arkansas Senator said, "that free transit between the two parts of Berlin was guaranteed under Four-Power Pact. If this agreement is being broken by unilateral action it could lead to serious consequences." [6]

With the exception of Senator Fulbright's comment, official Washington remained silent for the first seventeen hours after the East Berlin border was sealed. Leaders in London and Paris likewise declined comment although the British Foreign Office did make a brief announcement that the Communist moves were "contrary to the four-power status of Berlin and are therefore illegal." In the meantime, of course, the minions of Walter Ulbricht literally were leaving no stone unturned in their efforts to close whatever gaps might have remained in the newest extension of the Iron Curtain.

Shortly after twelve noon on Sunday, August 13, (5 P.M. Berlin time), Secretary of State Dean Rusk finally broke the silence which had enshrouded Washington. The Secretary issued a brief statement which did little more than call attention to the fact of which the entire

* See previous chapter.

world was now aware. The authorities in East Germany, Rusk said, had taken severe measures to deny their own people access to West Berlin. "These measures have doubtless been prompted by the increased flow of refugees in recent weeks." Rusk then added what has since become known as the American sigh of relief—Western rights had not been affected! "Available information," Rusk said, "indicates that measures taken thus far are aimed at residents of East Berlin and East Germany and not at the Allied position in West Berlin or access thereto."

Almost as an afterthought, Rusk added that the East German action was a violation of the four-power status of Berlin. This violation, he said, would be "the subject of vigorous protest through appropriate channels." [7]

With that the statement concluded. There was no demand that the admittedly illegal East German measures be halted or that the right of free circulation within the city be restored. There was no threat of Western counteraction nor indeed, anything which might indicate that the United States planned to intervene. It was, in fact, almost as if the American government welcomed the East German move. The refugee flow finally had been shut off and deplorable though this may have been for those affected, a dangerous source of tension in Berlin had been removed. The formal protest to which Rusk referred, a State Department aide later announced, "would probably be made tomorrow." [8]

Before making his statement, Rusk had discussed the Berlin situation by telephone with President Kennedy who was spending the weekend at Hyannis Port. The President approved Rusk's statement and agreed with the Secretary that the most serious aspect of the border closure was the possibility that an insurrection might be touched off in East Germany.[9] If the President and the Secretary considered the effect of the East German action on the morale of the people of West Berlin and thereby on the Western position in Berlin, they gave no sign of it. The President and his Secretary of State were in complete agreement that nothing should be done to aggravate the situation further. Mr. Kennedy remained at Hyannis Port, declining to make public comment, and Dean Rusk went to a baseball game at Griffith Stadium.

Indeed, had the East German regime been worried about the possibility of Western intervention, the events on the afternoon of August 13 in Washington must have consoled them. The response at each of the Allied capitals, in fact, would hardly have given cause for alarm. In Paris, both President De Gaulle and Premier Debré were on vacation. In their absence, no official statement was forthcoming and certainly no counteraction could have been initiated. In London, Lord Home was away shooting grouse, and Prime Minister Macmillan was vacationing in Scotland. Only in Bonn was the head of the government on duty. Dr. Adenauer was informed during the night of the Communist action and afterwards called a hasty conference of his advisers at his Rhoendorf home. The Chancellor then issued a short official statement. "It is the law of the hour," he said, "to meet the challenge from the East firmly but calmly and to do nothing that can worsen the situation." Reports from Bonn indicate that Adenauer had definite countermeasures in mind. High on the list, it was felt, was the possibility of economic sanctions.[10] In the absence of guidance from his NATO partners, however, the Chancellor dared not act on his own.

Meanwhile, at Allied headquarters in Berlin, the casual unconcern of the first few hours gradually yielded to a grim realization that more was involved than originally had been believed. Although the total effect of the Communist measures were still not yet understood, the presence of heavily armored East German Army units along the sector border, and especially the movement of two Soviet armored divisions to positions surrounding the city, were enough to cause the Allied command to think in terms of tactical readiness. There still was no thought of action to reopen the border; indeed, it was still felt that the East German move was not totally undesirable, but the sudden appearance of so much Communist military power now caused the American, British, and French Commands to be concerned over the security of the Western sectors. Accordingly, the three Allied garrisons were alerted and confined to their barracks in a full state of combat readiness.

Shortly after the alert was ordered, the three Western Commandants began a series of meetings which lasted throughout the day. Mayor Brandt attended several of these and in no uncertain terms advised the military authorities that the entire Western position in Berlin was at stake. The Communists, he said, had physically absorbed East Berlin into the GDR and had unilaterally destroyed the four-power status of the city. It was a blatant act of aggression against the West he insisted and if nothing was done to counteract it, his people would feel betrayed. The Mayor pleaded for energetic action which would force the

Communists to "cancel their unlawful measures." Among other things, he asked for an immediate show of force along the border.

Prodded by Brandt's forceful arguments the Commandants began to revise their earlier estimates of the situation. The Mayor's proposals were forwarded to each of the three Western capitals but no action was taken. Even had they wanted to, it probably would have been impossible for the Allied Commandants to have taken the prompt action which Mayor Brandt desired. Unlike General Clay in June of 1948, the Allied Commandants in Berlin in 1961 were very junior members of the Western military directorate. Whereas, General Clay was the American Military Governor for all of Germany, and reported directly to the Secretaries of State and of the Army in Washington, Major General Albert Watson, II, had a command line running first to Army headquarters in Heidelberg, from there to NATO in Paris, and then to Washington. Even when his messages arrived in Washington it is certain that, coming as they did from a relatively junior official who had been in Berlin less than three months, they would not have received the same deferential treatment that Clay's did in 1948. Accordingly, on August 13 Watson carried out the orders he had been given and did nothing. The alert he called was for the protection of the Western sectors. It was not for possible counteraction. After dispatching Brandt's request forward, he declined all further public comment. The situation, he said, had been fully reported to the three Allied capitals and any comment would have to come from there.[11]

Later Sunday afternoon, Mayor Brandt addressed a special session of the West Berlin Parliament. He appealed to the Berliners to remain calm and reasonable. At the same time he let it be known that he considered prompt and vigorous Allied countermeasures essential. The right of free movement within the city, he said, was inherent in the very nature of its four-power status. This right had never been interfered with before, not even during the blockade of 1948–49 when the Russians had tried to starve the city into submission. The Communist action of last night, the Mayor continued, was therefore all the more serious and should be speedily resisted. Allied reaction, he concluded, should not be confined to protests. "Today," Brandt said, "the real test for our people begins." [12]

The reaction of the Berliners was much like that of Mayor Brandt. Having lived in the eye of a storm for over fifteen years, they were

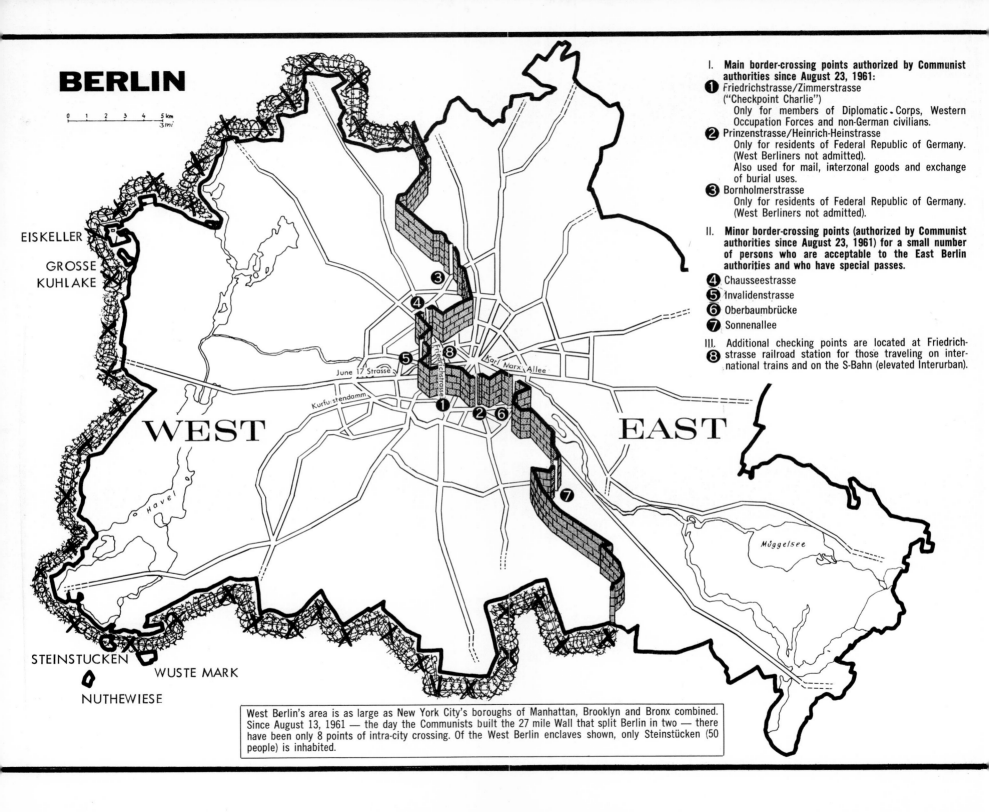

BERLIN

0 1 2 3 4 5 km
3 mi

WEST

EAST

EISKELLER

GROSSE KUHLAKE

June 17 Strasse

Kurfurstendamm

Friedrichstrasse

Karl Marx Allee

Havel

Müggelsee

STEINSTÜCKEN

WUSTE MARK

NUTHEWIESE

I. **Main border-crossing points authorized by Communist authorities since August 23, 1961:**

❶ Friedrichstrasse/Zimmerstrasse ("Checkpoint Charlie")
  Only for members of Diplomatic-Corps, Western Occupation Forces and non-German civilians.

❷ Prinzenstrasse/Heinrich-Heinstrasse
  Only for residents of Federal Republic of Germany. (West Berliners not admitted).
  Also used for mail, interzonal goods and exchange of burial uses.

❸ Bornholmerstrasse
  Only for residents of Federal Republic of Germany. (West Berliners not admitted).

II. **Minor border-crossing points (authorized by Communist authorities since August 23, 1961) for a small number of persons who are acceptable to the East Berlin authorities and who have special passes.**

❹ Chausseestrasse

❺ Invalidenstrasse

❻ Oberbaumbrücke

❼ Sonnenallee

III. Additional checking points are located at Friedrichstrasse railroad station for those traveling on international trains and on the S-Bahn (elevated Interurban).

West Berlin's area is as large as New York City's boroughs of Manhattan, Brooklyn and Bronx combined. Since August 13, 1961 — the day the Communists built the 27 mile Wall that split Berlin in two — there have been only 8 points of intra-city crossing. Of the West Berlin enclaves shown, only Steinstücken (50 people) is inhabited.

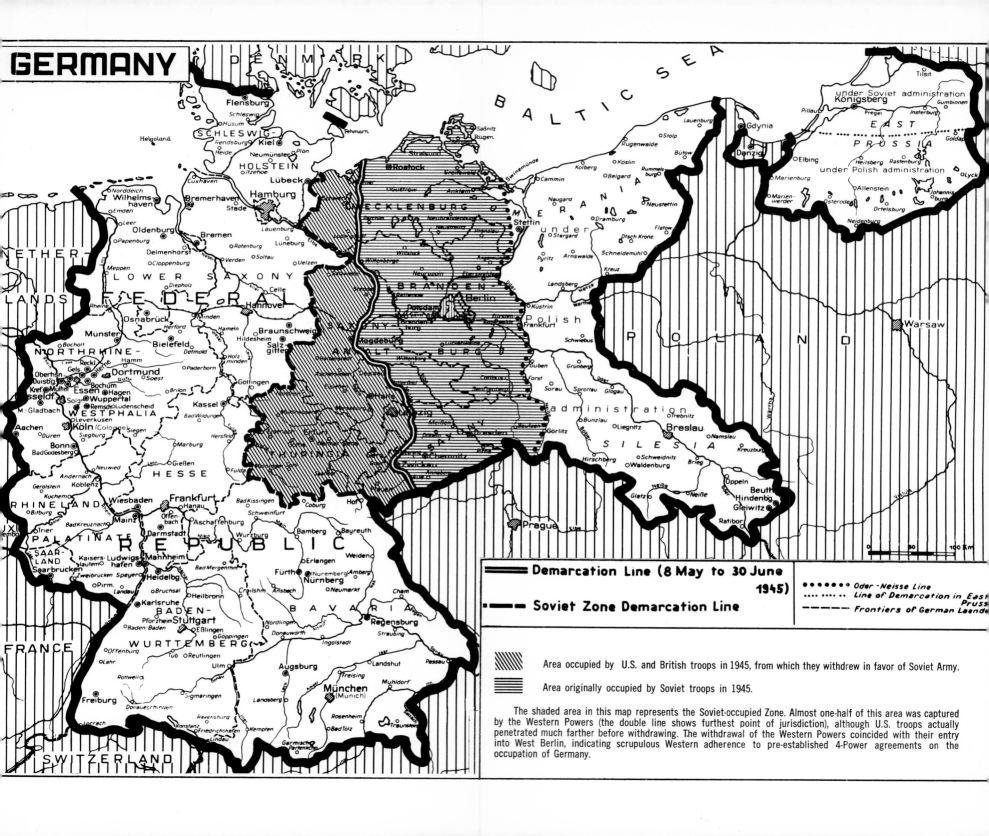

GERMANY

Demarcation Line (8 May to 30 June 1945)

Soviet Zone Demarcation Line

Oder-Neisse Line

Line of Demarcation in East Prussia

Frontiers of German Laender

Area occupied by U.S. and British troops in 1945, from which they withdrew in favor of Soviet Army.

Area originally occupied by Soviet troops in 1945.

The shaded area in this map represents the Soviet-occupied Zone. Almost one-half of this area was captured by the Western Powers (the double line shows furthest point of jurisdiction), although U.S. troops actually penetrated much farther before withdrawing. The withdrawal of the Western Powers coincided with their entry into West Berlin, indicating scrupulous Western adherence to pre-established 4-Power agreements on the occupation of Germany.

acutely sensitive to its various shifts and stresses and they knew that the Communist action was a threat to their existence. The closing of the border within the city—the total incorporation of the eastern sector of the city into the so-called German Democratic Republic—spelled for them the end of Berlin's role as a vigorous island of freedom in the midst of a Communist sea. West Berlin itself might remain, but only as a withered monument to a past civilization; without the free access to it by people in the East, its purpose would be ended. For Berlin was more than a haven for refugees. It was a place where people from the East could come for a visit, could see for themselves the good life in the free West, and could return home with this lesson when their visit was over. More than 150,000 such people came into West Berlin each day. Except for a few, all returned to East Berlin and East Germany in the evening. They returned, however, having experienced the freedom, the joy and the prosperity which West Berlin so cheerfully shared. Then too, as long as they knew they could leave East Germany whenever they wished, Ulbricht's power was limited. With the lifeline to Berlin open, communism could never consolidate its deadly grip on East Germany. But with it closed, sixteen million people were exiled into slavery.

Such were the feelings of the Berliners on the afternoon and evening of August 13, as they waited for American intervention; for America, since the days of the airlift, had come to symbolize for the Berliners the determination of a free people to defend the cause of freedom with whatever means were necessary. Not even their compatriots in West Germany held the same mystical place in the hearts of the Berliners as did the Americans. Considering the miracle of the airlift, this feeling was not without reason.

By Sunday evening, therefore, the disappointment in Berlin was all the keener when the *Amis* had failed to act. The appearance of even one American soldier in battle dress at the border probably would have soothed the Berliners. Clay would have recognized this; Brandt did recognize it; Watson may have recognized it but in the absence of orders from Washington he declined to act. Washington, of course, was unaware of it, much as they had been unaware of the possibilities of the airlift in 1948.

Along the sector border in West Berlin crowds of Berliners watched the Communist preparations all day. At dawn, a dozen or so gathered at the Brandenburg Gate. By noon, a thousand or more were on hand, each anxiously watching and waiting. Many West Berliners took advantage of the Communist decree which still allowed them to drive into East Berlin to see for themselves what was happening. What they saw was a shock. Between the *Unter den Linden* and the *Potsdamer Platz* they could count thirty-six Russian-made tanks with East German crews. In the *Marx-Engels Platz* stood twenty-seven military lorries, most of them loaded with uniformed People's Army troops carrying submachine guns.* Other vehicle parks were located nearby, and although no Russian troops were in sight, hard core factory militia (*Betriebskampfgruppen*) mounted a guard to the rear of the barricades and kept everyone 500 meters from the frontier. The rest of East Berlin was also an armed camp. Field kitchens and bivouac areas were placed in the middle of the streets. Meals were constantly being served to soldiers "back from the front." As one West Berliner reported it, it was as though the city was being occupied all over again.

By 10:30 Sunday evening a crowd of over five thousand West Berliners had gathered before the Brandenburg Gate. Their tempers were now on edge. All day long they had seen the barricades grow thicker. Reel after reel of barbed wire had been added to the first flimsy obstacles. All day long they had seen the East German army deployed in full battle array across the sector boundary. Shouts of "Hang Ulbricht," and "Put down your guns," began to be heard. Ten East German armored cars moved up to the other side of the gate. The West Berlin police succeeded in maintaining order but only with the greatest difficulty. When West Berlin went to bed that night, it went to bed angry and disappointed—angry that the Communists had acted, disappointed that the West had not.

Encouraged by the lack of Western response, the East German regime wasted little time in consolidating and extending their gains. At 4 A.M. Monday morning, August 14, 1961, all telephone and postal service with West Germany was severed. Although the trunk lines into West Berlin from West Germany were not affected, the East German action further isolated the people of the Soviet zone and now made it all but impossible for them to communicate with the outside world. A

---

* Testimony from defecting officers of the East German Army has subsequently revealed that Communist forces in East Berlin on August 13, were issued only blank ammunition and were under orders to give way should Allied troops intervene.

spokesman for the West German Postal Ministry in Bonn said that telegrams were the only communications still being accepted in East Germany from the West. No messages, he added, were coming out.

Later in the day, East zone authorities went one step further and closed the Brandenburg Gate. The number of crossing points into East Berlin was now reduced to twelve. Even at these twelve, steps were underway to restrict the flow of traffic further. At some, streets were torn up so that only one lane could proceed at a time; at others, movable barbed wire barricades were erected where previously only heavily armed soldiers had stood.

Karl Maron, the venomous East German Interior Minister, also announced on Monday that henceforth all West Berliners would be required to remain 100 meters from the barricades. East German forces, he said, would take appropriate action against all who did not. Western news photographers who violated the edict later in the afternoon on Monday were sprayed by Communist water trucks. Several other skirmishes were reported along the border and on three occasions *Vopos* hurled tear gas grenades into West Berlin.

Allied military headquarters in West Berlin still declined to intervene although Western troops were kept on a stand-by alert and only personnel living "off post" were allowed to leave the *kasernen*. The American Command also declined all public comment other than to say it was "watching the situation closely." [13]

Monday afternoon at the *Schöneberger Rathaus*, West Berlin's City Hall, five thousand West Berlin workers protested the lack of Western response. Carrying signs reading "We demand Counter-Measures," and "Reunification Fast," the workers listened sullenly as Mayor Brandt entreated them to remain calm. He had advised the Allies, Brandt said, of the need for urgent action. All they could do now was to wait. The workers departed slightly more comforted than when they had come. The Mayor, they knew, was on their side.

In the West, the critical position of West Berlin as a result of the border closure still was not recognized. President Kennedy returned from Hyannis Port late Monday morning and met with Secretary Rusk for more than an hour. The conference resulted only in the agreement that "there should be no move to provoke demonstrations against the Communist East German regime so long as Western access to isolated Berlin is unimpeded." [14] As before, the President and Rusk were still looking at the East German move as something which might serve to lessen tensions with the Soviet Union. The possibility of countermeasures was of little interest.

At the State Department in Washington on Monday, the diplomatic representatives of Great Britain, France, and Germany met with Assistant Secretary of State Foy Kohler to draft the text of the official Western protest. Countermeasures were discussed but only in general terms. British and American representatives argued gravely against any "rash action" which might upset the delicate balance in Berlin. A dispatch in the well-informed *Washington Evening Star* that day reported governmental reaction in Washington to the border closure to be one of disapproval but little more: "While the West deeply disapproves shutting off communications between East and West Berlin, American officials said it would not be to the West's advantage to do anything drastic about it." [15]

On Capitol Hill, reaction was much the same. Senate Democratic Leader Mike Mansfield advocated a policy of "let's keep our shirts on" and see what this is all about. "Berlin," he said, "is only one of the many difficulties that confront the President at this time."

Senator Hubert Humphrey, the Democratic Whip, said that we "must look for Mr. Khrushchev to be very difficult" in the months ahead.

Senator Bourke Hickenlooper of Iowa called the border closure "another and not unexpected step in the cold war." No voice was raised in the Senate of the United States on the day following the East German action, advocating anything other than a policy of watchful waiting.[16]

Reaction was about the same in the other Allied capitals. In London, Foreign Office spokesmen let it be known that the British government was opposed to an economic embargo. In Paris, the hush of August vacations continued to prevail at the Quai d'Orsay. In West Germany, Chancellor Adenauer took to the campaign trail and in Regensburg delivered one of the harshest personal attacks on Mayor Brandt that the German electorate had ever heard. The Chancellor alluded directly to Brandt's illegitimate birth and spoke of him as "Herr Brandt, alias Framm." Adenauer again mentioned that economic sanctions were being considered by the West but he carefully avoided an open endorsement of them. The trade agreement with East Germany, he said, would have to be "looked at" in light of the latest move on Berlin.

Thus, forty-eight hours after the border closure had been effected, the Western powers had yet to take a positive step. Indeed, there was virtual agreement in each of the Allied capitals that a positive step should not be taken. Not even a formal protest over the Communist action had been transmitted to the authorities in East Berlin. It is not surprising therefore that the East Germans rapidly grew bolder, for the West seemed very much a paper tiger.

At one o'clock Tuesday morning, August 15, 1961, East German authorities announced that West Berlin vehicles would no longer be allowed in East Berlin without a special permit. The East German move was especially significant since it represented a clear-cut attack on Western rights. The original Communist measures to seal the border had carefully avoided any interference with Western traffic. One can only assume that the move was taken because of the total lack of Western response to the previous Communist measures. Several hours later, East German police fired on an escaping couple attempting to make their way to the West by swimming the Teltow Canal. The shots missed and the refugees made it safely across but it was an ominous sign for the future.

Later in the day, while the West Berliners continued to seethe at the lack of Western response, the formal Allied protest to the measures of August 13 was finally delivered to Soviet Military Headquarters in Karlshorst. The message was not only three days late, but unlike other protests, it was delivered not by one of the Western Commandants but simply by a messenger from the Allied Staff. Its contents were exceedingly mild and polite. Like Rusk's earlier statement in Washington, it merely recited the events which had taken place. There was no demand that the border be reopened or that the East German military forces be withdrawn. Indeed, only in the last paragraph of the 350-word note were the Communist measures actually protested.[17]

The Ulbricht regime acknowledged the protest in a manner that might be expected. Several hours after its delivery, the East German Government stole the march on the West and announced that any attempt to apply economic sanctions against the GDR would be met with a total blockade of all West German traffic to Berlin. Since the possibility of an East German blockade had been mentioned the day before by both Washington and London in their appeals for restraint, it again is likely that the East German regime was gauging its moves by Allied reaction.

If this was the case, they once more were not disappointed. In Bonn, where sentiment for economic sanctions had been strongest, the Free Democrats led by Erich Mende now opposed an embargo and said the Communists should not be given a pretext for blocking Western access. Mende's comments were strongly seconded in London by unidentified high British Foreign Office officials who indicated in "off the record" statements that the Macmillan Government was "leery" of launching reprisals against the Soviet bloc for fear of provoking the Communists into further actions.[18]

In Paris, Foreign Minister Couve de Murville broke the official silence of the French government only to say that the East German action of August 13 was entirely against the four-power status of Berlin and must be taken very seriously. Significantly, de Murville added: "I would not say that it was entirely unexpected."

From Washington, the *New York Times* reported that despite pressure from the Adenauer government for a more vigorous response, the Kennedy Administration had "decided to make a world wide show of reasonableness" in dealing with the Berlin issue. As was now the vogue in Washington,* it was another case of the deliberate press leak being used to announce governmental policy. Said the *Times:*

> The Kennedy Administration set out today to portray East Germany's closing of the border between East and West Berlin as a dramatic confession of Communist failure.
> The highest officials here indicated that this would be the extent, for the time being, of the Allied response to Communist moves in Berlin. As long as Western rights of access to the divided city are respected, the officials said, protest and vigorous propaganda will be the primary form of retaliation.[19]

News of the American position was received in Berlin with alarm. Neither the man on the street nor responsible city officials could believe their ears when they heard that the West had won a propaganda victory in the border closure. One astonished official of the West Berlin government remarked that if the West won many more victories like that there would be very little left to defend in Berlin.[20]

Indeed, as the days wore on after the border closure it became increasingly apparent that Washington was hopelessly out of touch with the situation in Berlin. Part of this no doubt was due to the fact that

* See previous chapter.

the senior U.S. representatives in Berlin were relatively minor cogs in the American government. Every action of the Berlin Command, in fact, was minutely dictated at this time from Washington, either by the State Department or the Pentagon. General Watson's reports were lightly received as coming from someone too closely involved to have a proper perspective. In the absence of a senior Administration official in Berlin, American policy in the crisis was reduced to bumbling along as best it could, based on the educated guesses of political authorities 3,500 miles from the scene of action. The result was a near fatal misjudgment of the issues involved.

By Tuesday night, August 15, with Allied action confined so far to the rather feeble protest made that morning, and with a propaganda victory now claimed by Washington, the mood in West Berlin became one of despair. The city's 13,000 riot police were put on a full state of alert to guard against any possible violence by the citizens themselves, and Mayor Brandt called a mass meeting for the following day in front of the City Hall. East German military forces along the border were reinforced and 47 more Russian-built T–34 tanks were moved into tactical positions. At several points the flimsy wire barricades were replaced by prefabricated concrete slabs taken from nearby housing projects.

Wednesday morning, August 16, 1961, saw further inroads made in the Allied position. East German border guards installed raisable traffic barriers—the kind seen at many grade-level railroad crossings—at each of the remaining twelve crossing points. East zone functionaries began to boast publicly of their victory and one East Berlin official even remarked that it had been impossible to work with "open borders." [21] Colonel Andrei Solovyev, the Soviet Commandant in East Berlin, also chose Wednesday morning to reply to the Western protest of August 3 regarding the earlier East German measures against the so-called "border crossers." With heavy irony, Colonel Solovyev stated that the Allied protest was now "completely out of place." Solovyev charged that it simply was another attempt by the West to interfere in the domestic affairs of the German Democratic Republic. "If you intend by your letter to extend the outmoded occupation regime to the capital of the German Democratic Republic," he said, "then such demands cannot be taken seriously." [22]

A breakfast meeting between President Kennedy and Secretary Rusk in Washington on Wednesday morning resulted only in more leaks to the press that the United States intended to take no vigorous action.

In West Berlin on Wednesday, the cries for countermeasures became more furious. By early afternoon over a quarter of a million people had gathered in front of the West Berlin City Hall in response to Mayor Brandt's plea of the day before. By now, however, their mood was one of anger and bitterness. Almost all thought they had been betrayed by the West. Dozens of posters appeared protesting the West's inaction. One said "Munich–1938—Berlin–1961." Another, "Paper Protests Don't Stop Tanks." With equal vigor the crowd booed references to the East German border closure and to the perfunctory Allied protest which followed it.

Mayor Brandt, looking tired and worn, attempted to keep the crowd in check and carefully avoided any incendiary remarks. He informed the crowd that he had sent a personal message to President Kennedy advising him of the situation and stating that the city expected "not merely words but political action." "What happened here in the last three days," Brandt said, "is a new version of the occupation of the Rhineland by Hitler. The man today is called Ulbricht." The Mayor's words expressed the feelings of the people precisely. They listened attentively and went home. Many were already convinced that their cry for support had gone unheeded.

The measures which Brandt suggested that the Allies should take are worthy of notice. In subsequent days some were adopted and some were not. All, however, had been suggested by the Mayor in his earliest conferences with Allied officials in Berlin after the border closure had gone into effect. It is natural therefore that Brandt's greatest criticism that Wednesday afternoon was directed against the slowness with which the West was responding. Brandt's suggestions included:

1. The immediate reinforcement of the Allied garrison.

2. The immediate movement of Allied troops along the autobahn between Berlin and West Germany to emphasize the continued right of Allied access.

3. The indictment of the East German regime before the United Nations for the suppression of human rights.

4. A selective ban by the West German government on vital economic goods imported by East Germany.

5. The immediate arrival in West Berlin of a prominent American personality preferably a Cabinet Minister.

6. The appointment of General Lucius Clay as American Commandant.

7. The taking over of the West Berlin portion of the city's elevated railroad system which was still under the control of the East. (This suggestion previously had been denied by the Allied Commandants.)

8. Closing of the offices of the German Communist Party (SED) in West Berlin. (This also had been turned down.)

9. Allied refusal to issue travel documents to East German officials wishing to travel to the West. (This ban had been rescinded earlier in the year.)

10. The stationing of token Allied forces along the sector border. (This had been strongly urged by Brandt Sunday morning but had been refused.)

11. Immediate protest to the Russians at the continued presence of East German armed forces in East Berlin.

12. An immediate session of the West German Bundestag. (This also had been refused, this time by Bonn.)

The above list represented a carefully thought out program prepared by the West Berlin city government under Brandt's direction. It seems neither inflammatory nor provocative, and it certainly warranted immediate consideration. In Washington, however, the embattled Mayor's call for "political action" was greeted with a storm of political abuse. The State Department and the White House were incensed that Mayor Brandt had announced the letter before the President had received it. Almost immediately the propaganda organs of the Administration began decrying Brandt's letter as a cheap political trick designed to rally support in the forthcoming West German elections. Sophisticated Washington columnists commented that Kennedy himself had just been through a bitter election and well understood the "temptation a crisis offers politicians." [23] Virtually all segments of the American press took up the cry. The Scripps-Howard chain commented editorially that Brandt's statement was "rude and presumptuous." "West German campaign oratory," it said, "is an irresponsible complication of the crisis in

Berlin." [24] The *New York Times, The Washington Post,* and *The Washington Evening Star* were likewise critical of Brandt's letter.

William S. White, the traditionalist political commentator of *The Evening Star,* referred to Mayor Brandt as a "mere mayor" trying to "take over the foreign policy, not only of his own country but of all the West by addressing personal notes to the President of the United States." White accused the Mayor of "shamelessly using the world crisis" to promote his own campaign. "It is easy for demagogues to whip up excited crowds, as Mr. Brandt is doing, to pour scorn on the West for inaction." [25]

And so it went on the fourth day after the border closure. The Berlin crisis continued to drift, with the West still refusing to concede that an emergency existed. The *New York Times* reported that the Kennedy Administration felt the "long advertised crisis" in Berlin had not yet occurred. Other capitals were reported "in essential agreement" with Washington that "no rash sanctions or countermeasures should be applied at this time." [26]

The following day, Thursday, August 17, 1961, Mr. Kennedy's press secretary, Pierre Salinger, announced that Mayor Brandt's letter had arrived. Salinger made a point of saying, however, that it had not yet been decided whether the letter would be answered.[27] But in Western Europe by this time, doubts were beginning to arise over the wisdom of the "propaganda victory" approach advocated by the United States. Paris announced that President De Gaulle was cutting his vacation short and returning to the city because of the Berlin crisis. In Bonn, Konrad Adenauer and other CDU officials began to feel the pressure for more effective action and stepped up their pleas to Washington. A group of university students in Bonn sent President Kennedy a black umbrella reminiscent of Neville Chamberlain whose policy of appeasement in 1938 paved the way for Hitler's dismemberment of Czechoslovakia.* From Berlin, Edward R. Murrow, the new head of the United States Information Agency who was visiting the beleaguered

---

* Attached to the umbrella was the following message:

> We are sorry to say, Mr. President, that because of your reserved reaction to the happenings in Berlin you have at the moment become the most worthy possessor of this symbol of a fateful policy.
> Because your doubtlessly very determined words in this present crisis were not followed by equally determined actions, there arises a comfortless memory of an era of European history from which the world is still suffering.

city, sent back dire warnings of the total failure of the Administration's policy.

By Thursday afternoon, certain rumblings of regret could be heard even in Washington. Doris Fleeson, the syndicated columnist of *The Evening Star,* in what perhaps could be termed a press leak from the bottom, defended Brandt's "precedent-shattering letter" as coming from a man "standing on the barricades with a restless populace behind him." The very same approach she said had long been argued by the German experts of the State Department. "Up until now," Miss Fleeson continued, "the reply has come back from the top that they were not convinced." She went on to say that the fact that Brandt's letter was sent at all reflected an increasingly deteriorating situation; a situation that the news dispatches from Berlin were describing with increasing bluntness.[28] Although she did not disclose her source, it was obvious that Miss Fleeson had been talking to people in Foggy Bottom other than Dean Rusk.

In Berlin, meanwhile, the East Germans continued their efforts to complete the separation of East and West. Although "the Wall" itself had not yet made its appearance, East German workmen began tearing up rails along the S-Bahn system which had previously run into West Berlin. People living in houses along the border were evacuated and doors and windows facing West Berlin were sealed.

The continued lack of Allied response to the Communist moves was driving responsible officials in West Berlin to despair. Little secret was made of the breach which had developed between Berlin and Washington. In Moscow, the Kremlin, which was profiting immensely from the situation, broke its long silence on the border closure and announced that the East German measures would remain in effect until a peace treaty had been signed. Previously, Soviet officials had remained conspicuously noncommittal about the East German action, apparently content with allowing the Ulbricht regime and the Warsaw Pact to shoulder full responsibility.* By Thursday, it was obvious that the West planned no violent reaction and so Moscow hastened to join its ally already in the field. Lest there be any doubt of Soviet intentions, however, Andrei Smirnov, the Russian Ambassador in Bonn, called on Chancellor Adenauer the day before and advised him that Russia

---

* Khrushchev, interestingly, had been on vacation at his Black Sea villa in Sochi since August 12.

would do nothing to aggravate the crisis until after the September West German elections.

Later in the day on Thursday, the formal Allied protests of the East Berlin border closure were delivered in Moscow. It was reported by the *New York Times*, however, that the notes were being delivered largely to assuage West German feelings of disappointment.[29] Like the earlier note sent to the Soviet Commandant in East Berlin, the tone of the protest was restrained. In what must rank as one of the great understatements of diplomatic communication, the East German sealing of the frontier was said to have "the effect of limiting, to a degree approaching complete prohibition, passage from the Soviet sector to the Western sectors of the city." [30] The protest, of course, had been drafted in Washington by the Western representatives meeting with Foy Kohler at the State Department, and clearly reflected the Kennedy Administration's hesitation to increase the area of conflict.

Thursday evening Dean Rusk met with President Kennedy at the White House to review the situation. They stressed that Berlin was only one of the issues discussed, but it was no secret that the continuing reports from Berlin had had their effect. Mr. Kennedy clearly was unhappy at the way the situation was developing, and accordingly now gave Mayor Brandt's proposals close attention. Secretary Rusk, in fact, seized on the suggestion of sending a high ranking official to Berlin and reportedly recommended Vice President Lyndon Johnson.[31]

Friday saw additional signs of activity in Washington. President Kennedy conferred with Vice President Johnson at 11 A.M. and shortly afterwards announced that Mr. Johnson had agreed to go to Berlin as his personal representative. General Lucius Clay was contacted in New York and soon appeared at the White House. The President asked Clay, then chairman of the board of the Continental Can Corporation, to join the Vice President's mission. Clay instantly accepted. The President also announced that his own departure for Hyannis Port this weekend would be postponed.

At six P.M. Friday evening, just prior to Vice President Johnson's departure, the President convened another special policy meeting on Berlin at the White House. This time Lyndon Johnson and General Clay joined the conferees. With them, in addition to the President and Secretary Rusk, were Presidential military adviser General Maxwell Taylor; Special Assistants McGeorge Bundy and Walt Rostow; and

Charles Bohlen, former U.S. Ambassador to Moscow who, as Special Assistant to the Secretary of State, was to accompany the Vice President's mission. Once more Mayor Brandt's proposals were considered, and Generals Clay and Taylor urged that the American garrison be reinforced. An overland movement of troops from West Germany, the Generals said, would have the added advantage of demonstrating the continued right of Allied access. According to General Clay, most of the other participants were strongly opposed. Basic Western rights in the divided city, they claimed, had not been affected.[32] But the counsel of the generals prevailed. At 7:40 P.M. Pierre Salinger called in reporters for an official announcement. The garrison would be reinforced. "In view of recent developments, including the movement of East German military forces into East Berlin," Salinger stated, "the President has directed an appropriate increase of the U.S. garrison in Berlin. A battle group of approximately 1,500 men will proceed by way of the Helmstedt-Berlin Autobahn, arriving there on Sunday." [33]

At 9:14 P.M. Friday evening Vice President Johnson and General Clay departed from Andrews Air Base for Bonn. In a brief departure statement, Mr. Johnson said he was going to Berlin to assure the West Berliners of America's "firm determination to use whatever means may be necessary to fulfil our pledge to preserve their freedom and their ties with the free world." General Clay made no statement.

In Germany, announcement of Johnson's mission had an immediate and heartening effect. Chancellor Adenauer applauded the move and said that the West German government warmly welcomed the Vice President's visit. Mayor Brandt expressed his "unlimited pleasure" at the announcement. "The people of Berlin," he said, "will show President Kennedy's representative how welcome he is in Berlin, and the Soviet Union will correctly understand this trip."

Earlier in the day, both the Chancellor and Mayor Brandt spoke before a belatedly called special session of the Bundestag. Neither brought up the subject of economic reprisals, although Brandt repeated once more his appeal for "convincing, non-military countermeasures." He said he was not reproaching the Allies but that the situation demanded "visible signs of Allied presence and Allied rights and above all, political initiatives." The Mayor also repeated his request that the garrison in Berlin be reinforced.

For the Communists, Friday was also a busy day. Shortly after midnight East German workmen began construction of a six-foot high concrete wall in the *Potsdamer Platz*. During the day other stretches of the wall went up replacing the improvised barbed wire entanglements strung earlier in the week. Thousands of workmen were reported at work on the project. Defecting East German policemen said that orders had been issued to complete construction of the wall along the entire 28-mile sector border by Monday.[34] Allied officials watched the wall's progress without comment. In contrast to the afternoon of August 13, at no time did responsible officials in Berlin recommend to the various capitals that action be taken to interfere with the wall's construction.*

On Friday, Colonel Andrei Solovyev also rejected the protest of the Allied Commandants regarding the sealing of the East sector border. The protest, Solovyev said, was "completely unfounded."

At the same time Solovyev was acting, Moscow likewise was rejecting the Western notes of the day before. These notes, said Moscow, were "without foundation" and were "categorically rejected by the Soviet Government." The length of the Soviet reply, almost 3,000 words, indicates that it had been prepared sometime previously and had been kept on hand for the use at the proper time. For the most part it was another attempt to justify the Soviet stand on Berlin, and catalogued

---

* At his Press Conference on January 15, 1962, President Kennedy was asked specifically about the wall's construction and whether intervention had been recommended. The question, and Mr. Kennedy's answer, were as follows:

Q.—Mr. President, criticism that we did not tear down the Berlin wall seems to be increasing rather than decreasing. . . . I don't recall that you have ever publicly discussed this particular phase of the question. Do you think it would be helpful for you to do so now?

A.—Well, I haven't discussed it but I stated that no one at that time in any position of responsibility—and I would use that term—either in the West Berlin American contingent, in West Berlin, France, or Great Britain, suggested that the United States or other countries go in and tear down the wall.

The Soviet Union had had a de facto control for many years, stretching back to the late 40s in East Berlin. It has been turned over as a capital for East Germany a long time ago. And the United States has a very limited force surrounded by a great many divisions, and we are going to find ourselves severely challenged to maintain what we have considered to be our basic rights—which is our presence in West Berlin and the right of access to West Berlin, and the freedom of the people of West Berlin.

But in my judgment, I think that you could have had a very violent reaction which might have taken us down a very rocky road. And I think it was for that reason and because it was recognized by those people in positions of responsibility that no recommendation was made along the lines you have suggested at that time. Hindsight is . . .

in detail alleged Western violations to the city's four-power status. The responsibility for the East German sealing of the border between East and West Berlin was laid directly on the Western powers. Their subversive activities, Moscow said, had made the "protective measures on the border of the German Democratic Republic" necessary. The measures, it was announced once more, would remain in effect until the conclusion of a German peace treaty and "the normalization of the situation in West Berlin" on that basis.

Shortly after the delivery of the Russian notes, Walter Ulbricht delivered a victory address to the East German people. Ulbricht's tone was one of elation. The border closure he said had "cleansed the atmosphere." "We have succeeded in getting the war center of West Berlin under control." Ulbricht spoke for more than an hour. He made repeated attacks on the West, and especially on Mayor Brandt. In conclusion, Ulbricht stated that "our measures have shown even to those who did not believe it before the true balance of power in the world."

Fortunately, announcement of the visit of Vice President Johnson and General Clay took some of the sting out of Ulbricht's words. Western inaction at this point very definitely would have caused a major panic in Berlin. West Berlin officials already were reporting temporary shortages of certain staples in various retail stores because of anxious buying by excited housewives. While the city itself had supplies enough to last over nine months, popular morale would have sustained it for only a fraction of that time.

At six o'clock Saturday morning the battle group President Kennedy had ordered to Berlin began to roll. Shortly after six A.M. public information officers at USAREUR Headquarters in Heidelberg disclosed that the unit involved was the 1st Battle Group, 18th Infantry, from nearby Mannheim.* The route of march would take the battle group along the West German autobahn from Mannheim to Frankfurt and Kassel, and then along the Harz mountains to Braunschweig (Brunswick). It would bivouac in Braunschweig for the night, enter East Germany at Helmstedt early Sunday morning and be in Berlin shortly

---

* The 18th Infantry was the closest American battle group to Berlin. The northern portion of the U.S. defense area in Germany is held largely by armored units and while these could have been moved, it was no doubt felt easier to transport infantry troops in trucks than it would have been to place the tanks and personnel carriers of an armored battalion on the road. (A battle group, it should be noted, is a unit of organization peculiar to the American infantry. Armored units are grouped into battalions and combat commands.)

after noon. Although no difficulty was expected on the move through East Germany, United States Army Commander in Europe, General Bruce C. Clarke, moved with a small command group to the Helmstedt area Saturday afternoon. Military and West German police took over the problem of traffic control along the entire route from Mannheim to Helmstedt and energetically kept the column moving. Nineteen hours after leaving Mannheim the last vehicle of the 18th Infantry closed in Braunschweig.

While the 18th Infantry was on the road, Vice President Johnson and General Clay landed in Bonn. They conferred with Chancellor Adenauer for over two hours. After lunch Johnson and Clay departed for Berlin. The Chancellor, who himself had not yet been to Berlin since August 13, requested to accompany the mission but Vice President Johnson politely declined. The German election campaign was hot enough, Johnson felt, without making it appear that the United States was taking sides. The flight, he told Adenauer, had been intended as a purely American affair.

Vice President Johnson landed at Tempelhof airport in Berlin shortly after two P.M. As soon as the wheels of his plane touched down a massive demonstration of solidarity began. Mayor Brandt was on hand to meet him. Together they reviewed an honor guard of American troops and West Berlin police. The Vice President spoke briefly; his words were moving and to the point, and already the morale of the city was recovering. The United States, Johnson said, would stand with Berlin in the defense of freedom. "We remember your ordeals, we honor your fortitude, and we are with you in the determination to defend your liberty and the high and holy cause of human freedom."

The Vice President and Mayor Brandt then led a motorcade from Tempelhof to City Hall. In spite of a steady rain which had kept up all morning, more than 400,000 people lined the route, many openly weeping. When the motorcade had gone less than a mile, Johnson and Brandt stepped from their car and began to walk. They moved slowly through the huge crowd shaking hands as they went. It was a moment of intense emotion in a city long accustomed to great emotions.

The party moved on to the newly built wall in the *Potsdamer Platz;* Johnson studied it closely for over ten minutes and the cavalcade resumed. At City Hall waited 300,000 people in a mood even more charged than that of those who had lined the route. The Vice President himself was now close to tears. His presence had had an electric effect.

Mayor Brandt spoke first. "On Wednesday we stood here and called out to the world for our brothers in the East. The dispatch of American troops and this visit are the answer." The crowd raised a tremendous cheer.

Lyndon Johnson then spoke. The fact that he said nothing new nor promised any strikingly bold action did not bother the Berliners. They were happy that he was there and that their link to the free world had been demonstrated. Six days before, of course, would have been better but the important thing now was that America had acted.

To the crowd, and later that evening before a special session of the West Berlin Parliament, Vice President Johnson renewed America's pledge to stand by the city. His words were not the words of diplomatic nicety but of a man who now felt the importance of the events about him. Doubtless, they were also words which the Communists would understand. Quoting the American *Declaration of Independence,* Johnson said—"To the survival and to the creative future of this city we Americans have pledged, in effect, what our ancestors pledged in forming the United States: 'our lives, our fortunes, and our sacred honor.'"

After Vice President Johnson had spoken Mayor Brandt introduced General Clay. Although the Vice President was the star of the day, the Berliners had a special, and perhaps, a much deeper affection for their old friend. Their ovation was tumultuous. "Here stands the man," Brandt said, "who helped to save our lives then, together with the unforgotten Ernst Reuter." According to nearby witnesses the General was also close to tears. Blushing at the personal demonstration for himself, Clay told the crowd:

> I want to say how wonderful it is to see proud and still free looks on the faces of the people of West Berlin. Thanks to your courage, with the support of my own countrymen and the support of all freedom-loving people, what we started together twelve years ago we will finish together and Berlin will still be free.

When the speeches were over, the German police band broke into the *Star Spangled Banner* followed by the *Deutschland Lied* and *Berliner Luft*. From the tower of the *Schöneberger Rathaus* waved four flags: two American, one German and one from Berlin. From inside the tower, the Freedom Bell, installed after the blockade, rang out loudly. For the Berliners, and indeed, for the entire free world, it had been a great day.[35]

If possible, Sunday was even greater. Shortly before one P.M. the first elements of the 18th Infantry rolled into Berlin. Vice President Johnson and thousands of enthusiastic Berliners were on hand to greet them. People once more lined the streets and pelted the trucks with bouquets of flowers as the column quickly made its way from the American checkpoint at Drei Linden to McNair Barracks. From a reviewing stand on the parade ground at McNair Barracks—the same reviewing stand from which General Omar Bradley had welcomed the Second Armored Division into Berlin sixteen years before—Vice President Johnson told the arriving troops that they were there as a symbol of America's promise to remain in Berlin "no matter what course things run."

After a short rest, the soldiers remounted their vehicles for a parade through the city. Up *Clay Allee,* down the *Kurfürstendamm,* into the *Tauentzienstrasse* the column moved, everywhere accompanied by ringing ovations from a grateful populace. Colonel Grover S. Johns, the veteran commander of the battle group, said it was "the most exciting and impressive reception I've ever seen with the possible exception of the liberation of France." [36]

Sunday evening, as the emotion packed day drew to a close, Vice President Johnson remarked that "we all feel better now." In addition to welcoming the reinforcements from the 18th Infantry, Johnson had kept up an almost round-the-clock tour of the city. He also managed a seventy-five minute private talk with Mayor Brandt from which both emerged beaming. "There are absolutely no differences between us," the Vice President told waiting newsmen. Johnson had advised Mayor Brandt that the United States planned no additional measures at this time in Berlin and also handed him President Kennedy's reply to the Mayor's earlier letter. Although its contents were never made public, little secret has been made that the President's message contained some rather sharp language. It had been drafted at Mr. Rusk's special direction in Washington and to a large extent reflected the views which had dictated the earlier policy of the Administration. Lyndon Johnson by this time had formed perhaps a better judgment of the situation and advised the Mayor not to be too upset about the letter.

At four A.M. Monday morning Vice President Johnson's party departed for home. The two and a half days had been well spent, and the morale of the Berliners—"our first line of defense"—had been restored. More important perhaps, a responsible member of the Administration had seen for himself the situation in Berlin and could add his voice to the President's councils. General Clay, of course, was no stranger to the problems of dealing with the Russians over the divided city and no doubt contributed his own advice that we should take a firm stand.

Official American thinking regarding the situation in Berlin at this time actually was divided into two schools. The first, and the dominant school within the Administration, nominally headed by Mr. Rusk, included Adlai Stevenson, "Chip" Bohlen, Senators Fulbright and Mansfield, most of the political appointees in the State Department at the level of Assistant Secretary and above, and Ted Sorensen, Walt Rostow and Arthur Schlesinger, Jr., on the President's personal staff. Generally speaking, they believed that the Allied position in Berlin was based on three things: first, the right of free access; second, the right to keep troops there; and third, the continued economic and political viability of the Western sectors. In Mr. Rusk's terminology, these items were the "heart of the matter" in Berlin and therefore what the West should defend. The border closure, it was felt, did not affect these basic points. Indeed, now that the refugee problem had finally been settled, the Rusk-Stevenson-Bohlen school believed that it might be possible to conclude a mutually acceptable arrangement over West Berlin with the Russians on a long term basis. These negotiations would naturally involve some give and take but this was thought to be justified if a lasting settlement could be achieved. Among those items that might be conceded—and these limits varied—were a reduction in the size of the garrison (the recent increase would make this even easier); the liquidation of RIAS and other related "irritants"; the total separation of West Berlin from the Federal Republic; and perhaps, reconsideration of the Rapacki Plan for a neutralized zone in Central Europe.

Seen in the larger framework of foreign policy in general, the advocates of the "soft-line" urgently sought to improve diplomatic relations with the Soviet Union and felt that this could be achieved through "meaningful" negotiations. Indeed, to these advisers the absolute horror of nuclear war made any other course unthinkable. Thus, since there was no "rational" alternative to negotiations, the mere fact that discussions were going on was considered a virtue; as having an intrinsic value of its own regardless of the subject discussed. It was this sacramental view of negotiations that characterized the Rusk-Stevenson-Bohlen school within the Administration, and all of its members were ranged somewhere along this continuum. The Soviet Union was looked on as a tough but nevertheless reasonable adversary with whom one could carry on a meaningful dialogue—just as Disraeli or Palmerston could have done with the Czars. This view was supported by the numerous Kremlinologists who professed to see in the post-Stalinist development of Russia a significant liberalization of communism, as well as by the serious internal rifts within the Sino-Soviet bloc which were everyday becoming more evident. Khrushchev's pleas for "peaceful coexistence" thus tended to be accepted at face value. In Secretary Rusk's phrase, the United States should "always be willing to go the last mile" to make negotiations possible.

Also, many of the members of this "soft-line" school were occupying high executive positions for the first time. An overwhelming preponderance of them hailed directly from university campuses, or were writers and men of letters—all honorable professions, but professions (in the words of one contemporary critic) "preoccupied with words, prone to regard verbalizing as completed action." The propensity to debate was thus an inborn characteristic of many on the New Frontier, and even President Kennedy traced his governmental experience to the United States Senate, a body long distinguished for its rhetorical tradition, where responsibility rarely transcends the oral level. It was perhaps only natural then that during the first year of their stewardship many in the Administration should look at the cold war simply as another dispute amenable to discursive solution. According to the Rusk-Stevenson-Bohlen school, "brinkmanship" in any form was to be avoided; detachment and objectivity to be encouraged. But the detached and disinterested approach was particularly subject to error when it came to dealing with Berlin. The questions of sector boundaries, free access, troop levels, etc., were charged with a significance penetrating to the very roots of the Western Alliance, and could not be looked at "with the calm detachment . . . of a city planner talking about the defects of the municipal franchise of Montclair, New Jersey." *

* Dean Acheson to the Legislators of the North Atlantic Treaty Organization, November 18, 1959.

At the time of the border closure in East Berlin, however, it was the Stevenson-Bohlen view that prevailed in Washington. Its proponents considered the continued stream of refugees as perhaps the major source of tension in Berlin, and therefore the major stumbling block to reopening negotiations. If this exodus could somehow be shut off, then the way would be open for fruitful discussions. Since every sign pointed to an eventual East German border closure anyway, it was tacitly agreed between Washington and the other Allied capitals that no Western opposition should be offered when the move was finally made. This agreement was ratified at the meeting of the Foreign Ministers in Paris, and dictated the initial Allied response on August 13 and the days immediately following. Great Britain and the Adenauer government were in complete accord with the Administration position although for political reasons the West Germans were considerably more circumspect in saying so. France, though opposed to opening negotiations, was not opposed to shutting off the flow of refugees for its own sake. First, General De Gaulle agreed that tensions might be reduced. Second, and here one must appreciate De Gaulle's overriding sense of history, the movement of German peoples out of Central Germany, he felt, must be checked so that a vacuum for Slavic expansion would not be created. In the long run, according to De Gaulle, a halting of the westward migration of the East German refugees might be important in securing the German frontier on the Oder—a scheme he had long advocated.

Thus, when the East Germans did strike, the West stood by and did nothing. The formal protest sent three days later was strictly for appearances. No concerted effort to reopen the border was ever considered and the idea of countermeasures caused only alarm. Not until the situation in West Berlin became truly critical was this policy seriously questioned. Then, it was questioned not by the school that had developed it but by the opposing group which had reluctantly acquiesced to its adoption. For Stevenson and Schlesinger, Willy Brandt was still a wild man shouting fire in a crowded theater. The best indication that a shift had occurred, however, was the return of General De Gaulle to Paris on Wednesday. By this time it was obvious that all was not well.

Opposed to the Rusk-Stevenson-Bohlen group on Berlin was the so-called "hard-line school." This school centered on the various "cold war" planning staffs in Washington, and for the most part represented a continuation of the policies of the two previous Administrations. Undisputed leader of the hard-line school was former Secretary of State Dean Acheson. Other prominent members included Paul Nitze, General Taylor, the uniformed service chiefs, many of the civilian leaders in the Pentagon, and the pick and shovel men on the German desk in the State Department.

The influence of the hard-line school on American policy was probably greatest during the early days of the Kennedy Administration. Certain of the hard-line advocates, the Joint Chiefs of Staff in particular, later became seriously discredited in the eyes of the White House as a result of the Cuban episode. Their views on Berlin were therefore discounted accordingly. Former Secretary Acheson, who up until Vienna had been the President's personal adviser on Berlin, became the victim of a palace vendetta and fell from grace shortly after the President's return. President Kennedy himself had been severely shaken by his meeting with Khrushchev in Vienna and afterwards desperately sought to reduce whatever tensions might exist in U.S.-Soviet relations. As a result, by the middle of July the influence of the hard-line school had become minimal. The Stevenson-Bohlen policy leading toward negotiations was adopted, and the possibility of an East German border closure was accepted as a contribution to that end.

The position of the hard-line advisers was about the same as that of General De Gaulle * and Mayor Brandt. Negotiations with Russia over Berlin were not considered desirable since the West could go no way but down. The status quo in Berlin represented a major victory for the West. As long as the status quo remained, Ulbricht could not consolidate his hold on East Germany, and without East Germany, Khrushchev could not consolidate his hold on Eastern Europe. Berlin, in short, was an offensive weapon—an asset rather than a liability. It was therefore in our interests to do everything possible to maintain the present situation and to keep the bone in Khrushchev's throat where it belonged. Admittedly, to do this involved a willingness to "go to the brink" if necessary. The continuing pressure on Khrushchev that Berlin represented, however, made this risk worth while.

This reasoning was based on the belief that the Western position in

* While General De Gaulle may have favored ending the flow of refugees for its own sake, he strongly opposed negotiations over Berlin and was firmly against Western concessions. It is in this latter, and indeed, more fundamental connection, that his position was similar to the hard-line school in Washington.

Berlin included a great deal more than the so-called "heart of the matter" items listed by Secretary Rusk. In fact, every element of the existing four-power status in Berlin was considered essential. As soon as the first dent was made, it was felt, a never ending process of attrition would begin and Berlin's value would be nullified. It goes without saying that the right of free movement within the city, the right which insured the continued access to West Berlin by the peoples of the East, was one of the major points to be preserved. The complete adoption of the Stevenson-Bohlen policy following Vienna therefore represented a major defeat for the hard-line advocates. The West's position in Berlin came to be looked on by the Kennedy Administration as a burden rather than an advantage. Accordingly, American policy became directed toward unloading that burden.

But none of this should be considered as ameliorating the role of President Kennedy as the final arbiter of American foreign policy. No President in history has been so vocal in his determination to be "his own Secretary of State," and never before have deskmen at the State Department had their work so well supervised "all the way to the top." [*] Indeed, it would be a disservice both to the President and to his advisers (both "hard-line" and "soft-line") if anything in this discussion should be taken to indicate that U.S. policy on the New Frontier is anything other than that desired by the President himself.

As has been indicated, immediate Western action—or rather, immediate Western inaction—following the border closure was a direct result of this policy. With the flow of refugees halted, the way to negotiations with Khrushchev was felt to be open. As Chalmers Roberts of *The Washington Post* wrote of the border closure on August 18:

> No one is saying so out loud but there is a considerable belief here that the Communist move in effect removes one of the issues in dispute at any future East–West negotiations. Nikita Khrushchev has been demanding that the West end the use of Berlin as an escape route for East Germans. Now he has done it himself.

The delayed *pro-forma* Western protest, the long period of official silence, the belated attempt to portray the Communist action as a "sign of weakness" were all natural adjuncts of this policy. Kennedy's sting-

[*] Charles Burton Marshall, "Organizing Foreign Policy," *New Republic*, December 25, 1961.

ing reply to Mayor Brandt likewise resulted from assuming that the closing of the border had been to the West's advantage. The reports from West Berlin speaking of the need for action and of the deteriorating popular morale were at first dismissed as momentary phenomena. Only when these reports persisted, and indeed, grew ever more urgent, was anything other than tacit acknowledgment of the East German action ever considered. The proposals of the West Berlin government were then scrutinized with care. Vice President Johnson was dispatched to Berlin and, over the reported objections of the Stevenson-Bohlen school, the 18th Infantry moved to the city's reinforcement.

On his arrival in Berlin, Vice President Johnson shared the feeling that the border closure could be made to work to the West's advantage. His purpose, as he expressed it, was to reassure the Berliners and to have a look for himself. He did both, and as a result, when he reported to President Kennedy in Washington, Johnson was in a position to advise the President of the extreme precariousness of the West's new position. The West Berliners, he emphasized, were disenchanted, and the whole episode had been woefully misjudged from Washington. It would be some time, perhaps even years, he indicated, before the West Berliners would recover from the shocks of the past week. Indeed, whether West Berlin would ever recover from the shock of Western inaction was at best, problematical. If Communist pressure should suddenly tighten again, a full blown panic would likely ensue.[37]

Clearly, Lyndon Johnson had been deeply moved by his visit to Berlin. He returned, as he said, "with a feeling of unlimited gratitude to the people of West Berlin and West Germany and with a feeling of unlimited compassion for the suffering now being endured by the people of East Berlin and East Germany. . . ." His arrival statement at Andrews Air Base eloquently expressed this feeling; it stands in marked contrast both to the announcement of Mr. Rusk eight days before, and to the policy which Washington had pursued up until his visit. Said Johnson:

> It is impossible to give an adequate picture, in these few words, of the courage and the dedication to freedom which sustain the people of West Berlin in these difficult days. They are being tested and harassed by Communist power; but their heroic conduct in this emergency has become one of the major assets of the free world. . . .

No one who has seen and talked with the refugees from East Germany, as I have done, can fail to realize what a profound human tragedy is involved.

That realization must heighten the urgency with which we consider our own responsibilities, and the responsibilities of our Allies, in dealing with the issues raised by the Berlin crisis.[38]

Following Vice President Johnson's first-hand report, the Western attitude stiffened considerably. President Kennedy announced from the White House that the next weeks and months would be difficult "in maintaining the freedom of West Berlin, but maintain it we will." [39] This remark represented a decided departure from the earlier idea that the border closure had represented a net gain for the West, and indeed, was the first public statement made by the President since the border closure went into effect nine days before.

Although the pressure for negotiations continued, a number of new actions were now taken to buttress the Allied position in West Berlin. On August 21, when a battalion of the East German Army suddenly appeared across the border, the British military command in Berlin dispatched a company of combat infantry and four fifty-ton Centurion tanks to the West Berlin sector boundary. The British action represented the first appearance of Allied military forces along the West Berlin border since the East German operations of August 13 had begun. The company remained in place overnight and was joined the following day by the entire British garrison. As a spokesman at British Headquarters in Berlin was quoted as saying, "we decided to show the flag." [40]

In Washington on August 21, the State Department also announced that a previously negotiated commercial air pact with the Soviet Union would not be signed "in the light of the over-all world situation." The following day, West German Chancellor Konrad Adenauer flew to Berlin to inspect the Wall and discuss the situation with West Berlin officials. The Chancellor was met at Tempelhof by Mayor Brandt, but the atmosphere between the two was reported as distinctly "cool." [41] At several stops along the sector boundary the Chancellor was greeted by an East German loudspeaker car hurling abuse. At other points, however, where Communist police were fewer, he was greeted by crowds of several hundred East Berliners who had gathered to wave handkerchiefs across the border. According to Flora Lewis, the indefatigable correspondent of the *Washington Post Foreign Service,* many could be seen openly weeping.[42]

As the West was moving to counteract the effects of the border closure, the East Germans stepped-up their measures to complete the separation of the city. Many of these measures were clearly designed to probe the willingness of the West to respond. On August 21, all residents of East Berlin whose houses fronted on the sector border were dispossessed and relocated. Two days later the East German Interior Ministry announced that the number of crossing points into East Berlin was being reduced from twelve to seven. Of the seven, four would be for West Berliners, two for West Germans, and one for "foreigners" and Allied personnel. The East German decree was accompanied by a new order banning all persons in the West from approaching the Wall closer than a distance of 100 meters. This ban, the announcement said, would be rigidly enforced by East German police with whatever means were necessary.

This time, Western reaction was immediate, and within hours after the 100-meter ban was announced, the three Allied Commandants had met, ordered a full alert of Western forces and dispatched 1,000 troops supported by tanks to defend the integrity of the sector boundaries up to the very wall itself. By one P.M., Wednesday afternoon, a vigorous protest note had been drafted and delivered to Soviet Headquarters in Karlshorst. The protest concluded with the statement that the East German ban was illegal and that "the Commandants are taking the necessary action to insure the security and integrity of the sector borders."

The decision of the Commandants to take immediate action over the 100-meter ban had not been referred to their governments for approval.[43] The question of the reduction of crossing points, however, was another matter. In Washington, despite Vice President Johnson's urgent report of Monday, the Administration had decided to accept this latest East German affront as merely an extension of the earlier restrictions. While Paris and London were both reported adamant for firm countermeasures, the *New York Times* said that Washington had decided vital Western rights still had not been affected. After describing the so-called "heart of the matter" views of the Administration, the *Times* said:

In the view of the highest policy makers here, the new limitations on the movements of West Germans, West Berliners and Allied diplomats and soldiers who wish to enter East Berlin do not compromise any of these vital interests.

On the contrary, the policymakers tended at first to regard the new restrictions as merely an extension of the erection of Communist barricades between the two parts of Berlin.[44]

On Thursday, August 24, the probing action of the East German regime continued. Three American Army buses were held up for over an hour at the *Friedrichstrasse* checkpoint—the only checkpoint still open to Allied personnel—when East German police demanded to inspect the identity papers of the soldiers aboard. Later in the day, two American soldiers on duty at the border were sprayed with water from a Communist water truck. The stream of water subsided only when a nearby American officer reached for a tear gas grenade strapped to his uniform. That evening, East German border guards fired on and killed a refugee trying to make his escape to the British sector across a canal near the Reichstag. Although shots had been fired before, it was the first time a refugee had been killed since the border was closed eleven days before.

The following day, August 25, 1961, East German police fired warning shots over the heads of a crowd in the French sector when they did not respond to an order to move back from the wall. West Berlin police then stepped in and moved the crowd "for their own safety." In two other incidents, East German police threw tear gas grenades into crowds of West Berliners along the border who were jeering at a speech of Walter Ulbricht being broadcast over East German loudspeakers. Ulbricht had returned to his old game of announcing that following a peace treaty, all access to Berlin would be placed in the hands of the East German regime.

In Washington meanwhile, pressure for negotiations was mounting. Following the movement of Allied troops to the sector boundary, Secretary Rusk became worried that a major conflict would be touched off in Berlin by "some PFC on the border." Senator Mansfield once more advocated that the West begin negotiations on Berlin immediately,[45] and at the White House, Administration spokesman Pierre Salinger, reflecting the Rusk position which had been adopted by the U.S., denied a report that General Clay was being considered for reassignment to Berlin.[46]

But in Berlin the renewed Communist offensive was taking its toll. Morale, which had been given so great a boost by Vice President Johnson's visit, was beginning to sag dangerously. And the persistence with which Washington pressed for negotiations in the face of continuing Communist encroachments was again being equated in Berlin with a willingness to surrender vital Western rights. The lack of more positive Western countermeasures to the latest East German assaults, and particularly, the acceptance of the reduction of crossing points from 12 to 7, was once more giving the West Berliners a feeling of alarm.

On August 26, the West attempted to calm these fears. The three Western Ambassadors in Bonn delivered identical personal notes to the Soviet Ambassador in East Berlin protesting the latest East German moves and announcing that any attempt to enforce the 100-meter ban "could only have the most serious consequences." Heartening though the protests were, the Berliners could not help noticing that they were made in the form of personal letters from the Ambassadors and not as official communications from their respective capitals.* Instead of raising the city's spirits, the protests thus served to lower West Berlin morale all the more.

Two days later Secretary Rusk announced from New York that negotiations with Russia over Berlin were definite. Mr. Rusk's announcement came following a two-hour meeting with Adlai Stevenson in the latter's Waldorf-Astoria apartment. The time and place of the negotiations, Rusk said, had not been worked out but they would probably take place when the UN General Assembly session convened on September 19. Since President De Gaulle was still adamantly against negotiations, it was assumed that the conversations would be begun by the United States alone.[47]

Rusk's announcement indicated once more that the basic policy of the Administration had not changed. Negotiations were still being considered by Washington as the surest way of reaching a settlement in Berlin. Whatever may have been the results of Vice President Johnson's visit, it did not dissuade the President from this basic tenet.

The following day, on August 29, in what may have been a severe

---

* The fact that the protests were delivered to the Soviet Ambassador in East Berlin rather than the Soviet Ambassador in Bonn was also considered dangerously close to a diplomatic recognition of the East German regime.

shock to the Administration, Chancellor Adenauer wrote to President Kennedy advising him that the continuation of Western reverses in Berlin was leading to a dangerous revival in neutralist sentiment throughout West Germany. According to Adenauer, and certainly De Gaulle and Brandt would have agreed, the present Western policy in Berlin was endangering the entire Western alliance. The dangers, as Adenauer was reported to have listed them, were that the Communists would continue to nibble away at West Berlin, or that the Allied position there would "be seriously weakened through negotiations with the Soviet Union." If the Communists were allowed to get away with any new attacks on the city after their success in sealing the border, the Chancellor said that a panic flight of West Berliners would probably result. The impact of such an event in West Germany he said was of great concern.[48]

Already, according to Adenauer, the failure of the West to react to the border closing had been followed in West Germany by the sprouting of neutralist sentiment. Some people he said were once more beginning to question whether Germany should have joined the North Atlantic Community. Indeed, although he did not say so directly, the Chancellor himself was being vigorously attacked in West Germany for the weak Allied stand and was again being referred to in the scornful phrase of the late Kurt Schumacher as the "Chancellor of the Allies." Adenauer concluded his message by saying that unless the West showed a noticeable ability to defend its position in West Berlin, a desire for some kind of an accommodation with Russia, perhaps even a neutral role between East and West, would become a serious factor in West German politics. Immediate countermeasures, he suggested, were essential.[49]

With the West German election less than three weeks off, Adenauer's letter had a profound impact in Washington. Within twenty-four hours President Kennedy announced that Lucius Clay was returning to Berlin. At a news conference attended by a record 437 newsmen, the President said that he was appointing General Clay as his personal representative in Berlin "to add to our resources of judgment and action." The appointment would become effective immediately following the West German election.

In Berlin and West Germany the news of Clay's appointment was greeted with universal acclaim. To every West German and West

Berliner General Lucius D. Clay was a personal hero. If General Eisenhower could be said to be their conqueror, General Clay was their savior. In West Berlin, Mayor Brandt said that the city would welcome him "like a home-coming son." The appointment said Brandt, "makes unmistakably clear the determination of the United States to defend the freedom of Berlin."

With the appointment of General Clay the defense of Berlin had come full circle. The man who had saved the city for the West once before was again being called into service. This time, however, he would find his role more difficult. No longer the American proconsul of a conquered country, General Clay was to go to Berlin as a largely unofficial Presidential Ambassador. His appointment, it was stressed, would not offset the existing Command structure in Berlin. Unlike the crisis of 1948, Lucius Clay would now find himself at the operating end of a chain-of-command stretching through a myriad of bureaucratic labyrinths. His every action would be minutely controlled from a seat of government more than three thousand miles away. From a seat of government, it perhaps should be added, that no longer saw the Berlin crisis in the same manner as did he.

14

"No Concessions
Without Counter-Concessions"

ANNOUNCEMENT of General Clay's return halted the drift of Germany toward neutralism. It did not, however, restore Chancellor Adenauer's waning prestige. Indeed, it is unlikely that this was intended. The aging Chancellor was viewed by most of the new young men in Washington as the principal stumbling block to reopening negotiations. Should he gently be retired from office, a new overture could be made toward the East; an overture with double chance of success now that the refugee problem had been solved.

Early election returns on September 17 encouraged this view. Clearly, the Chancellor had lost his majority. When the counting was over, Adenauer's Christian Democratic Union had received but forty-five percent of the total vote. Its seats in the Bundestag numbered 242—eight less than necessary to form a government and thirty-seven less than the previous session. The SPD of Willy Brandt had won 190 seats (versus 169 in the previous session) and the Free Democrats 67 (versus 49). A coalition government would have to be formed.

For Adenauer, the results were particularly galling. He, of all people, had been blamed by the German electorate for events in Berlin. Ironically, part of the criticism was justified. When the Western Foreign Ministers met in Paris on August 7 and 8, Adenauer had accepted the Anglo-American view that a closing of the sector boundary would ease tensions in Berlin. When Mayor Brandt advised the Chancellor's Foreign Minister, Dr. Heinrich von Brentano, of the inherent danger of such a move, the latter had turned a deaf ear.* When the border closure did come, Ernst Lemmer, Adenauer's leader in Berlin, announced over a television hookup on the evening of August 13 that the measures were not a surprise. From Bonn, Dr. Adenauer himself pleaded for calm and the following day in Regensburg gave his now famous diatribe against "Herr Brandt, alias Framm."

During the week following August 13, Adenauer stuck closely to Washington's line that the border closure represented a propaganda victory for the West; that it was not something to get excited about. He at first denied Brandt's request for a special session of the Bundestag and continued campaigning as though nothing had happened. Belatedly, on Saturday, August 19, he asked to accompany Vice President Johnson to Berlin but was turned down. This was a severe blow to the Chancellor, for he had staked his future on American support. Having acquiesced to Anglo-American insistence on the border closure, *der Alte* could not understand the refusal of the American Administration to bail him out. Four years before, in 1957, when there was still some doubt as to West German interest in rearmament and when the *ohne mich* movement was at its height, John Foster Dulles had outspokenly endorsed Adenauer's re-election and the Chancellor undoubtedly was remembering this. But now there was a new group in Washington and no support was tendered. When he arrived at Tempelhof three days later, it was understood throughout Germany that the Chancellor had come too late.**

* After his advice had been turned down by Bonn, Brandt spoke out repeatedly during the next several days warning against a splitting of the city. His comments in Frankfurt on August 7, have already been mentioned, see Chapter 12. On August 11, Brandt once more met with von Brentano and once more warned him of impending events in Berlin. On August 12, in a speech on the Market Platz in Nuremberg, the Mayor specifically referred to the continued flight of refugees and said that measures already were underway to close it off. The purpose of Brandt's remarks was to mobilize public opinion against the impending East German move and force Bonn to recant, but, of course, his efforts were too late.
** There is little question in Bonn that Adenauer feels he was double-crossed by Washington. Without rendering a judgment, it would seem that he did have a

During the next several weeks Dr. Adenauer energetically tried to recoup his losses and did eventually succeed in curtailing the bitterness in the Federal Republic which had arisen over Allied inaction on August 13. Over the undoubted discomfiture of numerous Presidential advisers he prevailed upon Washington to return General Clay to Berlin, and all but thought he had weathered the storm.

But the resentment which most West Germans felt over the border closure perhaps subconsciously had been transferred to the Chancellor. Inside his own party there was widespread dissatisfaction at the way *der Alte* had handled the events of August 13, and an increasing demand for his retirement. The failure of the party to retain its absolute majority in the Bundestag was universally attributed to the Chancellor's attitude of "politics as usual."

Accordingly, when the votes were counted and it was determined that a coalition would be necessary, the cries for Adenauer's head rose to a crescendo. The heirs apparent within the CDU—Ludwig Ehrhard, Franz Josef Strauss, and Gerhard Schroeder—openly announced they would not support the Chancellor's re-election in the party caucus. Erich Mende, leader of the FDP, the party with whom the coalition would have to be formed, had made the air black during the campaign with repeated avowals that his party would never join a coalition headed by Chancellor Adenauer, and now repeated this liturgy to every newsman in Bonn who would listen. The White House, which already had relegated *der Alte* to a place among the "has beens," once more made no efforts on his behalf. The rumor was current in Bonn, in fact, that Washington would welcome a change to someone "more tractable" and more willing to recognize the "new realities" of the international situation—a description equally applicable to Ehrhard or Schroeder. While it would perhaps be too much to say that the wily Chancellor had been mousetrapped by Washington, it was clear that his defeat was not being looked on with alarm.

In Great Britain, where *der Alte* had never been popular anyway, both major parties were filled with glee at the prospect of the Chancellor's replacement. Following a conference of Labour leader Hugh Gaitskill with Prime Minister Macmillan at Chequers, *New York Times*

---

rather strong call on the Administration. While certainly there was never an explicit *quid pro quo*, Adenauer's acceptance of the Kennedy program for Berlin would seem to have obligated the Administration to his support. It is unlikely that *der Alte* has forgotten (or forgiven) this.

London correspondent Drew Middleton reported that both parties "discern an opportunity for a 'basic' discussion of the future of Germany" in light of the Chancellor's defeat. According to Middleton: "The British have always believed that Dr. Adenauer's dominant personality inhibited a free discussion of Germany's future by the Western powers." [1]

But if Washington and London had counted Adenauer out, it was a short count. His fighting spirit revived, the Chancellor faced down the revolt in his own party and then set about forming a new government. After receiving the backing of an admittedly reluctant caucus, he found an ally in his old adversary, the *Regierende Bürgermeister* of Berlin.

Perhaps also smarting over the cavalier treatment he had received from Washington, Willy Brandt now played a willing foil to the Chancellor's efforts to force the FDP into the coalition. More important, of course, Brandt feared the "new realists" more than the Old Fox. Whenever the Free Democrats balked at taking Dr. Adenauer as leader, Brandt and his lieutenants dutifully trundled over to the Palais Schaumburg for their own coalition talks with *der Alte*. Caught in between, Mende and the FDP quickly capitulated. The only casualty was the Chancellor's *alter ego*, Dr. von Brentano, as Foreign Minister —plus a rather innocuous statement from Adenauer that he would step down "before the next election."

The replacement of von Brentano was a public sop to the FDP. Conscious that much of their campaign had been waged on a platform of "standing up to the Chancellor," the Free Democrats desperately needed a face-saving concession. The sacrifice of von Brentano for someone not so "subservient" to the Chancellor's will was pictured as a likely device. A sensitive man, Brentano amicably bowed out rather than delay formation of the coalition.

To succeed Brentano, the FDP proposed Gerhard Schroeder, Minister of Interior in Adenauer's previous cabinet, and leader of the CDU faction most "tractable" in Washington's eyes. Since Brentano is extremely astute as well as sensitive, it is not unlikely that his voluntary withdrawal reflected his recognition that Schroeder might receive a better reception in certain Western capitals.

Schroeder's appointment was fought vigorously both by Mayor Brandt and the Berlin faction of CDU. Before being suggested by the

Free Democrats, Schroeder had confided to certain Western newsmen that he favored a "realistic appraisal" of the Berlin problem. According to Sydney Gruson of the *New York Times,* Schroeder's remark was interpreted as a "willingness to find a settlement with the Soviet Union that would separate West Berlin and West Germany," and supposedly, was based on Schroeder's assumption "that the Allies . . . were committed beyond their strength to maintain Berlin's present status." [2]

Faced with von Brentano's somewhat precipitant resignation, the Chancellor reluctantly accepted Dr. Schroeder as Foreign Minister. Shortly afterwards, the new Government took office. Adenauer had won, but his powers looked greatly diminished.

Two days after the West German election General Clay arrived in Berlin. Before leaving for Germany he had visited Washington for a round of top level conferences. As the President said afterwards, he felt "unusual confidence" in General Clay. All the same, the Administration was careful to keep the retired General out of any position of actual authority. His duties, as explained by the White House, would be to "report, recommend, and advise." He would have no command function.

The reception of General Clay in Berlin was impressive. The entire eleven mile route from Tempelhof to his quarters in Wannsee was lined with cheering Berliners, frequently packed three and four deep. Enthusiastic well-wishers repeatedly crashed the police barriers to press flowers in his hand. Since the airlift, of course, the West Berliners have regarded General Clay as their personal protector. For them, the General's return was a touching reunion. But even more, it was a guarantee of American determination.

As expected, Clay lost little time before going into action. His purpose for being in Berlin, as he explained it, was to "demonstrate United States strength and determination . . . and to force the Soviets to acknowledge responsibility for their sector." One day later, on September 21, he set out to prove the former. Informed during a tour of the border that the three hundred families of the isolated West Berlin enclave of Steinstuecken had been marooned there since August 13, the General flew by helicopter over a half-mile of East German territory to visit the tiny community. Until then, the village had lost contact with the West. Technically a part of the American sector, Steinstuecken is geographically separated from the rest of Berlin by an intervening portion of East Germany. Following the construction of the Wall, the residents of the village had been virtually imprisoned. It had been ten years, in fact, since an American official had visited the enclave. In the face of the latest Communist measures, many of its residents had given up hope.

But the General's flight quickly demonstrated U.S. resolve. Clay spent a total of forty-five minutes in Steinstuecken, chatted individually with numerous citizens, and visited publicly with the mayor in the shop-front window of the latter's grocery. Afterwards, Clay announced he was assigning a three-man military police detachment to Steinstuecken permanently. Berlin's morale began to revive.

The East Germans immediately attacked Clay's flight as provocative; an infringement on the supposed sovereignty of the GDR. According to the East zone's controlled press, it was "a warlike move in an otherwise calm situation." The British also had doubts, and George Bailey, foreign correspondent for *The Reporter*, states that their objections to Washington were strenuous. "They affirmed their support of the United States in all major issues but questioned the wisdom of risking an incident over such a trifling matter." [3]

General Clay, however, was not dissuaded. It was exactly such matters, he said, that would restore Allied prestige in the divided city if exploited properly. The Soviets, he argued, "would not allow a minor issue to become an international incident through mishandling by their East German puppets."

Every day for the next several weeks the helicopter flights to Steinstuecken were repeated. On one occasion, seven refugees who had sought shelter there were evacuated. Again the East Germans protested, threatening even to shoot the helicopters down. Clay ignored the protests and the flights continued. More refugees were evacuated. The GDR did not intervene; no shots were fired; indeed, the flights soon became routine. As Clay had predicted, when confronted by a show of Western determination the Communists backed down.

Clay's flight to Steinstuecken was only one example of his determination to place Allied relations in Berlin on an even keel. The day afterwards, at a cocktail party which he gave for Western newsmen, the General partially disclosed some of the Administration's plans for a negotiated settlement between East and West. It is unlikely that Clay's statement was a trial balloon. More probably, it was an attempt to acquaint Western opinion, and in particular, West German opinion, with the possibilities then being considered.

The conversation at the party supposedly was "off the record." Clay did attempt, however, to provide the newsmen with some background information as to how the crisis was being viewed in Washington and suggested, among other things, that West Germany finally "must recognize the reality of the existence of two German states." Regardless of the "off the record" nature of his remarks, the General's statement rated headlines in all major papers the following morning. Although Clay himself was not initially identified—the *New York Times* referred to the speaker as an "authoritative United States source in Berlin"—the story caused a major sensation. Was the United States reneging on its promise to support German reunification? It certainly seemed so.

Later in the day Clay himself was linked to the statement by the West Berlin *Tagesspiegel*, and the reaction in West Germany was immediate. The Federal Republic was being sold out, many charged, and Clay was being used as window dressing to conceal the transaction.

Only gradually did the storm subside. Following a frantic cable from Washington, General Clay issued an official denial. "There is no change in United States policy," he said, "and no change was announced by any United States spokesman in Berlin. . . . We believe in and support the reunification of Germany." [4]

But if this were true, why had the General spoken out the evening before? The real answer may never be known. But it is not likely that Clay was speaking "off the record" to a group of newsmen with whom he was scarcely acquainted, not expecting to see the story again. It is also unlikely that Clay was unaware of the explosive content of his remarks. Indeed, the most likely explanation is that Clay intentionally released his bombshell and fully expected the reaction which followed.

It is well to remember that at the time Clay spoke, the Rusk-Gromyko talks at the UN were in their second day. One of the principal items being considered in these talks was the question of Allied access to Berlin. Clay was aware of this. He was also aware of European fears about these talks, and the day prior to his arrival in Berlin he had discussed the situation at length with his old friend in Bonn, Konrad Adenauer. The day before that he was in Paris. Certainly he also knew that without the support of France and West Germany the talks at the UN would be fruitless. Thus, it is likely that Clay's statement was designed to focus attention on the U.S. position in the hope of reducing later opposition should an agreement be reached. In other words, Clay was telling the West Germans that they might have to accept a greater degree of East German control over the access routes to Berlin if a permanent accord was to be hoped for.*

If it was General Clay's purpose to call attention to the package then being prepared, Washington was not pleased. Following a round of high-level interviews in the capital, Max Frankel of the *New York Times* reported on September 24, that to the "chagrin" of the Kennedy Administration, "some of the specific points it considers as negotiable are being represented and misrepresented as official policy." This was a direct reference to Clay's comments.

Also, there is little question that Clay had correctly pictured Washington thinking. The day afterward, Assistant Senate Majority Leader Hubert Humphrey, in what was explicitly identified as an Administration policy statement, strongly endorsed a "new approach" to the East. "Talk of weakness or appeasement to describe a genuine meaningful negotiation," he said, "would be mischievous folly." According to the *Times,* Humphrey's speech "obviously was another attempt to prepare the country for a reasonable 'give and take' with the Communists." [5]

But if negotiations with Russia were now at a serious stage, General Clay continued to consolidate the Western position in Berlin as though nothing had happened. Before the smoke had cleared from his cocktail party remarks the General announced that U.S. military patrols along the autobahn were being resumed. Once more, Clay's action was a case of selecting a minor issue to demonstrate American rights and thus, to restore American prestige. The autobahn patrols had been discontinued six years earlier in the face of Soviet harassment. With the increasing interference to which the East Germans were now subjecting American motorists,** Clay said the patrols were being resumed in the Allied interest.

---

* It has also been suggested that Clay may have been speaking out to mobilize West German opposition against Washington's plan. While possible, it is unlikely that this was the primary reason, although the General's purpose may have been two-fold: first, to show Germany how Washington felt, and at the same time, to show Washington how Germany felt.

** Two American G.I.'s who were travelling on the autobahn had been seized and detained for six hours the day before by GDR authorities for no apparent reason.

According to the General: "We are in Berlin by right of victory and we propose to maintain the right of access on the ground for Allied personnel and completely free access in the air corridors."

At first there was little reaction to Clay's move. The Soviets allowed the patrols to pass unimpeded and Allied traffic was no longer subjected to East German interference. Washington, however, saw little future in the course Clay was pursuing and continued to seek other means of settlement. Reportedly, President Kennedy sent detailed memoranda to his various lieutenants asking why his policy on Berlin was being misunderstood. To Scotty Reston, who apparently had seen the memo, the answer was obvious. According to Reston, the President "has talked like Churchill and acted like Chamberlain."

Reston, in analyzing the Kennedy Administration's concern over Berlin, further commented: "The pressure by Moscow on Berlin has forced President Kennedy and his principal aides from the universities to examine their assumptions about the cold war. . . . They came to power last January determined to put an end to the angry dialogue with Moscow, and were inclined to believe that the Eisenhower Administration had not paid enough attention to the sophisticated views of Allies or the yearnings of neutrals." [6] This, of course, was a clear reference to earlier British sentiment for concessions in Berlin and properly reflected the thinking of many of the President's top level advisers.

The day following Reston's article, President Kennedy journeyed to New York to address the United Nations. Once more Mr. Kennedy spoke in Churchillian tones. As was the case on July 25, however, the offer of concessions was thinly veiled.* Said Kennedy: "We are committed to no rigid formulas. We seek no perfect solution. . . . We believe a peaceful agreement is possible which protects the freedom of West Berlin . . . while recognizing the historic and legitimate interest of others in assuring European security."

The President did not mention German reunification. He made no request for free all-German elections. He neither demanded that the right of free circulation be restored in Berlin or that the Wall come down. He did not refer to the city's four-power status. Once more it

---

Clay assumed that this was an East German probing action which if not countered swiftly would lead to more such acts.

* See Chapter 12.

was as if the United States had written off the sixteen million people of East Germany; had acquiesced to Ulbricht's annexation of East Berlin.*

In West Germany, reaction to Kennedy's speech was one of bitter disappointment. While Mike Mansfield hailed it as "one of the great speeches of our generation," the Hamburg *Bild Zeitung* asked whether in referring to the "historic and legitimate interest of others," Mr. Kennedy meant the right of Russia "to split Germany or that reunification must be renounced?" Heinrich von Brentano, who at that time was still West Germany's Foreign Minister, told a CDU caucus in Bonn that the Federal Republic must "brace itself with all its strength against tendencies to get a Berlin settlement at West Germany's expense."

East German response to the President's speech was noticeably different. The Ulbricht regime pulled all the stops in its propaganda organ and hailed the President's address as a new milestone toward peaceful coexistence. According to *Neues Deutschland,* the official Party newspaper in East Berlin, Mr. Kennedy's speech was "remarkable; remarkable because it showed American willingness to negotiate."

Interestingly, President Kennedy's speech also awoke the long slumbering dinosaurs of the Republican Party. Virtually inert since the border closure on August 13, Barry Goldwater finally broke the GOP moratorium on criticism of the President's Berlin policy to state that West German fears of Administration concessions were "perfectly justified." "Any time diplomats begin talking of negotiations in a Soviet-created situation where there is nothing to negotiate," said Goldwater, ". . . it is the time for the defenders of freedom to become wary." [7] But Goldwater had waited so long to raise his voice against Administration policy over Berlin that his criticism had little effect.

---

* The propensity of the Administration to seek a negotiated settlement in Berlin at almost any cost was manifested by more than President Kennedy's speech to the UN. During this same period, the White House overruled the Department of Defense regarding a previously approved build-up of U.S. ground forces by six or eight divisions. The earlier call-ups of August 25 and September 19 were to have been only the first increments of this program. But in the face of resumption of nuclear testing by the Soviet Union, the President reversed his field and canceled the call-up. See S. L. A. Marshall, "The Real Reserve Mess," *New Republic,* January 29, 1962, pp. 13–14.

Washington continued its quest for an accord with Russia, and at the same time, moved to reduce Clay's influence on the problem.

As has been mentioned, official Washington was becoming disturbed at the General's resolute actions in the isolated city. Accustomed to dealing with minor representatives in Berlin who would simply carry out orders, the State Department and numerous Presidential advisers —the Bohlen-Stevenson-Schlesinger group—now found it uncomfortable with a man of Clay's stature there. Prevented from dictating policy henceforth, these advisers determined to place further limitations on what the President's ambassador could do. On September 27, ten days after Clay had arrived in Berlin, General Bruce C. Clarke, Commander of the U.S. Army in Europe, visited the isolated city. After a ceremonial lunch with Clay, General Clarke advised Major General Watson that the Berlin Command could no longer use U.S. forces to counteract Communist measures without clearing each action with Heidelberg. Although the prohibition was delivered to General Watson, it was a direct slap at Clay's activities.

The Soviets were quickly apprised of the effects of Clarke's visit. The East German press began to play up Clay's differences with the Administration and three days afterward, the Soviet Commander in East Germany, Marshal Ivan S. Konev, delivered a sharp note to American headquarters demanding an end to the "illegal" autobahn patrols which Clay had instituted. It is more than coincidental that Konev's demand did not come until after Washington had acted to curtail Clay's power. The autobahn patrols had been functioning for over a week without Russian interference, and only when it became clear that Clay did not have Washington's full support did Konev move. Then, he moved firmly. The patrols, his note stated, would have to be ended immediately. His message, he said, "was not a protest but a warning," implying that dire consequences might follow. For Washington, this was too much. Clay was ordered to desist from the autobahn patrolling operations and another chance for a tactical victory was surrendered. Even in defeat, however, Clay had proved a point. By once more asserting his authority for autobahn operations, Marshal Konev, who until now had been conspicuously silent about East German activities, acknowledged Soviet responsibility for dealing with the Western powers.

As had been the case in 1948, however, Washington continued to press for a compromise in Berlin. Indeed, the illusion of compromise was pursued to the point of seriously endangering the Western Alliance. A Foreign Minister's conference scheduled for London on October 15, was canceled at the last moment when France, fearing she would not be able to block the proposed concessions over Berlin, declined to attend. Two weeks before, General De Gaulle had urged the West to stand firm. Speaking to a nationwide television audience, De Gaulle stated:

> Since we are France, a country that is essential to Europe and necessary to the free world, it is our duty to stand firm . . . and to urge our Allies to do the same.
> For nothing would be more dangerous to our cause, our safety, our alliance, and our peace than to retreat step by step before those who are menacing us.[8]

But De Gaulle's counsel had been ignored, and so to prevent the negotiations from continuing, the President of the Fifth Republic ordered his Foreign Minister to stay home.

The major bargaining points which the U.S. was ready to offer the East at this time are worth noting. Most important, as Clay had suggested earlier, was recognition of Soviet control of eastern Germany (in Washington's phrase, "the precise demarcation of the Communist Empire"), and de facto acceptance of the Ulbricht regime. Acceptance of the GDR, of course, would not include actual pro forma diplomatic recognition but would acknowledge East Germany's control of the access lanes to Berlin and would mark the end of Western demands for German reunification. Indeed, renunciation of German reunification was central to the Administration's position.

There were several reasons for this. First, most top Administration officials still saw in Germany the old scourge of Europe which had twice plunged the world into war. Many of these officials—Rusk, Stevenson, Schlesinger, Rostow—had only returned to government during the past year. Except for Rusk, their earlier service had been during the war, during the Roosevelt Administration when Germany was still Public Enemy No. 1. It is possible that this experience was still fresh. The decade of West Germany's peaceful development, of her attachment to the West and the revival of her democratic ideals, was only something they had read about. None had participated in the formation of the new Germany and it is likely that the old prejudices lingered on. Senators Fulbright and Mansfield, who shared the Stevenson-Schlesinger view, had been in official opposition to the party in Executive power during most of these years. To them, John Foster Dulles, who together with Adenauer was the architect of the new Germany, was a personal anathema and so were his policies.

Not morally committed to the idea of German reunification, it was only natural that the new men in Washington should have seen in it a valuable chattel which could be bartered to the East. The ensuing cries of anguish from West Germany which greeted these plans, only convinced those in the capital who had conceived them that they had been right all along about incipient "Pan-Germanism" and the rebirth of revanchist dogma.

The dismemberment of Germany was only one of Washington's bargaining points. On September 30, Senate Foreign Relations Committee Chairman J. William Fulbright, in an interview from London, suggested that the U.S. might formalize an agreement withholding nuclear weapons from West Germany. In a surprisingly all-inclusive statement, Fulbright said that atomic weapons should not be given to the Federal Republic "if there was any reasonable prospect of progress in reaching an acceptable agreement with the Soviet Union." [9] Clearly, this was another concession which Washington was dangling before Russia; a concession expressed explicitly by President Kennedy two months later.*

In addition to the acceptance of the Ulbricht regime and the explicit withholding of nuclear weapons, other possible U.S. concessions included permanent recognition of the Oder–Neisse line, negotiation of a new "contractual" arrangement for West Berlin replacing the oc-

---

* On November 28, Mr. Kennedy told Aleksie Adzhubei, Khrushchev's son-in-law, that "the United States, as a matter of national policy . . . will not give nuclear weapons to any country, and I would be extremely reluctant to see West Germany acquire a nuclear capacity of its own. Chancellor Adenauer stated that they would not in 1954. That is still the policy of that government and I think it is a wise policy."

Since both Chancellor Adenauer and the Bonn government are on record repeatedly against individual nuclear arsenals and, as the President said, since West Germany does not desire a nuclear capacity of its own, the formalization of an agreement between the U.S. and Russia specifically denying such weapons to the Federal Republic would appear to be not only unnecessary but also as though Bonn —one of America's strongest Allies—was being singled-out for special discriminatory treatment. As former West German Defense Minister Franz Josef Strauss once advised Washington, "there can be no second-class allies."

cupation agreement, and perhaps, a loosening of ties between West Berlin and the Federal Republic. The possibility of a larger deal involving mass disarmament and a neutralized buffer zone was considered even more desirable. Indeed, the American government, for the first time since the war, was negotiating seriously with Moscow for an accord in Central Europe—an accord which could be concluded only at free Germany's expense.

Bonn was well aware of Washington's attitude. An indication of the strain which now existed between the Kennedy Administration and the Federal Republic occurred the week after Fulbright's announcement when Willy Brandt arrived in New York to receive the 1961 Freedom House Award. When Brandt landed there was no representative of the U.S. Government to meet him. Similarly, and although the Lord Mayor had made his availability pointedly clear, no invitation to Washington was tendered. The following day, while Brandt addressed the luncheon in his honor (and remarked, incidentally, that "the Wall in Berlin must come down"), President Kennedy played host in the White House to Soviet Foreign Minister Gromyko. The day afterward, Mr. Kennedy did find time to call Brandt by telephone but the conversation was brief. Afterwards, the Lord Mayor ironically told waiting newsmen: "It is reassuring that the President was able to identify himself to some degree with the ideas I expressed yesterday." [10]

Clearly, however, Brandt was not referring to his remarks about the Wall. While he was in New York, in fact, the American government ordered U.S. forces in Berlin pulled back from patrolling the Wall. Allied troops, it should be remembered, had first been ordered to the sector boundary on August 23, following the GDR's attempt to impose a 100-meter "no-man's land" on the Western side. Although the size of the contingents had been gradually decreased since then, U.S. military forces were still on guard. But as shootings by East German police grew increasingly frequent, Washington became alarmed about the danger of a major incident. To reduce this possibility, the troops were therefore withdrawn.

Announcement of Washington's action had a serious effect in Berlin. Most West Berliners saw the move as another Western retreat. The number of people quitting the city for West Germany—an average of 1,700 per week since the Wall—now rose even higher. The value of personal savings accounts already was down four percent from the pre-August 13th level. Writing from Berlin shortly afterwards, Sydney Gruson reported that the West Berliners were not hopeful. "The people a visitor speaks with—taxi drivers, the diners in a restaurant or sidewalk cafe, German newsmen and even some officials—think the Communists are winning the battle of Berlin. There is no shock, as there was right after the border was closed August 13. There is resignation and a great deal of bitterness." [11]

The Allied soldiers in Berlin also were discouraged by their governments' hesitation. The U.S. garrison, for example, is composed of eighty-five percent regular troops. The French and British contingents are similarly structured. These are professional soldiers, and they do not take risks lightly. But they appreciate the importance of their assignment and were willing, indeed eager, to do their part in the city's defense.* Patrolling its borders was such a function, and when they were recalled, military morale hit rock bottom. As General Clay pointed out later, "to be effective, a soldier has to know he can walk a straight line."

To head off an impending crisis, Clay moved swiftly. First, he recommended that the West Berlin border police be armed with automatic weapons. This would at least put them on an equal footing with the East German border guards. Then, seeking to regain the initiative, he decided to force the Soviets back into the city as soon as possible.

An opportunity quickly presented itself. On Sunday evening, October 22, U.S. deputy chief of mission in Berlin, Mr. Allen Lightner, drove with his wife through the *Friedrichstrasse* checkpoint to East Berlin. No sooner had Lightner's car crossed the sector boundary, however, then it was stopped by East German police (*Volkspolizei*) demanding the diplomat's identification. Previously, as has been mentioned,** members of the Allied occupation traveled freely from one sector of the city to another simply by virtue of the license plates on their cars. No effort was made by the East sector police to stop Western vehicles and similarly, the West Berlin police allowed Russian cars to pass uninspected. This was true whether the occupants were in uniform or ci-

---

* The reenlistment rate of the Berlin Command has consistently been the highest of any other geographical area in the U.S. Army. According to military officials on the spot, this is a direct reflection not only of the "professionalism" of the unit, but of its efficiency and esprit as well.

** See Chapter 10.

vilian clothes. The license plates were deemed sufficient. This had been the practice since 1945, and was a reflection of Berlin's occupied status. Accordingly, the East German demand to inspect Mr. Lightner's papers was extremely significant. It was another Communist attempt to end the few remaining vestiges of four-power control.

As was customary, Lightner refused to produce his identification, stating that the United States did not recognize East German authority. When he attempted to drive on, however, several *Vopos* stepped in front of his car. Lightner thereupon demanded to see a Russian officer —the normal request in such circumstances—but the *Vopos* refused. All persons in civilian clothes entering the "capital of the German Democratic Republic," they said, would have to show their identification to East German authority. Lightner once more refused, and for almost an hour he and his wife waited for the East Germans to open the way, but without success. Lightner thereupon turned his car around and returned to the American checkpoint.

By this time the U.S. command was aware of Lightner's detention and an alert had been ordered. Waiting for him at Checkpoint Charlie when he returned were Lieutenant Colonel Robert H. Sabolyk, U.S. provost marshal for Berlin, and the alert platoon of the 2d Battle Group. Shortly afterwards, four M–48 medium tanks and two armored personnel carriers arrived. Operating under its own initiative, the Berlin Command was closely following Clay's instructions.

After letting his wife out at the American checkpoint, Lightner once more drove back into East Berlin. Once more his vehicle was stopped and once more his identification was demanded. Again Lightner refused to produce it and demanded a Soviet officer. For thirty minutes Lightner waited. No Soviet officer. The *Vopos* still refused to allow the car to proceed. At this point, Colonel Sabolyk, who was patiently watching the episode, ordered a squad from the alert platoon to escort Lightner's car through the barrier. With bayonets fixed, the eight men of the battle group moved out smartly, took up positions flanking the car, and then walked slowly but firmly beyond the East German barrier into East Berlin. The *Vopos* made no effort to interfere. Lightner drove on for a block, turned around and came back. Again the car was stopped. Again the eight-man escort moved out and conduct him back through the barrier. The East German police sullenly stepped aside.

As if to prove the right of Allied access, Lightner now repeated the process. This time his car was allowed to proceed by the East Germans uninspected. After driving about a mile through East Berlin Lightner returned through the checkpoint, again without difficulty. U.S. determination had carried the day.

On Monday, however, the GDR reacted with vigor. In a special announcement, the East German news agency (ADN) said that henceforth all "foreigners" wishing to enter East Berlin must show their identification papers to the *Volkspolizei* on duty. A Communist spokesman later clarified the announcement and said that military officials in uniform would be exempted. But the East German intent was clear. The issue raised by Lightner's crossing the previous evening had now been joined.

In Washington, as at the time of the blockade, indecision prevailed. An urgent message from General Watson requesting instructions as to how to handle the East German announcement drew only the laconic comment from the State Department that U.S. citizens should be "advised" to "go slow" on entering East Berlin.

Confronted with an impending collapse in the face of the Communist announcement, General Clay now took charge. Where Watson had merely asked for instructions, Clay went directly to the White House. As in 1948, Clay advised Washington that a failure to meet the Communist threat would have the most serious consequences. Only by forcing the Communists to back down, he said, could Allied prestige be salvaged. Refusal to meet the issue head-on would be interpreted as surrender.

Clay's appeal was successful. As the General later advised the author, "Whenever I carried my case directly to the President, I was supported." Over the strenuous objections of numerous high level advisers, General Watson was authorized to protest the East German announcement to Soviet authorities and, failing to receive satisfaction, to demonstrate once more U.S. intentions.

Wednesday morning, October 25, General Watson delivered his protest to Colonel Solovyev in East Berlin. Shortly afterwards, and as if to indicate Washington's support, State Department press officer Lincoln White announced that "when General Watson made his protest this morning he had behind him the full authority of the United States Government."

But the Soviets were in no mood to back down. Already, in fact, they had discerned a crack in Western ranks. On the day following Lightner's entry into East Berlin, British diplomats passing through the East German barrier had scrupulously showed their passports to East Berlin officials. Accordingly, General Watson's protest was denied and American headquarters was told that U.S. officials would have to comply with the East German regulations.

Having failed in their protest, U.S. officials in Berlin now began a systematic show of force. At 10:30 A.M. an American vehicle with two mission representatives attempted to enter East Berlin. When the *Vopos* refused to allow the car to pass, twelve U.S. military policemen escorted it through. Forty-five minutes later ten M–48 medium tanks lumbered up to Checkpoint Charlie and took up positions. Twice more that day American cars were escorted through the East Berlin checkpoint by military police. The East Germans, chagrined and humiliated, made no effort to interfere.

By now the Ulbricht regime was close to panic. The Deputy Defense Minister of the GDR announced in an emergency television broadcast that the "People's Army" was prepared to crush the American provocateurs. *Neues Deutschland* said the American action could not be tolerated. Other Communist spokesmen openly threatened war. But the East Germans were bluffing. Their attempt to curtail Allied rights had been turned against them. By vigorously contesting the GDR's encroachment, Clay was about ready to prove what had been his objective all along. Namely, that it was the Soviets and not the East Germans who were responsible for East Berlin.

The appearance of U.S. tanks at Checkpoint Charlie came close to doing that. Washington, of course, was now extremely jittery. But so was Moscow. On Thursday evening, October 26, after U.S. military police had forced the barrier twice more, thirty-three Soviet tanks with Russian crews rolled into East Berlin and bivouacked just off the *Unter den Linden*—less than a mile away. Earlier that afternoon General Clay had told newsmen that the "United States was determined to continue showing force, if necessary, until the issue was resolved with the Soviet Union."

The following day, Friday, October 27, the confrontation was achieved. Late in the afternoon, after the U.S. had forced the barrier once more (the East Germans now were thoroughly disgraced), ten of the Soviet tanks from the *Unter den Linden* rolled down *Friedrich-*

strasse toward the checkpoint. They stopped shortly before reaching it and took up a two-three-three-two position facing the West. Clay's point was proved, and the four-power status of Greater Berlin was still in effect.

Immediately after the Soviet tanks appeared, General Clay held a press conference at Berlin Command. His manner, though not jubilant, was that of a man whose arguments had been vindicated. Said Clay:

> The fiction that it was the East Germans who were responsible for trying to prevent Allied access to East Berlin is now destroyed.
>
> The fact that the Soviet tanks appeared on the scene proves that the harassments which were taking place at *Friedrichstrasse* were not those of the self-styled East German government but ordered by its Soviet masters.

Shortly after 10:30 the following morning the Soviet tanks withdrew. The American armor moved back thirty minutes later. The confrontation had lasted sixteen hours. For the first time since 1958, the West had successfully exposed the puppet relationship between Ulbricht and Moscow. A vital Communist argument had been demolished. The East Germans were not a sovereign state and could not be trusted, even by the Kremlin. The Communist gambit of a separate peace treaty with the GDR was thus revealed as meaningless. And once more, when confronted by a show of American determination, the East had backed down. Most important, however, by exposing the inherent weakness of the Ulbricht regime, General Clay had recouped much of the prestige which the West had lost in Berlin on August 13. Popular morale in the Western sectors began to revive, and the tide of Communist encroachment temporarily had been checked.

But Clay's victory was not without its drawbacks. As in 1948, the risks seemed to multiply the further one moved from the scene of action. NATO members wondered whether the United States had changed its policy in Berlin.* London regarded the show of force as "foolish posturing over an essentially minor issue." Official Washington, except perhaps for the President, was beside itself with indignation.

---

* As noted in Chapter 12, the NATO Council had approved U.S. plans for Berlin on August 10—three days before the Communist border closure. These plans encompassed the East German move and provided that no action would be taken to contest it. Indeed, according to the reports now coming from Paris, the NATO Council gave it as their understanding "that while the United States was determined to fight if necessary to uphold its rights of access to West Berlin, no such risk would be taken in regard to East Berlin." (*New York Times*, November 6, 1961.)

The proponents of negotiation charged that Clay had gone to the brink of war. Indeed, as soon as the Soviet tanks appeared, there was anguished hand-wringing even in the Pentagon. Clay was ordered to withdraw the U.S. forces from Checkpoint Charlie as soon as possible.

As a result of Washington's timidity, a second Western victory was discarded. No further efforts were made by U.S. officials to force the East German barrier. To all intents and purposes, the GDR had at least won a stand-off in its claim to deny entry to Allied diplomats except upon presentation of their papers. Negotiations over access to East Berlin were transferred to U.S. Ambassador Thompson in Moscow. In the interim, American diplomats were ordered to stay out of the Soviet sector.

The affair at Checkpoint Charlie marked the height of Clay's authority in Berlin. As soon as the tanks were withdrawn, senior Administration spokesmen began to decry the way the General had handled the issue. Leaks from Washington describing official "dissatisfaction" over the events at *Friedrichstrasse* soon turned into a deluge.* But Washington, of course, was completely out of touch with the daily situation in Berlin and could not understand how Clay's action had been necessary. Had the United States backed away from the confrontation at Checkpoint Charlie, a crisis of morale similar to that which occurred in August would have ensued. In such an event, it is unlikely that our position in Berlin could have been held.

The British, of course, shared Washington's view. The day after the tanks had been withdrawn from Checkpoint Charlie, the senior representative of the British Foreign Office in Berlin visited the Soviet sector and assured Russian officials that Clay would soon be recalled.[12]

The Administration's anti-Clay campaign had an immediate effect in Berlin. Less than three days after the visit of the British deputy chief

---

* The *New York Times*, for example, on November 5, printed a feature story by E. W. Kenworthy about the rift between Clay and Washington. According to Mr. Kenworthy, and again, the lack of identifiable sources is striking:

> Officials here [in Washington] readily concede that responsible officers on the spot must be allowed some leeway to make decisions. But some of them doubt whether the United States Mission acted wisely in "melodramatizing" the incident with fixed bayonets and tanks.
>
> They point out that it takes only a few minutes to get on the telephone to Washington. In their view . . . Clay . . . should have immediately got Washington's advice on how to proceed.
>
> Having swallowed the camel . . . some officials ask, why should the United States now strain at the gnat. . . .

of mission to East Berlin, the Communists once more were on the offensive. Convinced no doubt that Clay was firmly shackled, East German authorities on November 3, detained four separate U.S. Army vehicles in East Berlin for periods varying from 35 to 70 minutes. The day previous, Danish and Norwegian military mission chiefs were denied entrance to East Berlin until they produced their personal passports—thus acknowledging that East Berlin's occupation status had ended. One day later, two members of the U.S. Mission were detained for twenty minutes while on official business. By seeking to undercut Clay's prestige, Washington very nearly opened a Pandora's Box. Fortunately for the West, Clay withstood the assault and continued to operate as though nothing had happened. When the Communists saw that Clay was not leaving, they soon desisted from further encroachments.

There were other reasons too why Communist pressure subsided. In Moscow, the talks between Ambassador Thompson and the Kremlin were in high gear. The entire package which the Kennedy Administration had prepared on Berlin was being presented. In this situation, there was little reason for the Soviets to apply pressure on the West. With Washington now leading the dash to the conference table, there was good reason for Moscow to believe that its demands in Germany would be met; that regardless of the cruelty of the Wall, the United States was prepared to accept it, along with the Ulbricht regime, as the price for "easing tensions." And so, as he had done in a similar mood of anticipation two years before at Camp David, Nikita Khrushchev once more called off his East German stooges and modified his ultimatum. Temporarily, Communist pressure would be relaxed.

But once more Mr. Khrushchev was to be disappointed. As in 1960, the prize he sought was to be denied him. For standing firmly in the path of the Western retreat were the aging figures of Charles De Gaulle and Konrad Adenauer. And though the United States may occupy the leading position in the West, it dare not ratify an accord in Europe unacceptable to its two most resolute Allies.

For a while, however, the situation hung perilously in the balance. In spite of West European opposition, the United States seemed determined to ram through an agreement with Russia at all costs. During the winter and spring of 1961–62, a negotiated settlement in Berlin became the *sine qua non* of American policy. Only gradually did this policy yield to the perhaps wiser counsel of our continental Allies.

In November, as the Thompson-Gromyko talks were beginning, President Kennedy tendered a personal invitation to Dr. Adenauer to visit him, and the meeting was quickly arranged for November 20. The purpose of the meeting, in Washington's eyes, would be to convince the Chancellor of the American position. As the Administration would have it, Adenauer would be asked by Kennedy what was the alternative to negotiations? In short, Washington hoped to bring pressure on *der Alte* to support the talks which were then in progress.[13]

Adenauer, however, had his own reasons for coming to Washington. If the White House was eager for the Chancellor to visit in order to convince him of the necessity for negotiations, Dr. Adenauer was equally eager for the visit in order to stiffen American resolve, for Bonn was deeply troubled at this time about the course that the U.S. was following. The Kennedy Administration, it seems, had lost the confidence of West Germany, and Chancellor Adenauer wanted to explore the differences at first hand.

The meeting in Washington lasted three days, and when it ended, the President and Dr. Adenauer issued a joint communique. In spite of the communique's harmonious language, however, the differences remained.* The Chancellor had recognized that he could not stop the Administration from negotiating with the Kremlin. Rather than attempt to, he had insisted that before any overture was made, the Western powers should agree among themselves precisely what their offer would be. This served as a temporary brake on the discussions in Moscow because the Federal Republic certainly was not prepared to accept what Washington was offering.

Also, Dr. Adenauer, who found his worst suspicions now confirmed, firmly insisted that any discussions with Moscow be limited solely to Berlin. This was a complete turn-about from what Bonn had been saying since 1958, but the atmosphere in Washington had so shaken the Chancellor that he now sought anything to limit the scope of the Mos-

* The communique's most important passage clearly revealed these differences. According to its text, "Berlin, over which the Soviet Union has created an international crisis, was the subject of earnest consultation. The President and the Chancellor . . . are in accord on the basic elements which will permit a peaceful resolution of this crisis through negotiation, if there is reasonableness on the part of the Soviet Union."

Reference to the "reasonableness" of the Soviet Union was a virtual restatement of the position espoused earlier by De Gaulle. In effect, the Chancellor had agreed to the U.S. continuing its approach to Moscow only "if there is reasonableness on the part of the Soviet Union."

cow talks. If they were confined simply to Berlin, he felt, there would not be quite so much danger of recognizing the Ulbricht regime, or worse, of formally agreeing to Germany's continued division.

Even on Berlin, however, the position of the Kennedy Administration was extremely upsetting to Adenauer. Not only would the U.S. not agree to make removal of the Wall a condition for negotiation, but now Washington desired to formulate a new agreement with Russia over the isolated city which would supersede the Allies' right of occupation. According to the State Department, the plan would provide a new "contractual arrangement" for Western rights. To the West Germans, this seemed fearfully close to exchanging war won rights—the true legal basis for the Western position in Berlin—for a bilateral agreement with Russia; an agreement that there was no guarantee the Soviets would honor. The feeling was unmistakable, in fact, that the American proposal was simply a device for loosening Allied ties to Berlin and decreasing the extent of U.S. involvement.

To slow Washington's interest in the so-called "new contractual arrangement," Adenauer mobilized a united front. On the day of the Chancellor's departure from Washington, Foreign Minister Schroeder told a luncheon group at the National Press Club that it would be extremely dangerous "to renounce the rights vested in the Allies as the result of the miltiary occupation" for an agreement based purely on Russian good faith. Later, from Bonn, Lord Mayor Willy Brandt went even further. Any change in Berlin's status, Brandt said, would require an amendment to West Germany's Basic Law; an amendment, he added, which the SPD would never permit to pass.

In spite of the Chancellor's determined resistance, however, the Kennedy Administration stuck to its basic position that a negotiated settlement in Berlin could be achieved. Once more the feeling was current that Adenauer, like De Gaulle, was an anachronism on the world scene who would soon be gone. His views were written off accordingly.

Less than a week later, in fact, President Kennedy told Aleksie Adzhubei, Mr. Khrushchev's son-in-law, that an agreement was still possible in Germany which would "recognize" Germany's division. According to the President: "Germany today is divided. Germany today is not a threat to the Soviet Union militarily."

The important thing is to reach an accord which recognizes the interests of all. . . . I recognize that there are going to be two

Germanies as long as the Soviet Union thinks that that is in her interest. The problem now is to make sure that, in any treaty which the Soviet Union reaches with East Germany, the rights of the other powers are recognized in Berlin.

As in his UN speech earlier, Mr. Kennedy made no request that the freedom of movement in Berlin be restored. He did not demand that the Wall come down. Except in the past tense, he did not refer to Greater Berlin's four-power status. Based on the interview, there could be little doubt but that Washington regarded the Wall as permanent.

The Berliners accepted Kennedy's position stoically. When the President's brother visited the city in February, the people turned out in great numbers to see him. Few had any illusions that he was bringing salvation. Robert Kennedy reassured the Berliners that the U.S. would not forsake them. As for the division of the city, however, the Attorney General was more circumspect. The Wall, he said, was tragic, but they should not expect "miracles" that might bring it down.

The Berliners applauded Kennedy—not because of what he said, but because they felt he had told them the truth. It was an indication perhaps that the morale of the city was no longer on edge. For this, the tribute can go to Lucius Clay. The General had been in Berlin for five months when the President's brother arrived. His differences with Washington still existed, but his presence had had a tonic effect. In his actions, Clay had carefully avoided giving the Berliners any reason to feel that his disagreements with the Administration were serious. To them, he was the President's Ambassador acting with the President's full confidence—as indeed he was. For the general public, the machinations of the anti-Clay axis passed almost unnoticed.

All the same, however, official Washington continued to worry about the possibility of an incident in Berlin. In mid-December, for example, the State Department furnished a new and detailed set of directives to General Watson supposedly designed to cover any possible contingency. The directives were so complete, in fact, that the Berlin Commander was afforded no discretion whatever. Henceforth, Watson was to clear his actions—even those taken in the face of an obvious emergency—first with USAREUR headquarters in Heidelberg, and then with NATO.

General Clay vigorously protested the directives at the time, calling them a new high water mark in the discretionary limits placed on a tactical commander. Such orders, he said, would make it all but impossible for the local commander to take effective action should the Western sectors be threatened by a sudden incident. But it was this very limitation that Washington wanted. Clay received no satisfaction from his cables and therefore, on January 6, flew to Washington to place the issue directly before the President and Secretary Rusk. Before the General could arrive in Washington, however, news of his coming had been leaked to the press. Clay went through with the trip, saw both Kennedy and Rusk, but returned to Berlin with no additional authority.

Shortly after Robert Kennedy's visit, the Soviets abruptly ended the three-month calm that had prevailed in Berlin and began a series of harassing actions in the Allied air corridors. Exactly why the Kremlin suddenly reversed its tactics is difficult to explain, except in the context of the negotiations which were then in progress. Shortly after Christmas, Ambassador Thompson had presented to the Kremlin a U.S. plan calling for an "international authority" to control access to Berlin. Although the exact composition of the authority was not specified (President Kennedy had suggested such an idea in his interview with Khrushchev's son-in-law), the United States proposed that such a body be created and given full sovereignty over the means of Allied access to West Berlin. This would include the Helmstedt-Berlin autobahn, the three air corridors, and the airports in West Berlin.

To a large extent, the American plan was another outgrowth of the Kennedy Administration's haunting fear of an incident in the isolated city. As Washington saw it, Allied access to West Berlin was dependent entirely on the detailed set of working arrangements which had been developed over the years by the local military commanders. The functioning of this system required constant and direct contact between the Russians and ourselves. There were no buffers in between. Should a misunderstanding occur—even a legitimate misunderstanding—it would be the Soviets and the particular Western power, once more in a dangerous confrontation. To the White House, and to the State Department and the Foreign Office who quickly agreed, the possibility of such a confrontation brought back unhappy memories of Checkpoint Charlie. A lack of caution on either side, as they saw it, could easily escalate into nuclear war. Accordingly, to reduce the possibility of a direct confrontation, the Administration had come up with the idea of an "international authority" to control access. As explained by the State Department, it would be "something like the New York Port Authority," with representatives from all sides.

To the Administration's dismay, however, no sooner had Ambassador Thompson suggested the plan to Moscow than the Russians launched a deliberate campaign to harass Allied air traffic. Responsible opinion in West Berlin saw a direct link between the Russian move and Washington's proposal. For until Thompson had raised the matter with the Kremlin, the right of Western access always had been considered immutable. By now suggesting changes, Washington was indicating that this was not true. And so to probe Allied determination, the Soviets began to fly their own planes in the air corridors, to buzz commercial airliners, to threaten training flights at the same times and altitudes as Western flights, and to drop radar-jamming metal chaff.

Also, in addition to probing Western intentions, the Russians perhaps were demonstrating to Washington how easily an incident in the air corridors could arise. Such a demonstration would clearly encourage the Administration's desire for a new arrangement and thus facilitate the negotiations which were then in progress.

Washington's reaction to the Soviet harassment certainly gave the Kremlin no cause for alarm. No attempt was made to counter the Russian encroachments although the West did continue to fly its planes on schedule. Indeed, not to have done so would have amounted to a major defeat. By not countering the Russian moves, however, the United States left its intentions in the air corridors somewhat in doubt. General Clay, for example, had recommended the use of fighter escorts to prove Western determination but was turned down. Another possible counter would have been to fly C–130's into Berlin at altitudes above 10,000 feet. This had been done three years earlier and had brought the Russians quickly to heel. But this also was turned down. As a result, the Russians were allowed to harass Allied air traffic during the months of February and March, completely unopposed. A dangerous precedent was being set. The Russians demonstrated the right to fly in the Western corridors, to challenge Allied aircraft and to interfere with navigation controls. In the event of another blockade, the West would reap a bitter harvest.

Despite the Soviet harassment, Washington now pressed harder than ever for negotiations. The anomaly of meeting with the Russians at the conference table while the Soviet government was doing everything possible to interfere with Allied air traffic into Berlin seems to have made no impression on the Administration. Secretary Rusk went to Geneva for the disarmament conference in mid-March, and beginning on March 11, kept up a daily round of informal consultations with Soviet Foreign Minister Gromyko. In the days immediately preceding the first Rusk-Gromyko chat, however, Soviet harassment in the corridors was at its height. Metal chaff was dropped repeatedly in the air lanes and individual buzzings became the rule rather than the exception.[14]

Soviet activity in the air corridors stopped as abruptly as it had begun. The cut-off date came on March 29—two days after the final Rusk-Gromyko session in Geneva. Reportedly, Mr. Rusk had advised Gromyko that the Soviet Union could best prove its interest in negotiations over Berlin by leaving the air corridors alone. Rusk's statement, however, did not represent a new or firm approach by Washington and had, in fact, been told to the Soviets repeatedly since the harassment began. What was significant was that in their final meeting, Rusk and Gromyko had compiled a "position paper" on Berlin listing their various agreements and disagreements. According to reliable reports, the agreements were that West Berlin should be free, viable, and have links to the West. All of which, it should be noted, were phrases that fit neatly into the Soviet idea of a neutralized "free-city." The disagreements included U.S. insistence on the maintenance of Western troops in West Berlin, the question of access, and the role of the GDR.[15]

Because of the far-reaching implications of the "agreements," however, Gromyko must have felt that he had his foot in the door. Thus, the Soviets willingly curtailed their air corridor harassment content, perhaps, to consolidate their gains. For based on the Rusk accord, the Kremlin now knew positively that the United States no longer was interested in East Berlin. In effect, the United States had formally ratified Ulbricht's *fait accompli.*

The Rusk-Gromyko memorandum marked the opening of a new round of negotiations on Berlin. It also marked the end of General Clay's tenure in the isolated city. The reasons for Clay's leaving are obvious. First, the Rusk-Gromyko accord marked a temporary easing of tensions in Berlin. Second, and more important perhaps, the General was extremely dissatisfied with his position in Berlin. It was no secret that he and Washington saw the Berlin problem differently, and the

Rusk-Gromyko memorandum represented the culmination of this difference. Where Clay felt that the best way to discourage Communist encroachments was through prompt and effective countermeasures, the Kennedy Administration did not. As a result, his recommendations for a firm stand frequently were turned down. Thus, unable to have an effective voice in U.S. policy, the General perhaps felt he was being used as a cover by Washington to mollify the Berliners—as a front man to shield a policy with which he basically disagreed.

Also, American insistence on negotiations in the face of continuing Soviet affronts in the air corridors must have galled the General considerably. The implications of the American negotiating package—increased recognition for the GDR, renunciation of German reunification, and recognition of the Oder-Neisse line—were probably equally distasteful. In addition, General Clay has always esteemed the position in which the Berliners hold him; perhaps to some degree he felt he was not being fair to them to continue on. The temporary calm produced by the Rusk-Gromyko talks gave him the opportunity to bow out gracefully.*

In the following weeks, whenever Clay spoke in Berlin, he referred to the fact that the situation had eased, that West Berlin's morale had recovered, and that his presence was no longer needed. In the existing situation, he said, he could do more for Berlin's defense by returning home than by staying on. It is questionable, however, whether the General was giving an accurate picture of the situation or attempting to reassure the Berliners that his leaving was justified.

Indeed, in terms of Western unity, Berlin's defenses were now in serious disrepair. On April 12, the day following Clay's departure to

---

* But even in leaving, Clay once more became the victim of an Administration vendetta. Originally, the General had planned to fly to Washington, discuss the details of his leaving with the President, and then return to Berlin to wind up his affairs. For reasons of West Berlin morale, announcement of his resignation would be held up until Clay had returned to the isolated city. This would allow Mayor Brandt to take part in the announcement and would help ease the Berliners' feeling of anxiety.

Certain Presidential advisers, however, saw the situation differently. Seeking to preempt the General's own announcement, perhaps even to further the idea of Clay's differences with Washington, or that he was being recalled, the anti-Clay axis caused the news of his resignation to be leaked to the press as soon as Clay departed to see the President. Washington's action may also have been another attempt to embarrass Clay or to confront him with a *fait accompli*. Mayor Brandt, for example, had not yet been told of the General's plans and found it necessary to answer questions about Clay's leaving based merely on guess work.

see the President, the United States had submitted to each of the major Western powers (France, Britain, and the Federal Republic) its detailed proposals for an accord in Berlin. These proposals were an outgrowth of the Thompson talks in Moscow and the more recent Rusk-Gromyko conversations in Geneva. They were to be used as a basis for a new round of negotiations scheduled to begin in Washington on April 16, when Secretary Rusk met Soviet Ambassador Anatoly Dobrynin. Attached to the U.S. proposals was a curt demand from the State Department requesting approval within twenty-four hours.

Specifically, the U.S. proposals provided for: (1) the establishment of an "international access authority" to control traffic to Berlin; (2) an exchange of "non-aggression declarations" between NATO and the Warsaw Pact in which each side would pledge not to violate "existing borders or demarcation lines"; (3) a U.S.-Soviet agreement to prevent the spread of nuclear weapons; and (4) the establishment of official bilateral committees between East Germany and the Federal Republic at the governmental level. These committees would deal with trade, communications, cultural exchanges and travel—all of which were matters then handled by the two states on a purely "technical" basis at the lowest level. As Washington saw it, the establishment of these committees would force the Federal Republic into official dealings with the Ulbricht regime, and would encourage the realization in West Germany that the two states would have to work together. There were no provisions for later reunification under the U.S. plan.[16]

In Bonn, the arrival of the American *"diktat"* caused a flurry of reaction. To begin with, responsible West German officials considered the twenty-four-hour deadline requested by Washington to be unreasonable. Although this difficulty did not arise in Paris or London (the French automatically rejected and the British automatically accepted the U.S. plan), the Federal Republic wanted time to give the proposals the mature consideration which they deserved and strongly resented being pressured. Chancellor Adenauer, in fact, was away from Bonn at the time the U.S. proposals arrived and had rushed back to place them before his Cabinet. He requested an extension of the original ultimatum and was reluctantly granted another twenty-four hours.

The blatant pressure represented by the extremely short time limit was not nearly as upsetting to Bonn, however, as the substance of the American proposals. First, the Federal Republic had doubts about the

U.S. access plan. Under Washington's proposal, access to West Berlin would be entrusted to an international authority, one of whose principal members would be the spurious German Democratic Republic. To Bonn, this seemed dangerously close to entrusting a major degree of political control over Berlin's access to the Ulbricht regime. Indeed, the inclusion of East Germany in such an "authority," it was feared, would merely foreshadow a separate Soviet peace treaty with the GDR, the assumption being that the Allies would now have a *modus operandi* should the Russians choose to do so.[17]

Also, the request for joint East-West committees with no provision for eventual reunification seemed to place the Federal Republic in the position of formally recognizing the GDR. The pledge of respect for "existing demarcation lines" between NATO and the Warsaw Pact appeared to be not only an acceptance of the Wall in Berlin but a permanent denial of the right of self-determination to the people of East Germany, and a *de jure* acceptance of the Oder-Neisse line as well.

Equally important perhaps, in no place had the American proposals referred to East Berlin. This was a significant departure from all previous Western proposals, including even the Geneva low-water mark of 1959. Indeed, to Bonn, three out of the four U.S. proposals dangerously enhanced the position of the East while gaining nothing in return.

Washington's ultimatum, however, made the Federal Republic's reply imperative. Pressed for time and thus unable to prepare a set of alternatives—there are many in Bonn who think the time limit was decreed precisely for this purpose—the Federal Republic advised Washington that while it had reservations, it would reluctantly go along with the package. As subsequent events were to reveal, Chancellor Adenauer thought there would be no chance of Russia accepting the proposals and therefore, rather than cast his Government in an obstructionist light, it was decided to go along with the plan. But the key to this position, of course, was that the Soviets would reject the package. To help insure this, Bonn began its own guerrilla campaign against the proposals. Immediately following the Federal Republic's official reply to Washington, Dr. Heinrich von Brentano, now leader of the CDU's parliamentary majority, reportedly caused the precise details of the American plan to be leaked to the press. The following day, April 13, both the *New York Times* and the *Washington Post* carried front page stories from Bonn describing the exact nature of the U.S. proposals.

The repercussions were immediate. In the White House, President Kennedy reportedly flew into a finger-pointing rage. Assorted Presidential advisers and the State Department were indignant. West German Ambassador Wilhelm Grewe was summoned to the office of Assistant Secretary of State Foy Kohler and chided in language frequently exceeding the bounds of diplomatic nicety. Rusk himself dispatched a seething cable to German Foreign Minister Schroeder which was so heated in its accusations that Chancellor Adenauer wanted to return it unanswered. According to Washington, the leak in Bonn had made a unified Western position "practically impossible" on the eve of the Dobrynin talks and represented a deliberate attempt "to sabotage East-West negotiations."[18]

The following day, Saturday, April 14, the Bonn government expressed its "deep regrets" over U.S. "irritation" at the leak. The difficulty, according to West German Press Secretary Felix von Eckhardt, was due to "thoughtless" reports written by certain correspondents— thoughtless because of the political consequences aroused.[19]

In spite of the leak from Bonn, the Rusk-Dobrynin talks began as scheduled on April 16. The American package proposal was presented, and afterward, Ambassador Dobrynin remarked that the session had been fruitful. Three days later, in a surprise move, the Soviet Union announced that Marshal Ivan Konev was being recalled from East Germany. To informed observers, the evidence seemed clear that the Kremlin was impressed by the American offer and was putting on a new face. The East Berlin newspaper *Neues Deutschland*, for example, reported that the American plan was "an approach to reality."

In West Germany, however, opposition to the U.S. proposals now began to crystalize. For the next several weeks the air was filled with transatlantic sniping as both Bonn and Washington battered away at each other's position. Chancellor Adenauer—now back in Cadenabbia —began to advise visitors that the Federal Republic had consented to Washington's proposals confident that Russia would reject them. The State Department issued statement after statement explaining that the Administration's proposals, and particularly those regarding access, would only give the East Germans "local responsibilities"—responsibilities which Secretary Rusk maintained they already enjoyed.[20]

Of all the issues that divided Bonn and Washington, however, it was the question of access that was now the most serious. As more and more details of the U.S. plan were revealed, it became increasingly plain that major concessions to the Ulbricht regime were involved. First, the fact that only one autobahn, that between Helmstedt and Berlin, would come under the jurisdiction of the proposed international authority meant that the remaining two autobahns between Berlin and West Germany,* plus all the rail lines and canal routes, would remain under exclusive East German control. Since these other routes carried virtually eighty-five percent of the traffic to Berlin, the American proposal appeared in Bonn not as a way to guarantee West Berlin's continued viability but merely as a means of reducing U.S. involvement. The Berlin-Helmstedt autobahn, it should be remembered, is the only one used by Allied forces.

Thus, to Bonn, the price which Washington was prepared to pay for this limited agreement seemed excessive. The fact that the public had never been explicitly advised that only the routes used by the Western powers would be included under the U.S. plan tended to confirm Bonn's suspicions. In Washington, the State Department explained the omission on technical grounds. To try to set up international control of rail and canal traffic, they said, would mean creating international "pockets" all over East Germany.[21] Presumably, this would also have been true of the other two autobahns. The fact that the United States was prepared to discontinue its military trains into Berlin once the access authority came into existence, however, was extremely disquieting.

Another West German objection related to the composition of the proposed authority. Under Washington's latest draft, reportedly developed by President Kennedy himself,[22] the authority would be made up of thirteen member states, each possessing one vote. These states would include: for the West—the United States, Great Britain, France, the Federal Republic, and West Berlin; for the Communists—the Soviet Union, Poland, Czechoslovakia, the German Democratic Republic, and East Berlin; and three neutrals—Austria, Sweden and Switzerland. Since this arrangement would give the Communist bloc parity with the West, the ultimate responsibility for Berlin traffic thus would be shifted to the three neutrals, i.e., to Austria, Sweden and Switzerland. To renounce Allied rights presently guaranteed by the Big Four themselves

* Nuremberg-Berlin and Frankfurt (Eisenach)-Berlin.

in favor of an agreement resting in the final analysis on the political courage of three relatively weak neutrals seemed an unhappy bargain. Also, the fact that both West Berlin and West Germany would be included as political equals on the Western side seemed to lend credence to the Communist claim that there was no legal connection between the two—a claim clearly contrary to established fact.

But the West German misgivings counted for little in Washington. The Rusk-Dobrynin talks continued at the State Department and the Russians evidently felt encouraged by the U.S. proposals. Not only was the pressure on West Berlin now relaxed completely, but Nikita Khrushchev advised Gardner Cowles, in an exclusive Kremlin interview, that he was "cautiously optimistic" of a settlement in Berlin. Since Mr. Khrushchev's mood was reported by Cowles as "calm, relaxed and confident," it is unlikely that the Soviet leader felt he was getting a bad bargain.[23]

Because of Russia's new conciliatory attitude, the West German government now became seriously concerned that the U.S. might consummate its deal on Berlin. On April 27, preparatory to the convening of the NATO conference of Foreign Ministers in Athens, Chancellor Adenauer called a top-level policy meeting of his principal foreign policy advisers at Cadenabbia. To Foreign Minister Schroeder, whose public statements were tending to support Washington's line, the Chancellor conveyed his own feelings in no uncertain terms. Afterward, and despite the fact that Schroeder was going to see Rusk in Athens, Dr. Heinrich von Brentano flew to Washington to restate the West German case. Brentano arrived in the capital on April 29. If Schroeder had unintentionally allowed Washington to believe that Bonn would accept the new arrangement, the former foreign minister pointedly advised otherwise. "It is not reasonable to belittle the differences that do exist," he said. "The situation is too serious for that, and it would only make the task of East-West negotiations more difficult to gloss them over."

There is no reason to believe that Dr. Brentano's presentation met with success. Before leaving Washington he told reporters in especially guarded terms that while the U.S. and West Germany agreed on "final goals," they still differed as to "means" and "methods." In fact, Brentano's skillful terminology cloaked a rift that was increasing rather than decreasing. The extent of this rift, and of the difference between Washington and Bonn as to "means" and "methods," was illustrated in Brentano's luncheon address to the National Press Club. Referring to the Kennedy Administration's plan for an international access authority, Brentano said that he "and the Federal Government" supported the concept of such an authority, but that questions about its composition and function "are very important and decisive."

According to Brentano, the "original idea" was to have the United States, Britain, France and the Soviet Union "carry the political responsibility" for access. Acting under them in a "purely technical capacity," he said, would be an "administrative group" which could include East Germany. That, said Dr. Brentano, was and remains "a good and a sound idea." [24] But it was an idea considerably removed from the thirteen nation authority which Washington was now proposing. Thus, when he returned to Bonn, von Brentano told Adenauer that the United States was still pursuing an illusory settlement and one which West Germany must not accept.

From Athens, the Chancellor received similar reports from Dr. Schroeder. Despite the rosy press reports that Secretary Rusk and the West German Foreign Minister had agreed on all substantive issues, it was another case of diplomatic subterfuge. In reality, the "basic agreement" that was reported related only to the idea of an international authority, not to its details. Schroeder, in fact, firmly advised Rusk that the West German Government felt that the U.S. proposal would undermine vital Allied rights in Berlin and would make the situation worse rather than better. French Foreign Minister Couve de Murville added his voice to that of Schroeder's, remarking that there was no logical reason for continuing the negotiations. Again, however, the French and West German objections were brushed aside.

But by the beginning of May, the French and West Germans were not alone in questioning the Kennedy Administration's preoccupation with negotiations. Suddenly finding its tongue, the liberal wing of the Republican Party now began to speak out against concessions in Berlin. In a concerted Senate appearance, three Republican liberals—Ken Keating of New York, Hugh Scott of Pennsylvania, and Jake Javits of New York—warned the White House over any deal which would dilute Western rights.

"To enter into negotiations in which the East German government may have some say over access rights to West Berlin would be a bitter renunciation of our position," said Keating. "No matter what cloak of plausibility may be pulled over this maneuver, it is in essence catastrophic."

Scott and Javits were equally critical. To Scott, the "secrecy" surrounding the Administration's activities was "lamentable." It would be fatal, he said, to "bargain away part of, or perhaps ultimately all of, the present free access guaranteed by postwar settlement." Javits said it was "disquieting" that the Administration "appears to believe that a new agreement on Berlin is the immediate and primary objective of our current policy."

Several days earlier, General Clay himself had expressed similar doubts about the Administration's access proposals. Appearing on the West Berlin television version of "Meet the Press," the General was asked whether he shared the German reservations about the inclusion of the Ulbricht regime in the suggested international authority. "I am not happy, of course, at this thought, or this prospect," Clay replied. "I think that this needs to be carefully discussed and carefully thought out between the Allies and the Federal Republic of Germany, but I don't think we should condemn it until we know a great deal more about it." [25]

Asked whether he thought the United States could avoid recognition of the Ulbricht regime in the course of the negotiations, Clay answered as follows:

> I think if you are speaking of diplomatic recognition that this will not be done. When you get into this so-called *de facto* recognition it is very difficult for me to know at what stage *de facto* recognition becomes highly objectionable and at what stage it is a fact of life we have to live with. . . .
>
> I think this is a field in which there must be complete unanimity of thinking among the Allies, where there must be complete discussion.
>
> Certainly it would be self-defeating for the U.S. to adopt any proposal along this line that had not been fully discussed with and accepted by the Federal Republic of Germany. After all, the creation of unity of thought, of economic, of political unity in Western Europe has been a part of our European policy for many, many years.
>
> If this should fail, if we should lose our friendship of France and the friendship of West Germany because of overtures in these negotiations, it would destroy our entire policy. It would be unthinkable that this would occur. . . .

The overall tenor of Clay's remarks was moderate. There was little question, however, that he had great apprehensions about the U.S. access proposals, and indeed, about the total drift of American policy on Berlin. Clearly, General Lucius D. Clay was glad to be going home. As he explained it to the Berliners, with the Soviet pressure on Berlin temporarily slackened, he now could do more for the city's defense in the United States. Implicit in Clay's comment, of course, was the underlying friction with Washington which had hampered his role in Berlin. Perhaps in America, he could bring his weight to bear more fully on Washington.

As for the existing calm in Berlin, Clay said he thought it would continue, "except for the inevitable tension along the Wall, as long as the talks go on." "But obviously," he added, "it is only an interlude."

Shortly afterwards, on May 1, General Clay made his last public appearance in Berlin. The occasion was West Berlin's traditional May Day celebration in the *Platz der Republic*—the great amphitheater before the charred ruins of the Reichstag. For the Berliners, they knew that this would be their last chance to see General Clay before he departed. As a result, over 700,000 people—one out of every three persons living in West Berlin—turned out for the occasion. As far as the eye could see, was row after row of people, all standing silently and listening to the speeches.

The author was in the *Platz der Republic* that day. The impression is unforgettable. Three-quarters of a million people paying homage to one man, the man who to them personified American determination, who represented American strength, and who symbolized American honor.

The General, in fact, was not even scheduled to speak. He would just be there on the platform. But the emotional tie that unites Clay and the West Berliners had brought them out to see him. Clay himself was deeply moved. Mayor Brandt quickly sensed the mood of the crowd and asked the General to speak. The people raised a tremendous cheer. Those around us were applauding and weeping simultaneously.

Clay did speak. What he said was brief. It was not bitter, but at the same time the words were not the words of victory. It was almost as if the General was warning the Berliners to be watchful:

I am sure that President Kennedy, if he knew that I was speaking to you, [Clay began,] would want me to extend his greetings.

I need not remind you of his commitments to you on behalf of our people except to say to you that we live up to our commitments.

I leave Berlin because the time has come when I can serve its cause better at home. . . . I can, on a moment's notice, return to Berlin the moment I think I can be of better service here.

So I shall not now, or ever, say "goodby." For Berlin is too much a part of me to ever leave. I shall only say, as we say in America, "so long, thank you, and God bless you."

Footnote references in general have been made to primary sources. Insofar as possible I have attempted to avoid merely repetitious and cumulative listings of all relevant material and have restricted myself instead to the one or two most relevant items.

The material in the latter chapters, i.e., those pertaining to events in Berlin from 1958 onward, has been gathered by the author from first-hand research in Berlin, Bonn, Paris, and Washington. The author has interviewed numerous officials of all four Western powers and much of the material given to him has been on a "not for attribution" basis. Accordingly, many of the footnote citations in Chapters 12–14 are not intended as sources but rather as references where the general reader or scholar can find independent corroboration for the material which the author has presented.

Jean E. Smith

NOTES

CHAPTER 1—THE DEFENSE OF BERLIN (SETTING THE SCENE)

[1] *Neue Zürcher Zeitung*, August 13 and 14, 1961; *New York Times*, August 13, 1961; Bundesministerium für Gesamtdeutsche Fragen, *Die Flucht aus der Sowjetzone und die Sperrmassnahmen des Kommunistischen Regimes vom 13. August, 1961 in Berlin* (Bonn und Berlin: Bundesdruckerei, 1961), pp. 15–22, 32–34. The latter source contains an admirable collection of official statements made by ninety-five recent refugees from the Soviet zone concerning the reasons for their flight. See pp. 43–83.

[2] *Frankfurter Allgemeine Zeitung*, July 8, 1961; *Neues Deutschland* (East Berlin), July 19, 1961; *Volksstimme* (Magdeburg), July 22, 1961; *Leipziger Volkszeitung*, July 24, 1961.

[3] Brandt and Clay material; Federal Republic of Germany, Press and Information Office, *Facts about Germany*, 3d. ed. (Wiesbaden, 1960), p. 31; Federal Republic of Germany, Press and Information Office, *The Bulletin*, Vol. 9, No. 31 (Bonn: August 15, 1961), p. 7; United Nations, *Demographic Yearbook–1960*, Statistical Office, Department of Economic and Social Affairs (New York, 1960), pp. 146–47.

[4] Soviet aide-mémoire presented by Chairman Khrushchev to President Kennedy in Vienna, June 4, 1961. Reprinted in U.S. Department of State, *Berlin–1961*, Department of State Publication 7257 (Washington: Government Printing Office, 1961), pp. 30–31.

[5] *Neues Deutschland* (East Berlin), August 13, 1961.

[6] *Berlin–1961, op. cit.*, p. 38.

[7] Dwight D. Eisenhower, "My Views on Berlin," *Saturday Evening Post*, December 9, 1961, p. 19.

CHAPTER 2—WARTIME AGREEMENTS REGARDING THE OCCUPATION OF BERLIN

[1] Chester Wilmot, *The Struggle for Europe* (New York: Harper & Bros. 1952), p. 82.
William L. Shirer, *The Rise and Fall of the Third Reich* (New York: Simon and Schuster, 1960), pp. 851–66.

[2] Cables, Winant to Secretary of State, December 19, 1941 and January 19, 1942, contained in *The Papers of John Gilbert Winant, U.S. Ambassador to the Court of St. James During World War II* (Microfilm), Columbia University in the City of New York.
Winston Churchill, *The Grand Alliance* (Boston: Houghton Mifflin, 1951), pp. 637–41.
Herbert Feis, *Churchill, Roosevelt, Stalin: The War They Waged and the Peace They Sought* (Princeton: Princeton University Press, 1957), pp. 26–27.
Also see the Memorandum of Assistant Secretary of State A. A. Berle, Jr.

to Secretary Hull, September 15, 1941, reprinted in *Foreign Relations of the United States: Diplomatic Papers, 1941*, U.S. Department of State, Vol. 1 (Washington: Government Printing Office, 1958), p. 188.

³ Churchill, *The Grand Alliance, op. cit.*, pp. 630–31.

⁴ Anne Armstrong, *Unconditional Surrender: the Impact of the Casablanca Policy Upon World War II* (New Brunswick: Rutgers University Press, 1962); Sir Llewellyn Woodward, *British Foreign Policy in the Second World War* (London: H. M. Stationery Office, 1962), pp. 433–37.

⁵ Robert Sherwood, *Roosevelt and Hopkins* (New York: Harper & Bros., 1948), p. 716; Woodward, *op. cit.*, pp. 437–42.

⁶ Notes of Harry Hopkins, March 17, 1943, as quoted by Robert Sherwood, *ibid.*, pp. 714–15.

⁷ Cordell Hull, *Memoirs* (New York: Macmillan, 1948), p. 1285. Also see Feis, *op. cit.*, pp. 213–23. The full text of Secretary Hull's Moscow proposals is reproduced in Appendix III.

⁸ Hull, *op. cit.*, pp. 1284–89. Also see Philip Mosely, "The Occupation of Germany," *Foreign Affairs* (July, 1950), pp. 580–81; Feis, *op. cit.*, pp. 219–23; U.S. Department of State, *Foreign Relations of the United States: Conferences at Cairo and Tehran* (Washington: Government Printing Office, 1961), pp. 183–86. Hereafter cited as *Conferences at Cairo and Tehran*.

⁹ Feis, *op. cit.; Conferences at Cairo and Tehran, op. cit.*, pp. 116–17, 130–36, 152–55; Woodward, *op. cit.*, pp. 445–48.

¹⁰ Maurice Matloff, *Strategic Planning for Coalition Warfare, 1943–1944*, Office of the Chief of Military History, Department of the Army (Washington: Government Printing Office, 1959), pp. 335, 547–49.

¹¹ *Ibid.*, pp. 335–36.

¹² *Ibid.*, p. 338.

¹³ Minutes, Meeting of President and Joint Chiefs of Staff (126th mtg. JCS), 19 Nov 43. See Appendix IV.

¹⁴ Winston Churchill, *Triumph and Tragedy* (Boston: Houghton Mifflin, 1953), pp. 507–8; Woodward, *op. cit.*, pp. 445–48, 465–70.

¹⁵ Matloff, *op. cit.*, p. 341.

¹⁶ Mosely, *op. cit.*, pp. 589–90. Sir William Strang, *At Home and Abroad* (London: Andre Deutsch, 1956), pp. 213–14.

¹⁷ Memo of Major General Thomas T. Handy, 19 November 1943, cited in Matloff, *op. cit.*, pp. 341–42. Also see Forrest C. Pogue, *The Supreme Command*, Office of the Chief of Military History, Department of the Army (Washington: Government Printing Office, 1954), p. 349.

¹⁸ Matloff, *op. cit.*, pp. 341–42.

¹⁹ Sherwood, *op. cit.*, pp. 721–24, 755–57, 774–75.

²⁰ John L. Snell, *Wartime Origins of the East–West Dilemma over Germany* (New Orleans: Hauser, 1959), p. 72.

²¹ Churchill, *Triumph and Tragedy*, p. 508.

²² Matloff, *op. cit.*, p. 491.

²³ Wilmot, *op. cit.*, p. 644. The "Bohlen" minutes of the Tehran Conference are reprinted in Appendix V.

²⁴ Sherwood, *op. cit.*, p. 798; Woodward, *op. cit.*, pp. 447–48.

²⁵ See Mosely, "The Occupation of Germany," *op. cit.*; cf., *Conferences at Cairo and Tehran, op. cit.*, pp. 883–84.

²⁶ Matloff, *op. cit.*, p. 341, n.

²⁷ Strang, *op. cit.*, pp. 213–14; Mosely, *op. cit.*, pp. 589–91.

²⁸ Joint Chiefs of Staff Document 624/1, 29 December 1943, Title: Military and Naval Advisors for European Advisory Commission. Cited in Ray S. Cline, *Washington Command Post: The Operations Division*, Office of the Chief of Military History, Department of the Army (Washington: Government Printing Office, 1951), p. 323, n.

²⁹ Mosely, *op. cit.*, pp. 586–88.

³⁰ Cline, *op. cit.*, pp. 323–26.

[31] The discussion of the proceedings of the WSC presented by Mr. Philip Mosely, one of the State Department representatives, is indicative of spirit which prevailed. See Mosely, *op. cit.,* pp. 585–95.

[32] Cline, *op. cit.,* pp. 324–25.

[33] Mosely, *op. cit.,* p. 586.

[34] *Ibid.,* p. 591; Woodward, *op. cit.,* pp. 476–78.

[35] *Ibid.;* cf. Albert L. Warner, "Our Secret Deal Over Germany," *Saturday Evening Post,* August 2, 1952, pp. 66–68.

[36] Mosely, *op. cit.,* p. 591. But cf. Cable 1435, Secretary of State to Winant, February 26, 1944, contained in *Winant Papers, op. cit.*

[37] *Ibid.,* pp. 591–93; cf. Memorandum of Conversation, Eden–Morgenthau, August 13, 1944, in *Conferences at Cairo and Tehran, op. cit.,* pp. 881–82.

[38] Mosely, *op. cit.,* p. 592. Also see Feis, *op. cit.,* pp. 362–63.

[39] Feis, *op. cit.,* pp. 362–63; Matloff, *op. cit.,* pp. 335n., 492; Sherwood, *op. cit.,* pp. 755–57.

[40] General Lucius D. Clay, *Decision in Germany* (Garden City, N.Y.: Doubleday & Co., Inc., 1950), p. 15.

[41] See Mosely, *op. cit.,* p. 594.

[42] Strang, *op. cit.,* p. 265.

[43] U.S. Congress, Senate. *Documents on Germany 1944–1959,* Committee Print, Committee on Foreign Relations, U.S. Senate, 86th Congress, 1st Session (Washington: Government Printing Office, 1959), pp. 1–3. Cited hereafter as *Documents on Germany.*

[44] Churchill, *Triumph and Tragedy,* p. 156.

[45] *Ibid.*

[46] Matloff, *op. cit.,* p. 511, n; Woodward, *op. cit.,* pp. 471–76.

[47] Feis, *op. cit.,* p. 365.

[48] *Documents on Germany,* pp. 3–5.

[49] Hull, *op. cit.,* pp. 1619–20.

[50] Mosely, *op. cit.,* p. 596. Also see Snell, *op. cit.,* 105–6.

[51] Mosely, *op. cit.,* pp. 595–99.

[52] Edward R. Stettinius, *Roosevelt and The Russians—The Yalta Conference* (Garden City, N.Y.: Doubleday & Co., Inc., 1949), pp. 37–38.

[53] Sherwood, *op. cit.,* pp. 858–61.

[54] U.S. Department of State, *Foreign Relations of the United States: The Conferences at Malta and Yalta, 1945,* Department of State Publication 6199 (Washington: Government Printing Office, 1955), pp. 118, 121, 688.

[55] As quoted in Feis, *op. cit.,* p. 533.

[56] *Ibid.*

[57] Mosely, *op. cit.,* p. 600.

CHAPTER 3—THE MILITARY DECISION TO HALT AT THE ELBE

[1] Forrest C. Pogue, *Command Decisions* (Kent T. Greenfield, ed.), Office of the Chief of Military History, Department of the Army (Washington: Government Printing Office, 1960), p. 482.

[2] Walter Bedell Smith, *Eisenhower's Six Great Decisions* (New York: Longmans, Green & Co., 1956), p. 181.

[3] Field Marshal Montgomery, Viscount of Alamein, *Memoirs* (Cleveland: World Publishing Co., 1958), pp. 248–49, 296.

[4] Forrest C. Pogue, *The Supreme Command,* Office of the Chief of Military History, Department of the Army (Washington: Government Printing Office, 1954), p. 447.

[5] Dwight D. Eisenhower, "My Views on Berlin," *Saturday Evening Post,* December 9, 1961, p. 20.

[6] Dwight D. Eisenhower, *Crusade in Europe* (Garden City, N.Y.: Doubleday & Co., 1948), pp. 378–84.

[7] Omar Bradley, *A Soldier's Story*

(New York: Henry Holt & Co., 1951), p. 530f.

[8] Feis, *op. cit.*, p. 602.

[9] Captain Harry Butcher (USNR), *My Three Years With Eisenhower* (New York: Simon and Schuster, 1946), p. 814.

[10] SHAEF Intelligence Summary, March 11, 1945, as quoted in Shirer, *op. cit.*, pp. 1105–6. Also see Bedell Smith, *op. cit.*, pp. 186–90; Feis, *op. cit.*, p. 602.

[11] Bedell Smith, *op. cit.*, pp. 189–90.

[12] Butcher, *op. cit.*, pp. 809–10.

[13] Eisenhower, *Crusade in Europe*, p. 397.

[14] Feis, *op. cit.*, p. 602n.

[15] Bradley, *op. cit.*, p. 536.

[16] *Ibid.*, pp. 535–36.

[17] *Ibid.*, pp. 531–36.

[18] Bedell Smith, *op. cit.*, p. 182.

[19] Winston Churchill, *Triumph and Tragedy*, p. 455.

[20] *Ibid.*, p. 457.

[21] *Ibid.*

[22] Cable, Supreme Commander to Prime Minister, quoted in Churchill, *Triumph and Tragedy*, pp. 457–58.

[23] As quoted in Eisenhower, *Crusade in Europe*, p. 460

[24] Winston Churchill, *Triumph and Tragedy*, pp. 458–66.

[25] Prime Minister to General Ismay, 31 March 45, quoted in Churchill, *Triumph and Tragedy*, pp. 460–61.

[26] Eisenhower, *Crusade in Europe*, pp. 400–1.

[27] *Ibid.*, pp. 401–2.

[28] Prime Minister Churchill to General Eisenhower, 31 March 45, quoted in *Triumph and Tragedy*, pp. 463–64.

[29] Prime Minister to President Roosevelt, 1 Apr. 45, quoted in Churchill, *Triumph and Tragedy*, p. 465.

[30] *Ibid.*

[31] *Ibid.*

[32] Pogue, *The Supreme Command*, p. 443n.

[33] General Eisenhower to Prime Minister, 1 Apr. 45, quoted in Churchill, *Triumph and Tragedy*, p. 466.

[34] *Ibid.*, p. 467.

[35] Prime Minister to President Roosevelt, April 5, 1945, quoted in Churchill, *Triumph and Tragedy*, p. 468.

[36] Feis, *op. cit.*, p. 607.

[37] Pogue, *The Supreme Command*, p. 444.

[38] Eisenhower to Marshall, 7 April 45, quoted in Pogue, *The Supreme Command*, p. 446.

[39] *Ibid.*, p. 446. Also see William D. Leahy, *I Was There* (New York: Whittlesey House, 1950), pp. 350–51.

[40] Supreme Commander to F. M. Montgomery, 8 April 1945, quoted in Pogue, *The Supreme Command*, p. 446.

[41] Bedell Smith, *op. cit.*, p. 187.

[42] Pogue, *The Supreme Command*, p. 452.

[43] *Ibid.*

[44] *Ibid.*, pp. 452–53.

[45] *Ibid.*, pp. 446–47.

[46] Bradley, *op. cit.*, p. 537.

[47] *Ibid.*, pp. 537–39.

[48] Bedell Smith, *op. cit.*, pp. 185–86.

[49] Quoted in Pogue, *The Supreme Command*, p. 468.

[50] Pogue, *Command Decisions*, p. 481.

[51] Montgomery, *op. cit.*, p. 286.

[52] Bedell Smith, *op. cit.*, p. 186.

[53] William D. Leahy, *op. cit.*, pp. 350–51.

[54] Harry S Truman, *Year of Decisions* (Garden City, N.Y.: Doubleday & Co., 1955), p. 214.

[55] Churchill, *Triumph and Tragedy*, pp. 513–14.

[56] *Ibid.*, p. 506.

[57] Pogue, *Command Decisions*, p. 490. Also see Truman, *op. cit.*

[58] Bedell Smith, *op. cit.*, p. 222.

CHAPTER 4—"AN IRON CURTAIN IS DRAWN DOWN UPON THEIR FRONT"

[1] Eisenhower to Combined Chiefs of Staff, 5 April 1945, quoted in Pogue, *The Supreme Command*, p. 465.

[2] Prime Minister to General Ismay, 7 April 1945, in Churchill, *Triumph and Tragedy*, pp. 512–13.

[3] British Chiefs of Staff to Joint Staff Mission, Washington, 11 April 1945, cited in Pogue, *The Supreme Command*, p. 465n.

[4] Memo, Brig. Gen. George A. Lincoln for Gen. Hull, 13 April 1945, sub: Military Contacts with the Russians, quoted in Pogue, *The Supreme Command*, pp. 465–66.

[5] President Truman to Prime Minister, quoted in Wilmot, *op. cit.*, p. 696. Also see Leahy, *op. cit.*, p. 410.

[6] Truman, *op. cit.*, p. 214; Churchill, *Triumph and Tragedy*, p. 516; Feis, *op. cit.*, p. 634.

[7] Eisenhower to President Truman, 23 April 1945, quoted in Truman, *op. cit.*, p. 215.

[8] Churchill, *Triumph and Tragedy*, pp. 517–18; Truman, *op. cit.*, pp. 214–16.

[9] Feis, *op. cit.*, p. 634.

[10] Ministry of Foreign Affairs of the U.S.S.R., *Stalin's Correspondence With Churchill, Attlee, Roosevelt and Truman 1941–1945* (London: Lawrence & Wishert, 1958), p. 346.

[11] Prime Minister to Foreign Secretary, 4 May 1945, quoted in Churchill, *Triumph and Tragedy*, pp. 502–3.

[12] Churchill, *Triumph and Tragedy*, pp. 455–56.

[13] Stettinius, *op. cit.*, p. 278. Further indicative of President Roosevelt's attitude toward the Russians was the comment made by him shortly before this to William C. Bullitt: "I have a hunch that Stalin . . . doesn't want anything but security for his country, and I think that if I give him everything I possibly can and ask for nothing in return, *noblesse oblige.*" William C. Bullitt, "How We Won the War and Lost the Peace," *Life*, August 30, 1948, p. 94.

[14] Feis, *op. cit.*, p. 636.

[15] U.S. Congress, Senate, *Hearings 1953–1954* (Jenner Subcommittee), Committee on the Judiciary, U.S. Senate, 83rd Congress, 1st Session (Washington: Government Printing Office, 1955), July, 1953; November 12, 1953; December 2, 3, 10, 1953.

[16] Eugene Davidson, *The Death and Life of Germany* (New York: Alfred A. Knopf, 1958), p. 65.

[17] Walter Millis (ed.), *The Forrestal Diaries* (New York: Viking Press, 1951), pp. 48–51.

[18] Butcher, *op. cit.*, pp. 854–55.

[19] Prime Minister to President Truman, 12 May 1945, quoted in Churchill, *Triumph and Tragedy*, pp. 573–74.

[20] Feis, *op. cit.*, p. 637.

[21] *Ibid.*

[22] Federal Republic of Germany, Press and Information Office, *Germany Reports* (Wiesbaden, 1953), pp. 62–63; Clay, *op. cit.*, p. 32; Frank Howley, *Berlin Command* (New York: G. P. Putnam's Sons, 1950), pp. 42–45. Also see *Berlin im Neuaufbau: Das erste Jahr*, yearly report of the Berlin Magistrat (Berlin: 1946).

[23] Truman, *op. cit.*, p. 341.

[24] Leahy, *op. cit.*, pp. 355–56.

[25] Davidson, *op. cit.*, pp. 74–75.

[26] W. Phillips Davison, *The Berlin Blockade* (Princeton: Princeton University Press, 1958), p. 29.

CHAPTER 5—THE OCCUPATION BEGINS

[1] Truman, *Year of Decisions,* pp. 298–300; Herbert Feis, *Between War and Peace—The Potsdam Conference* (Princeton: Princeton University Press, 1960), pp. 74–76.

[2] Truman, *Year of Decisions,* pp. 300–1; Feis, *Between War and Peace,* p. 77.

[3] Cable, Eisenhower to Marshall, quoted in Truman, *Year of Decisions,* p. 300.

[4] Feis, *Between War and Peace,* p. 77.

[5] *Ibid.*

[6] Cable, Eisenhower to Combined Chiefs, 2 June 1945, quoted in Truman, *Year of Decisions,* p. 301.

[7] Cable, Combined Chiefs to Eisenhower, 3 June 1945, quoted in Truman, *Years of Decisions,* p. 301.

[8] Cable, Prime Minister to President, 4 June 1945, quoted in Churchill, *Triumph and Tragedy,* p. 603.

[9] Clay, *op. cit.,* p. 20.

[10] Montgomery, *op. cit.,* p. 338; cf., Clay, *op. cit.,* pp. 21–22.

[11] As quoted in Feis, *Between War and Peace,* p. 141.

[12] Truman, *Year of Decisions,* p. 302.

[13] Cable, Hopkins to President, quoted in Truman, *ibid.,* pp. 302–3. Also see Sherwood, *op. cit.,* pp. 913–15.

[14] Cable, Prime Minister to Foreign Office, 11 June 1945, quoted in Churchill, *Triumph and Tragedy,* p. 604.

[15] Cable, President to Prime Minister, 12 June 1945, quoted in Truman, *Year of Decisions,* p. 303.

[16] Cable, Prime Minister to President, 14 June 1945, quoted in Churchill, *Triumph and Tragedy,* pp. 605–6.

[17] Churchill, *Triumph and Tragedy,* pp. 605–6.

[18] Leahy, *op. cit.,* p. 382.

[19] Truman, *Year of Decisions,* pp. 305–6.

[20] *Ibid.*

[21] See Chapter 2, *supra.*

[22] Cable, Prime Minister to Stalin, 15 June 1945, quoted in Churchill, *Triumph and Tragedy,* p. 606.

[23] *Stalin's Correspondence with Churchill, Attlee, Roosevelt and Truman,* pp. 366–67. Also see Feis, *Between War and Peace,* p. 146.

[24] Cable, Marshall to Eisenhower, 25 June 1945, quoted in Truman, *Year of Decisions,* p. 306.

[25] Cable, Deane to Marshall, 25 June 1945, quoted in Truman, *Year of Decisions,* p. 307.

[26] Feis, *Between War and Peace,* p. 147; Clay, *op. cit.,* pp. 24–26.

[27] Howley, *op. cit.,* pp. 42–43; Montgomery, *op. cit.,* p. 344.

[28] Clay, *op. cit.,* p. 26.

[29] *Ibid.*

[30] Churchill, *Triumph and Tragedy,* p. 609.

[31] Howley, *op. cit.,* p. 43.

[32] *Ibid.,* p. 49.

[33] Clay, *op. cit.,* p. 31.

[34] *Ibid.,* p. 28.

CHAPTER 6—BLOCKADE

[1] U.S. Department of State, *Protocol of the Berlin (Potsdam) Conference, August 1, 1945,* Department of State press release 238, March 24, 1947. Reproduced in *Documents on Germany, op. cit.,* pp. 24–35.

[2] Clay, *op. cit.*, p. 45.

[3] *Ibid.*, p. 29.

[4] Howley, *op. cit.*, p. 93.

[5] *Ibid.*, p. 114.

[6] *Ibid.* The best single chronology of the first year Allied occupation in Berlin, together with many valuable documents, is to be found in, *Berlin: Kampf um Freiheit und Selbstverwaltung 1945–1946*, West Berlin Senat (Berlin: Heinz Spitzing, 1961).

[7] Howley, *op. cit.*, p. 106. Also see Willy Brandt and Richard Lowenthal, *Ernst Reuter: Ein Leben für die Freiheit* (Munich: Kindler, 1957), pp. 348–59.

[8] *Ibid.*, pp. 120–21. Also see Jacques Robichon and J. V. Ziegelmeyer, *L'Affaire de Berlin: 1945–1959* (Paris: Gallimard, 1959), pp. 85–134.

[9] Clay, *op. cit.*, p. 348.

[10] *Ibid.*, p. 354.

[11] Cable, Clay to Chamberlin, 5 March 1948, quoted in Walter Millis (ed.) *The Forrestal Diaries* (New York: Viking Press, 1951), p. 387.

[12] Millis, *op. cit.*, pp. 387ff.

[13] Teleconference, Clay and Department of the Army, quoted in Clay, *op. cit.*, p. 358.

[14] Teleconference, Clay and Department of the Army, 31 March 1948, quoted in Clay, *op. cit.*, p. 359.

[15] *Ibid.*, pp. 359–60.

[16] Clay, *op. cit.*, p. 359.

[17] Teleconference, Clay and Department of the Army, 2 April 1948, quoted in Clay, *op. cit.*, p. 360.

[18] Teleconference, Clay and Department of the Army, 10 April 1948, quoted in Clay, *op. cit.*, p. 361.

[19] Davison, *op. cit.*, p. 98. Also see *Berlin: Behauptung von Freiheit und Selbstverwaltung 1946–1948*, West Berlin Senat (Berlin: Heinz Spitzing, 1959), pp. 410–523.

[20] Howley, *op. cit.*, p. 202.

[21] Willy Brandt, *My Road to Berlin* (New York: Doubleday & Co., 1960), pp. 193–94.

[22] Teleconference, Clay and Department of the Army, 25 June 1948, quoted in Clay, *op. cit.*, p. 366.

[23] Harry S Truman, *Years of Trial and Hope* (New York: Doubleday & Co., 1956), p. 123.

[24] Millis, *op. cit.*, pp. 452–54.

[25] *Ibid.*, pp. 454–55. Also see Truman, *Years of Trial and Hope*, p. 123.

[26] As reproduced in Beate Ruhm von Oppen, *Documents on Germany Under Occupation 1945–1954* (London: Oxford University Press, 1955), p. 313.

[27] Truman, *Years of Trial and Hope*, pp. 125–26.

[28] Clay, *op. cit.*, p. 368.

CHAPTER 7—THE CITY IS SPLIT

[1] October 20, 1947. As cited in Davison, *op. cit.*, p. 83.

[2] *Neue Zeitung* (West Berlin), April 30, 1948.

[3] Clay, *op. cit.*, p. 364.

[4] *Ibid.*

[5] Davison, *op. cit.*, p. 97.

[6] *Ibid.*, p. 101.

[7] *Ibid.*, pp. 90–151.

[8] Clay, *op. cit.*, p. 367.

[9] *Ibid.*

[10] *Ibid.*, p. 374.

[11] *Ibid.*

[12] Davison, *op. cit.*, pp. 165–67.

[13] Truman, *Years of Trial and Hope*, p. 126.

[14] Clay, *op. cit.*, pp. 369–70; Brandt and Lowenthal, *op. cit.*, pp. 401–51.

[15] Truman, *Years of Trial and Hope*, p. 128.

[16] Clay, *op. cit.*, p. 376.

[17] Davison, *op. cit.*, p. 194.

[18] Clay, *op. cit.*, p. 375.

[19] Howley, *op. cit.*, pp. 214–16.

[20] *Ibid.*, pp. 217–18.

[21] Davison, *op. cit.*, pp. 204–8.

[22] Millis, *op. cit.*, p. 486; Davison, *op. cit.*, p. 248.

[23] Truman, *Years of Trial and Hope*, p. 130.

[24] *Ibid.*, p. 129.

[25] Trygve Lie, *In The Cause of Peace*

(New York: Macmillan, 1954), pp. 203, 210.

[26] Truman, *Years of Trial and Hope*, pp. 130–31. Also see Dean Acheson's extremely informative account of these negotiations in his article: "On Dealing With Russia: An Inside View," *New York Times Magazine*, April 12, 1959, pp. 27, 88–89.

[27] Davison, *op. cit.*, p. 273.

CHAPTER 8—RECOVERY (1949–1958)

[1] U.S. Congress, *Congressional Record*, Vol. 95, Part 5 (Washington: Government Printing Office, 1949), pp. 6313, 6339.

[2] U.S. Department of State, *Germany, 1947–1949: The Story in Documents* (Washington: Government Printing Office, 1950), pp. 69–70.

[3] Clay, *op. cit.*, pp. 397–98.

[4] *Germany, 1947–1949, op. cit.*, pp. 283–305.

[5] Davidson, *op. cit.*, p. 249.

[6] Clay, *op. cit.*, pp. 414–15.

[7] *Documents on Germany, op. cit.*, p. 459.

[8] *Germany, 1947–1949, op. cit.*, pp. 390–91.

[9] Quoted in von Oppen, *op. cit.*, pp. 390–91.

[10] *Ibid.*, p. 462.

[11] Dr. Rudolf Legien, *The Four Power Agreements on Berlin* (Berlin: Carl Heymanns Verlag, 1960), pp. 40–43.

[12] *Documents on Germany, op. cit.*, pp. 98–102. Also see von Oppen, *op. cit.*, p. 510.

[13] See especially Peter Rogge, *Die Amerikanische Hilfe für Berlin* (Tübingen: J. C. B. Mohr, 1959), and the article by Dieter Pohmer, "Wirtschaft-liche Probleme Berlins" in Hans Rothfels (ed.) *Berlin in Vergangenheit and Gegenwart* (Tübingen: J. C. B. Mohr, 1961), pp. 93–123.

[14] *Documents on Germany, op. cit.*, p. 461.

[15] *Ibid.*, p. 465.

[16] *Ibid.*, pp. 468–89.

[17] *Ibid.*, p. 472.

[18] Federal Republic of Germany, Ministry of All-German Affairs, *The Soviet Zone of Germany* (Cologne: Druckhaus Deutz, 1960), pp. 15–22.

[19] As quoted in Davidson, *op. cit.*, p. 341. For Reuters own account see Brandt and Lowenthal, *op. cit.*, pp. 670–98.

[20] Brandt, *My Road to Berlin, op. cit.*, pp. 245–46.

[21] *Documents on Germany, op. cit.*, p. 480.

[22] Brandt, *My Road to Berlin, op. cit.*, pp. 240–43.

[23] *Documents on Germany, op. cit.*, p. 123.

[24] *Ibid.*, pp. 158–59.

[25] *Ibid.*, pp. 159–60.

[26] See Brandt, *My Road to Berlin, op. cit.*

[27] *Ibid.*, p. 250.

CHAPTER 9—THE FIRST ULTIMATUM

[1] Letter, Premier Bulganin to President Eisenhower, December 10, 1957, republished in *Department of State Bulletin,* January 27, 1958, pp. 127–30.

[2] Statement of President Eisenhower to the First Plenary Session of the NATO Council, December 16, 1957, quoted in *Department of State Bulletin,* January 6, 1958, pp. 6–7.

[3] *New York Times,* January 10, 1958.

[4] Department of State Press Release #7, January 10, 1958.

[5] Letter, President Eisenhower to Premier Bulganin, January 12, 1958, republished in *Department of State Bulletin,* January 27, 1958, pp. 122–27.

[6] *Department of State Bulletin,* March 24, 1958, pp. 459–61.

[7] Letter, Bulganin to Eisenhower, March 3, 1958, republished in *Department of State Bulletin,* April 21, 1958, pp. 648–52.

[8] *New York Times,* January 16, 1958.

[9] See especially *New York Times,* January 19, 1958; February 5, 1958.

[10] *Department of State Bulletin,* April 21, 1958, pp. 652–55.

[11] Department of State Press Release #150, March 25, 1958.

[12] Department of State Press Release #159, March 31, 1958.

[13] *Department of State Bulletin,* July 7, 1958, pp. 17–22.

[14] *New York Times,* May 24, 1958.

[15] Department of State Press Release #330, June 16, 1958.

[16] Letter, Khrushchev to Eisenhower, June 11, 1958, republished in *Documents on Germany, op. cit.,* pp. 281–90.

[17] *Ibid.*

[18] The author accompanied Major Dansby to the Soviet Control Point.

[19] Letter, Eisenhower to Khrushchev, July 2, 1958, as reported in White House News Release, July 2, 1958.

[20] *Department of State Bulletin,* September 22, 1958, pp. 462–65.

[21] *New York Times,* July 16, 1958.

[22] *Ibid.,* August 8, 1958; August 13, 1958.

[23] *Department of State Bulletin,* October 20, 1958, pp. 616–17.

[24] Department of State Press Release #573, September 30, 1958.

[25] *New York Times,* October 30, 1958, p. 4.

[26] Department of State Press Release #676, November 7, 1958.

[27] *Documents on Germany, op. cit.,* pp. 308–12.

[28] Department of State Press Release #721, November 26, 1958.

[29] Note from the Soviet Foreign Ministry to the United States, Great Britain, and France, November 27, 1958. Official Translation. *Department of State Bulletin,* January 19, 1959, pp. 81–89.

CHAPTER 10—NEGOTIATIONS UNDER PRESSURE

[1] *Documents on Germany, op. cit.,* p. 332.

[2] *New York Times,* November 28, 1958.

[3] *Ibid.,* November 27, 1958.

[4] *Ibid.,* November 28, 1958.

[5] *Ibid.*

[6] *Ibid.*

[7] *Ibid.*

[8] *Ibid.,* November 19, 1958.

[9] *Ibid.*

[10] *Ibid.,* November 28, 1958.

[11] *Ibid.,* November 30, 1958.

[12] *Ibid.,* November 29, 1958.

[13] *Ibid.*, November 30, 1958.

[14] White House Press Release, November 30, 1958.

[15] *Tagesspiegel* (West Berlin), December 1, 1958.

[16] *New York Times*, December 1, 1958.

[17] *Ibid.*, December 2, 1958.

[18] *Ibid.*, December 4, 1958.

[19] *Ibid.*, December 9, 1958; January 13, 1959.

[20] *Ibid.*, December 9, 1958.

[21] *Ibid.*, December 11, 1958.

[22] *Documents on Germany, op. cit.*, p. 333.

[23] U.S. Department of State, *The Soviet Note on Berlin: An Analysis*, Department of State Publication 6757 (Washington: Government Printing Office, 1959), pp. 50–51.

[24] *Ibid.*, p. 51.

[25] *Documents on Germany*, pp. 336–47. Also see Quincy Wright, "Some Legal Aspects of The Berlin Crisis," *American Journal of International Law*, Vol. 55 (1961), pp. 959–65; and Wilhelm G. Grewe, "Other Legal Aspects of the Berlin Crisis," *American Journal of International Law*, Vol. 56, No. 2 (April, 1962), pp. 510–13.

[26] *The Soviet Note on Berlin: An Analysis*, pp. 32–36.

[27] *Department of State Bulletin*, March 9, 1959, pp. 333–43.

[28] Department of State Press Release #28, January 13, 1959.

[29] *New York Times*, January 25, 1959.

[30] *Documents on Germany*, pp. 378–80.

[31] *New York Times*, February 5, 1959.

[32] *Ibid.*

[33] *Ibid.*, February 10, 1959; Department of State Press Release #99, February 9, 1959.

[34] *Documents on Germany*, p. 382.

[35] *Department of State Bulletin*, April 13, 1959, pp. 508–11.

[36] *Documents on Germany*, pp. 389–99.

[37] *Ibid.*, pp. 399–405.

[38] White House Press Release, March 16, 1959.

[39] *Documents on Germany*, pp. 409–10.

[40] *New York Times*, April 1, 1959.

[41] *Department of State Bulletin*, April 27, 1959, p. 582.

[42] *New York Times*, April 18, 1959.

[43] Hans Speier, *Divided Berlin* (New York: Praeger, 1961), p. 50.

[44] *New York Times*, March 16, 1959; March 17, 1959; April 9, 1959.

[45] *Ibid.*, May 15, 1959; June 11, 1959.

[46] *Ibid.*, June 17, 1959.

[47] *Ibid.*, June 20, 1959.

[48] *Ibid.*

[49] *Ibid.*, July 26, 1959. One of the best analyses of the relative perils and prospects of negotiating with the Russians is found in Dean Acheson, "On Dealing With Russia; An Inside View," *op. cit.*

CHAPTER 11—THE TALE OF THREE SUMMITS (CAMP DAVID—PARIS—VIENNA)

[1] White House News Conference, August 3, 1959.

[2] *New York Times*, September 27, 1959.

[3] *Ibid.*, September 28, 1959.

[4] *Ibid.*

[5] *Ibid.*

[6] White House News Conference, September 28, 1959.

[7] *New York Times*, September 29, 1959. For West Berlin reaction to President Eisenhower's statement see *Neue Zürcher Zeitung*, October 1, 1959.

[8] *Ibid.*, October 7, 1959.

⁹ *Ibid.*, October 6, 1959; October 8, 1959; October 9, 1959.

¹⁰ *Neues Deutschland*, November 4, 1959. Also see *New York Times*, October 30, 1959; October 31, 1959; November 6, 1959.

¹¹ *Ibid.*, December 21, 1959.

¹² Warsaw Pact Communique, February 4, 1960.

¹³ *New York Times*, February 9, 1960.

¹⁴ *Ibid.*, February 18, 1960; February 20, 1960; February 21, 1960; February 25, 1960; March 12, 1960; March 15, 1960; March 16, 1960.

¹⁵ *Ibid.*, March 10, 1960.

¹⁶ *Neue Zürcher Zeitung*, March 9, 1960.

¹⁷ *Ibid.*, March 16, 1960.

¹⁸ Speier, *op. cit.*, p. 88.

¹⁹ *New York Times*, April 3, 1960.

²⁰ White House News Conference, April 27, 1960.

²¹ Eisenhower, "My Views on Berlin," *op. cit.*, p 28.

²² *New York Times*, May 17, 1960.

²³ See Speier, *op. cit.*, p. 105.

²⁴ *New York Times*, August 31, 1960. Also see *Frankfurter Allgemeine Zeitung*, August 30, 1960.

²⁵ Speier, *op. cit.*, p. 119.

²⁶ *New York Times*, September 1, 1960.

²⁷ *Die Welt* (Hamburg and Berlin), September 5, 1960.

²⁸ *Neues Deutschland*, September 13, 1960.

²⁹ *Ibid.*, September 22, 1960.

³⁰ *Ibid.*, September 24, 1960; *Neue Zürcher Zeitung*, September 23–24, 1960.

³¹ *New York Times*, September 29, 1960.

³² *Ibid.*, October 14, 1960.

³³ See press conference remarks of President Kennedy and Secretary Rusk reported in *New York Times*, February 2, 1961 and February 7, 1961, respectively.

³⁴ *New York Times*, May 21, 1961.

³⁵ *Ibid.*, March 11, 1961.

³⁶ *Ibid.*, March 31, 1961.

³⁷ *Ibid.*, June 7, 1961.

CHAPTER 12—FROM VIENNA TO AUGUST 13

¹ *New York Times*, June 10, 1961.

² *Ibid.*, June 12, 1961. Also see *Neue Zürcher Zeitung*, June 9, 1961; June 11, 1961; June 12, 1961.

³ *New York Times*, June 12, 1961.

⁴ *Ibid.*

⁵ *Ibid.*, June 15, 1961.

⁶ *Berlin–1961*, *op. cit.*, p. 41. Also see *Neues Deutschland*, June 16, 1961.

⁷ *New York Times*, June 21, 1961.

⁸ *Ibid.*

⁹ Nikita Khrushchev, *The Soviet Stand on Germany* (New York: Crosscurrents Press, 1961), pp. 22–23.

¹⁰ *Ibid.*, pp. 44–62.

¹¹ *New York Times*, June 24, 1961.

¹² *Ibid.*, July 11, 1961.

¹³ Khrushchev, *op. cit.*, pp. 74–92.

¹⁴ *New York Times*, July 13, 1961.

¹⁵ *Ibid.*

¹⁶ *Ibid.*, July 14, 1961.

¹⁷ Arthur Krock, *New York Times*, July 18, 1961.

¹⁸ *Ibid.*

¹⁹ *Berlin–1961*, *op. cit.*, p. 22.

²⁰ In this connection, see especially the article of Wallace Carroll in *New York Times*, July 19, 1961, p. 6.

²¹ *Berlin–1961*, *op. cit.*, pp. 36–37.

²² *New York Times*, July 24, 1961.

²³ *Berlin–1961*, *op. cit.*, pp. 37–41.

²⁴ Khrushchev, *op. cit.*, pp. 93–107.

²⁵ *New York Times*, August 6, 1961.

[26] *Ibid.*, August 8, 1961.

[27] *Ibid.*, August 7, 1961.

[28] Khrushchev, *op. cit.*, pp. 108–32.

[29] *The Soviet Zone of Germany, op. cit.*, pp. 1–32.

[30] *Berlin–1961, op. cit.*, p. 41.

[31] *New York Times*, June 24, 1961. This same dispatch also reported that Herr Ulbricht denied that his regime "intended to construct a wall to separate East and West Berlin"—a rumor which was current in Berlin at the time.

[32] *New York Times*, July 5, 1961; July 6, 1961; July 15, 1961.

[33] *Volksstimme* (Magdeburg), July 22, 1961.

[34] *Die Flucht aus der Sowjetzone, op. cit.*, pp. 64–82.

[35] *New York Times*, August 1, 1961; July 29, 1961.

[36] *Ibid.*, August 3, 1961.

[37] *Ibid.*, August 4, 1961.

[38] *Die Welt* (Hamburg and Berlin), August 4, 1961.

[39] *New York Times*, August 9, 1961.

[40] *Ibid.*, August 10, 1961.

[41] *Die Flucht aus der Sowjetzone, op. cit.*, p. 33.

[42] *New York Times*, August 12, 1961.

CHAPTER 13—THE WALL

[1] Communique of the Warsaw Pact, reprinted in the *New York Times*, August 14, 1961.

[2] Announcement of the Council of Ministers of the German Democratic Republic, reprinted in the *New York Times*, August 14, 1961.

[3] *New York Times*, August 14, 1961, p. 1.

[4] *Ibid.*, August 13, 1961, p. 3.

[5] *Ibid.*

[6] *Ibid.*, p. 1.

[7] U.S. Department of State, *Berlin–1961, op. cit.*, pp. 41–42.

[8] *New York Times*, August 14, 1961.

[9] *The Evening Star* (Washington, D.C.), August 14, 1961.

[10] *New York Times*, August 14, 1961.

[11] *Ibid.*

[12] *Ibid.*

[13] *The Evening Star* (Washington, D.C.), August 14, 1961.

[14] *Ibid.*, August 15, 1961.

[15] *Ibid.*

[16] *Ibid.*, August 14, 1961.

[17] U.S. Department of State, *Berlin–1961*, p. 42.

[35] *New York Times*, August 20, 1961.

The Evening Star (Washington, D.C.), August 15, 1961.

[19] *New York Times*, August 16, 1961.

[20] *The Washington Post*, August 17, 1961.

[21] *New York Times*, August 16, 1961.

[22] *The Washington Post*, August 17, 1961.

[23] R. H. Shackford, *Daily News* (Washington, D.C.), August 17, 1961.

[24] *Daily News* (Washington, D.C.), August 17, 1961.

[25] *The Evening Star* (Washington, D.C.), August 18, 1961.

[26] *New York Times*, August 16, 1961.

[27] *The Evening Star* (Washington, D.C.), August 17, 1961.

[28] *Ibid.*

[29] *New York Times*, August 18, 1961.

[30] U.S. Department of State, *Berlin–1961*, pp. 42–43.

[31] *New York Times*, August 18, 1961.

[32] *The Washington Post*, August 19, 1961.

[33] *Ibid.*

[34] *New York Herald Tribune*, August 19, 1961.

[18] *New York Times*, August 16, 1961.

The Washington Post, August 20, 1961.

[36] *The Washington Post,* August 21, 1961.

[37] *New York Times,* August 22, 1961.

[38] *Ibid.*

[39] *Ibid.*

[40] *Ibid.*

[41] *The Washington Post,* August 23, 1961.

[42] *Ibid.*

[43] *New York Times,* August 24, 1961.

[44] *Ibid.*

[45] *The Evening Star* (Washington, D.C.), August 27, 1961.

[46] *The Washington Post,* August 26, 1961.

[47] *Ibid.,* August 29, 1961.

[48] *New York Times,* August 30, 1961.

[49] *Ibid.* Also see Samuel H. Barnes, *et al.,* "The German Party System and the 1961 Federal Election," *American Political Science Review,* Vol. 56, No. 4 (December 1962), pp. 899–914.

CHAPTER 14—"NO CONCESSIONS WITHOUT COUNTER–CONCESSIONS"

[1] *New York Times,* September 21, 1961.

[2] *Ibid.,* November 3, 1961. For a thorough treatment of the maneuverings leading to the formation of the West German Government in 1961, see Peter H. Merkl, "Equilibrium, Structure of Interests and Leadership: Adenauer's Survival as Chancellor," *American Political Science Review,* Vol. 56, No. 3 (September, 1962), pp. 634–50.

[3] George Bailey, "The Gentle Erosion in Berlin," *The Reporter,* April 26, 1962, p. 15.

[4] *New York Times,* September 24, 1961.

[5] *Ibid.*

[6] *Ibid.,* September 25, 1961.

[7] *Ibid.,* September 26, 1961.

[8] *Ibid.,* October 3, 1961.

[9] *Ibid.,* October 1, 1961.

[10] *Ibid.,* October 8, 1961.

[11] *Ibid.,* November 1, 1961.

[12] Bailey, *op. cit.,* pp. 18–19.

[13] *New York Times,* November 19, 1961.

[14] Bailey, *op. cit.,* pp. 18–19.

[15] *Washington Post,* April 13, 1962.

[16] *Ibid.,* April 14, 1962. Also see *Washington Post,* April 16 and April 17, 1962; *The Evening Star* (Washington, D.C.), April 16, 1962, and the *New York Herald Tribune* (Paris Edition), April 27, 1962.

[17] George Bailey, "Adenauer Faces a Cruel Choice," *The Reporter,* June 7, 1962, p. 17.

[18] *New York Times,* April 15, 1962.

[19] *Washington Post,* April 15, 1962.

[20] *New York Herald Tribune* (Paris Edition), April 27, 1962.

[21] *Washington Post,* April 26, 1962.

[22] *Ibid.,* May 8, 1962.

[23] *Ibid.,* April 21, 1962.

[24] *Ibid.,* May 5, 1962.

[25] Transcript, *Sender Freies Berlin,* "*Die Fernseh, Pressekonferenz,*" 27 April 1962.

APPENDIX I

Berlin's Early History

1237—Town of Cölln established on left bank of the Spree River at the site of a former Wendish fishing village.

1244—Town of Berlin established on right bank of Spree opposite Cölln.

1307—Towns of Berlin and Cölln merged as independent city-state. Join Hanseatic League.

1380—Berlin partially destroyed by fire.

1412—Frederick, Duke of Nuremberg, head of the House of Hohenzollern, becomes representative of the Holy Roman Emperor (Sigismund) in Mark Brandenburg.

1415—Frederick of Hohenzollern becomes Elector (*Kurfürst*) of Brandenburg.

1415—Frederick II ends independence of Berlin after a brief military struggle.

1486—Berlin becomes official seat of the Hohenzollerns.

1517—Berlin undergoes commercial decline; withdraws from Hanseatic League.

1628—Berlin besieged by Wallenstein during Thirty Years War. Town partially destroyed.

1643—Frederick Wilhelm, the Great Elector (1643–1688), begins process of restoring and expanding Berlin.

1701—Prussia becomes Kingdom. Frederick III of Brandenburg becomes Frederick I of Prussia.

1710—Population of Berlin estimated at 56,000.

1740—Frederick the Great (d. 1786) ascends Prussian throne. Massive building program begun in Berlin.

1788—Carl Gottfried Langhans commissioned to build Brandenburg Gate.

1806—Napoleon enters Berlin following Battle of Jena.

1809—Humboldt University founded in Berlin.

1816—Population of Berlin 197,000.

1838—Construction of first railroad in Prussia, built between Berlin and Potsdam.

1848—Popular revolution in Berlin collapses following entreaties by Frederick Wilhelm IV.

1871—Wilhelm I of Prussia crowned Emperor of Germany following defeat of France in Franco-Prussian War. Berlin becomes capital of unified Germany. Population over 800,000.

1871–1914—

Berlin becomes largest manufacturing city in Germany as well as capital of government, industry and intellectual life. Population in 1914 numbers 3,000,000.

Nov. 9,—Wilhelm II abdicates. German Republic proclaimed in Berlin.
1918

Jan. 29,—Communist (Spartacist) uprising. Rosa Luxemburg and Karl Lieb-
1919   knecht executed.

June 28,—Germany signs Versailles Treaty.
1919

July 1,—Weimar Republic established.
1919

Sept. 8,—Germany admitted to League of Nations.
1926

Jan. 30,—Adolph Hitler becomes Chancellor of Germany.
1933

APPENDIX II

Chronology of Events

1941-1962

14 August 1941. Signing of the Atlantic Charter fixing Allied war aims.

16–28 December 1941. Visit of Anthony Eden to Moscow. Discussion of postwar Germany with Stalin.

26 January 1943. Doctrine of unconditional surrender announced by President Roosevelt at Casablanca.

17 March 1943. Visit of Anthony Eden to Washington. FDR agrees U.S. will take part in Germany's occupation.

19–30 October 1943. Moscow Conference of Foreign Ministers (Eden, Hull, and Molotov). Establishment of European Advisory Commission to consider postwar European problems.

19 November 1943. President Roosevelt discusses postwar zonal boundaries in Germany with military chiefs on board the *Iowa*.

28 November–1 December 1943. Big Three Conference at Tehran.

14 January 1944. First meeting of European Advisory Commission. Attlee proposals for zonal boundaries within Germany presented by Great Britain.

18 February 1944. Soviets accept Attlee proposals.

3 April 1944. FDR agrees to boundary of Soviet zone as proposed in the Attlee report.

11–16 September 1944. Second Quebec Conference. Tentative adoption of Morgenthau Plan by Roosevelt and Churchill, and agreement on the relative location of U.S. and British occupation zones in Germany.

12 September 1944. Completion of the protocol outlining occupation boundaries in Germany by the European Advisory Commission.

14 November 1944. European Advisory Commission approves revised plan of 12 September defining occupation boundaries in Germany and sector boundaries in Berlin.

1 February 1945. Formal approval of the occupation boundaries in Germany by the Combined Chiefs of Staff, meeting at Malta.

3–11 February 1945. Big Three Conference at Yalta formally approves occupation boundaries.

7 March 1945. U.S. forces cross Rhine at Remagen.

28 March 1945. Eisenhower cables Stalin that Allied forces will drive south of Berlin.

12 April 1945. U.S. Ninth Army crosses Elbe River fifty miles from Berlin.

17 April 1945. Major General (later General) Lucius D. Clay appointed deputy to Eisenhower for military government.

22 April 1945. Soviet armored forces reach the city limits of Berlin.

30 April 1945. Adolph Hitler commits suicide.

2 May 1945. All organized resistance ends in Berlin. Soviets complete occupation of city. European Advisory Commission adopts amended version of occupation plan allowing for French participation.

7 May 1945. Colonel General Jodl signs instrument of surrender at Rheims.

8 May 1945. Second surrender ceremony held in Berlin, Keitel, von Friedeburg, and Strumpf representing the German High Command and Zhukov, Tedder, de Tassigny and Spaatz the Allies.

17 May 1945. Soviet Commander in Berlin appoints sixteen member *Magistrat* to serve as principal city administrative body.

5 June 1945. First meeting of the Allied Control Council (Eisenhower, Montgomery, de Tassigny and Zhukov) in Berlin. Council officially promulgates occupation documents drafted by the European Advisory Commission.

14 June 1945. Letter of President Truman to Marshal Stalin setting date for withdrawal of Western forces from Soviet zone on June 21.

18 June 1945. Stalin replies to Truman but suggests July 1, as the date for withdrawal.

29 June 1945. Conference between Clay, Zhukov, and Weeks regarding withdrawal, and access of Allied forces to Berlin.

1–4 July 1945. U.S. and British occupation forces arrive in Berlin.

7 July 1945. Allied Kommandatura for the governing of Berlin established. Unrestricted movement and transportation between all sectors approved.

11 July 1945. First meeting of Allied Kommandatura; Colonel General Alexander V. Gorbatov (USSR), Major General Lewis Lyne (UK), Major General Floyd L. Parks (U.S.) and Brig. Gen. Geoffroi de Beauchesne (France), the latter not yet a voting member.

17 July–2 August 1945. Big Three Conference at Potsdam prescribes occupation policy for Germany.

20 July 1945. President Truman attends flag raising ceremony at American Headquarters in Berlin.

26 July 1945. Big Three reach agreement with Provisional Government of the French Republic regarding zones of occupation and the administration of Greater Berlin.

12 August 1945. French forces assume responsibility for their sector of Berlin.

30 August 1945. Four Power Allied Control Council for Germany formally established.

11 September–2 October 1945. London meeting of the Council of Foreign Ministers.

20 November 1945. Nuremburg trial of major war criminals begins. General McNarney succeeds Eisenhower as American Military Governor.

9 February 1946. Stalin announces that world revolution of communism is still going on.

28 March 1946. Kommandatura instructs Berlin *Magistrat* to draft a city constitution.

31 March 1946. Socialist party (SPD) in Berlin votes against merger with the Communists.

21 April 1946. Communist party and rump Socialist party form Socialist Unity Party (SED) throughout Soviet controlled territory.

25 April–12 July 1946. Paris meeting of the Council of Foreign Ministers.

26 May 1946. General Clay recommends bizonal merger with British.

13 August 1946. Draft Constitution for Greater Berlin accepted by Kommandatura to become effective following new elections in October.

5 September 1946. Radio in the American Sector (RIAS) established.

6 September 1946. Major foreign policy speech of Secretary of State Byrnes at Stuttgart announcing merger of U.S. and British zones.

20 October 1946. Results of first postwar election in Berlin give the SPD 63 seats, CDU 29 seats, SED 26 seats and the LPD 12 seats in the City Assembly.

5 December 1946. Berlin City Assembly elects new *Magistrat*, with 18 members, and Dr. Otto Ostrowski (SPD) as *Oberbürgermeister*.

15 March 1947. General Clay succeeds General McNarney as American Military Governor in Germany.

11 April 1947. City Assembly repudiates pact between Ostrowski and Soviet authorities.

17 April 1947. Oberbürgermeister Ostrowski resigns. Soviet Commandant refuses to recognize resignation.

5 June 1947. Secretary of State Marshall announces beginning of Marshall Plan in speech at Harvard.

24 June 1947.   Berlin City Assembly elects Professor Ernst Reuter (SPD) *Oberbürgermeister* 89–17.

27 June 1947.   Soviet Commandant vetoes election of Reuter. Deputy Mayors Louise Schroeder and Ferdinand Freidensburg serve in Reuter's place.

25 November–15 December 1947.   London meeting of the Council of Foreign Ministers.

21 February 1948.   Soviet sponsored Peoples Congress of Greater Berlin meets in Soviet sector.

25 February 1948.   Government of Czechoslovakia falls.

10 March 1948.   Soviet Military Administration in Soviet zone imposes severe restrictions on Germans traveling from East zone to Berlin.

17 March 1948.   Brussels mutual defense treaty signed. German People's Council established in East Berlin.

20 March 1948.   Marshal Sokolovsky walks out of Allied Control Council protesting action of Allies in western Germany.

30 March 1948.   Soviets impose rail and highway restrictions on Allied traffic between Western zones and Berlin. "Little Airlift" begun in response.

3 April 1948.   Soviet zone authorities close freight routes to Berlin from Munich and Hamburg.

9 April 1948.   Soviet Military Administration announces all freight trains on remaining line (Berlin-Helmstedt) will require individual clearances from the Soviet Kommandatura in Berlin.

13 April 1948.   Soviet authorities incorporate East Berlin police force into that of Soviet zone.

20 April 1948.   Soviet Military Administration imposes additional restrictions on barge traffic to and from Berlin.

9 June 1948.   Soviet authorities tighten individual travel requirements between Soviet zone and Berlin.

10 June 1948. Soviets attempt removal of locomotives and rolling stock from American sector. Halted by armed intervention.

11 June 1948. Soviets block all rail traffic between West Germany and Berlin for two days.

12 June 1948. Soviets close Elbe River highway bridge for repairs.

16 June 1948. Soviet Commandant walks out of Allied Kommandatura.

18 June 1948. Western powers announce currency reform for West Germany but not Berlin.

19 June 1948. Soviet authorities suspend all passenger traffic into Berlin.

23 June 1948. Warsaw Conference of Soviet and satellite Foreign Ministers.

Soviets order currency reform throughout Soviet zone and all Berlin.

Western powers order own currency reform in Western sectors of Berlin.

First of Soviet inspired riots outside of Berlin City Hall.

24 June 1948. Soviets impose complete blockade on all forms of traffic into Berlin alleging "technical difficulties." All electric power flowing from East Berlin and Soviet zone into Berlin interrupted. All mail and parcel post service suspended.

25 June 1948. Airlift begins.

3 July 1948. Three Western Commanders-in-Chief call on Marshal Sokolovsky to protest Soviet action.

6 July 1948. United States, British and French note delivered to Moscow protesting blockade.

8 July 1948. Western powers suspend reparations deliveries to Soviet Union.

2–17 August 1948. Negotiations held in Moscow between Western Ambassadors and Marshal Stalin.

26 August 1948. Five thousand Communist demonstrators storm meeting of Berlin City Assembly in Soviet sector.

31 August–7 September 1948. Four Military Governors meet in Berlin but are unable to reach agreement on currency issue.

1 September 1948. Parliamentary Council meets in Bonn to draft constitution for West Germany.

6 September 1948. City Assembly moves from Soviet to British Sector because of riots and refusal of Soviet authorities to provide protection.

9 September 1948. Mass meeting of 300,000 in front of Reichstag in Berlin protests Communist actions.

14 September 1948. Western *aide-mémoire* delivered to Marshal Stalin.

18 September 1948. Soviet Union replies to Western *aide-mémoire* alleging "technical difficulties."

29 September 1948. Western powers refer Berlin dispute to United Nations.

4 October 1948. UN Security Council meeting in Paris begins consideration of Berlin dispute.

19 October 1948. Dr. Philip Jessup presents Allied case to Security Council.

25 October 1948. UN Security Council resolution on Berlin vetoed by Soviet Union.

30 November 1948. Communists hold "extraordinary session" of City Assembly in East Berlin and establish separate city government. Friedrich Ebert elected *Oberbürgermeister* of East Berlin.

2 December 1948. Soviet Kommandatura recognizes East Berlin rump government "as the only legal organ of city government" in Berlin.

5 December 1948. Elections in the three Western Sectors of Berlin.

7 December 1948. Ernst Reuter reelected *Oberbürgermeister* by outgoing city assembly.

21 December 1948. Western Commandants reorganize Kommandatura on tripartite basis, extending Soviets an invitation to return at any time.

30 January 1949. Marshal Stalin in an interview with Kingsbury Smith states conditions for Berlin settlement.

4 February 1949. West tightens counterblockade. All truck traffic to Soviet zone stopped.

2 March 1949. West Military Governors take exception to provision of draft constitution of Federal Republic incorporating West Berlin into Federal Republic.

19 March 1949. Communist People's Council approves Constitution for East German government.

20 March 1949. Western powers announce that West mark will be only legal tender in West Berlin.

16 April 1949. Airlift 24 hour tonnage record set: 12,940 tons of food and coal.

25 April 1949. East Berlin government issues decree expropriating all houses and land in East Berlin.

1 May 1949. All banks and insurance companies in East Berlin expropriated.

4 May 1949. Four-power representatives to Security Council announce agreement to lift blockade 12 May 1949.

8 May 1949. Basic Law adopted by West German Federal Republic.

12 May 1949. Blockade lifted after ten months and twenty-three days.

15 May 1949. General Lucius D. Clay leaves Germany. Replaced by John J. McCloy.

23 May 1949. Sixth Session of Council of Foreign Ministers meets in Paris.

30 May 1949. People's Council adopts Constitution for GDR.

15 June 1949. Electoral Law for West Germany allows West Berlin eight nonvoting delegates in the Bundestag.

20 June 1949. Council of Foreign Ministers agrees to abide by 4 May 1949 agreement on Berlin.

8 July 1949. Soviet authorities in East Germany close all principal crossing points between East and West zones limiting traffic to one autobahn.

12 July 1949. Western Military Commandants protest Soviet action.

14 July 1949.   Soviets lift travel restrictions.

6 August 1949.   Three Western Commandants recommend inclusion of West Berlin in Marshall Plan.

14 August 1949.   First elections held in Federal Republic.

15 September 1949.   Dr. Konrad Adenauer elected Federal Chancellor.

21 September 1949.   Federal Republic of Germany officially comes into being.

30 September 1949.   Berlin airlift terminated.

8 October 1949.   West Berlin City Assembly invites Federal Republic to make West Berlin its capital.

15 December 1949.   West Germany and Berlin admitted as full members of Marshall Plan. West Berlin awarded 95,000,000 DM.

26 January 1950.   Western Commandants protest Soviet processing slow-down of Western military traffic on Helmstedt autobahn. Slow-down temporarily lifted but reimposed 30 January 1950.

5 February 1950.   Autobahn slow-down lifted.

23 February 1950.   Autobahn slow-down reimposed.

6 June 1950.   East German government announces acceptance of Oder-Neisse boundary.

25 June 1950.   North Korean People's Army invades South Korea.

2–3 July 1950.   Two-day nuisance restrictions imposed by Soviets on flow of water and electricity into West Berlin.

9 August 1950.   Electoral law of East German government incorporates East Berlin.

21 September 1950.   East Germany shuts off flow of electricity to West Berlin. West Berlin power plant built under Marshall Plan assumes load.

25 September 1950.   Soviets interrupt barge traffic to West Berlin. British retaliate and hold all barges in British sector bound for East Berlin.

1 October 1950.   New Constitution for West Berlin goes into effect.

5 October 1950. Barge traffic resumed by mutual agreement.

1 February 1951. Soviet authorities take over Western enclave of West Staaken. British lodge protest.

7 March 1951. Allied Kommandatura waives right to review acts of Berlin City Assembly.

1 September 1951. Soviet authorities impose heavy road tax on vehicles to Berlin.

20 September 1951. East-West German trade agreement signed. Soviets remove road tax.

18 October 1951. Soviet authorities attempt to take over enclave of Steinstuecken in American sector. United States files protest.

23 October 1951. Soviet authorities withdraw from Steinstuecken.

9 January 1952. West Berlin incorporated economically with Federal Republic.

17 January 1952. West Berlin representation in Bundestag increased from 8 to 19.

9 April 1952. Soviet authorities deny admission of UN Commission investigating free all-German elections to East Berlin.

29 April 1952. Russian MIG–15's attack Air-France plane in corridor. Allies file protest.

8 May 1952. Soviet military authorities deny clearance to American and British vehicles on Berlin-Helmstedt autobahn.

14 May 1952. Secretary of State Acheson attacks travel ban and reaffirms American intention to remain in Berlin.

16 May 1952. Soviets lift travel ban.

27 May 1952. European Defense Community treaty signed in Paris. Communique reaffirms Allied rights in Berlin. East German authorities cut all telephone service between West Berlin and both East Berlin and the East zone. Border between East and West Berlin also closed.

30 May 1952. Allies protest closing of border to Soviet Union.

19 June 1952.   Soviet Union rejects allied note.

29 June 1952.   Secretary of State Acheson visits West Berlin and reaffirms American pledge to remain.

8 October 1952.   Russian MIG–15's buzz and fire at U.S. hospital plane in corridor.

3 December 1952.   East sector police hold up road traffic into East Berlin searching for "illegal" goods purchased in West Berlin. Allies protest action.

8 December 1952.   East sector police cease searches.

5 March 1953.   Death of Marshal Stalin.

12 March 1953.   Russian MIG–15's shoot down British Lincoln bomber on routine training flight in corridor. British government protests announcing that if necessary, fighter escort will accompany planes.

16–17 June 1953.   East German uprising.

10 July 1953.   United States offers to supply food to East Germany.

11 July 1953.   Soviet government rejects U.S. offer.

26 July 1953.   Western powers begin issuing food in West Berlin to all those from East Germany who come over to get it.

1 August 1953.   East German government prohibits travel from East Germany to Berlin.

26 August 1953.   Three Western High Commissioners ask Soviets to remove all barriers to free movement throughout Germany.

1 September 1953.   Soviets reply stating it is a matter for the two German governments to settle.

29 September 1953.   Ernst Reuter dies.

22 October 1953.   Walter Schreiber (CDU) elected *Oberbürgermeister* of Berlin.

25 January–18 February 1954.   Council of Foreign Ministers meets in Berlin to discuss German peace treaty.

25 March 1954.   Soviet Union announces full transfer of sovereignty to East German Government.

30 March 1954.   East German government states all military missions operating in East Germany must be accredited to it.

23 October 1954.   Paris Protocol provides for end of occupation and West Germany's admission to NATO.

5 December 1954.   West Berlin elections. Otto Suhr (SPD) becomes *Oberbürgermeister.*

30 March 1955.   Highway tolls on autobahn increased 1,000 percent.

5 May 1955.   Occupation of West Germany officially ends.

14 May 1955.   Warsaw Pact signed.

15 May 1955.   Four Allies conclude Austrian peace treaty.

18–23 July 1955.   Big Four Summit Conference at Geneva.

14 September 1955.   Soviet Union grants full sovereignty to East Germany.

20 September 1955.   Soviet Union transfers control of all traffic to Berlin to East German government with the exception of Allied military traffic.

28 September 1955.   Western Foreign Minister meeting in New York states that Soviets are still responsible for control of military traffic to Berlin.

18 October 1955.   Soviet Union acknowledges control over Western military traffic until signing of peace treaty.

29 November 1955.   East German police hold two U.S. Congressmen and wives four hours at sector crossing point. U.S. Commandant protests to Soviet Commandant.

16 December 1955.   NATO Council in Paris reaffirms Western position in Berlin.

1 February 1956.   President Eisenhower and Prime Minister Eden renew Berlin pledge.

18 February 1956. Western Ambassadors in Bonn protest presence of paramilitary East German organizations in East Berlin.

23 October 1956. Hungarian uprising.

4 October 1957. Soviets launch Sputnik I.

14 February 1958. Formal promulgation of Rapacki Plan for denuclearized zone in Central Europe.

5 October 1958. Fifth Republic founded in France.

27 November 1958. Soviet Union denounces occupation agreements and demands West Berlin be made a free city.

1 April 1959. Western Foreign Ministers meeting in Washington express determination to maintain rights in Berlin. Soviet Embassy in East Berlin demands U.S. planes observe 10,000 feet ceiling in corridor.

4 April 1959. U.S. note rejects Soviet claim of 10,000 feet ceiling.

11 May 1959. Geneva Conference of Foreign Ministers convenes. East Germans present as witnesses.

26 May 1959. Secretary Dulles dies of cancer.

5 August 1959. Geneva Conference adjourns without reaching an agreement.

15 September 1959. Khrushchev arrives in Washington.

24–27 September 1959. Khrushchev and Eisenhower meet at Camp David. Khrushchev withdraws Berlin ultimatum.

6 October 1959. East Germans raise Communist flags in West Berlin.

1–6 November 1959. Show of force by General Hamlett prevents repeat of flag incident in Berlin.

3 February–15 March 1960. East Germans interfere with actions of Potsdam Military Missions.

4 February 1960. Warsaw Pact meeting in Moscow announces intention to conclude separate peace treaty with East Germany.

1 March 1960. Soviet spokesmen renew claim to 10,000 feet ceiling.

9 March 1960. Eisenhower orders flights above 10,000 feet halted.

15 March 1960. Eisenhower and Adenauer in joint communique reaffirm intention to remain in Berlin.

2 April 1960. Khrushchev in Paris press conference states that separate peace treaty with East Germany would end Allied rights in Berlin.

1 May 1960. U–2 shot down over Soviet Union.

17 May 1960. Paris Summit talks collapse.

1–30 June 1960. Communist pressure forces canceling of Bundestag session scheduled for Berlin.

24 August 1960. East German government announces U.S. spy ring smashed.

30 August–4 September 1960. East Germans block autobahn to participants in Homeland Day Rally. West Germans also barred from East Berlin.

5 September 1960. GDR interferes with barge traffic to Berlin.

8 September 1960. Restrictions on entry of West Germans to East Berlin reimposed.

13 September 1960. GDR announces it will not recognize West German passports issued to Berliners.

18 September 1960. Apostolic Nuncio to Germany barred from East Berlin.

21 September 1960. GDR bans all diplomats accredited in Bonn from East Berlin.

26 September 1960. East Berlin officials close sector boundary for period of 24 hours.

1 October 1960. West German spokesmen threaten trade ban on East Germany if pressure on Berlin continued. GDR abruptly discontinues harassing tactics.

20 January 1961. John F. Kennedy inaugurated 35th President of the United States.

22 February 1961. Kennedy suggests meeting to Khrushchev.

4 May 1961. Khrushchev accepts Kennedy invitation. Vienna selected as conference site.

3–4 June 1961. President Kennedy and Premier Khrushchev confer in Vienna. Khrushchev presents *aide-mémoire* outlining new Soviet demands on 4 June.

8 June 1961. Soviets protest meeting of Bundesrat in Berlin. Meeting canceled.

10 June 1961. Soviets publish *aide-mémoire*.

14 June 1961. Senator Mansfield advocates "third way" between East and West positions on Berlin.

23 June 1961. Washington announces first of series of reviews of defense posture.

8 July 1961. Khrushchev announces 25 percent increase in Soviet defense budget. Refugees from Soviet zone continue to increase.

17 July 1961. Torschlusspanik reported in East Germany.

30 July 1961. Senator Fulbright in TV interview questions why GDR has not closed border.

2–11 August 1961. GDR moves against "border crossers." Tightens restrictions. Allied note of 3 August goes unanswered.

3–4 August 1961. Warsaw Pact leaders meet in Moscow.

5–7 August 1961. Western Foreign Ministers meet in Paris.

13 August 1961. East German government closes sector border between East and West Berlin.

16 August 1961. Mayor Brandt requests political action to reopen border before mass meeting of 250,000 in Berlin. (Popular morale plummets.)

18 August 1961. Washington announces Berlin garrison will be reinforced.

19 August 1961. Vice President Johnson arrives in Berlin.

23 August 1961. East Germans reduce number of crossing points to seven; only one for Allied forces.

29 August 1961. Adenauer writes Kennedy about rise of neutralism in West Germany.

30 August 1961. Kennedy announces return of General Clay to Berlin.

17 September 1961. West German elections; CDU loses majority. Final returns give CDU 242 seats in Bundestag, SPD 190 seats and FDP 67.

19 September 1961. General Clay arrives in Berlin.

21 September 1961. Clay flies by helicopter to Steinstuecken.

26 September 1961. President Kennedy addresses UN. Says U.S. committed to no rigid formulas in Berlin.

22 October 1961. Mr. Allen Lightner, U.S. Deputy Chief of Mission in Berlin denied access to East Berlin.

27–28 October 1961. U.S. and Soviet tanks confront each other at Checkpoint Charlie for sixteen hours.

20 November 1961. Chancellor Adenauer visits Washington for discussions on Berlin.

25 November 1961. President Kennedy receives Aleksie Adzhubei, Khrushchev's son-in-law, for an extended interview on U.S.–Soviet relations.

14 February 1962. Soviets begin harassing Western planes in Berlin air corridors.

11 March 1962. Secretary Rusk and Soviet Foreign Minister Gromyko meet in Geneva.

11 April 1962. Washington announces General Clay's mission in Berlin has ended.

16 April 1962. Rusk–Dobrynin talks begin in Washington.

8 May 1962. General Clay leaves Berlin.

APPENDIX III

The Moscow Proposals, 1943

STATE DEPARTMENT MEMORANDUM PRESENTED
BY SECRETARY HULL TO THE FOREIGN MINISTERS'
CONFERENCE, MOSCOW, OCTOBER 23, 1943.*

IT IS PROPOSED that, in accordance with the declarations of the principal United Nations regarding the unconditional surrender of Germany, the terms of surrender to be accepted unconditionally by Germany shall be previously agreed upon jointly by the Governments of Great Britain, the U.S.S.R. and the United States; and that in coming to this agreement the three Governments be guided by the following principles:

1. That an instrument be signed which contains an admission of the total defeat of Germany.

2. That the instrument be signed both by an authorized agent of whatever German Government may exercise power *de jure* or *de facto* and by an authorized agent of the military authorities.

* The original of this document is located among the papers of President Roosevelt in the Franklin D. Roosevelt Library at Hyde Park, New York. It was sent by Mr. Cecil W. Gray, a Foreign Service Officer assigned to the Office of the Secretary of State, to Miss Grace Tully, the President's Secretary, on November 11, 1943. Attached to it was the following note: "Secretary Hull phoned that the President desired this document this afternoon. We apologize for its appearance but it is the only one we have to send you on this short notice."

The document is reproduced in: U.S. Department of State, *Foreign Relations of the United States—The Conferences at Cairo and Tehran* (Washington: Government Printing Office, 1961), pp. 183–86.

3. That the instrument empower the United Nations to exercise all the rights of an occupying power throughout Germany.

4. That the instrument bind the German Government to deliver, without reciprocity, all prisoners of war and such other nationals of United Nations states as may be held in detention.

5. That the instrument empower the United Nations to regulate the demobilization of the German armed forces.

6. That the instrument stipulate the release of the political prisoners held by the German Government, the abandonment of the concentration camps and the delivery to agents designated by the United Nations of persons who may subsequently be accused of actions within the United Nations' definition of war crimes.

7. That the instrument bind the German Government to the continued maintenance of all agencies of economic control, together with their staffs, complete records and other equipment, for subsequent disposition by the United Nations authorities.

8. That the instrument empower the United Nations to supervise the economic activities of Germany.

9. That the instrument bind the German Government to deliver, according to the stipulations of the United Nations High Command, all arms and armaments, other military and naval stores, and stocks of raw materials wherever located.

A. Treatment of Germany During the Armistice Period

Inter-Allied Control. It is proposed that, during the armistice period a strict international control—military, political and economic—be maintained; and that this control be exercised through an inter-Allied Control Commission charged with the carrying out of the terms of surrender and the policies agreed upon by Great Britain, the U.S.S.R. and the United States.

The Occupation of Germany. For the purpose of securing the execution of surrender terms and assuring the creation of conditions for a permanent system of security it is recommended that the occupation of Germany be effected by contingents of British, Soviet and American forces.

Local Government. It is recommended that policy with respect to local government (functions, agencies, personnel) be based upon the principle of minimum interference with established mechanisms and procedures. All Nazi government officials, in whatever capacity, should be promptly eliminated and every vestige of the Nazi regime should be uprooted.

It is recommended that effective supervision of local government be maintained by the occupation authorities and the Control Commission through the media of:

1. Mandatory and veto power over acts of key administrators.
2. Control of personnel administration.

3. Control over the administrative functions of the governmental authorities.

Treatment of National Socialist Party. The National Socialist Party should be dissolved forthwith. The functions of certain existing structures, such as those dealing with employment and social insurance, might be continued temporarily, subject to a thorough-going elimination of Nazi and other objectionable elements and to effective supervision by the occupation authorities.

Reparations. It is recommended that the principle be recognized that it is the duty of Germany to provide reparations for the physical damages inflicted by its armed forces upon the U.S.S.R. and other Allied and occupied countries; and that the forms, extent, and distribution of such reparations be determined through a Commission on German Reparations, consisting initially of representatives of the Governments of Great Britain, the U.S.S.R. and the United States, with provision for the representation of other directly interested governments.

Disarmament. For the purpose of providing a basis for a general security system, it is proposed that, on the cessation of hostilities:

1. All German armed forces should be disarmed and demobilized;

2. All arms, ammunition and military equipment and facilities wherever located should be surrendered to the United Nations;

3. Captured and surrendered arms should be scrapped;

4. Manufacture of war material should cease immediately;

5. For the armistice period at least the control of arms manufacturing facilities, as well as all economic facilities, in Germany should be transferred to the United Nations.

Among measures of permanent control of German military potential, the following are suggested for consideration:

1. Germany should be denied a standing army and military training should be prohibited;

2. The German General Staff should be disbanded and should not be reconstituted in any form;

3. The military caste system in all its phases should be eliminated;

4. Arms manufacturing facilities in Germany should be dismantled;

5. The importation and manufacture in Germany of arms, ammunition, and implements of war, and materials essential to their manufacture, including all types of aircraft, should be prohibited;

6. A permament audit and inspection system should be established and maintained under supervision of the United Nations.

B. PERMANENT STATUS OF GERMANY

Problem of German Political Unity. At the present time there is no indication whether the effect of defeat will be to strengthen the trend towards political unity within Germany, or whether the reaction against the defeated Hitler regime will lead to emergence of a spontaneous movement for the creation of several separate states out of the territory of the present Reich. Certain vital phases of this question continue under study.

Democratic Government. It is the view of the American Government that, in the long run, the most desirable form of government for Germany would be a broadly based democracy operating under a bill of rights to safeguard the civil and political liberties of the individual. Among the conditions required for the success of a new democratic experiment in Germany would be: a tolerable standard of living; restriction of measures of control to the requirements of general security; harmony of policy and purpose among the British, Soviet and American Governments. Since the administration of Germany will be controlled by the inter-Allied mechanisms during the armistice period, it is during that period that the bases of a democratic regime should be laid. Early steps should be taken to restore freedom of speech, religion, and of the press, freedom to organize political parties other than of Nazi-Facist doctrine, cultural associations and trade unions. When conditions permit, preparations should be made for the holding of free elections for the creation of a central German Government to which the occupation authorities would gradually transfer their responsibility for the internal administration of the country.

Decentralization. It is the view of the American Government that the potential threat of Germany to general security might be lessened through decentralization of the German political structure, through assigning to the federal units control over a wide range of administrative functions, and through encouraging any movement which may emerge within Germany in favor of the diminution of Prussian domination over the Reich.

Frontiers. This is a matter which should come within the purview of the general settlement.

APPENDIX IV

The *Iowa* Conference

MINUTES OF THE PRESIDENT'S MEETING WITH THE JOINT CHIEFS OF STAFF, NOVEMBER 19, 1943, 2 P.M., ADMIRAL'S CABIN, *U.S.S. IOWA* *

· · ·

3. SPHERES OF RESPONSIBILITY IN GERMANY

THE PRESIDENT observed that in the memorandum he received from Admiral Leahy on behalf of the Joint Chiefs of Staff asking for guidance regarding spheres of influence as a result of a European-wide RANKIN,** the paper makes certain suppositions without actually saying so. He felt that whatever territorial dispositions were made should conform to geographic subdivisions of Germany. He said that the Soviet Government will offer no objection to breaking up Germany after the war, that practically speaking there should be three German states after the war, possibly five. He said (1) we might take southern Germany, Baden, Wurtenburg [Wuerttem-

* Present were President Roosevelt; Harry Hopkins; Fleet Admiral William Leahy; Fleet Admiral Ernest J. King; General George C. Marshall; General H. H. Arnold; Rear Admiral Wilson Brown, Naval Aide to the President; and Captain Forrest B. Royal (USN), Secretary to the Joint Chiefs of Staff. The original copy of these minutes is contained in the files of the Joint Chiefs of Staff in Washington. It is reproduced in *The Conferences at Cairo and Tehran, op. cit.*, pp. 248–61.
** Code name for Allied plan in the event of a sudden German military collapse.

berg], Bavaria, everything south of the Rhine [Main?]. This area forms a
sort of southern state. (2) Take everything north and west of that area, including Hamburg and Hanover, and so forth, up to and including Berlin to
form a second state, and the northeastern part, that is, Prussia, Pomerania,
and south, to form a third state. He believed these general divisions were a
logical basis for splitting up Germany. Especially was this so because the
first or southern state was largely Roman Catholic; the northwestern portion
is Protestant, while it might be said that the religion of the northeastern part
is Prussianism. He felt that Marshal Stalin might "okay" such a division. He
believed that the Chiefs of Staff would want to make a European RANKIN
conform to such a division. Actually the British wanted the northwestern
part of Germany and would like to see the U.S. take France and Germany
south of the Moselle River. He said he did not like that arrangement. We do
not want to be concerned with reconstituting France. France is a British
"baby." United States is not popular in France at the present time. The
British should have France, Luxembourg, Belgium, Baden, Bavaria, and
Wurtenburg. The occupation of these places should be British. The United
States should take northwest Germany. We can get our ships into such ports
as Bremen and Hamburg, also Norway and Denmark, and we should go as
far as Berlin. The Soviets could then take the territory to the east thereof.
The United States should have Berlin. The British plan for the United States
to have southern Germany, and he (the President) did not like it.

GENERAL MARSHALL agreed that the matter should be gone into again. He
said the proposals in the paper before the President had devolved from a
consideration of the United States concentration on the right of the OVER-
LORD line from England. The conceptions for occupation were primarily
based on military considerations of OVERLORD. He said he saw a frank
approach to the matter in the paper from three points of view: (1) a normal
OVERLORD; (2) a partial OVERLORD, with some fighting; and (3)
RANKIN Case "C" (total collapse of Germany before OVERLORD got
underway).

ADMIRAL KING observed that if OVERLORD should be underway when
Germany collapsed, we would necessarily have a cross-over of our forces
under the President's plan. Particularly would this be so if we should have
reached the line of the Seine.

GENERAL MARSHALL said that when OVERLORD was launched we must
have U.S. forces on the right from a logistics point of view.

ADMIRAL KING observed that while the President's idea regarding areas
of occupation did not present insuperable difficulties, nevertheless there was
a problem which would have to be worked out.

GENERAL MARSHALL said if a break comes, we could split our forces into
two parts.

THE PRESIDENT observed that there were no ports south of Hamburg and
Bremen until the Dutch ports are reached.

ADMIRAL KING felt that the military plans for OVERLORD were so far

developed that it would not be practicable to accept any change in OVER-
LORD deployment.

GENERAL MARSHALL said that the whole matter goes back to the question
of ports in England. If we stick to OVERLORD we must have a scheme for
disengaging OVERLORD at any stage of development in order to comply
with the political considerations of occupation outlined by the President.

THE PRESIDENT said it was his idea we should use as many troops from
the United States in the occupation of Germany as possible. These can go
around Scotland.

ADMIRAL KING felt that we must have a special occupational army, in a
particular command, earmarked for occupation of northwest Germany.

GENERAL MARSHALL said that the OVERLORD conception was that the
United States forces would be progressing on the right and those should be
the divisions first to come home.

THE PRESIDENT said he felt that the divisions now in North Africa, Sicily
and Italy should be the divisions first to be sent back to the United States.
He said one reason for the political "headache" in France was that De Gaulle
hoped to be one mile behind the troops in taking over the government. He
felt that we should get out of France and Italy as soon as possible, letting the
British and the French handle their own problem together. There would
definitely be a race for Berlin. We may have to put the United States divisions into Berlin as soon as possible.

ADMIRAL LEAHY observed it would be easy to go directly into northwest
Germany. The problem of occupational troops proceeding to northwest Germany would certainly be less difficult than their fighting their way there
across the intervening territory from northwestern France.

GENERAL MARSHALL observed that it was most important to keep commands in homogeneous control.

THE PRESIDENT said he envisaged a railroad invasion of Germany with
little or no fighting.

GENERAL MARSHALL said he assumed there would be a difficult lack of
rolling stock and the land advance would have to be largely made on a
motor truck basis.

MR. HOPKINS suggested that we be ready to put an airborne division into
Berlin two hours after the collapse of Germany.

In reply to a question from the President as to Admiral Leahy's opinion
of the occupations area divisions, from a State Department point of view,
ADMIRAL LEAHY said that he felt we should definitely get out of France as
soon as possible. We should accept any difficulties in order to get out of
France at the earliest possible time. If we want to let De Gaulle have France,
all well and good. However, whatever troops there are in France at the time
of German collapse will certainly have to stay in order to supervise any
elections. General De Gaulle wants to start the French Government right
now. Possibly there will be civil war in France. The British should clear up

such a condition. On the other hand, it would be much easier for the United States to handle conditions in Germany. The Germans are easier to handle than would be the French under the chaotic conditions that could be expected in France.

THE PRESIDENT said he personally envisaged an occupational force of about one million United States troops. He expanded on the policy of "quarantine." He said that the four United Nations by their police power could, if necessary, maintain order in Europe by the "quarantine" method. For instance, we do not want to use our troops in settling local squabbles in such a place as Yugoslavia. We could use the Army and Navy as an economic blockade and preclude ingress or egress to any area where disorder prevailed.

In reply to a question from General Marshall as to how long the President contemplated it would be necessary to maintain one million men in Europe, THE PRESIDENT replied for at least one year, maybe two.

ADMIRAL LEAHY observed that there will certainly be civil wars in many parts of Europe when the Germans let go. If the French divisions could be properly controlled, they could doubtless put down civil war in France. If De Gaulle could control the troops, he could put down the civil war—but what then? France will require food and munitions. THE PRESIDENT said we may definitely have to keep certain divisions in France. He felt that Holland was no problem. The Queen will return there and all will be well. On the other hand, Belgium is a big question—it is a two-language country. Possibly a buffer state between Germany and France will be necessary. This buffer state could run from northern France, say, Calais, Lille, and Ardenne[s], through to Alsace and Lorraine—in other words, from Switzerland to the seacoast. This would be a single buffer state.

ADMIRAL LEAHY observed that this was also at one time a German proposal and called the interdicted zone.

THE PRESIDENT observed that if we take the RANKIN paper proposed by COSSAC, the British would undercut us in every move we make in the southern occupational area proposed for the United States. He said that it was quite evident that British political considerations were in the back of the proposals in this paper.

GENERAL MARSHALL said that the paper in the President's hands as regards occupational zones works out logically. There would be less entanglement in forces, supply lines would be shorter and more direct. The paper was worked out on that basis.

ADMIRAL KING said that it was evident from any stage of OVERLORD it is imperative to plan for what operations should be necessary in order to switch to the occupation areas proposed by the President.

· · ·

ADMIRAL LEAHY observed that the conference had been of great benefit to the Chiefs of Staff.

THE PRESIDENT then reiterated his idea of a U.S. occupational zone for Germany and drew out the proposed line of demarcation on a map. This map had been obtained from Rear Admiral Brown and was handed to General Marshall at the conclusion of the meeting.

APPENDIX V

Proceedings at Tehran

TRIPARTITE POLITICAL MEETING, DECEMBER 1, 1943,
6 P.M., CONFERENCE ROOM, SOVIET EMBASSY, TEHRAN.*

PRESENT

United States	United Kingdom	Soviet Union
President Roosevelt	Prime Minister Churchill	Marshal Stalin
Mr. Hopkins	Foreign Secretary Eden	Foreign Commissar Molo-
Mr. Harriman	Sir Archibald Clark Kerr	tov
Mr. Bohlen	Major Birse	Mr. Pavlov

· · ·

Turning to the question of Germany, THE PRESIDENT said that the question was whether or not to split up Germany.

MARSHAL STALIN replied that they preferred the dismemberment of Germany.

THE PRIME MINISTER said he was all for it but that he was primarily more interested in seeing Prussia, the evil core of German militarism, separated from the rest of Germany.

THE PRESIDENT said he had a plan that he had thought up some months ago for the division of Germany in five parts. These five parts were:

1. All Prussia to be rendered as small and weak as possible.
2. Hanover and Northwest section.
3. Saxony and Leipzig area.
4. Hesse-Darmstadt
   Hesse-Kassel and the area South of the Rhine.
5. Bavaria, Baden, and Wurtemburg [Wuerttemberg].

He proposed that these five areas should be self-governed and that there should be two regions under United Nations or some form of International control. These were:

* Minutes prepared by Charles Bohlen. Reprinted in *Conferences at Cairo and Tehran, op. cit.*, pp. 596–604.

385

1. The area of the Kiel Canal and the City of Hamburg.
2. The Ruhr and the Saar, the latter to be used for the benefit of all Europe.

THE PRIME MINISTER said, to use an American expression, "The President had said a mouthful."

He went on to say that in his mind there were two considerations, one destructive and the other constructive.

1. The separation of Prussia from the rest of the Reich.
2. To detach Bavaria, Baden, Wurtemburg [Wuerttemberg] and the Palatinate from the rest of Germany and make them part of the Confederation of the Danube.

MARSHAL STALIN said he felt if Germany was to be dismembered, it should really be dismembered, and it was neither a question of the division of Germany in five or six states and two areas as the President suggested. However, he said he preferred the President's plan to the suggestion of Mr. Churchill.

He felt that to include German areas within the framework of large confederations would merely offer an opportunity to the German elements to revive a great State.

He went on to say that he did not believe there was a difference among Germans; that all German soldiers fought like devils and the only exception was the Austrians.

He said that the Prussian Officers and Staffs should be eliminated, but as to the inhabitants, he saw little difference between one part of Germany and another.

He said he was against the idea of confederation as artificial and one that would not last in that area, and in addition would provide opportunity for the German elements to control.

Austria, for example, had existed as an independent state and should again. Hungary, Rumania, and Bulgaria likewise.

THE PRESIDENT said he agreed with the Marshal, particularly in regard to the absence of differences between Germans. He said fifty years ago there had been a difference but since the last war it was no longer so.

He said the only difference was that in Bavaria and the Southern part of Germany there was no officer cast[e] as there had been in Prussia. He agreed with Marshal Stalin that the Austrians were an exception.

THE PRIME MINISTER said he did not wish to be considered as against the dismemberment of Germany—quite the contrary, but he felt to separate the parts above would merely mean that sooner or later they will reunite into one nation and that the main thing was to keep Germany divided if only for fifty years.

MARSHAL STALIN repeated what he had said as to the danger of the reunification of Germany. He said no matter what measures were adopted there would always be a strong urge on the part of the Germans to unite.

He said it was a great mistake to unite Hungary with Germans since the Germans would merely control the Hungarians, and to create large frameworks within which the Germans could operate would be very dangerous.

He felt the whole purpose of any international organization to preserve peace would be to neutralize this tendency on the part of the Germans and apply against them economic and other measures, and if necessary, force, to prevent their unification and revival. He said the victorious nations must have the strength to beat the Germans if they ever start on the path of a new war.

THE PRIME MINISTER inquired whether Marshal Stalin contemplated a Europe composed of little states, disjoined, separated and weak.

MARSHAL STALIN replied not Europe but Germany

He supposed for example that Poland would be a strong country, and France, and Italy likewise; that Rumania and Bulgaria would remain as they always had; small States.

THE PRESIDENT remarked Germany had been less dangerous to civilization when in 107 provinces.

THE PRIME MINISTER said he hoped for larger units.

THE PRIME MINISTER then returned to the question of Poland and said he was not asking for any agreement nor was he set on the matter but he had a statement which he would like to have the Marshal examine.

This statement suggested that Poland should obtain equal compensation in the West, including Eastern Prussia and frontiers on the Oder to compensate for the areas which would be in the Soviet Union.

THE PRESIDENT interjected to say that one question in regard to Germany remained to be settled and that was what body should be empowered to study carefully the question of dismemberment of Germany.

It was agreed that the European Advisory Committee [Commission] would undertake this task.

BIBLIOGRAPHY

The documents, books and articles listed below have been useful to me. They by no means constitute a complete bibliography of all works on Germany and Berlin.

OFFICIAL PUBLICATIONS

Berlin Magistrat. *Berlin im Neuaufbau: Das erste Jahr.* Ein Rechenschaftsbericht des Magistrats der Stadt Berlin. Berlin: 1946.

Berlin Senat. *Berlin: Behauptung von Freiheit und Selbstverwaltung, 1946–1948.* Berlin: Heinz Spitzing Verlag, 1959. (Good bibliography.)

———. *Berlin: Facts and Figures.* Berlin: Berlin Press and Information Agency, 1959.

———. *Berlin: Kampf um Freiheit und Selbstverwaltung 1945–1946.* Berlin: Heinz Spitzing Verlag, 1961. (Good bibliography.)

———. *Berliner Schicksal 1945–1952.* Berlin: 1952.

Berlin Statistisches Landesamt. *Statistisches Jahrbuch Berlin.* Berlin: Kulturbuch-Verlag, 1960.

BYRNES, JAMES F. *Restatement of United States Policy in Germany. Address by the Secretary of State Delivered in Stuttgart, Germany, September 6, 1946.* State Department Publication 2616. Washington: Government Printing Office, 1946.

CLINE, RAY S. *Washington Command Post: The Operations Division.* Office of the Chief of Military History. Department of the Army. Washington: Government Printing Office, 1951.

EHRMAN, JOHN. *Grand Strategy.* Vol. V, August, 1943–September, 1944. London: H. M. Stationery Office, 1956.

———. *Grand Strategy.* Vol. VI, October, 1944–August, 1945. London: H. M. Stationery Office, 1956.

German Democratic Republic. *Memorandum of the Government of the German Democratic Republic on the Berlin Question.* Berlin: 1959.

German Federal Republic. *The Bulletin—A Weekly Survey of German Affairs.* Press and Information Office. Bonn: 1952–1963.

———. *Facts About Germany.* (2d ed.) Press and Information Office, Wiesbaden: 1959.

———. *The Flight from the Soviet Zone.* Ministry of Exiles, Refugees, and War Victims. Bonn: 1959.

———. *Four Power Conference in Berlin, 1954: Speeches and Documents.* Press and Information Office. Berlin: 1954.

———. German Information Center. *Berlin: Crisis and Challenge.* New York: 1962.

———. *Germany Reports.* Press and Information Office. Wiesbaden: 1953.

———. Ministry of All-German Affairs. *Die Flucht aus der Sowjetzone und die Sperrmassnahmen des Kommunistischen Regimes vom 13. August 1961 in Berlin.* Bonn: 1961.

———. *The Soviet Zone of Germany.* Ministry of All-German Affairs. Cologne: 1960.

Great Britain. *An Account of Events Leading Up to a Reference of the Berlin Question to the United Nations.* London: H. M. Stationery Office, 1948.

———. *Berlin and The Problem of German Reunification.* London: British Information Services, 1961.

———. *Conference of Foreign Ministers at Geneva, 1959.* London: H. M. Stationery Office, 1959.

———. *Documents About the Future of Germany.* London: H. M. Stationery Office, 1959.

———. *Selected Documents on Germany and the Question of Berlin 1944–1961.* London: H. M. Stationery Office, 1961.

GREENFIELD, KENT R. (ed.). *Command Decisions.* Office of the Chief of Military History. Department of the Army. Washington: Government Printing Office, 1960.

MARSHALL, GEORGE CATLETT. *The Problems of European Survival and German and Austrian Peace Settlements: Address by the Secretary of State.* State Department Publication 2990. Washington: Government Printing Office, 1947.

MATLOFF, MAURICE. *Strategic Planning for Coalition Warfare, 1943–1944.* Office of the Chief of Military History. Department of the Army. Washington: Government Printing Office, 1959.

NOTTER, HARLEY A. *Postwar Foreign Policy Preparation: 1939–1945.* Department of State. Washington: Government Printing Office, 1949.

PLISCHKE, ELMER. *Berlin: Development of Its Government and Administration.* Historical Section. Office of the U.S. High Commissioner for Germany. Bonn: 1952.

POGUE, FORREST C. *The Supreme Command.* Office of the Chief of Military History. Department of the Army. Washington: Government Printing Office, 1954.

ROTTMANN, JOACHIM. *Der Viermächte-Status Berlins.* Bundesministerium für Gesamtdeutsche Fragen. Bonn: 1959.

Union of Soviet Socialist Republics. *Stalin's Correspondence with Churchill Attlee, Roosevelt and Truman, 1941–1945.* New York: E. P. Dutton & Co., 1958.

———. *The Soviet Union and the Berlin Question.* Moscow: 1948.

U.S. Army. *Berlin*. Public Information Office, Berlin Command. Berlin: 1954.

U.S. Congress. *Congressional Record*. Washington: Government Printing Office, 1949–1963.

U.S. Congress, House of Representatives. *Special Study Mission to Berlin*. Committee Print, Committee on Foreign Affairs. Washington: Government Printing Office, 1959.

————. *Terminating the State of War Between the United States and the Government of Germany: Report to Accompany H.J. Res. 289*. Committee on Foreign Affairs. Washington: Government Printing Office, 1951.

U.S. Congress, Senate. *Administration of National Security—Basic Issues*. Committee on Government Operations. Washington: Government Printing Office, 1963.

————. *Berlin in a Changing World*. Report of Senator Mike Mansfield, *et al.*, to the Committee on Foreign Relations. Washington: Government Printing Office, 1963.

————. *Documents on Germany, 1944–1959*. Committee Print, Committee on Foreign Relations. Washington: Government Printing Office, 1959.

————. *Interlocking Subversion in Government Departments*. (The Harry Dexter White Papers). Committee on the Judiciary. Washington: Government Printing Office, 1956.

U.S. Office of Military Government for Germany. *Military Government Information Bulletin*. Berlin: 1945–1949.

————. *A Survey of Berlin*. Berlin: 1950.

U.S. Office of Military Government, U.S. Sector, Berlin. *A Four Year Report —July 1, 1945–September 1, 1949*. Berlin: 1949.

U.S. Department of State. *Berlin—City Between Two Worlds*. Washington: Government Printing Office, 1960.

————. *Berlin—1961*. Washington: Government Printing Office, 1961.

————. *The Berlin Crisis: A Report of the Moscow Discussions, 1948*. Washington: Government Printing Office, 1948.

————. *Department of State Bulletin*. Washington: Government Printing Office, 1958–1963.

————. *Documents on German Foreign Policy, 1918–1945*. Series D. 12 vols. Washington: Government Printing Office, 1948–1962.

————. *Foreign Relations of the United States: Conference of Berlin (Potsdam) 1945*. 2 vols. Washington: Government Printing Office, 1960.

————. *Foreign Relations of the United States: Conferences at Cairo and Tehran 1943*. Washington: Government Printing Office, 1961.

————. *Foreign Relations of the United States: Conferences at Malta and Yalta–1945*. Washington: Government Printing Office, 1955.

————. *Foreign Relations of the United States: Diplomatic Papers. 1941*, Vol. I. Washington: Government Printing Office, 1958.

————. *Foreign Relations of the United States: Diplomatic Papers. 1941*, Vol. IV. Washington: Government Printing Office, 1956.

――――. *Foreign Relations of the United States: Diplomatic Papers.* 1942, Vol. I. Washington: Government Printing Office, 1960.

――――. *Foreign Relations of the United States: Diplomatic Papers.* 1942, Vol. III. Washington: Government Printing Office, 1961.

――――. *Germany 1947–1949: The Story in Documents.* Washington: Government Printing Office, 1950.

――――. *Making the Peace Treaties, 1941–1947.* Washington: Government Printing Office, 1947.

――――. *Nazi Conspiracy and Aggression.* 10 vols. Washington: Government Printing Office, 1946.

――――. *Occupation of Germany, Policy and Progress, 1945–1946.* Washington: Government Printing Office, 1947.

――――. *The Soviet Note on Berlin: An Analysis.* Washington: Government Printing Office, 1959.

――――. *Toward the Peace, Documents.* Washington: Government Printing Office, 1945.

Trial of the Major War Criminals Before the International Military Tribunal. 42 vols. Nuremberg: 1947–1949.

Trials of War Criminals Before the Nuremberg Military Tribunals. 15 vols. Washington: Government Printing Office, 1951–1952.

United Nations. *Demographic Yearbook—1960.* Statistical Office, Department of Economics and Social Affairs. New York: 1960.

WOODWARD, SIR LLEWELLYN. *British Foreign Policy in the Second World War.* London: H.M. Stationery Office, 1962.

BOOKS, DIARIES, AND MEMOIRS

Historical Background

ARENDT, HANNAH. *The Origins of Totalitarianism.* New York: Harcourt, Brace & World, 1951.

BARRACLOUGH, GEOFFREY. *The Origins of Modern Germany.* (2d ed.) Oxford: Basil Blackwell, 1947.

BELOFF, MAX. *The Foreign Policy of Soviet Russia, 1929–1941.* 2 vols. London: Oxford University Press, 1947–1949.

BRACHER, KARL DIETRICH. *Die Aufloesung der Weimarer Republik.* (2d ed.) Stuttgart: Institut für Politische Wissenschaft, 1957.

――――, *et al. Die nationalsozialistische Machtergreifung.* Köln: Westdeutscher Verlag, 1960.

BRECHT, ARNOLD. *Prelude to Silence.* New York: Oxford University Press, 1944.

BULLOCK, ALAN. *Hitler: A Study in Tyranny.* New York: Harper & Bros., 1953.

CARR, E. H. *German-Soviet Relations between the Two World Wars, 1919–1939.* Baltimore: The Johns Hopkins Press, 1951.

CARR, E. H. *The Twenty Years Crisis.* London: Macmillan, 1939.

CARSTEN, F. L., *The Origins of Prussia.* Oxford: Clarendon Press, 1954.

CLARK, R. T. *The Fall of The German Republic.* London: Allen and Unwin, 1935.

CRAIG, GORDON A. *The Politics of The Prussian Army: 1640–1945.* New York: Oxford University Press, 1956.

DAHLMANN–WAITZ. *Quellenkunde der deutschen Geschichte.* 2 vols. Leipzig: K. F. Koehler, 1931–1932.

DEHIO, LUDWIG. *Germany and World Politics in the 20th Century.* New York: Alfred A. Knopf, 1959.

DICKINSON, ROBERT E. *Germany—A General and Regional Geography,* London: Methuen & Co., Ltd., 1953.

DILL, MARSHALL. *Germany—A Modern History.* Ann Arbor: University of Michigan Press, 1961.

EYCK, ERICH. *History of The Weimar Republic.* Vol. I. Cambridge, Mass.: Harvard University Press, 1962.

FAY, SIDNEY B. *The Rise of Brandenburg-Prussia to 1786.* New York: Henry Holt & Co., 1937.

FIX, W. *Die Territorialgeschichte des Preussischen Staates.* Berlin: Simon Schropp, 1869.

FONTANE, THEODOR. *Havelland.* Stuttgart and Berlin: Cotta, 1914.

———. *Oderland.* Stuttgart and Berlin: Cotta, 1907.

———. *Spreeland.* Stuttgart and Berlin: Cotta, 1903.

GOOCH, GEORGE P. *Germany.* New York: Scribners, 1925.

———. *Studies in German History.* London: Longmans, Green & Co., 1948.

HALL, WALTER P. *Europe in the Twentieth Century.* New York: Appleton-Century-Crofts, 1957.

HALPERIN, S. WILLIAM. *Germany Tried Democracy.* New York: Crowell, 1946.

HENDERSON, SIR NEVILE. *Failure of a Mission: Berlin 1937–1939.* New York: G. P. Putnam's Sons, 1940.

KOHN, HANS. *German History—Some New German Views.* Boston: The Beacon Press, 1954.

———. *The Mind of Germany.* New York: Charles Scribner's Sons, 1958.

———. *West Germany: New Era for German People.* New York: Foreign Policy Association, 1958.

KRIEGER, LEONARD. *The German Idea of Freedom.* Boston: The Beacon Press, 1957.

MEINECKE, FRIEDRICH. *The German Catastrophe.* Cambridge, Mass.: Harvard University Press, 1950.

NEUMANN, FRANZ. *Behemoth: The Structure and Practice of National Socialism.* New York: Oxford University Press, 1942.

PINSON, KOPPEL S. *Modern Germany. Its History and Civilization.* New York: Macmillan, 1954.

ROSENBERG, ARTHUR. *The Birth of the German Republic*. London: Oxford University Press, 1931.

ROTHFELS, HANS. *German Opposition To Hitler*. Chicago: Regnery, 1948.

SCHECHTMANN, JOSEPH B. *European Population Transfers, 1939–1945*. New York: Oxford University Press, 1946.

SCHULTZ, JOACHIM. *Die letzten 30 Tage—aus dem Kriegstagebuch des O.K.W.* Stuttgart: Steingrüben Verlag, 1951.

SHIRER, WILLIAM L. *Berlin Diary*. New York: Alfred A. Knopf, 1943.

————. *End of a Berlin Diary*. New York: Alfred A. Knopf, 1947.

————. *The Rise and Fall of the Third Reich*. New York: Simon and Schuster, 1960.

SZAZ, ZOLTAN MICHAEL. *Germany's Eastern Frontiers*. Chicago: Regnery, 1960.

TAYLOR, A. J. P. *The Course of German History*. New York: Hamilton, 1946.

TAYLOR, TELFORD. *Sword and Swastika*. New York: Simon and Schuster, 1952.

TREVOR–ROPER, H. R. *The Last Days of Hitler*. (3d ed.) New York: Collier, 1962.

VALENTIN, VEIT. *The German People*. New York: Alfred A. Knopf, 1946.

WHEELER–BENNETT, JOHN. *The Nemesis of Power*. New York: St. Martin's Press, 1954.

WILMOT, CHESTER. *The Struggle for Europe*. New York: Harper & Bros., 1952.

Wartime Agreements

AMBRUSTER, HOWARD WATSON. *Treason's Peace*. New York: Beachhurst, 1947.

ARMSTRONG, ANNE. *Unconditional Surrender: The Impact of the Casablanca Policy on World War II*. New Brunswick: Rutgers University Press, 1962.

BALDWIN, HANSON W. *Great Mistakes of the War*. New York: Harper & Bros., 1950.

BILAINKIN, GEORGE. *Second Diary of a Diplomatic Correspondent*. London: Sampson Law, Marston, 1946.

BRADLEY, OMAR N. *A Soldier's Story*. New York: Henry Holt, 1951.

BRYANT, ARTHUR. *The Turn of the Tide*. Based on the War Diaries of Field Marshal Viscount Alanbrooke. London: Collins, 1957.

————. *Triumph in the West*. Garden City: Doubleday & Co., 1959.

BUTCHER, CAPTAIN HARRY. *My Three Years with Eisenhower*. New York: Simon and Schuster, 1946.

BYRNES, JAMES F. *Speaking Frankly*. New York: Harper & Bros., 1947.

CHURCHILL, WINSTON S. *Closing the Ring*. Boston: Houghton Mifflin, 1951.

————. *The Grand Alliance*. Boston: Houghton Mifflin, 1950.

CHURCHILL, WINSTON S. *The Hinge of Fate.* Boston: Houghton Mifflin, 1950.
————. *Triumph and Tragedy.* Boston: Houghton Mifflin, 1953.
CLARK, GENERAL MARK. *Calculated Risk.* New York: Harper & Bros., 1950.
CLAUSS, MAX WALTER. *Der Weg nach Jalta: President Roosevelt's Verant-wortung.* Heidelberg: Vowinckel, 1952.
CORBETT, PERCY E. *War Aims and Postwar Plans.* London: Royal Institute of International Affairs, 1941.
DALLIN, ALEXANDER. *German Rule in Russia, 1941–1945.* New York: St. Martin's Press, 1957.
DALLIN, DAVID J. *Russia and Postwar Europe.* New York: Yale University Press, 1943.
DEANE, JOHN R. *The Strange Alliance: The Story of Our Efforts at Wartime Cooperation With Russia.* New York: Viking, 1947.
DENNETT, RAYMOND and JOHNSON, JOSEPH E. (eds.). *Negotiating With the Russians.* Boston: World Peace Foundation, 1951.
EISENHOWER, DWIGHT D. *Crusade in Europe.* Garden City: Doubleday & Co., 1948.
FEIS, HERBERT. *Between War and Peace—The Potsdam Conference.* Princeton: Princeton University Press, 1960.
————. *Churchill, Roosevelt, Stalin—The War They Waged and the Peace They Sought.* Princeton: Princeton University Press, 1957.
GOODRICH, LELAND M. and CARROLL, MARIE J. *Documents on American Foreign Relations.* Vol. VI, July, 1943–June, 1944. Boston: World Peace Foundation, 1945. Vol. VII, June, 1944–June, 1945. Princeton: Princeton University Press, 1947.
GOTTLIEB, MANUEL. *The German Peace Settlement and the Berlin Crisis.* New York: Paine Whitman, 1960.
HASSETT, WILLIAM D. *Off The Record With FDR.* New Brunswick: Rutgers University Press, 1958.
HOLBORN, LOUISE W. (ed.). *War and Peace Aims of the United Nations.* Boston: World Peace Foundation, 1943, 1948.
HOLLES, EVERETT. *Unconditional Surrender.* New York: Howell Soskin, 1945.
HULL, CORDELL. *Memoirs.* 2 vols. New York: Macmillan, 1948.
Infantry Journal Press. *Conquer—The Story of the Ninth Army 1944–1945.* Washington: 1947.
ISMAY, LORD. *The Memoirs of Lord Ismay.* New York: Viking Press, 1960.
KECSKEMETI, PAUL. *Strategic Surrender: The Politics of Victory and Defeat.* Stanford: Stanford University Press, 1958.
KENNAN, GEORGE F. *Russia and The West under Lenin and Stalin.* Boston: Atlantic–Little, Brown, 1961.
LEAHY, WILLIAM D. *I Was There.* New York: Whittlesey House, 1950
LEGIEN, RUDOLF. *The Four Power Agreements on Berlin.* Berlin: Carl Hey-mann Verlag, 1960.
LIPPMANN, WALTER. *U.S. War Aims.* Boston: Little, Brown & Co., 1944.

MARSHALL, GEN. GEORGE C. *General Marshall's Report, the Winning of the War in Europe and the Pacific: Biennial Report of the Chief of Staff of the U.S. Army, July 1, 1943–June 30, 1945*. New York: Simon & Schuster, 1945.

———. *Report on the Army: Biennial Reports of Gen. George C. Marshall to the Secretary of War; July 1, 1939–June 20, 1943*. Washington: Infantry Journal Press, 1943.

———. *Selected Speeches and Statements of General of the Army George C. Marshall*. Washington: Infantry Journal Press, 1945.

McCARTHY, JOSEPH R. *America's Retreat from Victory (The Story of George Catlett Marshall)*. New York: Devin-Adair, 1951.

MIKSCHE, F. O. *Unconditional Surrender: The Roots of World War III*. London: Faber, 1952.

MILLIS, WALTER (ed.). *The Forrestal Diaries*. New York: The Viking Press, 1951.

MONTGOMERY, VISCOUNT. *The Memories of Montgomery of Alamein*. Cleveland: World Publishing Co., 1958.

MORGENTHAU, HENRY J. *Germany Is Our Problem*. New York: Harper & Bros., 1945.

MOSELY, PHILIP E. *The Kremlin and World Politics* (Vintage Russian Library). New York: Random House and Alfred A. Knopf, 1960

MURALT, LEONARD VON. *From Versailles to Potsdam*. Chicago: Regnery, 1948.

NEUMANNN, WILLIAM L. *Making the Peace: 1941–1945*. Washington, D.C.: Foundation for Foreign Affairs, 1950.

NIZER, LOUIS. *What to do with Germany*. New York and Chicago: Ziff-Davis, 1944.

OPIE, REDVERS. *The Search for Peace Settlements*. Washington: Brookings Institution, 1951.

PICH, F. W. *Peacemaking in Perspective*. Oxford: Pen-in-Hand, 1950.

ROOSEVELT, ELEANOR. *This I Remember*. New York: Harper & Bros., 1949.

ROOSEVELT, ELLIOTT. *As He Saw It*. New York: Duell, Sloan & Pearce, 1946.

ROSENMAN, SAMUEL I. (ed.). *The Public Papers and Addresses of Franklin D. Roosevelt*. 13 vols. New York: Random House, 1938–1950.

ROZEK, EDWARD J. *Allied Wartime Diplomacy: A Pattern in Poland*. New York: John Wiley & Sons, 1958.

SAYRES, MICHAEL, and KAHN, ALBERT E. *The Plot Against Peace*. New York: Dial Press, 1945.

SHERWOOD, ROBERT E. *Roosevelt and Hopkins*. New York: Harper & Bros., 1948.

SMITH, GENERAL WALTER BEDELL. *Eisenhower's Six Great Decisions*. New York: Longmans, Green & Co., 1950.

———. *My Three Years in Moscow*. Philadelphia: J. B. Lippincott Co., 1950.

SNELL, JOHN L. (ed.). *The Meaning of Yalta.* Baton Rouge: Louisiana State University Press, 1956.

―――. *Wartime Origins of the East-West Dilemma over Germany.* New Orleans: Hauser, 1959.

STETTINIUS, EDWARD R., JR. *Roosevelt and the Russians―The Yalta Conference.* Garden City: Doubleday & Co., 1949.

STIMSON, HENRY L. and BUNDY, MCGEORGE. *On Active Service in Peace and War.* New York: Harper & Bros., 1950.

STRANG, LORD. *Home and Abroad.* London: Andre Deutsch, 1956.

STRAUSS, HAROLD. *The Division and Dismemberment of Germany.* Geneva: Les Presses de Savoie, 1952.

VANDENBERG, ARTHUR H. *The Private Papers of Senator Vandenberg.* Boston: Houghton Mifflin, 1952.

WEDEMEYER, GENERAL ALBERT C. *Wedemeyer Reports.* New York: Henry Holt, 1958.

WELLES, SUMNER. *An Intelligent American's Guide to Peace.* New York: Dryden Press, 1945.

―――. *Seven Decisions That Shaped History.* New York: Harper & Bros., 1950.

―――. *The Time for Decision.* New York: Harper & Bros., 1944.

WINANT, JOHN G. *Letters from Grosvenor Square.* Boston: Houghton Mifflin, 1947.

WITTMER, FELIX. *The Yalta Betrayal.* Idaho: Caxton, 1954.

The Post War Era

ACHESON, DEAN. *Power and Diplomacy.* Cambridge, Mass.: Harvard University Press, 1958.

―――. *Sketches from Life.* New York: Harper & Bros., 1961.

ADENAUER, KONRAD. *World Indivisible: With Liberty and Justice for All.* Translated by Richard and Clara Winston. New York: Harper & Bros., 1955.

ALBRECHT, GUNTER. *Berlin im Blickpunkt der Welt.* Berlin: Deutscher Zentralverlag, 1959.

ALEXANDER, EDGAR. *Adenauer and the New Germany.* New York: Farrar, Straus & Cudahy, 1957.

ALLEMANN, RENÉ. *Bonn ist nicht Weimar.* Köln-Berlin: Kiepenheuer und Witsch, 1956.

ALMOND, GABRIEL A. (ed.). *The Struggle for Democracy in Germany.* Chapel Hill: University of North Carolina Press, 1949.

ALTMANN, RUEDIGER. *Das Erbe Adenauers.* Stuttgart-Degerloch: Seewald, 1960.

BALFOUR, M., and MAIR, J. *Four Power Control in Germany and Austria, 1945-1946.* London: Oxford University Press, 1956.

BATHURST, M. E. and SIMPSON, J. L. *Germany and the North Atlantic Community.* New York: Praeger, 1956.

BELGION, MONTGOMERY. *Victor's Justice.* Chicago: Regnery, 1949.

BENNETT, LOWELL. *Berlin Bastion.* Frankfurt/Main: Rudl, 1951.

BRANDT, KARL. *Germany: Key to Peace in Europe.* Claremont: Claremont College, 1949.

————. *Is There Still a Chance for Germany.* Chicago: Regnery, 1948.

BRANDT, WILLY (as told to Leo Lania). *My Road to Berlin.* New York: Doubleday & Co., 1960.

———— and LOWENTHAL, RICHARD. *Ernst Reuter: Ein Leben für die Freiheit.* Munich: 1958.

BRANDT, STEFAN. *The East German Rising.* London: Thames and Hudson, 1955.

BUTLER, EWAN. *City Divided: Berlin 1955.* New York: Praeger, 1955.

BUTZ, OTTO. *Germany: Dilemma for American Foreign Policy.* New York: Doubleday & Co., 1954.

CASTELLAN, GEORGES. *D.D.R.—Allemagne de l'Est.* Paris: Seuil, 1955.

————. *La Republique Democratique Allemagne.* Paris: 1961.

CHARLES, MAX. *Berlin Blockade.* London: Wingate, 1959.

CLARK, DELBERT. *Again The Goose Step.* Indianapolis: Bobbs–Merrill, 1949.

CLAY, LUCIUS D. *Decision in Germany.* Garden City: Doubleday & Co., 1950.

————. *Germany and the Fight for Freedom.* Cambridge, Mass.: Harvard University Press, 1950.

COLE, TAYLOR (ed.). *European Political Systems* (2d rev. ed.). New York: Alfred A. Knopf, 1960.

COLEGROVE, KENNETH. *Democracy Versus Communism.* Princeton: Van Nostrand Co., 1957.

CONANT, JAMES B. *Federal Republic of Germany—Our New Ally.* Minneapolis: University of Minnesota Press, 1957.

————. *Germany and Freedom: A Personal Appraisal.* Cambridge, Mass.: Harvard University Press, 1958.

CONNELL, BRIAN. *Watcher on The Rhine.* New York: Morrow & Co., 1959.

CRAIG, GORDON A. *From Bismark to Adenauer—Aspects of German Statecraft.* Baltimore: The Johns Hopkins Press, 1958.

DAHRENDORF, RALF. *Class and Class Conflict in Industrial Society.* Stanford: Stanford University Press, 1959.

DALLIN, ALEXANDER (ed.). *Soviet Conduct in World Affairs.* New York: Columbia University Press, 1960.

DAVIDSON, EUGENE. *The Death and Life of Germany.* New York: Alfred A. Knopf, 1959.

DAVISON, W. PHILLIPS. *The Berlin Blockade: A Study in Cold War Politics.* Princeton: Princeton University Press, 1958.

DEUTSCH, HAROLD C. *New Crisis on Berlin.* Toronto: Canadian Institute of International Affairs, 1959.

DEUTSCH, KARL W. and EDINGER, LEWIS J. *Germany Rejoins The Powers.* Stanford: Stanford University Press, 1959.

DORNBERG, JOHN. *Schizophrenic Germany.* New York: Macmillan, 1961.

DRUMMOND, ROSCOE, and COBLENTZ, GASTON. *Duel At The Brink.* Garden City: Doubleday & Co., 1960.

ELLWEIN, THOMAS. *Klerikalismus in der deutschen Politik.* Munich: Isar Verlag, 1955.

ERHARD, LUDWIG. *Germany's Comeback in the World Market.* Translated by W. H. Johnston. New York: Macmillan, 1954.

————. *Prosperity through Competition.* Translated by E. T. Roberts and S. B. Wood. New York: Praeger, 1958.

ERMAN, HANS. *Weltgeschichte auf berlinisch.* Herrenalb Schwarzwald: Verlag für Internationalen Kulturaustausch, 1960.

FINLETTER, THOMAS K. *Foreign Policy—The Next Phase.* New York: Harper & Bros., 1957.

FISHMAN, JACK. *The Seven Men of Spandau.* New York: Rinehart, 1954.

FREUND, GERALD. *Germany Between Two Worlds.* New York: Harcourt, Brace & Co., 1961.

FRIEDMANN, WOLFGANG. *Allied Military Government in Germany.* London: Stevens, 1947.

FRIEDRICH, CARL J. (and associates). *American Experiences in Military Government in Germany.* New York: Rinehart, 1948.

GABLENTZ, O. M. VON DER. *Documents on the Status of Berlin, 1944–1959.* Munich: R. Oldenbourg Verlag, 1959.

GIMBEL, JOHN. *A German Community Under American Occupation.* Stanford: Stanford University Press, 1961.

GOLAY, JOHN FORD. *The Founding of The Federal Republic of Germany.* Chicago: University of Chicago Press, 1958.

GRENFELL, RUSSELL. *Unconditional Hatred: German War Guilt and the Future of Europe.* New York: Devin-Adair, 1953.

GREWE, WILHELM G. *Deutsche Aussenpolitik der Nachkriegszeit.* Stuttgart: Deutsche Verlags-Anstalt, 1960.

GROSSER, ALFRED. *Die Bonner Demokratie.* Dusseldorf: Rauch, 1960.

————. *The Colossus Again.* New York: Praeger, 1955.

GUNTHER, JOHN. *Inside Europe Today.* New York: Harper & Bros., 1961.

HABE, HANS. *Our Love Affair With Germany.* New York: G. P. Putnam's Sons, 1953.

HARTMANN, HEINZ. *Authority and Organization in German Management.* Princeton: Princeton University Press, 1959.

HEIDENHEIMER, ARNOLD J. *Adenauer and the CDU.* The Hague: Nijhoff, 1960.

————. *The Governments of Germany.* New York: Crowell, 1961.

HELLER, DEANE and DAVID. *The Berlin Crisis.* Derby, Conn.: Monarch Books, 1961.

————. *The Berlin Wall.* New York: Walker, 1962.

HENKIN, LOUIS. *The Berlin Crisis and the United Nations.* New York: Carnegie Endowment for International Peace, 1959.

HIRSCH-WEBER, WOLFGANG, and SCHUTZ, KLAUS. *Wähler and Gewählte.* Berlin: F. Vahlen, 1957.

HISCOCKS, RICHARD. *Democracy in Western Germany.* New York: Oxford University Press, 1957.

HOLBORN, HAJO. *American Military Government:—Its Organization and and Policies.* Washington: Infantry Journal Press, 1947.

————. *The Political Collapse of Europe.* New York: Alfred A. Knopf, 1951.

HOLBROOK, SABRA. *Capital Without a Country.* New York: Coward-McCann, 1961.

HORNE, ALISTAIR. *Return to Power: A Report on the New Germany.* New York: Praeger, 1956.

HOWLEY, FRANK. *Berlin Command.* New York: G. P. Putnam's Sons, 1950.

KAHN, HERMAN. *On Thermonuclear War.* Princeton: Princeton University Press, 1961.

KENNAN, GEORGE F. *Russia, The Atom, and The West.* New York: Harper & Bros., 1957.

KERTESZ, STEPHEN D. *The Fate of East Central Europe.* Notre Dame: University of Notre Dame Press, 1956.

KHRUSHCHEV, NIKITA. *The Soviet Stand on Germany.* New York: Crosscurrents Press, 1961.

KIAULEHN, WALTHER. *Berlin: Schicksal einer Weltstadt.* Munich: Biederstein, 1958.

KIRCHHEIMER, OTTO. *Political Justice.* Princeton: Princeton University Press, 1961.

KISSINGER, HENRY A. *Nuclear Weapons and Foreign Policy.* New York: Harper & Bros., 1957.

————. *The Necessity for Choice.* New York: Harper & Bros., 1960.

KITZINGER, UWE W. *German Electoral Politics.* London: Oxford University Press, 1960.

KLEMPERER, KLEMENS VON. *Germany's New Conservatism.* Princeton: Princeton University Press, 1957.

KLIMOV, GREGORY. *The Terror Machine: The Inside Story of the Soviet Administration in Germany.* (Originally published in German as *Berliner Kreml.*) New York: Henry A. Praeger, 1958.

KNAPPEN, MARSHALL. *And Call It Peace.* Chicago: University of Chicago Press, 1947.

KUBY, ERICH. *Das ist des Deutschen Vaterland: 70 Millionen in 2 Wartesälen.* Hamburg: Rowohlt, 1959.

LANGE, MAX GUSTAV (ed.). *Parteien in der Bundesrepublik.* Stuttgart: Ring–Verlag, 1955.

LEONHARD, WOLFGANG. *Child of the Revolution.* Translated by C. M. Woodhouse. Chicago: Regnery, 1958.

LEWIS, H. O. *New Constitutions in Occupied Germany.* Washington: Foundation for Foreign Affairs, 1948.

LIE, TRYGVE. *In the Cause of Peace.* New York: Macmillan, 1954.

LITCHFIELD, EDWARD H. (and associates). *Governing Postwar Germany.* Ithaca, N.Y.: Cornell University Press, 1953.

LOCHNER, L. P. *Tycoons and Tyrants: German History from Hitler to Adenauer.* Chicago: Regnery, 1954.

LOWIE, ROBERT H. *Toward Understanding Germany.* Chicago: University of Chicago Press, 1954.

MANDER, JOHN. *Berlin: Hostage for the West.* London: Penguin, 1962.

————. *The Eagle and The Bear.* London: Barrie and Rockcliff, 1959.

MARSHALL, CHARLES BURTON. *The Limits of Foreign Policy.* New York: Henry Holt, 1954.

MARTIN, JOHN STEWART. *All Honorable Men.* Boston: Little, Brown & Co., 1950.

MCINNIS, EDGAR (ed.). *The Shaping of Postwar Germany.* New York: Praeger, 1960.

MEISSNER, BORIS. *Russland, die Westmächte und Deutschland: die sowjetische Deutschlandpolitik, 1943–1953.* Hamburg: Nolke, 1953.

MENDERSHAUSEN, HORST. *Two Postwar Recoveries of the German Economy.* Amsterdam: North-Holland Pub. Co., 1955.

MERKATZ, DR. HANS JOACHIM VON, and METZNER, DR. WOLFGANG. *Germany Today—Facts and Figures.* Frankfurt am Main: Alfred Metzner Verlag, 1954.

MIDDLETON, DREW. *The Struggle for Germany.* London and New York: Allan Wingate, 1950.

MONTGOMERY, JOHN D. *Forced To Be Free: The Artificial Revolution in Germany and Japan.* Chicago: University of Chicago Press, 1957.

MOORE, B. T. *NATO and the Future of Europe.* New York: Harper & Bros., 1958.

MORGENTHAU, HANS. *Germany and the Future of Europe.* Chicago: University of Chicago Press, 1951.

MORLEY, FELIX. *The Foreign Policy of the United States.* New York: Alfred A. Knopf, 1951.

NEAL, FRED WARNER. *War and Peace and Germany.* New York: W. W. Norton & Co., 1962.

NETTL, J. P. *The Eastern Zone and Soviet Policy in Germany, 1945–1950.* London: Oxford University Press, 1951.

NEUMANN, BERNARD. *The Three Germanies.* London: Hale, 1957.

NEUMANN, SIGMUND (ed.). *Modern Political Parties.* Chicago: University of Chicago Press, 1957.

NORMAN, ALBERT. *Our German Policy: Propaganda and Culture.* New York: Vantage, 1951.

OPPEN, BEATE RUHM VON. *Documents on Germany Under Occupation 1945–1954.* London: Oxford University Press, 1955.

PAGEL, KARL (ed.). *The German East.* Berlin: K. Lemmer, 1954.

POLLOCK, JAMES K. *Germany in Power and Eclipse.* New York: Van Nostrand, 1952.

————; MEISEL, J. H.; and BRETTON, H. L. *Germany Under Occupation.* Ann Arbor: George Wahr, 1949.

————, et al. *German Democracy at Work.* Ann Arbor: University of Michigan Press, 1955.

POUNDS, NORMAN J. G. *Divided Germany and Berlin.* Princeton: Van Nostrand, 1962.

PRICE, HOYT and SCHORSKE, CARL. *The Problem of Germany.* New York: Council on Foreign Relations, 1947.

PRITTIE, TERENCE. *Germany Divided.* Boston: Atlantic-Little, 1960.

RATCHFORD, B. U., and ROSS, WM. D. *Berlin Reparations Assignment.* Chapel Hill: The University of North Carolina Press, 1947.

RICHART, ERNST. *Macht Ohne Mandat.* Cologne: Institut für Politische Wissenschaft, 1958.

RIESS, CURT. *Berlin—Berlin 1945–1953.* Berlin: Non-Stop Bücherei, 1954.

————. *The Berlin Story.* New York: The Dial Press, 1952.

ROBICHON, JACQUES and ZIEGELMEYER, J. V. *L'Affaire de Berlin: 1945–1959.* Paris: Gallimard, 1959.

ROBSON, CHARLES B. (ed.). *Berlin—Pivot of German Destiny.* Chapel Hill: University of North Carolina Press, 1960.

RODNICK, DAVID. *Postwar Germans.* New Haven: Yale University Press, 1948.

RODRIGO, ROBERT. *Berlin Airlift.* London: Cassell, 1960.

ROGGE, PETER G. *Die amerikanische Hilfe für West Berlin.* (Von der deutschen Kapitulation bis zur westdeutschen Souveränität.) Tübingen: J. C. B. Mohr, 1959.

RÖPKE, WILHELM. *The Solution of the German Problem.* New York: G. P. Putnam's Sons, 1946.

ROTHFELS, HANS (ed.). *Berlin in Vergangenheit und Gegenwart.* Tübingen: J. C. B. Mohr, 1961.

Royal Institute of International Affairs. *Documents on Germany Under Occupation.* London: Oxford University Press, 1955.

SAINTOGUE, R. A. CHAPUT DE. *Public Administration in West Germany.* London: 1961.

SALOMON, ERNST VON. *Fragebogen.* Garden City: Doubleday & Co., 1955.

SCHMIDT, HELMUT. *Defense or Retaliation—A German View.* New York: Praeger, 1962.

SCHULZ, KLAUS-PETER. *Berlin zwischen Freiheit und Diktatur.* Berlin: Staneck, 1962.

SETON-WATSON, HUGH. *The East European Revolution.* London: Meuthen, 1956.

SNYDER, LOUIS L. *Documents of German History.* New Brunswick: Rutgers University Press, 1958.

SPEIER, HANS. *Divided Berlin.* New York: Praeger, 1961.

———. *German Rearmament and Atomic War: The Views of German Military and Political Leaders.* Evanston: Row, Peterson & Co., 1957.

———. *The Soviet Threat to Berlin.* Santa Monica: The Rand Corp., 1960.

——— and DAVISON, W. P. (eds.). *West German Leadership and Foreign Policies.* Evanston: Row, Peterson & Co., 1957.

SPIRO, HERBERT J. *The Politics of German Co-Determination.* Cambridge, Mass.: Harvard University Press, 1958.

STARR, JOSEPH R. *United States Military Government in Germany.* Washington: U.S. Army Historical Division, 1950.

STEINIGER, PROF. DR. PETER ALFONS. *West Berlin—Ein Handbuch zur West Berlin Frage.* Berlin: Kongress-Verlag, 1959.

STOLPER, GUSTAV. *German Realities.* New York: Reynal and Hitchcock, 1948.

STOLPER, WOLFGANG. *Germany Between East and West.* Washington: National Planning Association, 1960.

———, and ROSKAMP, KARL W. *The Structure of The East German Economy.* Cambridge, Mass.: Harvard University Press, 1960.

THAYER, CHARLES W. *The Unquiet Germans.* New York: Harper & Bros., 1957.

TOYNBEE, ARNOLD (ed.). *Survey of International Affairs, 1939–1946.* Vol. III. *Four Power Control in Germany and Austria.* London: Oxford University Press, 1952.

TRUMAN, HARRY S. *Year of Decisions.* Garden City: Doubleday and Co., 1955.

———. *Years of Trial and Hope.* Garden City: Doubleday and Co., 1956.

ULBRICHT, WALTER. *Die Entwicklung des deutschen volksdemokratischen Staates 1945–1958.* Berlin: Dietz, 1958.

UTLEY, FREDA. *The High Cost of Vengeance.* Chicago: Regnery, 1949.

WALLICH, H. C. *Mainsprings of the German Revival.* New Haven: Yale University Press, 1955.

WARBURG, JAMES P. *Germany—Bridge or Battleground.* New York: Harcourt & Brace, 1947.

———. *Germany—Key to Peace.* Cambridge: Harvard University Press, 1953.

WEYMAR, PAUL. *Adenauer, His Authorized Biography.* New York: E. P. Dutton & Co., 1957.

WHITE, WILLIAM L. *Report on The Germans.* New York: Harcourt & Brace, 1947.

WILLIS, F. ROY. *The French in Germany 1945–1949.* Stanford: Stanford University Press, 1962.

WISKEMANN, ELIZABETH. *Germany's Eastern Neighbors.* London: Oxford University Press, 1956.

WOLFERS, ARNOLD. *Germany: Protectorate or Ally.* New Haven: Yale University Press, 1950.

WUNDERLICH, FRIEDA. *Farmer and Farm Labor in the Soviet Zone of Germany.* New York: Twayne, 1958.

ZINK, HAROLD. *American Military Government in Germany.* New York: Macmillan, 1947.

―――. *The United States in Germany 1944–1955.* Princeton: Van Nostrand Co., 1957.

ARTICLES

ACHESON, DEAN GOODERHAM. "On Dealing With Russia: An Inside View," *New York Times Magazine,* April 12, 1959, pp. 27, 88–89.

―――. "The Practice of Partnership," *Foreign Affairs,* Vol. 41, No. 2 (December, 1962), pp. 247–60.

ADENAUER, KONRAD. "The German Problem, A World Problem," *Foreign Affairs,* Vol. 41, No. 1 (October, 1962), pp. 59–65.

―――. "Germany: The New Partner," *Foreign Affairs,* Vol. 33 (1955), pp. 177–83.

ALEXANDER, EDGAR. "Church and Society in Germany," in J. Moody, ed., *Church and Society* (New York: 1953).

ALSOP, JOSEPH and STEWART. "How Our Foreign Policy is Made," *Saturday Evening Post,* April 30, 1949.

BARNES, SAMUEL H.; GRACE, FRANK; POLLOCK, JAMES K.; and SPERLICH, PETER W. "The German Party System and the 1961 Federal Election," *American Political Science Review,* Vol. 56, No. 4 (December, 1962), pp. 899–914.

BENTZIEN, JOACHIM. "Die Luftkorridore von und nach Berlin," *Aussenpolitik,* Vol. 12 (1961), pp. 685–90.

BRAUNTHAL, GERALD. "The Free Democratic Party in West German Politics," *Western Political Quarterly,* Vol. 13, June, 1960.

BUCERIUS, GERD. "Berlin ist ein Land der Bundesrepublik," *Die Zeit,* Vol. 15, No. 41, p. 4.

CHAMBERLIN, WILLIAM HENRY. "The Revival of Anti-Germanism," *Modern Age,* Vol. 6, No. 3 (Summer, 1962), pp. 277–84.

CLAY, LUCIUS D. "Berlin," *Foreign Affairs,* Vol. 41, No. 1 (October, 1962), pp. 47–58.

COLE, TAYLOR. "The Democratization of the German Civil Service," *Journal of Politics,* Vol. 14 (1952), pp. 3–18.

CRAIG, GORDON A. "NATO and the New German Army," in W. Kaufmann (ed.), *Military Policy and National Security,* Princeton: Princeton University Press, 1956.

CROAN, MELVIN, and FRIEDRICH, CARL J. "The East German Regime and Soviet Policy in Germany," *Journal of Politics,* Vol. 20 (1958), pp. 44–63.

DORN, WALTER L. "The Debate over American Occupation Policy in Germany in 1944–1945," *Political Science Quarterly*, December, 1957.

EDINGER, LEWIS J. "Post-Totalitarian Leadership," *American Political Science Review*, Vol. 54 (1960), pp. 58–82.

EISENHOWER, DWIGHT D. "My Views on Berlin," *Saturday Evening Post*, December 9, 1961.

ERLER, FRITZ. "The Struggle for German Unification," *Foreign Affairs*, Vol. 34 (1956), pp. 380–93.

FAHY, CHARLES. "Legal Problems of German Occupation," *Michigan Law Review*, Vol. 47 (November, 1948), pp. 11–22.

GLASER, KURT. "Die politische Falle," *Schlesische Rundschau*, Vol. 13, No. 34 (1961), p. 2.

GREWE, WILHELM G. "Other Legal Aspects of the Berlin Crisis," *American Journal of International Law*, Vol. 56, No. 2 (April, 1962), pp. 510–13.

HEIDENHEIMER, ARNOLD J. "Federalism and the Party System: The Case of West Germany," *American Political Science Review*, Vol. 52 (1952), pp. 809–28.

———. "Der starke Regierungschef und das Parteiensystem: der Kanzler-effekt in der Bundesrepublik," *Politische Vierteljahresschrift*, Vol. 2 (Sept., 1961).

HEIDLER, M. "Der 13. August 1961," *Hochschulwesen*, 1961, pp. 621–28.

HOWLEY, FRANK P. "I've Talked 1600 Hours with the Russians," *Readers Digest*, May, 1949.

JANOWITZ, MORRIS. "Social Stratification and Mobility in West Germany," *American Journal of Sociology*, Vol. 64 (1958), pp. 6–24.

KAUPER, PAUL G. "The Constitutions of West Germany and the U.S.: A Comparative Study," *Michigan Law Review*, Vol. 58 (1960).

KIRCHHEIMER, OTTO. "The Administration of Justice and the Concept of Legality in East Germany," *Yale Law Journal*, Vol. 68 (1959), pp. 705–59.

———. "The Composition of The German Bundestag," *Western Political Quarterly*, Vol. 3 (1950), pp. 590–601.

———. "German Democracy in the 1950's," *World Politics*, Vol. XIII (1961), pp. 254–66.

KISSINGER, HENRY A. "The Search for Stability," *Foreign Affairs*, Vol. 37 (1959), pp. 537–60.

———. "Strains on The Alliance," *Foreign Affairs*, Vol. 41 (1962), pp. 261–85.

LEBEDEW, VALERIAN P. "Berlin in der Sowjet Literatur," *Kultur*, Vol. 1960–61, No. 165, pp. 6–7.

LOEWENBERG, GERHARD. "Parliamentarism in Western Germany: The Functioning of the Bundestag," *American Political Science Review*, Vol. 55 (March, 1961), pp. 87–102.

LOEWENSTEIN, KARL. "The Bonn Constitution and the European Defense Community Treaty," *Yale Law Journal*, Vol. 54 (1955), pp. 805–39.

MERKL, PETER H. "Equilibrium, Structure of Interests and Leadership: Adenauer's Survival as Chancellor," *American Political Science Review,* Vol. 56, No. 3 (September, 1962), pp. 634–50.

MIKSCHE, FERDINAND OTTO. "Sterben für Berlin," *Christ und Welt,* Vol. 14, No. 39 (1961), pp. 3–4.

"Military Government," *The Annals,* American Academy of Political Social Sciences, Vol. 267, January, 1950.

MORGENTHAU, HANS. "End of An Illusion," *Commentary,* November, 1961, pp. 422ff.

———. "The Trouble With Kennedy," *Commentary,* January, 1962, pp. 51–55.

MORGENTHAU, HENRY, JR. "Our Policy Toward Germany," *New York Post,* November 24, 1947.

MOSELY, PHILIP E. "Dismemberment of Germany," *Foreign Affairs,* Vol. 28 (April, 1950), pp. 487–98.

———. "The Occupation of Germany," *Foreign Affairs,* Vol. 28 (July, 1950), pp. 580–604.

NEUMANN, FRANZ. "Soviet Policy in Germany," *The Annals,* May, 1949.

NEUNREITHER, KARLHEINZ. "Politics and Bureaucracy in the West German Bundesrat," *American Political Science Review,* Vol. 53 (1959), pp. 713–31.

POLLOCK, JAMES K. "The West German Electoral Law of 1953," *American Political Science Review,* Vol. 49 (March, 1955), pp. 107–30.

PRITTIE, TERENCE. "The German Federal Parliament," *Parliamentary Affairs,* Spring, 1955, pp. 235–39. Mr. Prittie's articles also appear regularly in the *New Republic.*

PULZER, PGJ. "West Germany and the Three Party System," *Political Quarterly,* Vol. 33, No. 4 (1962), pp. 414–25.

SCHUMANN, ROBERT. "France and Germany in the New Europe," *Foreign Affairs,* Vol. 41, No. 1 (October, 1962), pp. 66–77.

SCHWENK, HANS. "Das Recht auf ein freies Berlin," *Die Bundeswehr,* 1961, pp. 229f.

TAUBER, KURT P. "German Nationalists and European Union," *Political Science Quarterly,* Vol. 74 (1959), pp. 564–89.

WAGNER, HELMUT R. "The Cultural Sovietization of East Germany," *Social Research,* Vol. 24 (1957), pp. 395–426.

WARNER, ALBERT L. "Our Secret Deal Over Germany," *Saturday Evening Post,* August 2, 1952.

WRIGHT, QUINCY. "Some Legal Aspects of The Berlin Crisis," *American Journal of International Law,* Vol. 55 (1961), pp. 959–65.

UNPUBLISHED MATERIAL

BRANDT, LORD MAYOR WILLY. *Material zum 13. August 1961.*

DORN, PROFESSOR WALTER. Unpublished manuscripts of the late Professor

Walter Dorn of Columbia University relating to America's role in the occupation of Germany. Columbia University Library.

WINANT, JOHN GILBERT. *The Papers of John Gilbert Winant, U.S. Ambassador to the Court of St. James During World War II*. Microfilm. Columbia University Library.

NEWSPAPERS AND JOURNALS

The best daily treatments of events in Germany appear in the *New York Times* and the *Washington Post*. (Until recently these were written by a unique husband-and-wife team, Sydney Gruson for the *Times* and Mrs. Gruson (Flora Lewis) for the *Post*.) I have also found the coverage of the *New York Herald Tribune* and *The Evening Star* (Washington, D.C.) useful.

The best German language account appears in the *Neue Zürcher Zeitung*. Also of value are the *Frankfurter Allgemeine Zeitung* and *Die Welt* (Hamburg and Berlin). For Berlin itself I have used the *Tagesspiegel* and the *Morgenpost*. The Party line in East Germany is authoritatively reported in the Ulbricht house organ, *Neues Deutschland*.

In addition to the articles cited previously, I have found the following periodicals to be especially helpful: *The Reporter, New Republic, Commentary, Saturday Evening Post, Foreign Affairs, Orbis, World Politics*, and the *American Political Science Review*. The news weeklies—*Time, Newsweek*, and *U.S. News and World Report*—also frequently contain worthwhile articles on Berlin. Among German journals I have used *Der Spiegel, Der Monat, Die Zeit, Deutsche Rundschau* and *Die Frankfurter Hefte*.

Index

THE DEFENSE OF BERLIN

Jean Edward Smith

designer:	Edward D. King
typesetter:	Vail-Ballou Press, Inc.
typefaces:	Text: Linotype Caledonia. Display: Bulmer
printer:	Vail-Ballou Press, Inc.
paper:	Warren's 1854 Medium Finish
binder:	Vail-Ballou Press, Inc.
cover material:	Bancroft Arrestox C